T0386101

DUMBARTON OAKS
MEDIEVAL LIBRARY

Jan M. Ziolkowski, General Editor

CHRISTIAN NOVELS FROM THE

MENOLOGION OF

SYMEON METAPHRASTES

DOML 45

Christian Novels from the *Menologion* of Symeon Metaphrastes

Edited and Translated by

STRATIS PAPAIOANNOU

DUMBARTON OAKS
MEDIEVAL LIBRARY

HARVARD UNIVERSITY PRESS
CAMBRIDGE, MASSACHUSETTS
LONDON, ENGLAND
2017

Library of Congress Cataloging-in-Publication Data
Names: Symeon, Metaphrastes, active 10th century, author. |
Papaioannou, Stratis, editor, translator. | Container of (expression):
Symeon, Metaphrastes, active 10th century. Works. Selections. |
Container of (expression): Symeon, Metaphrastes, active 10th century.
Works. English Selections.
    Title: Christian novels from the *menologion* of Symeon Metaphrastes /
edited and translated by Stratis Papaioannou.
    Other titles: Dumbarton Oaks medieval library ; 45.
    Description: Cambridge, Massachusetts : Harvard University Press,
2017.|
    Series: Dumbarton Oaks medieval library ; 45 | Texts in Greek with
English translations on facing pages ; introduction and notes in English. |
Includes bibliographical references and index.
    Identifiers: LCCN 2016048602 | ISBN 9780674975064 (alk. paper)
    Subjects: LCSH: Christian hagiography. | Christian women saints. |
Christian saints. | Orthodox Eastern Church—Liturgy.
    Classification: LCC BX380 .S96 2017 | DDC 270.3092/2 [B]—dc23 LC
record available at https://lccn.loc.gov/2016048602

Contents

CONTENTS

Introduction

About four hundred years after his death, pilgrims in Constantinople were paying their respects to the relics of
Symeon Metaphrastes, the author of the six texts edited and
translated into English for the first time in this volume.
"You go east from St. Sophia toward the sea; on the right
is the monastery called Hodegetria . . . The body of St.
Symeon is in this church," we read in a late fourteenth-
century Russian guidebook to the capital of Byzantium,
while Markos Eugenikos, writing some decades later, in-
forms us that Metaphrastes's body was preserved "intact
and unmouldered."[1] This miraculous preservation was just
one more aspect, perhaps the most spectacular, of the long
tradition of reverence and admiration for Symeon Metaphrastes, whose epithet means "reviser" in Greek. His primary, if not his only, saintly achievement was the composition of a *menologion:* a ten-volume liturgical collection of
saints' lives and martyrdom accounts, mostly by earlier authors, that he rewrote, revising their content and style. This
grand effort merited Metaphrastes the fame of a rescuer
who salvaged the biographies of the saints from oblivion.

A landmark of orthodox Christianity, Metaphrastes's
tenth-century *Menologion* could be regarded as—and we can
say this without exaggeration—one of the most important
Byzantine literary creations. It was the culmination of a

long history of Christian storytelling in Greek, ensuring the popularity of certain stories that satisfied the need of Byzantines for moral edification as well as their appetite for entertainment in the context of worship and beyond. It also represented a major Byzantine literary trend, that of rewriting in a rhetorical register *(metaphrasis);* this trend reflected the tastes and interests of the Constantinopolitan upper classes, which were formed during a period of revival for Byzantine political and cultural authority, in the ninth through the twelfth centuries. Given that the predilections of this social group were influential for the solidification of what we identify as Byzantine Christianity, Metaphrastes's rewriting project came to play a seminal role in the creation of a religious and cultural tradition with an immense appeal and longevity.

Metaphrastes's *Menologion* enjoyed popularity for several centuries, surpassed only by the Bible and some of the great early Byzantine fathers of the Church and comparable to Jacobus de Voragine's hagiographical bestseller, the late medieval *Golden Legend,* in Western Europe.[2] All together, the manuscripts that preserve different parts of Metaphrastes's *Menologion* number well over seven hundred. Metaphrastes's work thus affected generations of Byzantine readers and listeners as well as writers, even if it remains virtually unknown to the wider (even Byzantinophile) public.

It is easy to state the importance of Metaphrastes in the Byzantine world. But how does one introduce him and his texts to modern readers? Several challenges await us. The details of Metaphrastes's own life and the precise context of his literary creation still elude clear comprehension. His

wider sociohistorical setting is particularly complex: a whole
series of projects that aimed at military, economic, and cultural revival and expansion, not all of them successful or
long-lasting, defined the politics of the Byzantine imperial
court in the tenth century.

Orienting Metaphrastes in literary history presents us
with similar complexity, since the place of the *Menologion*'s
version of each hagiographical story requires an in-depth investigation into the multiple trajectories of Christian storytelling. The enormous appeal of the stories would have been
self-evident to Byzantine audiences, but to modern readers
their emphasis on the supernatural and their devotion to
certain recurrent motifs and character types may be puz-
zling. Equally, the sophistication of Metaphrastes's literary style would have been obvious to Byzantine (especially
learned) audiences, but modern readers may be put off by
his preoccupation with rhythm and wordplay or extravagant
eulogy and descriptions that favor the melodramatic. Finally, since the *Menologion* survives in numerous manuscripts
(more than one hundred for each of our texts), the re-
creation of the "original edition" as well as of its subsequent
textual history poses a corresponding number of difficulties.

None of these issues can be treated here satisfactorily.[3]
Yet a brief elaboration of these matters can provide the necessary background so that some of the appeal of these texts
may be restored as they search for new, dedicated readers.

SYMEON METAPHRASTES

Byzantine sources offer us only sparse biographical data
about the creator of the *Menologion,* which is attributed by
manuscript colophons, dedicatory poems, and Byzantine

authors to a Symeon who is accompanied by the identifiers *magistros, logothetes (tou dromou),* and *metaphrastes* in various combinations.[4] He was born in Constantinople into a well-to-do family during the reign of Leo VI (r. 886–912) and received a good education in both rhetoric (the art of discourse) and probably philosophy, which in Byzantium encompassed all forms of knowledge, from logic and the sciences to metaphysics. From at least the late 950s, he was employed in the imperial court and bureaucracy under several emperors, from Romanos II (r. 959–963) to Basil II (r. 976–1025), and held high titles and offices (*magistros* and *logothetes* were the last ones he acquired). In this capacity and at imperial behest, he authored several documents, texts, and collections, including the *Menologion* and a chronicle. He died (perhaps having become a monk in old age) on November 28 of an unspecified year, probably during the last decade of the tenth century.[5]

Almost none of this information can be confirmed with certainty; we know neither whether our biographical sources are accurate nor if they pertain to the same Symeon, the author of the *Menologion.* Even so, time of composition and his status at the imperial court seem incontrovertible. Internal evidence from the *Menologion* itself confirms that parts of its composition date to after 976 and that its author was certainly well-versed in the Byzantine tradition of learnedness. The consistent usage of the epithets *magistros* and *logothetes* in manuscripts of the *Menologion,* as well as details from a dirge composed soon after Metaphrastes's death by Nikephoros Ouranos (who died after 1007), also suggest that Metaphrastes was indeed a high functionary in the imperial court. Finally, the scale and type of the enterprise can be ex-

plained best if it was supported by either the emperor himself or by the highest echelons of Constantinopolitan society—the powerful eunuch minister Basil Lekapenos, active
from before 959 until 985 when he was deposed by Basil II,
has been proposed as Metaphrastes's possible patron.[6]

From the mid-eleventh century onward, Metaphrastes
was certainly viewed as a towering figure of the recent past.
His *Menologion* was copied in what was apparently mass production (by premodern standards) and was imitated, further
reworked, and expanded, though never supplanted or surpassed. He himself was considered an author-saint, on a par
with early Byzantine authorities such as Gregory of Nazianzos and John Chrysostom—the two other most copied and
studied authors in Byzantium.[7]

Metaphrastes's *Menologion*

Due to the monumental work of Albert Ehrhard, we know
a great deal about the so-called *Menologion* itself.[8] This modern designation refers to a liturgical book, usually in multiple volumes, that included various texts on saints—mostly
Passions (martyrdom accounts, or *martyria*) and *Lives* (biographies, or *bioi*)—arranged according to the sequence of
feast days in the Byzantine liturgical year that began on September 1. Its primary purpose was the provision of a text
dedicated to each saint on his or her feast day to be read
aloud during liturgical services (usually vigils, especially in
monasteries, but also in urban churches).

Such collections had appeared in Byzantium by the end
of the eighth century; yet the *menologion* was to reach its authoritative form in the work of Metaphrastes. Metaphras-

tes's collection gathered together 148 hagiographical texts in ten volumes: eight volumes for the months September through January, and two volumes for the months February through August. With the exception of eight texts that were new compositions by Metaphrastes and at least fourteen earlier texts that were adopted virtually without alteration, the rest of the texts included in the collection were versions by earlier, usually anonymous, authors that Metaphrastes selected, reworking and correcting their content and style according to the literary and theological standards of his day.[9]

It is this undertaking that earned him the title *metaphrastes,* namely, someone who "metaphrased," or rewrote and revised. Thus, though earlier *menologia* also contained primarily early Byzantine hagiographical texts, the point of Metaphrastes's collection was not simply to match a feast day with a text, but, more so, to identify or, in most cases, create the authoritative *right* text for each feast. As such, Metaphrastes's *Menologion* fits well into a period when the Byzantine ruling elite encouraged efforts to reorganize and essentially reinvent the early Byzantine tradition for ideological purposes, for internal consumption as well as for cultural export. The translation of Metaphrastic texts into medieval Georgian, old Slavonic, and Arabic attests to the latter activity.

Two further aspects of Metaphrastes's *Menologion* deserve mention. The first is that his compilation seems to have been left incomplete—perhaps because he lost favor at the court of Basil II.[10] The second is that when we speak of Metaphrastes we should not think of a single author. As we learn from the only detailed Byzantine description that we

have of Metaphrastes's working methods (that of Michael Psellos [1018–1078]), it is clear that he did not work alone.[11] Rather, he seems to have directed a group of collaborators, though whether they were scribes or coauthors is unclear. Because of this, it would be futile to search for a single authorial voice behind every aspect of his *Menologion,* even if a certain consistent approach to style and content can be identified more or less throughout—perhaps the result of review of the final product by Metaphrastes himself.

CHRISTIAN NOVELS

From the vast corpus of Metaphrastes's *menologion,* the following six texts were selected for this volume:

1. Kyprianos and Ioustina (October 2), *Life and Conduct and Passion* (*BHG* 456)
2. Pelagia of Antioch (October 8), *Life and Conduct* (*BHG* 1479)
3. Galaktion and Episteme (November 5), *Life and Conduct and Passion* (*BHG* 666)
4. Euphemia the Young Maiden (November 15), *Miracle* (*BHG* 738)
5. Barbara (December 4), *Passion* (*BHG* 216)
6. Eugenia (December 24), *Life and Conduct and Passion* (*BHG* 608)

These texts are united by the central role played by female protagonists; women who test social expectations take center stage. More important, these texts belong to a particular type of hagiographical story included in the original Metaphrastic collection, which I propose to view as "Christian

novels." The Christianity of our stories hardly needs explanation; the reader is confronted with it at every turn of the page. What do I mean, however, by the term "novel"? This designation, though not unproblematic when applied to Metaphrastes (as we shall see), has been adopted here because it captures two seminal features: (1) as in modern novels and fictional storytelling in general, the persons and events narrated by these stories are invented and imagined, carrying only refracted relationships to actual historical reality; and (2) parts of their plots (including the highlighted agency of female characters), narrative patterns, and rhetorical form—in the Metaphrastic version—bear resemblances to an earlier, specific type of prose fiction, the late antique "Greek novel."

Let us clarify these two features, starting with fictionality. The stories recounted in our texts, both at their core but also in several of their details (for instance, the superhuman endurance of all the martyrs under unbearable torture), are fictional. Unlike the case of other Byzantine saints' *Lives* (several of which were also included in Metaphrastes's *Menologion*), we can assume with some certainty that none of our stories' main characters ever existed and that few actions attributed to them ever occurred. Rather, these legendary tales derive perhaps from oral traditions and, as literary narrative does universally, retain only echoes of certain plausible social scenarios. In our stories, these scenarios take a rather extreme form and are enacted in the context of the late antique, pre-Christian, or early Christian Roman empire, a world which provides the setting for all our stories and which would have been far removed from Metaphrastes's audiences—notably, all the stories take place in the

southeastern parts of the Roman empire (*Eugenia* also takes place in Rome), which were either outside or at the borders of Byzantine territory at the time of Metaphrastes.

These are the main scenarios: the sorcerer and intellectual who converts to Christianity after failing to seduce a resisting Christian virgin (*Kyprianos and Ioustina*—a story later echoed in the German legend of Faust); the prostitute who is transformed into an ascetic *(Pelagia);* the pious wife who overcomes her infertility as a result of a monk's prayers, then persuades her husband to convert to Christianity, while their son marries a devout woman and makes an agreement with his wife to abandon marital life *(Galaktion and Episteme);* the foreign mercenary who marries the daughter of a widow in a town where he resides temporarily, only to take her away and treat her as a captive slave (*Euphemia*—a tale that may be compared to the ancient Greek story of Cassandra, Agamemnon's ill-fated captive); the daughter of a rich aristocrat who rebels against his authority (*Barbara*—a story similar to the ancient myth of Danaë, a virgin daughter imprisoned by her father); a similar virgin who leaves her family for a holier life *(Eugenia)*.

These scenarios are furthermore fused with a series of Byzantine cultural expectations, especially in relation to violence and power, family relations, and gender roles. Three such expectations stand out, though it would be hard to separate the one from the other: I am referring to (1) social morality, (2) the rules of the hagiographical genre, and (3) what we might call the Byzantine utopian imaginary, namely collective and personal fears and desires projected onto imagined plots. In four of our texts, for instance, our heroes meet their deaths after enduring extreme torture. Other forms

of violence (such as sexual violence) are also depicted; in this context, supernatural evil forces are seminal agents of action. The tension between Roman imperial power and Christian faith is explored throughout; only in the story of Euphemia is Byzantine authority, as embodied by a local general and a bishop, presented as guarantor of Christian order. In five of the stories, the negotiation of family ties lies at the epicenter, especially the relationship between an adolescent girl and her parents *(Barbara; Eugenia)*. Finally, as noted above, women take center stage (even if men—usually bishops—are instrumental for their sanctification) and often transcend their assigned social roles, inhabiting the innermost male spaces and social positions and even assuming the appearance of men *(Pelagia; Eugenia)*.

This literary reworking of plausible scenarios and the projection of cultural expectations onto imagined characters and plots align our stories with universal *fictional* storytelling (modern prose fiction included) and thus justify the designation "novels." Additionally, however, our texts contain a series of thematic and formal features that reflect and, occasionally, evoke the discourse of a specific type of fiction: the late antique "Greek novel," by which we refer to a popular genre of Greek prose (five complete texts survive as well as several fragments) that flourished during the Roman Imperial period and continued to attract readers throughout the Byzantine era; these texts narrated the romance between a young man and a young woman, their tribulations, and final union, and were set in a fictional past or in a chronologically indeterminate setting.[12]

The principal shared theme between our stories and the

Greek novels is the focus on personal relations and emotions: from erotic desire *(Kyprianos and Ioustina; Pelagia; Eugenia)* to marital love *(Galaktion and Episteme*—indeed Saint Galaktion's parents bear the names of the two protagonists of Achilleus Tatios's novel, *Leukippe and Kleitophon)*;[13] from family love *(Euphemia* and her mother; or in *Eugenia* where a beautiful daughter escapes her pagan household only to be miraculously reunited with them in Christian faith and martyrdom) to friendships between masters and servants (Eutolmios in *Galaktion and Episteme;* the two eunuchs Protas and Hyacinth, Eugenia's spiritual brothers) or among women *(Pelagia; Barbara; Eugenia).*

But there are other thematic similarities as well: the accentuated agency of women; the high value placed on the preservation of the virginity of female characters; the generally elevated social standing of the protagonists; the presence of antiheroes, especially sexually aggressive men and women, who challenge the virtue of the main characters; the significant names that characters bear (for instance, Pelagia is linked to the sea, or *pelagos,* of God's love and *Eugenia* evokes her good *genes* and noble *genealogy);* or the usage of dreams and letters for prefiguring or promoting narrative action.

As will be discussed in the following section, in Metaphrastes these thematic similarities are further enhanced by his adoption of a rhetorical register that is also reminiscent of the late antique Greek novels. Before we look at that topic, however, we must offer our readers three warnings. The first is that the six stories included in this volume are a mere selection, though hopefully a representative one, of

only a few of those Metaphrastic texts whose features warrant the term "Christian novel"; Metaphrastes's *Indes and Domna* (BHG 823), *Xenophon and Maria* (BHG 1878), or *Boniphatios* (BHG 281–82), for instance, contain many of the same features. A different selection from Metaphrastes would present a very different world of Byzantine storytelling.

The second warning is that, though resemblance to and even direct dependence on the late antique novels may be discerned, the principal theme of the late antique novel, namely the glorification of heterosexual romance in a world that threatens it with violence, is radically replaced by homage to personal devotion (sometimes presented as the most intense erotic desire) toward God, who restores perfect order and grants a happy ending, namely eternal glory, to his exemplary devotees.[14]

Third, though our six stories are in essence fictional and, at that, novelistic, they were not created nor were they read as fiction in Byzantium and beyond. In their original contexts of creation and their later reception by Christian readers, these texts related *true* stories. As such, they satisfied (and to some perhaps still do) personal hopes for a better world and a better self and carried real value for believers who associated with their saintly heroes not only through these tales but also through religious images, ritual cults, and, in many cases, relics — such as those of Saint Barbara, perhaps the most popular in our group. Thus the stories of these saints have earned the reverence they inspired over the centuries and, in this regard, the volume's title should not mislead readers into thinking that they are reading novels in precisely the modern sense of the term.

METAPHRASTES'S REWRITING

As already mentioned, the *Lives* and *Passions* of Metaphrastes usually reworked earlier versions, sometimes indeed through the usage of several earlier texts on the same saint. This is the case also with this volume's texts, all of which represent the most popular version of each story as attested by manuscript diffusion and readership. In the Notes to the Translation, I point out important differences between the pre-Metaphrastic and the Metaphrastic versions, to the extent that this is possible, as only a few pre-Metaphrastic versions have been edited or studied properly. Here, let us explore some general characteristics.

Metaphrastes amplifies rhetorically the earlier texts, often in a style and with narrative strategies that are reminiscent of the late antique Greek novels. For instance, as in the Greek novels and Byzantine rhetoric in general, Metaphrastes highlights intense emotions, whenever these are mentioned in the story. Like the earlier novelists and other rhetoricians, he also inserts personal comments and observations or offers directions to the reader/listener, while he simultaneously suppresses a feature of orality in the earlier versions, namely first-person narration (as previously featured in *Pelagia* and in *Galaktion and Episteme*). Similarly, indirect retelling or eloquent speeches often replace the intense but simple dialogue of the pre-Metaphrastic version. Furthermore, Metaphrastes's attempts, not always successful, to create the effect of historicity by inserting historical or pseudohistorical details also resemble novelistic writing. This is paralleled by another method of grafting the stories to universal truths: as in the late antique novels (especially

those of Achilleus Tatios and Heliodoros), Metaphrastes frequently interjects brief digressions in order to present maxims (*gnomai*) that are presented as Byzantine common sense, a shared, universal morality; later readers, with remarkable frequency, highlighted these maxims in the margins of Metaphrastic manuscripts.[15]

The further stylistic amplification at the level of vocabulary, syntax, and rhetorical figures, such as the replacement of Latin or vernacular words of the pre-Metaphrastic version, the preference for classical morphology and word arrangement, and the frequent usage of various figures of speech, have been studied well elsewhere.[16] It may suffice to stress here three general aspects of Metaphrastes's style which became apparent during the preparation of this volume and which may be regarded as distinctive of his approach. The first is that, while high Byzantine rhetoric (as evident also in the late antique novels) demanded that the author insert frequent allusions to other literary texts (usually from the rhetorical canon, but also obscure references), Metaphrastes avoided burdening his writing with such intertextuality—with the exception of biblical references. He thus created rhetorically sophisticated but still accessible texts.

The second noteworthy aspect is that, though a consistent rhetorical approach to style is evident, rarely do we find Metaphrastes repeating himself by using the same pun, metaphor, maxim, or biblical phrase. His purpose, that is, seems to have been first and foremost variation.

Finally, the rhetorical amplification of the stories seems to create particularly an acoustic effect, intended as Metaphrastes's texts were for regular public recitation. The pre-Metaphrastic versions may thus sometimes be more dra-

matic in narrative and dialogue. Yet his rhetorically reworked texts abound in aural theatricality, as they were meant to be read aloud.

TRANSMISSION, RECEPTION, AND THE PRESENT VOLUME

The edition of the Greek texts offered in this volume reconstructs, as much as possible, Metaphrastes's *Lives* and *Passions* in their likely state in the late eleventh century and thus as they would have been experienced by the majority of their Byzantine audience. By this time, the Metaphrastic texts had become remarkably stable and more or less "fixed" —without, that is, significant variation from manuscript to manuscript (see Note on the Text). Furthermore, Metaphrastes's collection had reached the peak of its popularity and circulation, as is clear from both the number and the high quality of eleventh-century manuscripts,[17] as well as from frequent references to the collection in contemporary lists of library holdings and in monastic *typika,* the rules that regulated daily services and appropriate readings in monasteries.[18] In the late tenth century, Metaphrastes's texts were already employed extensively by Euthymios the Hagiorite in his popular hagiographical text titled *Barlaam and Ioasaph;*[19] by the middle of the eleventh century, Paul Evergetinos had culled broadly from Metaphrastes's *Menologion* in order to create a similarly popular anthology for monastic audiences (the *Evergetinos*); and, sometime in the 1050s or 1060s, Michael Psellos wrote his encomium of Metaphrastes's rhetoric, a eulogy that testifies to the admiration for the Metaphrastic project among learned circles as well.[20] Metaphrastes, therefore, quickly became a classic.

A seminal feature of this *classical* form of Metaphrastes's

work in its Byzantine context was the performativity inherent in the makeup of the texts themselves and the manuscripts that transmit them, which this edition and translation attempt to retain as much as possible—even if syntax and rhythm rarely can be replicated exactly from one language to another. Metaphrastes's texts were meant primarily, as mentioned above, for public recitation. The format of the manuscripts consulted for this edition is telling: relatively large in size; with pages generally laid out in two columns; in a calligraphic script, easily legible (various forms of the so-called *Perlschrift*); with several phrases and passages marked with quotation marks in order to direct the reader responsible for the public recital—usually these are citations from the Bible, but occasionally they also include indirect speech (for example, *Kyprianos and Ioustina* 43), letters (*Kyprianos and Ioustina* 56–57; *Eugenia* 57), prayers (*Euphemia* 25; *Barbara* 32; *Eugenia* 79), and a dream (*Eugenia* 22). Most important, the manuscripts are fairly consistent in their punctuation, demarcating shorter syntactical units, sentences, and paragraphs, and they reflect an oral aesthetic that highlighted rhythm, sound, and rhetorical wit. I have followed closely this punctuation, with some flexibility so as to accommodate also the expectations of the modern reader.[21]

In general, both the critical edition and the translation offered here aim to retain the rhetoricality of Metaphrastes's original compositions, and this includes elements that might aesthetically challenge our criteria of what is good literary prose—such as repetitions of the same word or frequent statements that start with "for." I have thus preferred to err on the side of literalism and faithfulness to the original. Finally, since the Greek text has been thoroughly re-

vised, earlier translations into other modern languages, though consulted, have offered only limited benefit (with the exception of the French translation of *Pelagia*).[22]

Metaphrastes remained a classic for centuries. Public recitation and the popularity of Metaphrastes among lay and monastic audiences, as well as appreciation by learned readers, continued well into the fifteenth century and beyond: several of the manuscripts are post-Byzantine, and his texts seem to have served as the basis for a later, second rewriting for new audiences. The history of this reception would deserve its own study and a very different introduction. What is beyond doubt is that when Byzantine pilgrims and non-Byzantine travelers were advised to visit the Hodegetria monastery in Constantinople and see Metaphrastes's holy body, many of them knew that they were about to see the relics of a master writer of the past, whose stories and style inspired emulation and stimulated pleasure in his audience.

My debts of gratitude are multiple. The volume originated in discussions with Charis Messis, who offered guidance throughout its making. A course on translation at Brown University kick-started the project; its participants, Stevie Hull, Daria Resh, and Zachary Rothstein-Dowden, inspired ways of translating Metaphrastes and, with much labor and insight, collaborated with me on the translation of *Eugenia* (published here after later reworkings)—Daria Resh also researched extensively *Eugenia*'s manuscript history. Louis Zweig made a provisional, but helpful, draft of the edition and translation of *Barbara* for his senior thesis; he also tran-

scribed the PG versions of *Kyprianos, Pelagia, Galaktion,* and *Euphemia.* Nadia Kavrus-Hoffmann offered generously her expertise on paleography. Stephanie Larson reviewed the translation of *Kyprianos,* while Annie McDonald reviewed *Pelagia;* both helped improve the English with acumen. Adele Scafuro read early drafts of parts of *Eugenia* and made recommendations. Lorenzo Ciolfi helped with obtaining manuscript microfilms. Ansel Rothstein-Dowden transcribed the PG version of *Eugenia.* The Classics Department at Brown provided funding. Above all, Alice-Mary Talbot and John Duffy reviewed closely the entire volume and made numerous suggestions that improved the work immensely. Finally, Nate Aschenbrenner, under the incomparable editorial supervision of Alice-Mary Talbot, prepared the volume for publication with precision and care. I could not have hoped for better editors.

NOTES

1 On the Russian text, possibly a translation of a lost Greek guidebook dated to the years 1389 to 1391, see George P. Majeska, *Russian Travelers to Constantinople in the Fourteenth and Fifteenth Centuries* (Washington, D.C., 1984), 114–54 (citation on 138–39). Markos Eugenikos's (1394?–1445) phrase derives from a biographical notice that formed part of Eugenikos's holy service dedicated to Metaphrastes; see Athanasios Papadopoulos-Kerameus, Ἀνέκδοτα ἑλληνικὰ συγγραμμάτια ἔγγραφά τε καὶ ἄλλα κείμενα κατ' ἐκλογὴν συλλεγέντα ἐκ τῶν ἐν τῇ "Μαυροκορδατείῳ Βιβλιοθήκῃ" ἀναγραφομένων χειρογράφων καὶ νῦν τὸ πρῶτον ἐκδιδόμενα (Constantinople, 1884), 100–101.

2 For Jacobus de Voragine's (ca. 1260) collection of hagiographical stories titled *Legenda Aurea (Golden Legend),* see Brenda Dunn-Lardeau, ed., *Legenda aurea, sept siècles de diffusion – actes du colloque international sur la Legenda aurea, texte latin et branches vernaculaires* (Montreal, 1986).

3 For Byzantine hagiography in general, see now Efthymiadis, *Ashgate*

Research Companion, including the following chapter: Christian Høgel, "Symeon Metaphrastes and the Metaphrastic Movement," 181–96; for the middle Byzantine period in general, see *Le monde byzantin,* vol. 2, *L'Empire byzantin 641–1204,* ed. Jean-Claude Cheynet (Paris, 2006).

4 *Magistros,* from Latin *magister,* was a high-ranking dignity granted by the Byzantine emperor. *Logothetes (tou dromou)* was a high office within the Byzantine imperial administration; its holder was originally in charge of the public post but, in Metaphrastes's time, was also entrusted with several other duties and often functioned as the emperor's advisor.

5 For this biographical information, see Beck, *Kirche und theologische Literatur,* 570–75; Høgel, *Metaphrastes,* 61–88; *PmbZ* 2, no. 27504. The first attempt at a complete biography and survey of the works of Metaphrastes was made by the erudite Leo Allatius (1586–1669), a scholar of Greek descent and Italo-Greek education and head librarian of the Vatican library; see Leo Allatius, *De Symeonum scriptis diatriba* (Paris, 1664).

6 Paul Magdalino, "Byzantine Encyclopaedism of the Ninth and Tenth Centuries," in *Encyclopaedism from Antiquity to the Renaissance,* ed. Jason König and Greg Woolf (Cambridge, 2013), 223; it should be noted, however, that Metaphrastes's close friend, Nikephoros Ouranos (mentioned also above), was apparently an opponent of Basil Lekapenos in the court of Basil II.

7 For Gregory and Metaphrastes specifically, see Stratis Papaioannou, *Michael Psellos: Rhetoric and Authorship in Byzantium* (Cambridge, 2013), 46–48, 56–63, and 158–62.

8 Ehrhard, *Überlieferung* I, II, and III.

9 The best description of the project is found in Høgel, *Metaphrastes.* See further Kazhdan, *A History of Byzantine Literature,* 2:231–47; and Stratis Papaioannou, "Voice, Signature, Mask: The Byzantine Author," in *The Author in Middle Byzantine Literature,* ed. Aglaë Pizzone (Berlin, 2014), 35–39.

10 Høgel, *Metaphrastes,* 118–23 and 127–29.

11 Høgel, *Metaphrastes,* 93–96, with the comments by Nigel G. Wilson, "Symeon Metaphrastes at Work," *Νέα Ῥώμη: Rivista di ricerche bizantinistiche* 11 (2014): 105–7.

12 Of course, the term "novel" is a modern convention also in the case of late antique prose fiction; for discussions of this issue and a general introduction to the "Greek (and Latin) novels," see Tim Whitmarsh, ed., *The Cambridge Companion to the Greek and Roman Novel* (Cambridge, 2008).

13 For the story of Galaktion and Episteme, its novelistic features, and their hagiographical tradition, see Anne P. Alwis, *Celibate Marriages in Late Antique and Byzantine Hagiography: The Lives of Saints Julian and Basilissa, Andronikos and Athanasia, and Galaktion and Episteme* (London, 2011).

14 See Messis, "Fiction and/or Novelization," a seminal article with further bibliography.

15 I have counted sixty such marginal notes in the manuscripts (especially manuscript *C*) used for this edition; they usually direct the reader to maxims or to key moments in the action, while a few provide some minimal commentary. A few representative such comments are recorded in the Notes to the Translation.

16 Usefully summarized in Høgel, *Metaphrastes,* 139–40, following earlier scholarship.

17 More than two hundred Metaphrastic manuscripts date to the eleventh century, when also most of the numerous decorated and illustrated copies were produced; see Patterson Ševčenko, *Illustrated Manuscripts.* Almost all the manuscripts used for the DOML edition are in parchment and are decorated with ornamental headpieces, historiated initials, and, in a few cases, deluxe illustrations of saints.

18 Høgel, *Metaphrastes,* 152–54.

19 Rather than the other way around; see Johannes K. Grossmann, "Die Abhängigkeit der Vita des Barlaam und Ioasaph vom Menologion des Symeon Metaphrastes," *Jahrbuch der österreichischen Byzantinistik* 59 (2009): 87–94. On Euthymios's translation into Greek and expansion of the Georgian version of an originally Indian tale, see *Die Schriften des Johannes von Damaskos,* vol. 6/1: *Historia animae utilis de Barlaam et Ioasaph (spuria). Einführung,* ed. Robert Volk (Berlin, 2009).

20 For a recent translation of the Life of Metaphrastes by Psellos, see the online version of Elizabeth A. Fisher (http://chs.harvard.edu/CHS/article/display/5584) reproduced with some changes in Charles Barber and Stratis Papaioannou, *Michael Psellos on Literature and Art* (Notre Dame, Ind., 2017).

21 Regarding the manuscripts, see the Note on the Text below.

22 For the modern translations (where available), see the first note to the translation of each text.

LIFE, CONDUCT, AND PASSION OF SAINTS KYPRIANOS AND IOUSTINA

Βίος καὶ πολιτεία καὶ μαρτύριον τῶν ἁγίων Κυπριανοῦ καὶ Ἰουστίνης

Εὐλόγησον, πάτερ.

Πολλὰ καὶ μεγάλα με τὴν Ἀντιόχου θαυμάζειν παρακαλοῦσιν, ὅτι τε τῆς οἰκουμένης ἐπίπροσθεν τὸν παρὰ τῶν ἱεροκηρύκων Χριστοῦ μαθητῶν περιχαρῶς καταβληθέντα σπόρον ἐδέξατο· καὶ Χριστιανοὶ πρῶτον ἐν αὐτῇ κατὰ τὸν μέγαν Λουκᾶν ἐχρημάτισαν· καὶ ὅτι περ ἄνδρας τῷ βίῳ προήνεγκεν, *εἰς τριάκοντα καὶ ἑκατὸν καὶ ἑξήκοντα* τῆς ἀρετῆς εὐαγγελικῶς τὸν στάχυν ἐκθρέψαντας—οὐκ ἄνδρας δὲ μόνον, ἀλλὰ καὶ τῶν γυναικῶν οὐκ ὀλίγας. Ἀφεὶς οὖν κάλλη θαυμάζειν ναῶν, καὶ μεγέθη τειχῶν, καὶ πλήθη φυτῶν, εὐθηνοῦσάν τε γῆν ἀγαθοῖς, ἣν ἄρδει παρρέων Ὀρόντης, Ἰουστίναν τῷ λόγῳ διήγημα θήσομαι· ἥ, τὴν καρδίαν μετὰ μακροὺς τῶν ἱερῶν ἀποστόλων χρόνους νεώσασα τοῖς ἐκείνων διδάγμασι, στάχυν ἀθλητικὸν ἀνεβλάστησε, μάλα μὲν ὡραῖον, μάλα δὲ τῷ καρπῷ βρίθοντα.

2   Ταύτῃ πατρὶς μέν, ἣν ἐδηλώσαμεν, Ἀντιόχεια· Αἰδέσιος δὲ καὶ Κληδονία γεννήτορες. Ἀλλὰ τουτὶ τὸ καλὸν φυτὸν πολλαῖς ἐκόμα πρότερον ταῖς ἀκάνθαις· καὶ γὰρ καὶ αὐτὴ τῶν πατέρων ἀκολουθοῦσα τῇ πλάνῃ (εἰδώλων δὲ οὗτοι θεραπευταὶ καὶ ἀντίθεοι), τὰ ἐκείνων τιμῶσα ἦν καὶ σεβομένη τὰ εἴδωλα. Ἐπεὶ δέ, τῷ χρόνῳ τὴν ἡλικίαν

Life, Conduct, and Passion of Saints Kyprianos and Ioustina

Father, give the blessing.

Many and great things invite my amazement with regard to Antioch: it was first in the world to eagerly receive the seed implanted by the holy preaching disciples of Christ; it was first there, according to the great Luke, that people became Christians; and it produced men who cultivated the harvest of virtue following the gospel: *some thirty-fold, some hundred, some sixty* — indeed not only men, but also a great number of women. Leaving aside my amazement at the beauty of its churches, the magnitude of its walls, the abundance of its vegetation, or its soil which, watered by Orontes that flows by, abounds in good produce, I will set Ioustina as the subject of my story. Many years after the holy apostles, Ioustina renewed her heart with their teachings and brought forth a martyr's harvest of great beauty, brimming with fruit.

Her fatherland was, as we mentioned, Antioch; Aidesios 2 and Kledonia were her parents. At first, however, many thorns surrounded this beautiful flower, for she too was following her parents' erroneous path (they were devotees of idols, enemies of God), venerating their religion and worshipping their idols. When with time she advanced in age

προκόπτουσα, καὶ στερροτέρου φρονήματος ἥπτετο, φέγ-
γος αὐτὴν εἰσήει θεογνωσίας, ἅτε δοχεῖον οὖσαν φωτι-
σμοῦ τοιούτου καὶ χάριτος ἄξιον. Καὶ τῶν μὲν εἰδώλων
ἀσθένειαν καταγινώσκειν ἤρξατο, τὸν ἀληθῆ δὲ καὶ μόνον
ἐπιγινώσκειν Θεόν.

3   Ταῖς τοιαύταις οὖν τῶν λογισμῶν ἀναβάσεσι τὴν ψυχὴν
ἡ παρθένος προεκκαθαίρουσα, εἰς τὴν τοῦ σωτηρίου σπό-
ρου καταβολὴν ηὐτρεπίζετο. Ἐν ᾧ δὲ καθ' ἑαυτὴν ἔστρεφε
ταῦτα καί, σχολάζουσα, τὴν ἀκριβῆ γνῶσιν ἐζήτει παρὰ
Θεοῦ, Πραΰλιός τις τῶν ἐν Ἀντιοχείᾳ διάκονος, ἐν ἐπη-
κόῳ τῆς κόρης, οὕτω συμβάν, τὰ περὶ τῆς τοῦ Σωτῆρος
ἡμῶν καὶ Θεοῦ οἰκονομίας τε καὶ σαρκώσεως διεξήει·
ὅπως μὲν ὁ τῶν αἰώνων Δημιουργὸς εἰς οἶκτον ἦλθε τοῦ
πλαστουργήματος· ὅπως δὲ Γαβριὴλ ὁ τῶν ἄνω τάξεων
ἀρχηγὸς τῇ πρὸ γενεῶν τετηρημένῃ Παρθένῳ τοῦ μυστηρίου κῆρυξ εὐάγγελος γέγονε· καὶ ὡς συνέλαβεν ἐν γαστρὶ
καὶ ὠδινήσασα τέτοκε· καὶ ὡς τὴν τοῦ παιδίου γέννησιν
ἀστὴρ τῶν ἄλλων ἐπιδηλότατος τοῖς μάγοις ἐγνώρισε.
Τούτοις ἐπεξήει τὴν ἐν τῷ ἰδίῳ κόσμῳ φανερὰν αὐτοῦ
ἐπιφάνειαν· τὴν ἐν τούτῳ διατριβήν· τὰ σωτηριώδη δι-
δάγματα· τὰ θαύματα· τὸν διὰ ταῦτα φθόνον· τὸν σταυρόν·
τὴν ταφήν· καὶ τέλος, αὐτὴν τὴν θείαν ἀνάστασιν. Καὶ
ταῦτα μὲν ὁ Πραΰλιος.

4   Ἰούστα δὲ τῇ ἑαυτῆς ψυχῇ τὰ ἀκούσματα ταῦτα, ὡς
ἀγαθῇ γῇ σπέρματα, παρεδίδου. Καὶ οὕτως ἀκριβέστερον
ὅσαι ὧραι πρὸς τὴν ἀλήθειαν ἐμβαθύνουσα, τῶν μὲν εἰδώλων πολὺ κατέχεε γέλωτα· τὰ δὲ τῆς ὑγιοῦς πίστεως ταῖς
πλαξὶν ἐνέγραφε τῆς καρδίας. Ὅθεν ἠθέλησε μὲν εἰς ὄψιν

and also acquired a firmer spirit, the light of divine understanding entered her as a vessel worthy of such enlightenment and grace. And she began to disparage the malady of
idol worship and to recognize the one true God.

By cleansing her soul in advance with such ascents of her   3
mind, the virgin was preparing herself to receive the seed
of salvation. While she was turning over these thoughts in
her mind and, eager for learning, she was seeking from God
perfect knowledge, it so happened that, within her hearing,
a deacon in Antioch called Prailios was explaining everything about the dispensation and incarnation of God our
Savior: how the Creator of the ages showed mercy for His
creation; how Gabriel, the leader of the heavenly orders, announced the good news of this mystery to the Virgin who
had been predestined for generations; how she conceived in
her womb and gave birth in labor pains; and how a star, the
brightest of all others, made the birth of the child known to
the magi. To these he added His manifest appearance in His
own creation; His life in the world; His salvific teachings;
His miracles; the envy He attracted because of them; the
cross; the burial; and, finally, the most important, the divine
resurrection. This was what Prailios presented.

Iousta delivered into her own soul the words she was   4
hearing, like seeds to good soil. As time passed, delving further into the truth, she began to pour much scorn on the
idols, inscribing a sound faith on the *tablets of her heart*. She

ὀφθῆναι τῷ Πραϋλίῳ· καὶ γὰρ ἀκούσασα μόνον ἦν τῶν παρ' αὐτοῦ λεγομένων, καὶ τὴν περὶ τούτων γνῶσιν τελεώτερον ἐζήτει μυηθῆναι. Ἔτι δὲ τὴν παρθενικὴν ὄψιν ἀθέατον εἶναι βουλομένη, οὐκ ἔκρινε μὲν ἰδεῖν τὸν διάκονον· φοιτῶσα δὲ λάθρα παρὰ τὴν ἐκκλησίαν, ἰδεῖν οὕτως ἐπεθύμει τὸν τοῖς ζητοῦσιν ἐγγίζοντα Κύριον.

5 Βραχὺ τὸ ἐν μέσῳ, καὶ κοινωνὸν συνεῖδε ποιήσασθαι τὴν μητέρα τῶν ἐγνωσμένων. "Καὶ ἵνα τί, ὦ μῆτερ," εἶπε, "θεοῖς προσανέχομεν, οὓς συνιστῶσι χεῖρες ἡμέτεραι; Ἵνα τί τεχνιτῶν ποιήμασι προσκυνοῦμεν; Ἵνα τί δὲ τὸ μὲν ἐπιβώμιον ὑφάπτομεν, τὴν λαμπάδα δὲ τῆς ψυχῆς οὐκ ἀνάπτομεν οὐδὲ τὸν μαργαρίτην ἐμπορευόμεθα; Οὐκ οἶσθα τοὺς Γαλιλαίους (οὕτω γὰρ τοὺς τοῦ Χριστοῦ θιασώτας τοῖς ἐγχωρίοις καλεῖν σύνηθες); Πολλῷ οὗτοι τῶν παρ' ἡμῖν νομιζομένων θεῶν φοβερώτεροι· τούτων γὰρ εἴ ποτέ τις τοῖς εἰδώλοις ἐπιφανῇ, εὐθὺς οἱ παρ' ἡμῶν προσκυνούμενοι κλέπταις ὁμοίως ἢ δραπέταις δεδοίκασί τε καὶ ὑποφρίττουσι. Καὶ δικαίως· κλέπτουσι γὰρ ἐκεῖνοι τὴν τοῦ Θεοῦ τιμήν, ἔτι καὶ τὰς ἡμετέρας παραπολλύντες ψυχάς."

6 Ταῦτα ἔλεγε μὲν Ἰούστα. Ἡ μήτηρ δὲ τοῖς λεγομένοις οὐ κατετίθετο· πάνυ γὰρ ὑπὸ τῆς μωρᾶς κεκράτητο δυσσεβείας. Ὅθεν, "Μηδὲ ὁ πατήρ," ἔφη, "γνώτω τὴν ἐπιγενομένην σοι πρὸς τοὺς θεοὺς περιφρόνησιν." Ἰούστα δέ, "Ἀγαπητόν μοι μᾶλλον, εἰ καὶ τῷ πατρί," ἔλεγε, "καὶ παντὶ γνωρισθήσεται ταῦτα· οὐδὲ γὰρ ἐν τῇ σκοτίᾳ ἔτι πορεύεσθαι τὸ λοιπὸν ἀνέξομαι, καθότι μόνον τὸν διὰ Πραϋλίου γνωρισθέντα μοι Κύριον Θεὸν ἰσχυρὸν ἔγνων εἶναι, ζῶντά τε, καὶ τοὺς ἐκ πλάνης ἐπιστρέφοντας εἰσδεχόμενον."

thus desired to meet Prailios face to face; since she had only heard his words, she now sought to be initiated in their understanding in a more perfected fashion. But she wished to still preserve her maidenly face unseen, and thus decided not to go and see the deacon; rather, she secretly frequented the church, longing to see the Lord who approaches those who seek Him.

A short time had passed, and she resolved to share what 5 she had learned with her mother. "Why, O mother," she said, "do we devote ourselves to gods made by human hands? Why do we worship the creations of artisans? Why do we kindle the fire under the offerings on the altar, but do not ignite the torch of our soul? And why don't we purchase the precious pearl? Don't you know about the Galileans (this is how the locals used to call the followers of Christ)? They are much more fearsome than those so-called gods of ours. If one of the Christians appears in front of our idols, immediately the gods that we worship grow fearful and tremble like thieves or fugitives. And rightly so; for these idol-gods steal the honor that belongs to God, while also destroying our souls."

These were the words of Iousta. Her mother, however, 6 did not concur, for she was very much in the grip of that foolish impiety. Because of it, she said: "Do not let your father learn about your newfangled scorn for the gods." "It would actually be dearer to me if both my father," Iousta replied, "and everyone else would learn about it. Indeed, I will no longer bear to walk in darkness, since I have come to recognize only the Lord God, with whom Prailios acquainted me, as mighty, living, and accepting of those who turn back from error."

7 Ἠρέμα γοῦν συνιοῦσα ἡ μήτηρ, οὐδὲν μὲν ἀντετίθει τοῖς λεγομένοις· τῇ σιωπῇ δὲ μᾶλλον τὴν συγκατάθεσιν ὑπεσήμαινεν. Ὕστερον δὲ μιᾷ τῶν νυκτῶν, ἃ παρὰ τῆς θυγατρὸς ἤκουσε, καὶ τῷ ἀνδρὶ διεσάφησεν. Ὁ δὲ τὴν ἀκοὴν οὔτε τελέως ἀπώσατο, οὔτε πάλιν εὐπαραδέκτως πρὸς αὐτὴν ἔσχεν. Ὑπνομαχῶν δέ, φροντίσιν ἐπάλαιεν, ἕως ὕπνῳ ληφθείς, ἀγγελικῆς ἐπιφανείσης αὐτῷ παρεμβολῆς, ἐν μέσῳ Χριστὸν ἐχούσης δορυφορούμενον, κατεπλάγη μὲν ἐπὶ τῷ ὁράματι, αὐτοῦ δὲ καλοῦντος ἐπήκουσεν εἰρηκότος, "Δεῦτε πρός με, καὶ τὴν τῶν οὐρανῶν ὑμῖν χαρίσομαι βασιλείαν." Εἶτα διαναστάς, ἑτέραν οὐκ ἐζήτησε μαρτυρίαν· ἀλλὰ σὺν γυναικὶ καὶ τὴν θυγατέρα λαβών, διάκονόν τινα τῆς ἐκκλησίας ἠξίωσεν Ὀπτάτῳ τούτους προσαγαγεῖν, ὃς τηνικαῦτα τῆς ἐκκλησίας ἐπίσκοπος ἦν. Οἱ μὲν οὖν τῇ τοῦ Χριστοῦ σφραγῖδι σημειωθῆναι ἱκέτευον· ὁ δὲ ἀνεβάλλετο ἕως Αἰδέσιος ὁ πατὴρ αὐτῷ τήν τε τῆς θυγατρὸς αὐτόματον ἐπιστροφὴν πρὸς τὸν Κύριον, καὶ τὰ τῆς ὀπτασίας ἀκριβῶς ἐξηγήσατο.

8 Ὧν ἐκεῖνος ἀκούσας, οὐκέτι διαμφιβάλλων ἦν· οὐδὲ πολλῶν ἐδεήθη τῶν βουλευμάτων. Ἀλλ᾽ ἅμα μὲν τῷ τύπῳ τοῦ σταυροῦ καθάπερ τινὶ φρουρίῳ τούτους περιτειχίζει, ἅμα δὲ τοῦ φωτίσματος ἀξιοῖ. Καὶ διετέλει Αἰδέσιος τὸ λοιπὸν χλευάζων καὶ διασύρων τὰ τῆς ἀπάτης ἰδρύματα (ἱερεὺς γὰρ πρὸ τοῦ τῶν εἰδώλων ἐτύγχανεν ὤν). Ἔπειτα βαθμοῦ τοιοῦδε καταξιωθείς, καὶ *ἐν καθέδρᾳ πρεσβυτέρων*—τὸ τοῦ θείου φάναι Δαυίδ—τὸν Χριστὸν *αἰνέσας*, ἑλόμενός τε βίον τῷ Θεῷ φίλον καὶ καθαρώτατον, ἐξ

Slowly but surely her mother understood and made no 7
objection to her daughter's words; rather, in silence she indicated her consent. Then one night, she explained to her
husband what she had heard from her daughter. He neither
rejected outright what he heard, nor again did he readily accept it. Fighting with sleep, however, he battled with worry,
until he fell asleep and a band of angels appeared to him
guarding Christ in their midst. He was astounded by the
vision and heard Christ calling him and saying, "*Come to me,
and I will grant you the heavenly kingdom.*" He then woke
up and sought no other testimony. He took his wife and
daughter and asked a deacon of the church to bring them to
Optatos, the bishop at that time. They pleaded to be sealed
with the sign of Christ's seal, but Optatos delayed until
Aidesios, the father, narrated in detail his daughter's self-
enacted conversion to the Lord as well as everything about
his own vision.

Once the bishop heard their story, he was no longer in 8
doubt, nor did he require any more deliberations. Immediately, he fortified them with the sign of the cross, just as a
citadel with a wall; immediately, he deemed them worthy of
baptism. From then on, Aidesios would deride and mock
the shrines of deceit (for, in fact, up to that point, he was a
priest of the idols). Then, blessed with the same office, *he
praised* Christ *in the assembly of the elders*—to use the words of
the divine David—and chose the purest life, dear to God.

CHRISTIAN NOVELS FROM THE *MENOLOGION*

μῆνας ἐπιβιοὺς πρὸς τοῖς δώδεκα, πρὸς ὃν ἐπόθησε Κύριον ἐξεδήμησεν.

9 Ἡ μέντοι παρθένος οὐδὲν ἔπαθεν ἀγεννές, οὐδὲ ψυχῆς εὐγενοῦς ἀνάξιον· ἀλλὰ τῷ θεμελίῳ μᾶλλον τῆς πίστεως τὰς χρυσοῦ καὶ λίθων τιμίων πολὺ τιμιωτέρας ἀρετὰς ἐποικοδομοῦσα, προέκοπτε. Πάντως δὲ οὐκ ἦν οὕτω βιοῦσαν διαδρᾶναι τὰ τοῦ Πονηροῦ σκάνδαλα. Ὅθεν οὐδὲ διέδρα· ἀλλὰ καὶ πειρᾶται ταύτης· καὶ πολεμίως ἄγαν προσφέρεται. Πλὴν ἀλλὰ προσεκτέον· ὅτι τε οὐκ ἄχαρι τὸ διήγημα, καὶ ὅτι δεῖ μαθεῖν, καὶ ὅπως αὐτῇ τὴν πεῖραν ἐπήνεγκεν.

10 Ἀγλαΐδας τις σχολαστικὸς (ὥσπερ ἐκ τοῦ κάλλους ἴσως καὶ τὸ τοιοῦτον ἔλαχεν ὄνομα), Ἀγλαΐδας οὖν οὗτος, γένους ὢν τῶν εὐπατρίδων, καὶ πλούτῳ κομῶν, ἀφορμὰς εἶχε ταῦτα πρὸς ἡδονάς· καὶ ἀκολάστοις ὁρμαῖς ἐξεδίδοτο. Διὸ καὶ τὴν παρθένον πολλάκις ἰδὼν παροδεύουσαν, καὶ πρὸς τὸν τοῦ Θεοῦ οἶκον ἀφικνουμένην, τῷ κάλλει ταύτης οἷα βέλει δεινῶς βάλλεται—καίτοι μαραίνειν αὐτὸ καὶ ἀμαυροῦν ἐκείνης, ἅτε σφαλερὸν καὶ ἐπίβουλον, νηστείαις ἅμα καὶ προσευχαῖς δι' ὅλου μηχανωμένης. Ἀλλ' οὗτος πάνυ λίχνους ἔχων τοὺς ὀφθαλμούς, πρότερον μὲν τὰς ὁδοὺς ἐτήρει καὶ παρεφύλαττε· καὶ ὑπαντῶν εὐφήμει ταύτην, ἐπῄνει τοῦ κάλλους, μακαρίαν ἐκάλει τοῦ εὐτυχήματος. Εἶτα τὸν πόθον καὶ διὰ συμβόλων τινῶν ἐπεσήμαινε· καὶ πολλοῖς δικτύοις (ὡς ἂν εἴποι τις) τὴν θήραν προκατελάμβανεν. Ἀλλὰ τῇ παρθένῳ ταυτὶ πάντα λῆρος ἀκριβὴς καὶ νέμεσις ἐλογίζετο· καὶ γελᾶν μᾶλλον, ἢ προσέχειν σώφροσιν ὀφθαλμοῖς καὶ ἀκοαῖς ἐδόκει ἄξια.

11 Ἀπορήσας οὖν Ἀγλαΐδας τοῦ τοιοῦδε σκοποῦ, ἑτέραν

After living another eighteen months, he departed to the Lord for whom he longed.

The virgin showed no ignoble emotion, nor felt anything 9 unworthy of a noble soul. Instead, she became better and better, building on the foundation of her faith virtues that were much more precious than gold and precious stones. Of course, living in this way, it was impossible to escape the snares of the Evil One. Hence, she indeed did not escape them, but rather he brought her into temptation, acting against her in the most hostile fashion. Pay attention! The story is not without its grace, and you should learn also how the Devil led her into temptation.

There was a certain lawyer, Aglaïdas (allotted such a name 10 perhaps due to his beauty). This Aglaïdas was a man who used his high birth and great wealth as pretexts for pleasure and thus surrendered himself to his dissolute urges. Therefore, seeing often also the virgin, when she passed by on her way to the house of God, he was fiercely stricken by her beauty as if by an arrow—even though, with fasting and prayer, she did everything in her power to make her beauty wither and disappear as a perilous and dangerous thing. Still, with his lascivious eyes, at first he would watch the streets and wait for her; and when he came face to face with her, he would shower praises on her, extol her beauty, and laud her good fortune. Then he would slowly indicate his longing through some signals, casting many nets (as one might say) and preparing for the catch. Yet for the virgin all these ploys were nothing but sheer nonsense and an annoyance; she considered them as worthy of laughter rather than attention by chaste eyes and ears.

Thwarted in his ploy, Aglaïdas decided to change course 11

ὁδεύειν ἔγνω· καὶ πρὸς γάμου κοινωνίαν ἀγαγέσθαι ταύτην ἐζήτει. Ἰουστίνα δέ, νύμφην ἑαυτὴν μόνῳ τῷ Χριστῷ καθομολογήσασα, τοὺς ἄλλους εὐγενῶς ἀπηξίου, "Ἀρκετός," λέγουσα, "νύμφιος ὁ τὴν παρθενίαν ἐμοὶ φυλάττων, καὶ μολυσμοῦ τηρῶν ἀνεπίμικτον." Τούτοις Ἀγλαΐδας τοῖς ῥήμασι πλέον ἢ βέλεσι τιτρωσκόμενος (καὶ γὰρ ἀποτυγχάνων ἔρως βαρύτερός τε καὶ βιαιότερος), ἐπεί, πάντα λίθον (ὃ λέγεται) κινήσας, εὕρισκε τὴν παρθένον ἀκίνητον καὶ στερρὰν καὶ λόγοις ἀπατηλοῖς ἀθήρατον, χεῖρα συναγαγὼν οὐκ ὀλίγην, καὶ τοὺς περὶ τὰ ἐρωτικὰ ταῦτα δεινοὺς προσεταιρισάμενος, καθ᾽ ὁδὸν αὐτῇ ἐπετίθετο· καὶ ἀπαγαγεῖν ἐβιάζετο, ἔνθα δὴ καὶ ἠβούλετο.

12   Ἀλλ᾽ εὐθὺς εἰς τὴν πόλιν καὶ τὴν τῆς μητρὸς οἰκίαν διαδοθέντος τοῦ ἀτόπου τοῦδε τολμήματος, ἅμα πλεῖστοι καὶ κράτιστοι σὺν ὅπλοις ἐξῆεσαν· οἵ, καὶ μόνον ὀφθέντες, τοὺς βδελυροὺς ἐκείνους ἀφανεῖς ἔθεντο, οὐ χειρὶ μᾶλλον εἴκοντας, ἢ τῇ τοῦ πράγματος αἰσχύνῃ κραταιῶς ἀπελαυνομένους. Ἀγλαΐδας δὲ (καὶ γὰρ αἰσχύνης πάσης τὸ πάθος ἦν αὐτῷ βιαιότερον), οὔτε ξιφῶν, οὔτε πλήθους, οὔτ᾽ ἄλλου τινὸς φροντίσας, ἀλλὰ τῇ παρθένῳ περιπλακείς, πάντα παθεῖν ἕτοιμος ἦν μᾶλλον ἢ αὐτῆς ἀποστῆναι. Ἡ δὲ Ἰωσὴφ αὐτόχρημα ἦν, ὁ σωφρονικώτατός τε καὶ γενναιότατος· καὶ τὸν τοῦ σταυροῦ τύπον ὥσπερ ὅπλον προβαλλομένη, οὐ κατ᾽ ἐκείνου μᾶλλον ἢ τοῦ δι᾽ ἐκείνου πολεμεῖν αὐτὴν κρυπτῶς πειρωμένου, διεκρούσατό τε παραχρῆμα τὸν μιαρὸν καὶ ἀπώσατο· ὕβρεις τε ὅσας αὐτοῦ κατέχεε· καὶ τὴν ὄψιν (ἀξία γὰρ ἦν) πυγμῶν ἐνεπίμπλα καὶ ἐμπτυσμάτων.

and asked her to marry him. But Ioustina, having declared herself a bride of Christ alone, dismissed all other suitors nobly. "For me," she said, "He who protects my virginity and preserves it pure of all defilement is a sufficient bridegroom." Wounded by these words more than by arrows (since unrequited desire is heavier and more violent), and as he found the maiden to be immovable, staunch, and impossible to capture with deceptive words (though he had moved every stone, as the proverb says), he gathered abundant help, hired those specialized in matters of love, and ambushed her on the road; he thus carried her off by force to wherever he wished.

As soon as news of this outrageous daring spread in the city and to the household of her mother, many strong men, armed with weapons, rushed to meet the brigands. With their appearance alone, they made those appalling abductors flee out of sight—not so much because they yielded to force but rather because they were driven powerfully away by the shame of the deed. Yet Aglaïdas (as his passion was more violent than any feeling of shame) cared neither for the swords nor the crowd nor anything else; instead, he embraced the maiden and was ready to suffer anything rather than be separated from her. Ioustina became instantly like Joseph, that most chaste and most courageous man; holding the sign of the cross before her like a weapon—not against Aglaïdas, but rather against the one who was stealthily attempting to wage war against her through him—, she immediately repelled and pushed back that abominable man. She also poured all sorts of curses upon him and rained blows and spittle upon his face that deserved it.

12

13   Ἀλλ' ἐκείνῳ πρὸς ἔσχατον ἀνοίας ἐλθόντι, μᾶλλον δὲ
μανίας καὶ λύσσης ἐρωτικῆς, ταῦτα μὲν ὀλίγη φροντίς· ἐν
δὲ καὶ αὐτοῦ θανάτου βαρύτερον, τὸ Ἰουστίνης ἀποτυχεῖν.
Διὰ τοῦτο καὶ πρὸς βραχὺ κατήφειά τε αὐτὸν εἶχε· καὶ
λύπη συνέστελλεν. Ἐπεὶ δὲ τὰ τῆς ἐπιθυμίας αὖθις (εἰπεῖν)
ἀνεφλέγετο, ὁ δὲ περὶ τὴν ταύτης ἀντίστασιν ἀμελέτητός
τε ἦν καὶ λίαν ἀπαιδαγώγητος, καὶ οὐκ εἶχεν ἀναπαλαῖσαι
λογισμῷ γενναίῳ τὴν ἔφεσιν, ἐποίει πάντως ἅπερ αὐτῷ
τὸ πάθος ἐπέταττε· καὶ πρὸς ἀγῶνας ἑτέρους ἀφανεῖς ἀπεδύετο.

14   Ὧδε δὲ τοῦ λόγου γενόμενος, ἁπλοϊκῶς βούλομαι πάλιν καὶ σαφῶς ποιήσασθαι τὴν διήγησιν, ἐκεῖνα φθεγγόμε-
νος, ἅπερ ὡμολογημένην ἔχει καὶ φανερὰν τὴν ἀλήθειαν.

15   Κυπριανός τις ἐν τῇ Ἀντιοχέων διέτριβεν, ἡνίκα τὰ τῆς
βασιλείας σκῆπτρα Δέκιος εἶχεν. Ὃς πατρίδα μὲν ηὔχει
Καρχηδόνα τὴν ἐν Λιβύῃ· γεννήτορας δὲ τῶν εὐγενῶν καὶ
πλουσίων. Φιλοσοφία δὲ ἦν αὐτῷ καὶ τέχνη μαγικὴ τὸ φι-
λοπονούμενον· ταύταις ἐκ νέου προσέχων, εἰς ἀμφοτέρων
ἀκρότητα ἤλασε, σπουδὴν ἅμα καὶ φύσιν ὀξυτάτην εἰσ-
ενεγκών. Ὀνόματος δὲ μεγάλου τυχών, οὐ μόνην Καρχηδόνα χωρῆσαι τὸ ἐκείνου κλέος ἠξίωσεν, ἀλλὰ καὶ τὴν
περίβλεπτον Ἀντιόχειαν μάρτυρα τῆς αὐτοῦ σοφίας καὶ
τῆς περὶ τὰ μαγικὰ δεξιότητος ἠθέλησεν ἔχειν, ἴσως δὲ καὶ
μαθεῖν τι προσδοκήσας ἐκεῖθεν, ὃ μὴ μέχρι τότε μεμάθη-
κεν.

16   Πρὸς τοῦτον οὖν Ἀγλαΐδας ἐλθών, καὶ τὰ τοῦ πάθους
ὅπως εἶχε διηγησάμενος, καὶ ὅτι "Καὶ τέχνην πᾶσαν καὶ
χεῖρα κινήσας, οὐδεμίαν εὗρον τοῦ κακοῦ θεραπείαν, ἀλλὰ

Even so, having reached the peak of folly, or rather of madness and erotic rage, Aglaïdas cared little about all this. One thing was for him worse than death itself: losing Ioustina. For a short while, sadness overtook him and desolation depressed him. But as soon as his desire was again (so to speak) rekindled, untrained as he was and rather unschooled in its resistance, he could not wrestle his lust with gentlemanly reasoning, but was doing exactly as his passion demanded and thus prepared himself for new, secret endeavors. 13

Having reached this part of the story, I wish to resume my narrative in simple style and with clarity, relating only those facts whose truth is generally accepted and obvious. 14

There was a certain Kyprianos who lived in the city of Antioch, at the time when Decius held the imperial reins. Kyprianos boasted Carthage in Libya as his fatherland and his parents were among the noble and wealthy. His occupation was philosophy and the art of magic and, by devoting attention to these subjects from his youth, he brought them both to perfection, having applied his studiousness as well as his natural sharpness of mind. When he became famous, he thought that he deserved that not only Carthage should contain his glory, but that also the renowned Antioch should become a witness to his wisdom and his skill in matters of magic; perhaps, he also expected to learn there something new, which he had not yet learned. 15

It is to this man that Aglaïdas came and narrated everything about his passion; he said, "I employed every device and did everything in my power, yet found no remedy for 16

πάντων κρείττονα τὴν παρθένον ἐθεασάμην," τὸ τελευταῖον προστίθησιν, ὅτι "Σὺ μόνος μοι ὑπελείφθης τῆς συμφορᾶς παραμύθιον· καὶ ἐπὶ σοὶ μόνῳ θαρρήσας, τοῦ μὴ προκρῖναι μέχρι καὶ νῦν τὸν θάνατον τῆς ζωῆς τὴν ὁρμὴν ἐπέσχον. Πάντως δὲ οὐδὲ φροντίσεις, ὅσον ἄρα πλοῦτον καὶ χρυσίον παρ᾽ ἡμῶν ἕξεις, τῆς τοιαύτης ἀπολύσας με συμφορᾶς, ὡς ἔγωγε ἄφθονά σοι ταῦτα παρέξω καὶ ἐλπίδων πασῶν ἄμεινον."

17   Εἶπε· καὶ Κυπριανὸν ἐπακούοντα ἔσχε, καὶ ὡς τάχος λύσειν αὐτῷ τὴν λύπην ἐπαγγελλόμενον. Ὁ μὲν οὖν ἀπήει χαίρων, καὶ ὅσον οὔπω τὴν παρθένον διὰ χειρὸς ἕξειν φανταζόμενος. Κυπριανὸς δὲ εἰς τὰς βίβλους εὐθὺς ἔβλεπε, τὰς τοιαῦτα ἐνεργεῖν δυναμένας. Καὶ ἓν τῶν πονηρῶν πνευμάτων καλέσας, ἃ πρὸς τὰ φαῦλα ταῦτα συνεργεῖν οἶδε προθύμως, καὶ οἷς ἐκεῖνος διακόνοις ἐχρῆτο, μέγα τι καὶ τερατῶδες ἀνύειν βουλόμενος, "Εἰ καλῶς μοι καὶ ταχέως," ἔφη, "τελέσεις τὸ ὑπούργημα τόδε, τὸ μετὰ ταῦτα χαριοῦμαί σοι τὰ μέγιστα· καὶ τῶν ἄλλων πάντων θήσω προέχειν."

18   Τὸ δὲ τὰ προσφιλῆ καὶ συνήθη τῆς ὑπερηφανίας φθεγγόμενον, "Καὶ τί," εἶπεν, "ὃ μὴ ῥᾳδίως ἐμοὶ πεπράξεται βουλομένῳ; Πολλάκις μὲν γὰρ ὅλας πόλεις κατέσεισα· πολλάκις δὲ χεῖρα πατροκτόνον ὀξεῖαν ὀφθῆναι πρὸς τοῦτο καὶ τολμηρὰν παρεσκεύασα· μῖσος ἀδελφοῖς τε καὶ ὁμοζύγοις ἄσπονδον ἐνῆκα· παρθενεύειν πολλοὺς βουλομένους ἀπεῖρξα· μοναχοῖς ἐν ὄρεσι διαιτωμένοις, καὶ νηστείᾳ πάσῃ συνειθισμένοις, καὶ μικροῦ μηδὲ σαρκὸς ὅλως μνείαν ποιουμένοις, ἐπιθυμίαν σαρκὸς ἐνέσπειρα καὶ

this evil; rather, I watched the virgin defeat me in every respect." Then he added this last point: "You are the only consolation left to me for this misfortune; placing my trust in you alone, I restrained my urge to choose death over life until this very instant. Worry not about the amount of wealth and gold you will obtain from me if you release me from this misfortune, as I will provide them to you abundantly and exceeding all your hopes."

These were his words and Kyprianos heard his plea and promised to release him from this anguish as soon as possible. Aglaïdas left a happy man, imagining that in no time the virgin would be his. Meanwhile, Kyprianos immediately looked into his books, wherein lay the power to enact such hopes. He then summoned one of the evil spirits, one of his helpers who know how to eagerly collaborate on such wicked plans, with the wish that he perform a great and shocking deed. "If you do this service for me well and quickly," he said to the spirit, "from then on, you will be my favorite and I will prefer you over all the others." 17

The spirit responded with his dear and usual words of arrogance: "What is there," he said, "that cannot be done easily if I so wish? Many times I shook down entire cities, many times I turned a man's hand against his father into a fast and bold patricide, I instilled implacable hatred among brothers and between spouses, I prevented many from remaining virgins despite their wishes, I implanted the desire for the flesh into monks inhabiting mountains and used to every sort of fasting, people who had almost lost all memory of the flesh, 18

εὐμενὲς βλέψαι πρὸς ἡδονὰς παρεσκεύασα. Ἄλλους ἀπο-
τάξασθαι τοῖς σαρκικοῖς πᾶσι καὶ οἷς ἡμεῖς χαίρομεν καὶ
πρὸς ἀρετὴν μεταθέσθαι βουλομένους, ἀντικρούσας, ἑτέ-
ρωθεν ἀπογνῶναι τούσδε τοὺς λογισμοὺς πεποίηκα, καὶ
τῶν συνήθων πάλιν ἐπιμελῶς ἔχεσθαι. Ὅμως, τί πολλὰ
λέγειν προῆγμαι; Αὐτὸ δείξει τὸ πρᾶγμα καὶ νῦν, ὁποῖός
εἰμι τὴν διακονίαν ἀνυσιμώτατος. Λαβὼν οὖν τουτὶ τὸ
φάρμακον"—ἄγγος δέ τι ἦν τὸ διδόμενον πλῆρες—, "τῷ
οἴκῳ ἐπίρρανον τῆς παρθένου. Καὶ εἰ μὴ πάντα ἕξει σοι
κατὰ γνώμην, παροπτέος ἐγώ σοι τὸ λοιπὸν καὶ ἄχρηστος·
καὶ ἀσθένειαν ἡμῶν κατάγνωθι τὴν ἐσχάτην."

19   Ἐγίνετο μὲν οὕτω ταῦτα. Ἡ δὲ παρθένος, ἀναστᾶσα
περὶ τρίτην τῆς νυκτὸς ὥραν τὰς εὐχὰς ἀποδοῦναι Θεῷ,
διεθερμαίνετο μὲν τοὺς νεφροὺς ἤδη, καὶ τῆς προσβολῆς
ἠσθάνετο τοῦ Πειράζοντος. Ὅσῳ δὲ ταῦτα ἦν, κἀκείνη πάλιν τὰ τῆς εὐχῆς παρετείνετο. Ἐπεὶ δὲ δαψιλῶς ὑπετύφετο
τὸ τοῦ ἀντικειμένου πνεύματος πῦρ, ἐκείνη βιαζομένη,
"Ἐμνήσθην ἐν νυκτὶ τοῦ ὀνόματός σου," ἔλεγε, "Κύριε, καὶ
εὐφράνθην. Παγίδα ἡτοίμασαν τοῖς ποσί μου καὶ κατέκαμ-
ψαν τὴν ψυχήν μου. Ἐγὼ δὲ ἐν τῷ αὐτοὺς παρενοχλεῖν μοι,
ἐνεδυόμην σάκκον· καὶ ἐταπείνουν ἐν νηστείᾳ τὴν ψυχήν μου·
καὶ ἡ προσευχή μου εἰς κόλπον μου ἀποστραφήσεται. Ἐν
τούτῳ ἔγνων ὅτι τεθέληκάς με ὅτι οὐ μὴ ἐπιχαρῇ ὁ ἐχθρός
μου ἐπ᾽ ἐμέ. Ἡ ρομφαία αὐτῶν εἰσέλθοι εἰς τὰς καρδίας αὐτῶν, καὶ τὰ τόξα αὐτῶν συντριβείη. Σοὶ γὰρ τῷ ζῶντι Θεῷ
ὅλῃ ψυχῇ καὶ καρδίᾳ ἐμαυτὴν ἀνατέθεικα." Τούτοις χρη-
σαμένη τοῖς ὅπλοις κατὰ τοῦ Πειράζοντος ἡ γενναία, εἶτα
καὶ τὸ τοῖς ἐχθροῖς ἀνυπόστατον, τὸ τοῦ σταυροῦ σημεῖον,

and I made them look favorably on pleasures. Others who wished to renounce all matters of the flesh—the sort of things in which we delight—and devote themselves to virtue, I opposed and made them abandon such thoughts and persist diligently in their earlier bad habits. But why do I go on and on? In this case as well, the deed itself will demonstrate how effective I am in my service. Take this drug"—he offered a filled vessel—"and sprinkle with it the house of the virgin. If everything does not go according to your wishes, you may pass over me in the future as useless, and accuse me of the utmost impotence."

And so he did. Thus, when the virgin woke up around the 19
third hour of the night to offer her prayers to God, already she began to suffer an inflammation in her kidneys and to feel the attack of the Tempter. As long as this lasted, she too intensified her prayer. Pressured by the obstinate and smoldering fire caused by the adversary spirit, she prayed: "*I remembered Your name in the night, O Lord, and felt delight. They have prepared a trap for my steps and have overwhelmed my soul. While they troubled me, I wore sackcloth and humbled my soul with fasting and my prayer shall return into my lap. In this, I knew that You wanted me: since my enemy will not rejoice on my behalf. May their sword enter into their own hearts, and may their bows be crushed.* For with my entire soul and heart I have dedicated myself to You, the living God." Using these weapons against the Tempter, and then brandishing against him what is unbearable to these foes, namely the sign of the cross, the

αὐτῷ ἐπαφεῖσα, αἰσχύνῃ καλυψάμενον σὺν πολλῷ τῷ δέει, ἐξήλασε τὸ δαιμόνιον.

20 Ἐπανελθὸν δὲ πρὸς Κυπριανόν ἐκεῖνο, ἠσχύνετο μὲν τὴν ἧτταν ὁμολογῆσαι, καί, πολλὰς ἐλίττον πλοκάς, ταύτην ᾔει κἀκείνην μετατρεπόμενον. Ἐρωτώμενον δὲ ὅμως ἀκριβῶς καὶ λεπτολογούμενον, καίτοι φιλοψευδὲς ὄν, καὶ ἄκον φιλάληθες γίνεται· καὶ φανερῶς ἐκκαλύπτει ὃ λίαν κρύπτειν ἠβούλετο, "Εἶδόν τι σημεῖον," εἰρηκός, "καὶ ἰσχυρῶς ἔφριξα· καὶ τὴν ἐκείνου δύναμιν οὐχ ὑπέστην."

21 Οὕτως οὖν ἐκεῖνο καταγνωσθέν, ἕτερος αὐτίκα δαίμων μετακαλεῖται, πολὺ τοῦ προτέρου τῷ δοκεῖν δραστικώτερος. Καὶ ὃς ἀπελθών, αὐτίκα τὰ ὅμοια δράσας, τοῖς ὁμοίοις ὅπλοις ἐξεκρούετό τε καὶ ἀπεπέμπετο· καὶ τῷ πέμψαντι μετ' αἰσχύνης παρίστατο. Ἐπὶ τούτοις αὐτὸς παρῆν ὁ πατήρ τε καὶ ἄρχων τῶν δαιμόνων εἶναι λεγόμενος. Ὃς τοῖς μὲν πρότερον ἐκπεμφθεῖσιν ἠπείλει κόλασιν, οἷα μὴ τεχνικῶς μηδ' ἐπιτηδείως περὶ τοῦτο διαγενομένοις ὡς ᾤετο· πλεονάζει γὰρ τοῖς δαίμοσι τῶν ἄλλων κακῶν τὸ ἀλαζονικὸν καὶ μεγάλαυχον. Κυπριανῷ δὲ θαρρεῖν ἐκέλευε, καὶ μηδὲν αὐτῷ μέλειν τοῦ προκειμένου.

22 Τί οὖν τὸ μετὰ ταῦτα; Νέον αὐτὸς ἀναρριπίζει καὶ διαλλάττοντα πόλεμον, πολὺ τὸ πανοῦργον καὶ δολερὸν ἔχοντα. Καὶ ἀπελθὼν ἐν σχήματι γυναικείῳ τῇ κόρῃ παρεκαθέζετο· καὶ ὁ πάντολμος παρὰ Θεοῦ ἀπεστάλθαι πρὸς αὐτὴν οὐκ ἔφριξε λέγειν, "ὡς ἂν συνῶ σοι," φησί, "καὶ ἐπὶ μακρῷ καρτερήσω τὴν συνδιαίτησιν· τὸν γὰρ ἴσον τῆς παρθενίας ὠδίνω σοι καὶ αὐτὴ πόθον. Πλήν, ἀλλὰ τίνα μισθὸν ταύτης ἕνεκεν λήψομαι, βούλομαι μαθεῖν παρὰ

noble woman drove away the demon who covered himself with shame and much fright.

The demon returned to Kyprianos, but was ashamed to confess his defeat, and beat around the bush, now making one claim, and then another. When, however, he was submitted to exact and detailed questioning, although he was fond of lying, he unwillingly embraced the truth and clearly revealed that which he very much wanted to hide. "I saw a certain symbol," he said, "and was mightily terrified and I could not withstand its power." 20

As he was declared unfit, another demon was summoned immediately, supposedly much more effective than the previous one. He too went to Ioustina, did again the same sorts of things, and was repelled and driven away by the same sort of weapons. With shame, he stood before the one who had sent him. When this happened, he himself appeared, the one said to be the father and the leader of the demons. He threatened with punishment those who had been sent before, as they had gone about their task neither skillfully nor appropriately, in his opinion; for the most dominant vices of the demons are arrogance and haughtiness. And he ordered Kyprianos to take courage and not to worry about the endeavor at hand. 21

What happened next? He rekindled a new and different war with much cunning and guile. He went and sat next to the girl in the guise of a woman and the audacious one did not shrink from saying to Ioustina that (s)he was sent to her by God, "so that I may live with you," he said, "and endure this cohabitation for the duration; for, equally to you, I too feel the labor pains of desire for virginity. Nevertheless, I wish to learn from you what reward I will receive for this, as 22

σοῦ· μέγα γάρ μοι καὶ παρακεκινδυνευμένον τὸ πρᾶγμα δοκεῖ, καὶ πολλῶν δεόμενον τῶν ἀγώνων." Ἡ δὲ δεῖσθαι μὲν ἱδρώτων ἔλεγε τὸ πρᾶγμα ταῖς ἀληθείαις, "πλήν, ὅταν εἰς τὰς ἀμοιβὰς ἀπίδῃς καὶ τοὺς στεφάνους, πολλὴν καταγνώσῃ ῥαθυμίαν τῶν καλοῦ τοιούτου παραμελούντων."

23   Ἐντεῦθεν ἡ πονηρία, λαβομένη προφάσεως, ἐποίει τὰ ἑαυτῆς· καὶ "Τίς," ἔλεγε, "τῇ Εὔᾳ ὠφέλεια πρὸ τῆς τοῦ ξύλου γεύσεως; Πόθεν δὲ καὶ ὁ κόσμος ἐγένετο ἄν; Πόθεν οἱ νῦν ὄντες τὸ εἶναι εἶχον λαβεῖν, γάμου καὶ συναφείας ἀνῃρημένων, εἰ μὴ τοῦ ξύλου Εὔα τῆς γλυκείας ἐγεύσατο βρώσεως, εἰ μὴ τὸν ἄνδρα ἔγνω, τὸν διὰ τοῦτο δὴ καὶ γενόμενον; Εἰ πᾶσαι παρθενεύειν προείλοντο, πόθεν ἂν ἐτίκτοντο παῖδες, τὸ πᾶσιν ἀνθρώποις ἡδὺ παραμύθιον, ἡ τοῦ κατὰ μικρὸν ἐκλείποντος κόσμου ἀναζώωσις;"

24   Τούτων ἀκούσασα τῶν λόγων Ἰούστα, οὐ τὰ τῆς προμήτορος ὑπέμεινεν Εὔας, ἀλλ᾽ εὐθὺς ἐξανίστατο· καὶ τὸν πονηρὸν ἐξέκλινε σύμβουλον. Ὅθεν τὸ σύνηθες ὅπλον, τὸ τοῦ σταυροῦ σημεῖον, ἀφῆκε καὶ κατ᾽ αὐτοῦ. Καὶ ὁ μέν, πλείονι τῶν ἄλλων μεγαλαυχίᾳ σεσοβημένος, πλείονα καὶ τὴν αἰσχύνην ἔχων, εὐθὺς ἐξηλαύνετο. Αὐτὴ δὲ πάλιν ταῖς πρὸς Θεὸν εὐχαῖς καὶ δεήσεσιν ἑαυτὴν ἀνελάμβανεν. Ἐπὶ τούτοις ὁ τὰ μεγάλα φυσῶν ταπεινὸς ὤφθη Κυπριανῷ, καὶ σύμβολα σαφῆ τῆς ἥττης φέρων ἐπὶ τῆς ὄψεως. Ὁ δέ, "Καὶ ὁ τοσοῦτος," ἔφη, "σὺ τῆς τοιᾶσδε κόρης ἠλάττωσαι; Εἰς τί δὲ ἐκείνη τὸ θαρρεῖν ἔχουσα, μεγάλα τοιαῦτα κατὰ τῶν μεγάλων ὑμῶν δύναται;"

25   Τότε ὁ δαίμων (θεία δὲ ἦν πάντως ἡ κινοῦσα δύναμις ἔκφορα ταῦτα ποιεῖν τὸν τῆς ἀληθείας ἀντίπαλον), "Οὐχ

this way of life seems to me a serious matter and rather dangerous, requiring many struggles." And Ioustina responded that, in truth, virginity requires sweat, "nevertheless, when you look to the rewards and the crowns, you will condemn the great sloth of those who neglect such a good thing."

His slyness took this as pretext to set about its usual 23 work. "What benefit," (s)he said, "did Eve enjoy before tasting of the tree? How would the world have come into being? How would the people living today have obtained their existence, if marriage and intercourse were eradicated, if Eve did not taste the sweet savor of the tree, if she did not know her man, who was created for this very purpose? If every woman chose to remain a virgin, how would children be born, the sweet consolation for all mankind, the renewal of the world which wanes little by little?"

When she heard these words, Iousta did not submit to 24 the fate of Eve her foremother, but immediately resisted and shunned the evil counselor. She thus wielded her usual weapon, the sign of the cross, also against him. As he swaggered with more boastfulness than the rest, he was subject also to greater shame and was immediately driven away. Meanwhile, Iousta resumed her prayers and entreaties to God. After this, that very arrogant one appeared to Kyprianos humiliated, bearing on his face clear signs of his defeat. "Were you, the great one," Kyprianos asked, "also defeated by that extraordinary maiden? What is the source of her courage with which she overpowers your powerful lot in such fashion?"

Then, the demon replied (though it was definitely divine 25 power that made him, the adversary of truth, utter words against his nature): "We cannot stand," he said, "even to see

23

ὑπομένομεν," ἔφη, "τὸ τοῦ σταυροῦ σημεῖον οὐδὲ μόνον ἰδεῖν τυπούμενον· ἀλλὰ φθάνομεν ἀνὰ κράτος φεύγοντές τε καὶ διωθούμενοι, πρὶν ἢ τελείως αὐτὸ τυπωθῆναι." Πόσης ἀνάγκης ἦν τὸ ταῦτα ἐκκαλύψαι τὸν τοῦ ψεύδους πατέρα καὶ τῆς κακίας δημιουργόν τε καὶ πρόξενον; Ὥστε οὐδὲν ἔλαττον ὑπῆρξε θαῦμα τοῦ ἐκεῖνον οὕτως ὑπὸ κόρης καταβληθῆναι τὸ τὴν ἰδίαν ἧτταν ἀνακαλύψαι τὸν ὑπερήφανον. Πάντως δὲ πρὸς συνετὸν ἐλέγετο ταῦτα. Καὶ ἀφορμὴν λαβὼν ὁ σοφός, σοφώτερος ἦν· συνῆκε γὰρ εὐθέως ὡς, εἴ γε τοιαῦτα ὁ σταυρωθεὶς δύναται, πόση ἄνοια, τοῦτον ἀπολιπόντα, τοῖς ἐχθροῖς ἐκείνου, λίαν οὕτως εὐπτοήτοις οὖσι καὶ ἀδυνάτοις, προσέχειν.

26 Ταῦτα Κυπριανὸς ἐννοήσας, εὐθὺς κατὰ τῶν βίβλων ἐχώρει· καὶ ὡς κακῶν πηγάς, ὡς ὀργίων δαιμονικῶν θησαυρούς, ὡς τῆς αὐτῶν μοχθηρίας ἐντρυφήματά τε καὶ ἀναθήματα, δοῦναι πυρὶ ταύτας ἔγνω. Φέρειν οὖν εἰπὼν τοῖς θεράπουσι, καταλαμβάνει τὴν ἐκκλησίαν· καὶ τῷ ἐπισκόπῳ συγγενόμενος (Ἄνθιμος αὐτῷ ὄνομα), ἐγγραφῆναι τοῖς τοῦ Χριστοῦ προβάτοις ἠξίου. Ὁ δὲ (καὶ γὰρ τὸν ἄνδρα ἐγίνωσκε, καὶ λύκον αὐτὸν ἀτεχνῶς ᾔδει), τέχνην εἶναι τὸ πρᾶγμα νομίσας, τοὺς ἐκτὸς τῆς ἐκκλησίας ἀρκεῖν αὐτῷ παρηγγύα, μὴ καὶ τοῖς ἔνδον μελετᾶν ἐπιτίθεσθαι· "Μήποτέ σοι," φησί, "καὶ καλὸν τὸ πέρας οὐκ ἀπαντήσοι."

27 Ἤκουσε Κυπριανός. Καὶ πᾶσαν εἰσῆγε πίστιν μετὰ πολλοῦ τοῦ μετρίου, τήν τε τοῦ Χριστοῦ δύναμιν ἀνίκητον οὖσαν ἐπεμαρτύρει· Ἰούσταν γὰρ αὐτῷ ταύτην ἔναγχος ἔλεγε γνωρίσαι, δι᾽ ἧς ἐκείνη πολλοὺς ἐτρέψατο δαίμονας. "Λάβε δὲ καὶ τὰς βίβλους," ἔφη, "ταύτας, αἵ μοι τῶν κακῶν

the sign of the cross being made; rather, we flee with all our might and are pushed away even before the cross has been completed." What constraint there must have been for the father of lies, the creator and cause of evil, to reveal this? This confession of defeat by the arrogant one was a miracle equal to his being vanquished by the maiden. In any case, these words addressed a wise man, who took this opportunity and became wiser; for he immediately understood: if indeed the crucified one had such power, what inanity it was to abandon Him and pay attention to His enemies who are so easily scared and weak.

With these thoughts in mind, Kyprianos immediately 26 turned against his books and decided to burn them as sources of evil, as receptacles of demonic rites, as objects for demonic delight and devotion. He asked his servants to carry them and came to the church. There he met the bishop (his name was Anthimos) and asked to be registered among the flock of Christ's sheep. Anthimos (knowing Kyprianos, and considering him a veritable wolf), thinking the matter to be a trick, ordered him to limit himself to those outside the church and not plan to attack those inside it; "Lest," he said, "this not come to a good end for you."

Kyprianos heard the bishop, but introduced every sort of 27 proof with much moderation and attested to the invincibility of Christ's power. He said that Iousta recently introduced him to this power, through which she turned away many demons. "Take also these books," he said, "which

ἐξηγήσαντο· καὶ δίδου παρανάλωμα τῷ πυρί, ἵνα καὶ δαίμονες γνῶσιν, ὅτι μηδὲν κοινὸν ἐμοὶ κἀκείνοις τὸ μετὰ
ταῦτα· αὗται γάρ μοι τῷ φίλτρῳ τῷ εἰς αὐτοὺς ἐμεσίτευον."

28   Τούτοις μεταβεβλῆσθαι τὸν ἄνδρα πεισθεὶς ὁ ἐπίσκοπος, τὰς μὲν πυρὸς ἔργον (ὥσπερ ἄρα καὶ ἦσαν ἄξιαι) τὸ
τάχος ἐποίει· ἐκεῖνον δὲ εὐλογήσας ἀφῆκε, πολλὰ νουθε-
τήσας, καὶ τοῖς δεδογμένοις ἐμμένειν ἀσφαλισάμενος.
Αὐτίκα γοῦν πολὺς τῶν προτέρων εἰσῄει Κυπριανὸν ὁ
μετάμελος. Καί, τὸ ἀπ' ἐκείνου, οὕτως τῆς μοχθηρᾶς
ἀγωγῆς ἀπέστη, καὶ τοσοῦτον ἑαυτὸν τοῖς ἀτίμοις ἐξεπο-
λέμωσε πάθεσιν, ὅσην ἄρα, πρὸ τοῦ, τὴν πρὸς αὐτὰ φιλίαν
ἐσπείσατο. Οὐ μήν, ἀλλὰ καὶ περὶ τὰ καλὰ καὶ φίλα Θεῷ
τοσαύτην εἰσήνεγκε τὴν σπουδήν, ὅσην οὐδὲ περὶ τὰ πονηρὰ πρότερον. Δεῖγμα τῆς καλῆς ταύτης μεταβολῆς,
μετὰ τὴν τῶν βιβλίων καῦσιν, καὶ ἡ τῶν εἰδώλων κατάλυ-
σις, οὕτω γινομένη σὺν ἀκριβείᾳ, ὡς μηδὲ ἴχνος αὐτῶν τὸ
παράπαν ὑπολειφθῆναι, εἴ τι δὴ καὶ τοιοῦτον ὁ προλαβὼν
χρόνος παρ' αὐτῷ ἐθεάσατο.

29   Εἶτα τί; Κόνιν ἐφ' ὕβρει τῆς κεφαλῆς ἐκεῖνος καταχεά-
μενος, βαρεῖς τε ἀναφέρων τοὺς στεναγμούς, καὶ λούων
τοῖς δάκρυσιν ἑαυτόν, μόνος μόνῳ τῷ πανταχοῦ παρόντι
ὡμίλει. Τοσούτῳ τε τὴν καρδίαν τῷ τοῦ Θεοῦ περιεθέρ-
μαινεν ἔρωτι, καὶ οὕτως αὐτῆς πᾶν ὕψωμα καταβέβληκεν,
ὡς παραιτεῖσθαι καὶ αὐτὴν τὴν πρὸς Θεὸν ἱκετείαν προσφέρειν τῷ στόματι διὰ ταπεινοφροσύνης ὑπερβολήν. Διὰ
ταῦτα, μέγας μὲν Κυπριανὸς ἡνίκα δαίμοσι τὴν ὁρμὴν ἐδίδου, καὶ τὰ πρεσβεῖα τῆς τιμῆς παρ' αὐτοῖς ἔχων· μείζων

initiated me into evil, and burn them, so that also the demons may know that, after this, I will have nothing to do with them; for it is these books that mediated my love for the demons."

Persuaded by these words that the man had changed, Anthimos quickly set the books on fire (after all, this is what they deserved). He then blessed Kyprianos and dismissed him, after giving him much advice and encouraging him to abide by the teachings of the Church. Immediately, great remorse entered Kyprianos for his earlier self. From that point onward, he avoided wicked behavior and fought against dishonorable passions with intensity equal to the attachment he had maintained toward them until very recently. Indeed, not only that, but he also exerted even more zeal in good deeds that were pleasing to God than he had previously shown for wicked actions. Another evidence of this good conversion, was—after the burning of the books—the destruction of idols, which he conducted with such precision that not even a trace of them was left behind, whatever such idols times past had witnessed in his possession. 28

And then what? He poured the dust of shame on his head, voiced deep sighs, and bathed himself in tears. He thus conversed in solitude with God who is everywhere. He kindled such great desire for God in his heart and so demolished all his heart's haughtiness that he refrained from even uttering his supplications to God because of the excess of his humility. Due to this, Kyprianos, who had been great when he offered all his energy to the demons and had held the first place of honor among them, was even greater in the eyes of 29

δὲ παρὰ Θεῷ καὶ Χριστιανοῖς πάλιν, ὁπότε τὴν καλὴν ἀλλοίωσιν ἠλλοιώθη, καὶ τὴν πρὸς ἀρετὴν ἀπάγουσαν ὤδευσεν.

30   Οὕτως οὖν ἐν ἐξομολογήσει, στεναγμοῖς τε καὶ δάκρυσιν ὅλην τὴν νύκτα διηνεκῶς, περὶ τὸν ὄρθρον ὃς τὴν τοῦ Μεγάλου Σαββάτου εἶχεν ἡμέραν, εἰς τὸ κυριακὸν ἀφικνεῖται, πολλοὺς ἔχων τοὺς ἀντιφιλοτιμωμένους ἀλλήλοις, καὶ προφθάσαι τοῦτον ἐκεῖσε καὶ ἰδεῖν σπεύδοντας. Εἰσιὼν τοίνυν, δεξιὸν ἐποιεῖτο σύμβολον τῆς εἰς τὸν ναὸν εἰσόδου, εἰ τῷ σκοπῷ ἐκείνου καὶ τὰ τῆς ἀκροάσεως ῥήματα συμβαίνοντα ἔξοι.

31   Εἶχε μὲν οὖν τοὺς πόδας τῆς ἐκκλησίας ἐντός· εἶχε δὲ παραδόξως καὶ τὸν διάκονον, ταῦτα δὴ τὰ τοῦ ἀποστόλου διατρανοῦντα, "Χριστὸς ἡμᾶς ἐξηγόρασεν ἐκ τῆς κατάρας τοῦ Νόμου, γενόμενος ὑπὲρ ἡμῶν κατάρα"· ὡς δὲ καὶ τὰ τοῦ προφήτου· "Εἶδες, Κύριε, μὴ παρασιωπήσῃς· Κύριε, μὴ ἀποστῇς ἀπ᾽ ἐμοῦ." Κατ᾽ αὐτὸ δὲ καὶ τὸν Ἡσαΐαν ὑπανεγίνωσκεν ἕτερος, "Ἰδοὺ συνήσει," λέγων, "ὁ παῖς μου ὁ ἀγαπητὸς ὃν ἡρέτισα." Ἅπερ ἅπαντα συνᾴδοντα τῷ ἰδίῳ κρίνας σκόπῳ, ἐντελέστερον πρὸς τὴν εἰς Θεὸν πίστιν συνεβίβαζε τὴν ψυχήν, ἅτε συνετὸς ὢν ἄγαν καὶ τὸ δέον συνιδεῖν ὀξύτατος.

32   Ἐπεὶ δὲ καὶ ὁ καιρὸς ἐκάλει τοὺς κατηχουμένους τῆς ἐκκλησίας βαδίζειν ἐκτός, ὁ δὲ ἐπέμενεν ἔνδον ὤν, διάκονός τις (ᾧπερ Ἀστέριος ὄνομα) ἐπέτρεπεν ἐξιέναι. Ὁ δέ, κἀκεῖσε τὸ θερμὸν ὡς ἔοικε καὶ μεγαλόψυχον καὶ τὸ τοῦ φρονήματος ἀταπείνωτον δεῖξαι βουλόμενος, καὶ ὅτι μὴ εὔκολός ἐστι τῷ παντὶ μηδὲ πρόχειρος, οὐδέν τι μᾶλλον

God and the Christians, now that he experienced the good conversion, and traversed the path that leads to virtue.

After a whole night spent in confession of sins, in constant sighs and tears, Kyprianos came to the church around the time of the matins on Holy Saturday, while many vied with each other to arrive before him and observe him. When he entered, he thought that it would be a good sign for his entrance to the church, if the words of the reading would correspond with his purpose. 30

His feet had hardly entered the church, when, miraculously, the deacon started proclaiming aloud the following words of the apostle: "*Christ redeemed us from the curse of the Law, having become a curse for us*"; and also these words from the prophet: "*You saw, O Lord, do not pass by in silence! O Lord, do not stay far from me.*" Then, another deacon recited Isaiah saying: "*Behold, he will understand, my beloved son whom I have chosen.*" Since he was very wise and extremely sharp in recognizing what was right, Kyprianos considered all these to be in agreement with his own purpose, and thus advanced his soul to a more perfect faith in God. 31

As it was the time that the catechumens were asked to step outside the church, and he remained steadfastly inside, a deacon (whose name was Asterios) urged him to go out. Wishing, however, to show also, it seems, his fervent, high-minded, and unconquerable spirit, and that he was neither docile nor submissive to anyone, without yielding in the 32

ἐνδούς, "Τίνος χάριν," ἔφη, "διάκονε, δοῦλόν με γεγονότα Χριστοῦ, ἔξω βάλλειν τῆς ἐκκλησίας φιλονεικεῖς; Ἵνα τί δέ μου καὶ τὸν τόνον τῆς προθέσεως παραλύεις;" Ἐπὶ τούτοις ὁ διάκονος μὲν ἐφ᾽ οἷς ἔκρινεν ἔμενε· καὶ τῆς ἐκκλησίας ἐξῶσαι παρεβιάζετο, προσθεὶς οὕτως εἰπεῖν, "Οὔπω γέγονας τέλειος." Τὸν δὲ πληγῆναί τε ἰσχυρῶς τῷ ῥήματι, καὶ "Ζῇ μου ὁ Χριστός," φάναι, "ὁ τοὺς δαίμονας καταργήσας, ὁ τὴν παρθένον σώσας, ὁ τὸν ἀνάξιον οἰκτείρας ἐμέ. Οὐ τῆς προόδου τῆς ἐκκλησίας ἀπείρξεις με· οὐκ ἀποχωρήσω ταύτης, εἰ μὴ καὶ τέλειος γένωμαι."

33 Τοῖς ῥηθεῖσιν οὖν ὁ διάκονος σφόδρα καταπλαγείς, γνωρίζει ταῦτα τῷ ἐπισκόπῳ, καὶ ὅπως μὲν αὐτὸς ἐξώθει τῆς ἐκκλησίας Κυπριανόν, ὁ δὲ ἐντὸς μένειν ἠγάπα, καὶ μετὰ τῶν κατηχουμένων οὐκ ἠξίου χωρεῖν, ἑαυτὸν ἐθέλων οὐ τούτου μόνου, ἀλλὰ καὶ τῶν τελειοποιῶν μυστηρίων ἐπιτυχῆ γενέσθαι καὶ ἄξιον. Ὁ δὲ περὶ τὸ σῶσαι ψυχὴν εὐτεχνότατος Ἄνθιμος, τὸ πρᾶγμα θεῖον ἀκριβῶς λογισάμενος, μετακαλεῖται τάχιστα τὸν Κυπριανόν· καί, κατηχήσας, εἶτα καὶ τῷ θείῳ καθαίρει βαπτίσματι. Καὶ τῇ μὲν ὀγδόῃ τῶν ἡμερῶν ἱεροκήρυκα καὶ ἐξηγητὴν τῶν τοῦ Χριστοῦ μυστηρίων ἀποδεικνύει· τῇ εἰκοστῇ δὲ ὑποδιάκονον· τῇ δὲ τριακοστῇ τοῖς διακόνοις συναριθμεῖ.

34 Οὕτω μέντοι Κυπριανὸς καλῶς περὶ τὰ καλὰ διεγένετο. Καὶ οὕτω παρὰ τὴν πρώτην ὁρμὴν γέγονεν ἔνθεος· μεμένηκέ τε ἐπ᾽ αὐτῆς, πρὸς οὐδεμίαν ἀνθολκὴν τῆς φύσεως ταπεινὸν βλέπων καὶ ὑπ᾽ αὐτῆς καμπτόμενος, ὡς καὶ θείας ἄνωθεν τῆς ἐλλάμψεως καταξιωθῆναι, καὶ χάριν πλουτῆσαι

least Kyprianos said: "Deacon, why do you strive to throw me out of the church, when I have become a servant of Christ? Why do you mollify the force of my intent?" After these words, the deacon held fast to what he had judged to be right and tried to force and push him out of the church, adding the following words: "You have not yet become perfect." Kyprianos was mightily wounded by this remark, and replied: "Long live my Christ, who abolished the demons, who saved the virgin girl, who showed mercy to my unworthy self. You will not prevent me from stepping forward into the church and I will not leave, unless I also become perfect."

Greatly surprised by these words, the deacon informed the bishop about all this: how he tried to push Kyprianos out of the church, and how Kyprianos insisted on staying inside and would not leave with the catechumens, and that this was not the only wish of Kyprianos, but that he also wanted to achieve and become worthy of the perfecting rites. Anthimos, a man most skilled in saving a soul, understood perfectly that this behavior stemmed from God and summoned Kyprianos immediately; after instructing him as a catechumen, he purified him also with the holy baptism. On the eighth day, he made him a preacher and exegete of Christ's mysteries; on the twentieth, he made him a subdeacon; and, on the thirtieth, he included him among the deacons. 33

In this way, then, Kyprianos proceeded well toward what is good. And he became so inspired by this first motivation, and remained so steady in his drive, never becoming fainthearted or yielding when faced with the resistance of human nature, that he was deemed worthy also of divine illumination from heaven above, and became enriched with such 34

κατὰ παθῶν ὁμοῦ καὶ δαιμόνων ὑψηλοτέραν σχεδὸν ἀκοῆς καὶ πίστεως. Ἐπεὶ δὲ ἔτος ὅλον ἠνύετο, καὶ τῆς τῶν πρεσβυτέρων ἀξιοῦται καθέδρας, οὐ τοῦτο ἀνάβασιν ἁπλῶς κρίνων, ἀλλὰ τὴν πρὸς ἀρετὴν ἐπίδοσιν. Οὕτω προθύμως τὴν στενὴν καὶ τραχεῖαν ὁδεύων, καὶ οὕτως ὀξέως διὰ ταύτης φερόμενος, ὡς οὐδεὶς ἕτερος τὴν ὁμαλὴν καὶ πλατεῖαν καὶ τοῖς πολλοῖς βάσιμον, ἀμέλει καὶ δι' ὀλίγου, τοῦ ἄκρου τῆς ἀρετῆς ἐπελάβετο. Καὶ ποιμὴν κατέστη Καρχηδονίων· οὐ Καρχηδόνος δὲ μόνον, ἀλλὰ καὶ τῆς Ἑσπερίου πάσης· μᾶλλον δὲ καὶ Ἑῷαν ὅλην περιλαμβάνει τῷ κατ' αὐτὸν θαύματι. Οὗτος καὶ τὴν ἀληθῶς εὐγενῆ παρθένον Ἰοῦσταν, Ἰουστίναν μετονομάσας, καὶ ταῖς διακόνοις ἐγκαταλέξας, τὴν προστασίαν αὐτῇ τῶν κατὰ τὸ ἀσκητήριον ἐγχειρίζει καὶ ὡς μητέρα ταύταις ἐφίστησι.

35   Τοὺς δὲ τὴν ἐναντίαν τῷ ὀρθοδόξῳ τῆς πίστεως τεταγμένους, τῷ τε τοῦ βίου φωτὶ καὶ τῇ τῆς γλώττης ἡδονῇ ἐπαγόμενος, ἀριθμοῦ κρείττους ἑκάστης ἡμέρας προσετίθει τῇ Ἐκκλησίᾳ. Καί, συνελόντα φάναι, ὅσοις ἂν ἢ παρὼν τῇ γλώττῃ, ἢ ἀπὼν ὡμίλει τοῖς γράμμασι, τῆς ὀρθῆς ἐποιεῖτο μερίδος. Διόπερ ἀνθοῦντα τὰ τῶν Ἑλλήνων ἀπέσβη τότε· καὶ ὡς χλόη τις κατὰ μικρὸν ἐμαραίνετο.

36   Οὕτως αὐτῷ ἔχοντι παρὰ τοῦ Δολίου πόλεμος ἐπανέστη, οὐχ ἵνα τούτου ποτὲ κατισχύσῃ (ᾔδει γὰρ ὡς ἀδύνατον αὐτῷ περιγενέσθαι Κυπριανοῦ), ἀλλ' ἵνα, ποιμένος ἔρημα τὰ Χριστοῦ πρόβατα θέμενος, τότε καθάπερ λύκος ἐπιβάς, θύσῃ ταῦτα καὶ ἀπολέσῃ. Ὅλον τοίνυν τὸν Δέκιον ὑπελθὼν (αὐτὸς γὰρ τότε Ῥωμαίων ἐκράτει), πικρότατα

divine grace against the passions as well as against the demons that it almost exceeds the capacity of listeners to believe. After an entire year had passed, Kyprianos was deemed worthy also of priesthood, which he considered not simply a promotion, but a motivation toward progress in virtue. By following so eagerly the narrow and rough path, and advancing along this path faster than anyone else had ever traversed the smooth and broad way that is accessible to the many, he simply rose to the summit of virtue in a short time. He became bishop of the Carthaginians, indeed not only of Carthage, but of the entire West, while he encompassed the entire East as well with amazement. He also enrolled the truly noble virgin Iousta, whom he renamed Ioustina, among the deaconesses and entrusted her with the governance of their convent, appointing her as their spiritual mother.

As for those who were opposed to the orthodox faith, he 35 lured them with the light of his way of life and the pleasure of his eloquent tongue and each day added countless numbers of them to the Church. To put it concisely, with whomever he communicated, either orally when face to face, or in letters when absent, he converted them to orthodoxy. On account of this, paganism was extinguished, though it flourished previously, and like grass it gradually withered away.

As Kyprianos thrived, the Evil One raised a war against 36 him, not so that he would ever overpower Kyprianos (for he knew well that he could never defeat Kyprianos), but so that he would slaughter and destroy Christ's flock after removing its shepherd and attacking it like a wolf. He thus took full control over Decius (he was the ruler of the Romans at that time) and rendered him bitterly enraged

τοῦτον ἐκμαίνει κατὰ Χριστιανῶν. Τῷ δὲ τοσοῦτος ἀγὼν
ἦν ἴδιον αὐτοῦ θήραμα θέσθαι Κυπριανόν, ὅσον οὐδὲ Χριστιανοὺς ἑλεῖν ἅπαντας· ἤδει γὰρ οἶον ἐκείνου γλῶττα
Χριστιανοῖς ὄφελος, καὶ ὅτιπερ, ἐκεῖνον ἑλών, καὶ τοὺς ὑπ᾽
αὐτῷ ποιμαινομένους εὐκόλως ἂν παραστήσεται.

37   Πᾶσαν οὖν μηχανὴν καὶ πεῖραν κατ᾽ αὐτοῦ κινήσας, ὡς
οὔτε ἀγαθῶν ἐπαγγελίαις χαυνούμενον, οὔτε κακῶν ἀπειλαῖς πειθόμενον εἶδε, τέλος, ὑπερορίαν τοῦ ἀνδρὸς κατα-
κρίνει. Ὁ δὲ τοσοῦτον ἐδέησε τοῦ μέγα τι νομίσαι τὴν
τιμωρίαν (καίτοι κακῶν ἔσχατον οὖσαν), ὅσον, οὐδὲν τοῦ
οἰκείου φροντίσας, τῶν ἄλλων εἶχε τὴν ἐπιμέλειαν. Καὶ
οὐκ ἐπαύσατο γράφων, νουθετῶν, ὑπαλείφων, παρακαλῶν
πρὸς μόνους τοὺς ὑπὲρ τῆς ἀρετῆς ἄθλους ὁρᾶν, καὶ μόνης τῆς ἐκεῖθεν ἐκκρεμᾶσθαι δόξης· ξίφη δὲ καὶ πῦρ καὶ
θήρας ὡς ἀγαθῶν αἴτια μᾶλλον ἀσπάζεσθαι, καὶ ὀδύνης
οὕτω προσκαίρου καὶ βραχείας οὐρανῶν βασιλείαν ἀντι-
διδόντα.

38   Ταῦτα Κυπριανὸς οὐκ ἔλεγε μόνον, ἀλλὰ καὶ πρῶτος
ἐποίει, ἔργα λόγων εἰδὼς πολλῷ πλέον δυνάμενα πείθειν·
καὶ τῷ καθ᾽ ἑαυτὸν ὑποδείγματι πρὸς τὸν ὅμοιον ζῆλον
ἐκάλει. Καὶ ὅπως, ὁ λόγος δηλώσει. Ὁρῶν γὰρ ὁ Πονηρὸς
εἰς τέλος οὕτω Κυπριανὸν τὴν περὶ τὰ εἴδωλα πλάνην σβέ-
σαι φιλονεικοῦντα, δεινὰ ἐποίει· καὶ φορητὸν ἦν οὐδ᾽ ὅλως
αὐτῷ τὸ γινόμενον. Ἀμέλει, καί τινας τῶν τὴν ἀσέβειαν
θερμοτέρων ὑποδύς, πείθει κατηγορῆσαι αὐτοῦ πρὸς τὸν
τῆς Ἀνατολῆς κόμητα (Εὐτόλμιος ἦν ἐκείνῳ τὸ ὄνομα), ὡς
"Ἀναπείθει μὲν ἅπαντας, δεινῇ χρώμενος καὶ ἀφύκτῳ τῇ
γοητείᾳ· πολλοῦ δὲ κατὰ τῶν ἡμετέρων θεῶν ἐμπίπλησι

against the Christians. Decius's struggle became fiercer in trying to hunt down Kyprianos than in attempting to capture all other Christians; Decius knew, after all, what great benefit his eloquent tongue was for the Christians, and that if he caught Kyprianos, he could easily subdue those tended by him.

Decius set in motion every ploy and temptation against 37 him, but in the end, upon seeing that Kyprianos was neither enfeebled by promises of riches nor persuaded by threats of abuse, condemned him to exile. Yet Kyprianos downplayed the gravity of this punishment (even though it was indeed the worst of tribulations) in direct proportion to the care he bestowed on the others, without a thought for himself. He did not refrain from writing, admonishing, urging, exhorting people to gaze only at the prizes won on behalf of virtue, to depend only on the glory that comes from virtue, and to embrace death by sword, fire, and beasts as the cause of blessings, exchanging such temporary and brief pain for the kingdom of heaven.

Kyprianos did not only say these things but he was also 38 first to put them into action, knowing that works are much more effective than words in persuasion. By his own example, he invited people to show a similar zeal. How he did this, my story will reveal. As the Evil One recognized that Kyprianos was striving to extinguish entirely the error of idolatry, he was in distress and could not bear what was happening. At any rate, he entered the hearts of some men who were most fervent in their impiety and persuaded them to accuse Kyprianos to the *komes* of the East (his name was Eutolmios), saying the following: "He convinces everyone, using a dreadful and inescapable sorcery, and fills people with

τοῦ φρονήματος· καὶ τὸ δεινότερον, ὅτι μὴ πρὸς μόνους τοῦτο ποιεῖ οἷς ἂν εἰς ὄψιν ἔλθοι καὶ κατὰ τὸ λεληθὸς συγγένηται, ἀλλὰ καὶ οἷς ἂν ἀδεῶς ἐντύχῃ τοῖς γράμμασι"· καὶ ὅτι "Τὰ Χριστιανῶν μὲν πρεσβεύει μηδεμίαν φειδὼ ποιούμενος· τῆς ἡμετέρας δὲ καταπαίζει θρησκείας, καὶ εἰς τοὺς πατρίους ἐξυβρίζει θεούς." Τούτοις θερμότατα διακαυθεὶς εἰς θυμὸν ὁ κόμης, καὶ μάλιστα ὅτι μεμάθηκε καὶ τὴν παρθένον Ἰουστίναν τὰ ἴσα Κυπριανῷ φρονεῖν, δεσμοῖς αὐτοὺς καὶ φρουρᾷ τῇ ἄλλῃ παραδούς, τῷ ἐν Δαμασκῷ βήματι ταμιεύεται.

39   Ἀχθέντων τοιγαροῦν τῶν ἁγίων εἰς τήνδε τὴν πόλιν, "Σὺ εἶ ὁ τῶν Χριστιανῶν διδάσκαλος," τῷ Κυπριανῷ ὁ κόμης φησίν, ἀφ' ὑψηλοῦ τοῦ βήματος τοὺς λόγους κινῶν, "ὁ τοὺς προσανέχοντας τοῖς θεοῖς ἀναπείθων καὶ συνταράττων; Ὅς, τῷ ἀσθενεῖ τῆς γνώμης, πρὸς πᾶσαν εὐχερῶς δόξαν ἐκπίπτεις; Οὐ σὺ πολλοὺς μᾶλλον τοῖς θεοῖς προσήγαγες πρότερον, ἐπιδεξίοις ὡς ἐμάνθανον τοῖς περὶ αὐτῶν διηγήμασι; Πῶς οὖν ἄρτι μεταβέβλησαι; Καὶ τί τὸ τῆς μεταβολῆς αἴτιον; Ἵνα τί δὲ καί, τὸν ἐσταυρωμένον κηρύττων, ἀπατᾷν εἵλου τοὺς ἀνθρώπους διδάγμασιν ἀλλοκότοις;"

40   Ἐπὶ τούτοις ὁ ἅγιος, ἡσυχίαν ἄγων, ἑαυτὸν ἀνελάμβανέ τε καὶ ἀνεθάρρυνεν· εἶτα προσχὼν μετὰ πολλοῦ τοῦ κόσμου καὶ σεμνοῦ παραστήματος, πρὸς τὸν κόμητα ἔφη· "Ἐγὼ πολλήν, ὡς καὶ αὐτός μοι συμμαρτυρεῖς, τὴν περὶ τὰ Ἑλληνικὰ σπουδὴν ἔχων, καὶ περὶ λόγους καὶ τὴν τῶν μαγικῶν βίβλων μελέτην θερμότατα διακείμενος, οὐδὲν μέγα ἢ πρὸς ψυχὴν φέρον τὸ κέρδος ἐκεῖθεν ἐπορισάμην.

ardent spirit against our gods; and, what is worse, he does not do this only with those whom he might see face to face, meeting secretly, but also with those with whom he converses through letters without fear"; and that "He upholds the faith of the Christians without restraint, while he mocks our religion and heaps insults on the gods of our fathers." After hearing these words, the *komes* was inflamed with anger, especially because he learned that Ioustina the virgin also held the same beliefs as Kyprianos, and so he had them bound, put under separate guard, and delivered to the court in Damascus.

When the saints were led to that city, the *komes* questioned Kyprianos, hurling his words from a high throne, "Are you the teacher of the Christians, the one who advises people to change course and causes trouble to those who believe in the gods? Are you the one with the weak spirit who easily wavers toward any view? Aren't you the one who earlier actually made many believe in the gods by your most masterful, as I hear, stories about them? How did you now change? What is the cause of this change of mind? And why have you chosen to also deceive people with strange teachings, by preaching about the crucified one?" 39

After these words, the saint remained calm, restoring and reinforcing his courage. Then, stepping forward with much grace and solemn stature, he gave this response to the *komes:* "Indeed, as you too attest against me, I was devoted to pagan learning, and I pursued most zealously the study of discourse and of books pertaining to magic; yet, I gained nothing great nor anything beneficial to the soul from all that. 40

Οὕτω δέ μοι διακειμένῳ, καὶ τοῖς ματαίοις ἐνασχολουμένῳ πόνοις, οἰκτείρας ὁ Θεός με τῶν κενῶν ἱδρώτων καὶ τοῦ πρὸς τοὺς ἀνοήτους θεοὺς σεβάσματος, ὁδηγὸν ἀπλανῆ καὶ ἀγαθὴν ἡγεμόνα τῆς πρὸς αὐτὸν φερούσης ὁδοῦ τὴν παρθένον ταύτην ἐκπέμπει. Καὶ εἰ προσεχῶς ἀκοῦσαι θελήσειας, τὸν τρόπον οἶδα τῆς οἰκονομίας πάνυ θαυμάσεις.

41   "Ἔχει δὲ οὕτως. Ἀγλαΐδας τις τῶν ἐκ Κλαυδίου ἡττήθη τῆς παρθένου ταύτης ἔρωτι μανικῷ. Καὶ ὁ μὲν ἐς γάμον ἐζήτει· ἡ δὲ ἀπηξίου, τὴν σύζυγον στέργουσα παρθενίαν. Ὁ μὲν ἐπέμενε, τοῦτο μὲν ἱκετεύων, τοῦτο δὲ καὶ βίαν ἐπάγων· ἡ δὲ τῆς πρώτης οὐκ ἀπέστη βουλήσεως. Ὡς δὲ ἑώρα ταύτην ἀκλινῶς ἔχουσαν, καὶ πρὸς ἐκείνου πᾶσαν ἐπίνοιαν ἀντιπράττουσαν, ἡσυχίαν ἄγειν οὐδαμῶς ἴσχυσεν. Ἀλλ' ἐλθὼν ὡς ἐμὲ Ἀγλαΐδας, ἐξεῖπε μὲν τὸ ἀπόρρητον· ἐξεῖπε δὲ τὴν ἐκ τῆς παρθένου παρόρασιν. Καὶ τέλος, ἤξίου βοηθεῖν ὅση δύναμις τῇ ἀποτυχίᾳ, καὶ φίλτρον αὐτῇ ἀντίρροπον ἐπιπέμψαι, καὶ κινῆσαι πρὸς ἐπιθυμίαν τοῦ ἐραστοῦ τὴν οὕτως ὑπεροπτικῶς ἔχουσαν.

42   "Ταῦτα ἐκεῖνος μὲν ἤτει· ἐγὼ δὲ βίβλοις τὸ θαρρεῖν ἔχων ταῖς μαγικαῖς καὶ τοῖς δαίμοσιν, ἀμελεῖν ἐκέλευον, ταχεῖαν ὅσην ἐπαγγειλάμενος τὴν βοήθειαν. Ἕνα γοῦν τῶν δαιμόνων καλέσας, παραγυμνῶ τὸ πρᾶγμα· καὶ εἴ τις αὐτῷ δύναμις συμπράττειν ἤξίουν. Ὁ δέ, πρὸ μὲν τῆς πείρας, πολὺς ἦν τὴν ὀφρύν, καὶ θερμὸς τὴν ἐπαγγελίαν, καὶ πάντα πράττειν τῷ δοκεῖν δυνάμενος. Ἀπελθὼν δέ, καὶ τῇ κόρῃ συνάψας, μῦς ἐφάνη λέοντι προσβαλών, ἢ κάνθαρος ἀετῷ πρὸς πάλην ἐρίσας· φυγὰς γὰρ πρὸς ἡμᾶς ἐπανῆκε

While I was in that state of mind, occupied with those vain labors, God pitied my futile effort and veneration of unintelligent gods and sent this virgin as my unerring guide and good leader toward the way that leads to Him. If you would be willing to listen attentively, you would be greatly amazed, I am sure, about how He arranged my salvation.

"This is how it happened: a certain Aglaïdas, from Claudi-   41
us's clan, fell madly in love with this virgin. And he asked her to marry him, but she refused, desiring to remain wedded to her dear virginity. He insisted, first by begging, and then by using even force. Yet she did not depart from her earlier resolution. When he realized that she remained unswayed, as she continued to repel each and every one of his ploys, he could not bear to remain inactive. Aglaïdas came to me, told me his secret, and recounted how the virgin rejected him. In the end, he asked me to help him in his failure, as much as I could, by sending her a counteracting potion that would move that arrogant woman to desire her admirer.

"This was his request. With the boldness derived from   42
my books on magic and from the demons, I told him not to worry, promising him ample and speedy help. I then summoned one of the demons, revealed to him the matter at hand, and asked him to collaborate as much as he could. Before making his attempt, the demon was full of himself, ardent in making promises, and, in his own opinion, capable of achieving anything. When he went, however, and waged war against the maiden, he seemed like a mouse attacking a lion or a beetle challenging an eagle to fight; for he who,

καὶ λίαν καταδεὴς ὁ, πρὸ τοῦ, μέγας καὶ τὴν ὁρμὴν ἀνυ-
πόστατος.

43 "Ἐμὲ δὲ ἔκπληξις εἶχε. Πῶς οὕτως ἀπαλὴ παρθένος καὶ
τῷ παντὶ εὐπτόητος εἶναι μέλλουσα οὐ μόνον οὐκ εἶξε βίᾳ
καὶ περιαγωγῇ δαίμονος, ἀλλὰ καὶ φοβερὰ τούτῳ κατέστη; Τίνι δὲ καὶ ὅπλῳ ἐρειδομένη, οὐχ ὅπως ἀπώσατο,
ἀλλὰ καὶ φυγάδα τοῦτον ὡς ἡμᾶς παρεπέμψατο; Διὰ ταῦτα
μεστὸς ὑποψίας ἦν καὶ δειναῖς ἐννοίαις ἐπάλαιον. Ἐμοῦ δὲ
πυνθανομένου, καὶ διψῶντος μαθεῖν τὴν αἰτίαν, κρύπτειν
μὲν ἠβούλετο τὸ δαιμόνιον καὶ πάσῃ μηχανῇ συγκαλύ-
πτειν. Ὡς δὲ οὐκ ἀνίειν ἐγώ, μόλις ποτὲ καὶ ἄκον ὁμολογεῖ
καὶ τὸ ἀπόρρητον ἐκκαλύπτει, δύναμιν εἰπὸν θείαν παρ'
αὐτῇ εἶναι, καὶ ʻΜοί τι σημεῖον φανῆναι φρικτόν, οὗπερ
οὐδὲ μόνην ἁπλῶς τὴν θέαν ὑπέστην, ἀλλὰ φυγὰς ἐπάν-
ειμι.ʼ

44 "Οὕτως ἐκείνου καταγνωσθέντος, αὐτὸς οὐκ ἠμέλουν,
ἀλλὰ καὶ ἕτερον ἔπεμψα, τῇ μὲν οἰήσει πολλῷ τοῦ προλά-
βοντος ἰσχυρότερον, τῇ δυνάμει δὲ κατ' οὐδὲν ἀνόμοιον·
τὰ γὰρ αὐτὰ κἀκεῖνος ἰδών τε καὶ παθών, ἐπανῆκεν. Ἐγὼ
δὲ καὶ ἔτι βασάνῳ τὸ πρᾶγμα διδούς, αὐτὸν ἐκεῖνον τὸν
ἄρχοντα τῶν δαιμονίων ἐκπέμπω, ἀμαθεῖς καὶ νηπιώδεις
τοὺς πρὸ αὐτοῦ πεμφθέντας ἀποκαλοῦντα, καὶ οὐδὲν ἐπί-
κλοπον οὐδὲ τεχνικὸν πρὸς φρενῶν ἀπάτην ποιεῖν δυνα-
μένους. Ἐμὲ δὲ χρηστῶν ἐλπίδων ἐπλήρου· καὶ τὸ τὴν
παρθένον ἑλεῖν, καὶ ᾧ βούλομαι θᾶττον αὐτὴν καταπειθῆ
δεῖξαι, τίνος οὐκ ἔλεγεν εὐχερέστερον;

45 "Ἐπεὶ δὲ καὶ αὐτὸς προσέβαλεν ἀπελθών, τί μὲν οὐκ
ἔλεξε; Τί δὲ οὐκ ἔδρασε τῶν ἐπάγεσθαι δυναμένων; Ποῖον

until very recently, was formidable, possessing an irresistible force, returned to us in flight and a state of terror.

"I was taken by surprise: how could such a delicate virgin, 43 who was expected to be easily scared by anyone, not only withstand the force and attack of a demon but also terrify him? And what was her weapon with which not only she repelled him but also made him flee like a fugitive to me? Because of all this, I was full of disbelief and was struggling with difficult thoughts. So I started asking questions, thirsty to learn the cause of his retreat, but the demon wanted to conceal it and cover it up, using every trick. As I would not let go, he finally confessed with much unwillingness and revealed what he was hiding, saying that some divine power existed in her, and that 'She put in front of me a terrifying sign, whose sight not only could I not bear, but which made me return to you in flight.'

"When that demon was thwarted in this way, I did not 44 give up, but I sent against her another one who was much stronger in his arrogance than the previous one, yet identical in strength; for he too faced and suffered the same things and thus returned to me. I continued to probe the matter still more and sent that very master of the demons himself, who called those dispatched before him ignorant and infantile, as they were unable to do anything sly or cunning so as to deceive her wits. As for me, he filled me with good hope. Was there anything easier for him, he said, than to captivate the virgin and quickly render her submissive to whatever I wanted?

"When he too went and attacked her, what words did he 45 not use? What trick that could deceive her did he not

δὲ ἀπάτης ἐνέλιπεν εἶδος; Ἅπαντα ἐκείνη μάταια ἤλεγξε καὶ σαθρά. Καὶ τέλος, αὐτὸν ἐκεῖνον τὸν τὰ μεγάλα φυσῶντα οὕτω ταπεινὸν ἔδειξε καὶ φυγάδα, ὡς ἐπιδήλως ὁμολογεῖν τὴν τοῦ ἐσταυρωμένου δύναμιν ἄμαχον εἶναι, καὶ ὑπ᾽ ἐκείνης αὐτοὺς κραταιῶς ἐλαύνεσθαι.

46   "Πρὸς ταῦτα, τί με ἔδει ποιεῖν; Εἰπὲ πρὸς τῆς ἀληθείας αὐτῆς, ὁ δικάζων· εἰς νοῦν βάλλεσθαι τὸ πρᾶγμα, καὶ κρίνειν ἐπισκοπῆς ἄξιον, τίς ἡ θρυλλουμένη αὕτη τοῦ Χριστοῦ δύναμις, ᾗ καὶ δαίμονες κατάφοβοι γίνονται, καὶ μόνῳ τῷ φεύγειν σώζονται; Ἢ οὕτως ἀλόγως ἕπεσθαι τοῖς παραδεδομένοις, οἷα τῶν ῥινῶν ἑλκόμενον; Ἔγωγε οὖν ζητήσας, εὗρον· καὶ κρούοντι, διηνοίχθη μοι· καὶ φωτὸς γνώσεως ἐπιλάμψαντός μου τῇ καρδίᾳ, καθαρῶς ἔγνων ὅτι τὰ μὲν εἴδωλα ταυτὶ τὰ παρ᾽ ὑμῶν σεβόμενα ἀπάτη μόνον εἰσὶ καὶ ψεῦδος, ἐπ᾽ ὀνόματι θεοῦ προσκυνούμενα· εἷς δὲ ἀληθὴς Θεὸς ὁ Χριστός, τοὺς εἰς αὐτὸν πιστεύοντας δυνάμενος σώζειν."

47   Τούτοις ὁ κόμης εἰς ὀργὴν κινηθείς, μὴ ἔχων ὅ τι ποτὲ πρὸς τοιαύτην λόγων ἰσχὺν ἀντιφθέγξαιτο, τὸ πρόχειρον ἐποίει, καὶ τοῖς ὀργῇ νικηθεῖσιν ἀκόλουθον. Τὸν μὲν ἅγιον ἐκέλευε κρεμασθέντα ξέεσθαι, Ἰουστίναν δὲ κατὰ τὸ πρόσωπον καὶ τοὺς ὀφθαλμοὺς τύπτεσθαι—κἂν ἐκείνη τοὺς βασανιστὰς οὐκ αἰκίζειν ἐδόκει μᾶλλον, ἢ πρὸς Θεοῦ δοξολογίαν ὥσπερ ὑπομιμνήσκειν· τυπτομένη γὰρ οὕτω γεγονότερον ἐξεβόησε, "Δόξα σοι, ὁ Θεός, ὁ ἀναξίαν με οὖσαν οἰκειωσάμενος, καὶ ὑπὲρ τοῦ σοῦ παθεῖν με καταξιώσας ὀνόματος." Καὶ οὕτω πάσχουσα, γενναίως διεκαρτέρει, ὡς αὐτὴν μηδὲν ἀγεννὲς ἢ τῇ θηλείᾳ φύσει καὶ

pursue? What form of ploy did he leave out? Yet she proved all his schemes vain and flimsy. In the end, she humiliated him too, despite his great arrogance, and made him flee and admit openly that the power of the crucified one is unconquerable and that it was because of this that the demons were forcefully driven away.

"Confronted with all this, what should I have done? Tell me, judge, for the sake of truth. Should I have considered seriously and evaluated such a matter worthy of examination, namely what this notorious power of Christ is that petrifies even demons who save themselves only by fleeing? Or should I have foolishly abided by our traditions, like a man pulled by his nose? I sought, and I found; I knocked, and the door was opened for me; as the light of knowledge shone in my heart, I clearly understood that these idols which we revere are only deceit and lies, worshipped in the name of a god, but the one true God is Christ, who is able to save those who believe in Him."

The *komes* was enraged by these words and, unable to offer any retort to such a powerful speech, he did what was convenient and suitable for someone conquered by anger. He ordered that the holy Kyprianos be hanged and flayed, and that Ioustina be beaten on her face and eyes. She, however, thought that her torturers were not so much inflicting pain upon her, but rather prompting her to glorify God; while being beaten, she cried aloud, "Glory to You, O God, who made me Your own, though I am unworthy, and gave me the privilege to suffer on behalf of Your name." Suffering in this way, she endured so bravely that she showed nothing ignoble nor what one would expect of her female and weak

ἀσθενεῖ κατάλληλον ἐπιδείξασθαι, τοὺς τύπτοντας δέ, ἀτονήσαντας, τῆς βασάνου παύσασθαι.

48   Κυπριανὸς δὲ ὁ θεῖος ξεόμενος αὐτῆς κατὰ πρόσωπον, οὕτως ἦν ἀταπείνωτός τε καὶ μεγαλόφρων, καὶ τοιαύτας ἀνδρώδεις καὶ μακαρίας ἠφίει φωνάς, ὡς τοὺς περιεστῶτας ἀκούοντας εἰς ἑαυτὸν ἐπισπᾶσθαι, καὶ τοῦ τῆς ἀπιστίας βάθους ἀναλαμβάνειν· ἔλεγε γὰρ πρὸς τὸν κόμητα, ἀποβλέψας μάλα γενναῖον καὶ πλῆρες φρονήματος εὐγενοῦς, "Ἵνα τί οὕτως ἀπονενόησαι, ἀνάξιε δηλαδὴ τῆς τῶν οὐρανῶν βασιλείας, ὑπὲρ ἧς ἐγὼ πάντα παθεῖν εἱλόμην, ὡς καὶ αὐτοὶ μάρτυρες οἱ σοὶ μὴ βλέποντες ὀφθαλμοί; Οὐ συνήσεις; Οὐκ ἀναβλέψεις; Οὐκ εἴσῃ τί τὸ ἀληθινὸν φῶς, καὶ τὸ σκότος ἀπολιπὼν πρὸς αὐτὸ μεταπορευθήσῃ;"

49   Ἐπὶ τούτοις ὁ κόμης πρὸς ἕκαστον τῶν λεγομένων σφοδροτέραν αὐτῷ τὴν ὀδύνην ἐπιτιθείς, "Καὶ εἰ ἀθανάτου βασιλείας," ἔλεγε, "φαίνομαί σοι πρόξενος ὤν, ἔτι σοι πολλαπλασιάσω τὴν τιμωρίαν· καὶ μισθόν μοι πάντως ὀφλήσεις τῆς εὐεργεσίας καὶ τῶν χαρίτων, ὧν ἐγώ σοι πρόξενος γίνομαι." Ταῦτα εἰπών, καὶ μικρόν τι ξέειν παραχωρήσας, εἶτα τῆς τιμωρίας ἐπαύσατο, οὐκ ἐκ φιλανθρωπίας, ἀλλὰ ἐξ ἀπορίας, ἀπογνοὺς ὥσπερ τὴν τῶν ἁγίων μετάθεσιν. Διὰ δὴ ταῦτα καὶ εἰς φρουρὰν μὲν τὸν Κυπριανόν, Ἰουστίναν δὲ εἰς τὸ τῆς Τερεντίνης λεγόμενον φροντιστήριον ἀπαχθῆναι προστάττει.

50   Αὖθις δὲ μετὰ χρόνον οὐ πολυήμερον, εἰς ἐξέτασιν δευτέραν παραστησάμενος τοὺς ἁγίους, πραότητά τε ὑποκριθείς, "Μὴ θελήσητε," ἔφη, "ἀνθρώπῳ τεθνεῶτι ἀκολουθῆσαι, μηδὲ πιστεῦσαι τῷ τεθανατωμένῳ τὰ τῆς ὑμετέρας

gender; meanwhile, her tormentors ran out of energy and
stopped the torture.

The divine Kyprianos too, while being flayed facing her,   48
remained unfaltering and with such tenacious spirit and
voiced such manly and blessed thoughts that the bystanders
hearing him were persuaded to look inwardly and recover
from the depth of their faithlessness. For he kept saying to
the *komes,* gazing at him with a manly look, filled with noble
spirit, "Why have you lost your mind completely, O man unworthy of the kingdom of heaven, for which I have chosen
to suffer everything, as your very own unseeing eyes are wit-
nessing? Will you not understand? Will you not recover your
sight? Will you not recognize what is the true light and thus
change course in its pursuit, abandoning darkness?"

After each proclamation by Kyprianos, the *komes* intensi-   49
fied the torture, and would say to him: "If indeed you think
that I am the reason for your entrance into the immortal
kingdom, I will increase your punishment even more; and
you will definitely owe me for this benefaction and for all
your blessings for which I am the cause." Saying these words,
and letting the flaying continue for only a little more, he
then stopped the punishment, not out of mercy, but because
he was at a loss, despairing of ever achieving the saints' conversion. He thus ordered that Kyprianos be put in jail, and
Ioustina be taken to the so-called monastery of Terentine.

Then again, not many days later, he summoned the saints   50
for a second interrogation and, feigning benevolence, said:
"Renounce following a dead man and entrusting your life
to someone who was put to death; for he is certainly no

ζωῆς· οὐ γὰρ ζωοδότης πάντως ὁ μηδὲ ἑαυτῷ δυνηθεὶς
ἐπαρκέσαι καὶ τὴν οἰκείαν ψυχὴν περισώσασθαι."

51   Τὴν παραίνεσιν ταύτην οἱ ἅγιοι ὡς περιττὴν καὶ ἀσύνε-
τον, μᾶλλον δὲ κακοῦργον καὶ βλαβερὸν λογισάμενοι,
οὑτωσί πως πρὸς τὸν κόμητα εἶπον· "Τί δαί; Ὁ πολὺς σὺ
τὴν διάνοιαν καὶ ἀγχίνους, οὐ μεμάθηκας ὅτι θανάτου
χωρὶς οὐκ ἐπιγίνεται τὸ ἀθάνατον; Οὐδὲ συνῆκας, τί τὸ
μυστήριον τοῦ τῷ τριημέρῳ θανάτῳ νενικηκότος τὸν θάνατον; Ἀλλ' ἀμβλὺς σὺ τῷ ὄντι καὶ παχὺς τὴν διάνοιαν
περὶ τὰ μεγάλα τε καὶ χρηστά. Καὶ διὰ τοῦτο, βλέπων, οὐ
βλέψεις· καὶ ἀσύνετος ὤν, οὐ μὴ συνήσεις." Ἐπὶ τούτοις ὁ
κόμης, οὐδὲ τὸ τῶν λόγων ἀναμείνας τέλος, πρὸς ὀργὴν
εὐθέως ἐξήγετο· καὶ τὸ τῆς πρᾳότητος πεπλασμένον
εὐχερῶς διελύετο. Ὅθεν ηὐτρέπιζε καὶ τοῖς μάρτυσι ποινὴν
μάλα δεινήν, τήγανον αὐτοὺς κελεύσας σφόδρα διακαυθὲν
ὑποδέξασθαι.

52   Τοῦ θείου τοίνυν Κυπριανοῦ γενναίως πρότερον εἰσπη-
δήσαντος, Ἰουστίνα μετ' αὐτὸν ἀπήγετο. Ἥν, ἐπεὶ ὁ μάρτυς δειλίᾳ ληφθεῖσαν ὅσον εἰκάσαι εἶχε τῷ σχολαίῳ καὶ
νωθεῖ τοῦ βαδίσματος, λόγοις αὐτὴν ἀνελάμβανε, καὶ
μνήμῃ τῶν προτέρων κατορθωμάτων, οἷς ἐκείνη δαίμονάς
τε ἐτρέψατο, καὶ αὐτὸν τῆς ἀπιστίας ἀνεκαλέσατο.

53   Τοιούτοις θαρρύνας ῥήμασιν Ἰουστίναν, εἶτα καὶ ὡς
ὅπλῳ πάλιν τῷ τύπῳ τοῦ τιμίου σταυροῦ φραξάμενοι,
καθάπερ ἐπί τινος κατιούσης ἡσυχῇ δρόσου τῆς τοῦ σιδή-
ρου φλογώσεως ἀνεκλίνοντο. Ὅπερ ἄρα καὶ ὁ δικάζων,
οὐχ ἥκιστα ἐκπλαγείς, γοητείας οὐκ ἀληθείας εἶναι τὸ
γινόμενον ὑπελάμβανεν. Ὅθεν καὶ τὴν ἄνοιαν αὐτοῦ

life-giver, the one who is inadequate even for his own good, unable to save his own life."

The saints considered this exhortation pointless and un-   51
wise, or rather as malicious and harmful, and responded to the *komes* in more or less the following way: "What? Have you, a man of great mind and sharp intellect, not learned that, without death, immortality cannot be achieved? Have you not comprehended the mystery of the one who con-quered death by His three-day death? You must be really dull and thick-headed when it comes to great and beneficial matters. For this reason, though you have eyes, you will not be able to see; and since you are unwise, you will not com-prehend." When he heard this, the *komes* did not even wait for them to finish speaking before his anger was kindled; his feigned benevolence easily disappeared. Hence, he prepared another very harsh punishment for the martyrs: he ordered a frying pan to be put on a very hot fire for them.

The divine Kyprianos was the first to jump bravely in-   52
side; Ioustina was brought after him. When Kyprianos could guess from her slow and sluggish step that she was over-come by cowardice, he began to embolden her with words, reminding her of her earlier feats, of how she made demons flee and even saved him from faithlessness.

After Kyprianos encouraged Ioustina with such words,   53
they then shielded themselves again also with the sign of the holy cross, as if with a weapon, and lay down on the burning iron as if on some dew peacefully descending. Greatly surprised, the judge thought this to be the result of sor-cery rather than something real. To indulge his foolish

θεραπεύων, Ἀθανάσιός τις, εἷς τῶν συνεδριαζόντων αὐτῷ καὶ συνήθης ὑπάρχων, "Ἐγώ," ἔφη, "τὴν τοῦ Χριστοῦ ὑμῶν ἀσθένειαν ὡς τάχιστα διελέγξω." Εἶπε· καὶ ἅμα θρασύτερον τῆς τοῦ πυριφλεγοῦς τηγάνου καύσεως κατετόλμα, Δία καὶ Ἀσκληπιὸν ἐπιβοησάμενος—τὸν μέν, ὡς τοῦ αἰθερίου τε καὶ περιγείου πυρὸς ἄρχοντα· τὸν δέ, ὡς τοῦ ὑγιαίνειν χορηγὸν νομιζόμενον. Οὐκ ἔφθη δὲ τῷ πυρὶ προσψαῦσαι, καὶ τοῦ ζῆν εὐθὺς ὁ μάταιος ἀπηλλάττετο, ἀξίας ὧν κέκληκεν ὑπερασπιστῶν ἀπολαύσας τῆς βοηθείας. Οἱ ἅγιοι δὲ παρὰ πολὺ τῷ τηγάνῳ προσκαρτεροῦντες, ἀπαθεῖς ἔμενον, περιαυγαζόμενοι μᾶλλον ἢ φλεγόμενοι· καὶ γὰρ ὑπεχώρει τούτοις τὸ πῦρ καὶ ἣν εἶχεν ἐνέργειαν ἀπηρνεῖτο, καθάπερ τὸν ὑπὲρ οὗ ταῦτα πάσχειν εἵλοντο κοινὸν Δεσπότην καὶ Δημιουργὸν εὐλαβούμενον.

54   Ὁρῶν οὖν ὁ δικάζων πραγμάτων ἔκπληξιν καὶ καινοτομίαν, καὶ τὸ πῦρ ὡς ἕν τι τῶν λογικῶν φίλου καὶ δυσμενοῦς διάκρισιν ποιούμενον, καὶ τοὺς μὲν ἁγίους ἀπαθεῖς περιέπον καὶ συντηροῦν, Ἀθανάσιον δὲ τῷ θανάτῳ παραπέμψαν ὀξέως, μικροῦ καὶ αὐτὸς ἀπεπνίγετο. Καί, "Μέλει μοι τοῦ φίλου," ἔλεγε, "σφόδρα μέλει· καὶ λύπης ὅσης ἐπὶ τούτῳ αἰσθάνομαι."

55   Καλέσας δέ τινα τῶν συγγενῶν ᾧ Τερέντιος ὄνομα, τοῦτον ὅπως τὰ κατὰ τοὺς ἁγίους διάθηται χωρὶς τῶν ἄλλων εἰς συμβουλὴν ἀπελάμβανε. Τερέντιος δέ, "Μηδέν σοι καὶ τοῖς δικαίοις," ἔλεγε πρὸς αὐτόν, "μηδὲ οὕτως ἀβούλως ἀντιπίπτειν βούλου τῇ ἀληθείᾳ· ἡ τοῦ Χριστοῦ δύναμις φανερῶς ἄμαχος. Ἄριστα δὲ περὶ σαυτοῦ διασκέψῃ, εἰ τούτους τῷ βασιλεῖ παραπέμψεις, γνωρίσεις τε

misconception, a certain Athanasios, one of his fellow judges and a friend of his, declared: "I will very quickly prove the powerlessness of your Christ." Thus he spoke, and immediately dared to boldly enter the burning heat of the fiery frying pan, calling upon Zeus and Asklepios for help: the former as the master of the ethereal fire that surrounds the earth, the latter as the one thought to provide health. No sooner had he touched the fire than this foolish man lost his life right away, enjoying the help which was worthy of the helpers whom he summoned. The saints obstinately endured in the frying pan, suffering no harm, as they were being illuminated rather than burned; for in encountering them the fire retreated and denied its own force, as if it revered the Master and Creator whom it shared with them and for whom they had chosen to suffer all this.

Astonished by the unusual occurrence and seeing how the 54 fire, like a rational creature, distinguished between friend and foe, embracing and preserving the saints unharmed, while quickly sending Athanasios to death, the judge himself almost choked to death. "I am troubled for my friend," he kept saying, "I am deeply troubled; what great grief I feel for him!"

He then called one of his relatives whose name was 55 Terentios and, in private, sought his advice as to how to deal with the saints. Terentios said to him, "Have nothing to do with those two righteous ones! Do not choose to oppose the truth so imprudently! The power of Christ is clearly invincible. It would be best for your own sake if you sent them to the emperor, informing him in detail about how many

ἀκριβῶς ὅσα μὲν σὺ κατ' αὐτῶν διαπέπραξαι· ὅπως δὲ
οὗτοι μεγαλοψύχως πρὸς πάντα διαγεγόνασι· καὶ ὡς σὺ
μὲν οὐδὲν ἐνέλιπες ποιῶν τῶν εἰς τιμωρίαν ἡκόντων, ἀλλὰ
καὶ αὐτῶν ὠμότητα τῶν θηρίων κολάζων παρήλασας· ἐκείνων δὲ οὐδεμία τῶν τοιούτων ἥψατο βάσανος, ἀλλὰ ἄχρι
καὶ νῦν ἀπαθεῖς διαμεμενήκασι."

56   Τούτων ἀκούσας ὁ κόμης, ἐπιστολὴν ὧδέ πως ἔχουσαν
εἰς Νικομήδειαν πρὸς τὸν τότε κρατοῦντα (Κλαύδιος δὲ
ἦν) εὐθέως ἐκπέμπει. Εἶχε δὲ οὕτως· "Κόμης Εὐτόλμιος
Κλαυδίῳ Καίσαρι τῷ μεγάλῳ, γῆς καὶ θαλάσσης δεσπό-
ζοντι, χαίρειν. Γαλήνης πολλῆς τοὺς ὑπὸ τὴν σὴν ἐξουσίαν
ἀπολαύοντας ὁρῶν, μέγιστε βασιλεῦ, τῆς τῶν μεγάλων
θεῶν εὐνοίας ἣν περί σε διασώζουσι, καὶ τῆς προσούσης
σοι δεισιδαιμονίας ἄξιον, τοῦτο γινώσκω τὸ ἀνταπόδομα.
Ἐπεὶ δέ τινες τῶν λεγομένων Γαλιλαίων, τὰ εἰς αὐτοὺς
φρυαττόμενοι, Χριστὸν μᾶλλον, ὃν Ἰουδαίων παῖδες ὡς
κακοῦργον ἀνεσκολόπισαν, σέβουσί τε καὶ προσκυνοῦσι,
τούτου χάριν καὶ ἡμεῖς πᾶσι τρόποις ὡς στασιώδεις αὐτοὺς
καὶ λοιμούς, μετὰ τὴν εἰς τὸ βῆμα παράστασιν οὐ μετα-
τιθεμένους, ἐξελαύνειν τῶν πόλεων περὶ πολλοῦ ἐποιού-
μεθα. Καὶ οἷς μὲν ὀψέ ποτε μεταμέλειά τις ἐπὶ τοῖς κακῶς
δεδογμένοις ἐγένετο, τῇ τῶν μεγάλων εὐμενείᾳ θεῶν θαρροῦντες, εἰσδέχεσθαι τούτους καὶ τὴν προσήκουσαν ἀπο-
νέμειν χάριν οὐ παρῃτούμεθα. Οὓς δὲ ἀνιάτως ἔχοντας
διερευνώμενος εὕρισκον, τούτους αἰκίζειν, ἀνασταυροῦν,
ὄνυξι ξέειν, πᾶσι τρόποις κολάζειν, κατὰ τοὺς κειμένους
νόμους, οὐκ ἠμελήσαμεν· ἄλλως γὰρ οὐκ ἔνι περιγενέσθαι

actions you took against them; how they withstood everything valiantly; how you neglected no form of punishment,
but in torturing them you surpassed even the savagery of
wild beasts; and how, nevertheless, not a single such torture
affected them, but they remained unharmed until now."

When the *komes* heard this, he immediately sent a letter   56
to Nikomedeia, to the ruler at that time (this was Claudius).
This is roughly how the letter went: "Eutolmios *komes* to
Claudius the great Caesar, master of land and sea, greetings.
Seeing that those under your rule enjoy great peace, O greatest emperor, I know this to be a worthy requital for the favor that the great gods maintain toward you and for the piety you show toward them. Since, however, some of the
so-called Galileans became haughty in their religion, rever-
ing and venerating Christ whom the Jews hung on a gibbet
as a criminal, when they did not change their minds after
examination at court, I did everything in my power to expel
them from the cities as rebels and rogues. If some of them,
later on, regretted their wrong faith, I did not fail to welcome them back and to pardon them, encouraged by the benevolence of the great gods. Those, however, whom I found
after investigation to be incurable, I did not neglect to torture, crucify, flay with scrapers, and maltreat with every
form of punishment according to the existing laws; for it
is impossible to prevail otherwise over souls that have lost

ψυχῶν ἀπονενοημένων καὶ τὸ δύσερι πάθος προενῳκηκὸς
αὐταῖς ἐχουσῶν.

57 "Ἵνα δὲ μὴ λόγον ἄλλως ὑπολάβῃς με πλάττεσθαι, καὶ
Κυπριανὸν τοῦτον οὐχ ὑπ᾽ ἀνάγκης τινός, ἀλλ᾽ ἑκοντὶ τῶν
σωτήρων θεῶν μεταθέμενον, τῷ ἐσταυρωμένῳ τε ὅλον
ἑαυτὸν ἀναθέμενον, μετὰ τὸ σφοδρῶς αἰκίσαι, τῷ κράτει
σου νῦν ἐξαπέστειλα, ἄνθρωπον πιθανὸν τοῖς λόγοις, πονηρὸν τοῖς τρόποις, ἑτοιμότατον εἰς ἀπολογίαν. Τούτῳ εἰ
πράως ἐνέτυχον, οὐδὲ τὸν νοῦν μοι προσέχοντα ὅλως
εὕρισκον. Εἰ αὐστηρῶς ἐχρησάμην, καὶ βασάνοις ἐπήγα-
γον, οὐχ ὡς ἀνδρὶ μᾶλλον ἢ ἀνδριάντι καὶ ἄλλῳ τινὶ τῶν
ἀψύχων ἐπάγειν ταύτας ἐνομιζόμην. Εἰ φρουρᾷ κατα-
κλεῖσαι προσέταττον, ἀπορίας ἡγεῖτο τὸ προσταττόμενον,
οὐ φιλανθρωπίας. Καὶ οὐδὲ οὕτως ὁ μάταιος, ὅσα γε εἰς
θεοὺς καὶ τὸ ὑπήκοον, ἡσυχίαν ἄγειν ἠγάπα· ἀλλ᾽, ὑπὸ
κλεῖθρα τυγχάνων καὶ φύλακας, τῆς αὐτῶν ἀνοχῆς κατ-
ετρύφα· πολλούς τε τοῦ οἰκείου νοσήματος ἐμπιπλᾶν οὐκ
ἀπείχετο. Ἐπεὶ γοῦν καὶ χειρὸς ἐφάνη τιμωροῦ (τά γε παρ᾽
ἡμῖν) καὶ δημίων ὑπέρτερος, ἴσμεν δὲ πάντες ὅτι, ὅσην ὁ
ἥλιος ἐφορᾷ, σοί τε προσανέχει καὶ παρὰ σοῦ διϊθύνεται,
καὶ Κυπριανὸν πάντως συνάμα τινὶ Ἰουστίνῃ παρθένῳ, ἣν
καὶ αὐτὴν ἐξαπέστειλα, ἢ τῆς μισητῆς ἐκκλῖναι θρησκείας
παρασκευάσεις, ἢ τὰ τῷ μεγάλῳ Διῒ καὶ τοῖς ἄλλοις θεοῖς
ἀρέσκοντα καὶ ἐπ᾽ αὐτοῖς καταπράξῃ· ὧν τὸ δυσπειθὲς καὶ
τὰ περὶ αὐτῶν ὑπομνήματα κατὰ μέρος δηλώσει."

58 Διεξιόντα γοῦν τὰ γεγραμμένα τὸν βασιλέα θαυμάζειν
ἐπῄει· καί, πρὸ τῆς πείρας, τῆς καρτερᾶς αὐτῶν καὶ
μεγάλης ἡττᾶτο ψυχῆς. Ἐπεὶ οὖν ἱκανὰς ἐδόκει τὰς

their mind, souls inhabited by their inveterate passion for confrontation.

"So that you may not think that all this is made up, I   57
have now sent to your majesty, after severely torturing him,
also this Kyprianos, a man who, without being forced but of
his own free will, abandoned his faith in the gods of salvation and devoted himself entirely to the crucified one; a
man who is persuasive in words, wicked in his manners, and
most ready to make a defense on behalf of himself. When I
showed him leniency, I found him to be completely indiffer-
ent. If I treated him harshly, and subjected him to torture, I
did not seem to be dealing with a man, but rather with a
statue or some other inanimate object. If I ordered that he
be thrown into jail, he considered my ordinance to be the
result of despair, rather than mercy. Even so, the foolish man
did not choose to keep quiet, at least as far as the gods and
your subjects were concerned. Rather, while guarded under
lock and key, he indulged in the guards' tolerance and did
not refrain from infecting many of them with his disease.
Since, therefore, he has appeared to prevail over punishment—as far as I am concerned—and torturers, and since
we all know that the entire world under the sun relies on you
and is governed by you, you will definitely either make also
Kyprianos, as well as a virgin Ioustina, whom I also sent to
you, convert from their abominable religion, or you may do
with them whatever pleases the great Zeus and the rest of
the gods. My memorandum about them will explain in detail their disobedience."

As he read the letter, the emperor was brought to be-   58
wilderment and, before meeting the saints, he was already
overwhelmed by their great and tenacious souls. As he

53

προλαβούσας βασάνους, καὶ τὸ πλείονας ἐπιθεῖναι οὐκ ἄγριον μόνον, ἀλλὰ καὶ περιττὸν ἔκρινεν (ἐμάνθανε γὰρ αὐτοὺς πολλῷ τῷ περιόντι παντὸς τοῦ ἐπαγομένου καταφρονεῖν), κοινωσάμενος καὶ τοῖς φίλοις αὐτοῦ τὸ βούλευμα, ἐπεὶ κἀκείνους ἐπαινοῦντας εὗρε, τέλος, τοῖς φθάσασιν ἐπετίθει, "Κυπριανός," εἰπών, "καὶ Ἰουστίνα κατὰ θεῶν φρυαξάμενοι, καὶ μήτε κολάσεσι μεταγνῶναι πεισθέντες, μήτε μὴν ἀγαθῶν ὑποσχέσεσι, τὸν διὰ ξίφους ὑπομενέτωσαν θάνατον."

59   Τούτων ἀκούσαντες οἱ ἅγιοι, οὐ κατηφῆ ὄψιν, οὐκ ἀγεννὲς ῥῆμα, οὐκ ἄλλο τι μικρόψυχον ἐπεδείξαντο. Ἀλλὰ φαιδροὶ μᾶλλον καὶ πολλὴν τὴν τῆς ψυχῆς ἡδονὴν ἐπὶ τοῦ προσώπου σημαίνοντες, παρὰ τὸν ποταμὸν Γάλλον τὴν ἐπὶ θάνατον ἤγοντο, πλείστων ὅσων πρὸς τὴν θέαν ἐπειγομένων, ἅτε διατρεχούσης τῆς ἀκοῆς καὶ πάντας εὐθὺς καλούσης διὰ τὸ τῶν προσώπων ἐπίσημον.

60   Βραχὺν οὖν τινα καιρὸν εἰς εὐχὴν αἰτησάμενοι καὶ τυχόντες, εὐστάθειάν τε τῇ Ἐκκλησίᾳ καὶ εἰρήνην πᾶσι παρὰ Χριστοῦ αἰτησάμενοι, ὁ μέγας Κυπριανός, οὐδὲ θνήσκειν μέλλων, εἰς λήθην ἧκε τοῦ σοφοῦ τε καὶ μεγαλόφρονος· ἀλλὰ τὸ τοῦ θήλεως ἀσθενὲς ὑποπτεύων, τοὺς τὴν ἀναίρεσιν ἐπιτετραμμένους Ἰουστίναν ἠξίου διαχειρίσασθαι πρότερον. Οὗ γενομένου, καὶ τὸ μακάριον τέλος αὐτῆς δεξαμένης, πολλὴν ἐκεῖνος ὁμολογήσας τῷ Θεῷ χάριν τῆς καλῆς ταύτης καὶ ποθεινῆς κλήσεως, περιχαρῶς καὶ αὐτὸς διὰ ξίφους εὐθὺς τελειοῦται· καὶ πρὸς οὐρανὸν ἀναφέρεται.

considered the previous tortures to be sufficient and reckoned the addition of more punishments as not only cruel,
but also useless (for he learned that they disregarded every
punishment with much superiority), and as he found his
friends with whom he consulted in agreement with him, in
the end he added the following to what had already transpired: "Let Kyprianos," he said, "and Ioustina, who rebelled
against the gods, and were persuaded to repent neither by
punishments nor by promises of rewards, suffer death by
the sword."

When the saints heard this, they showed no lugubrious 59
face, uttered no ignoble word, displayed no other sign of
faintheartedness. Rather, expressing their inner delight on
their gleaming countenances, they were led to their execu-
tion near the river Gallos. Meanwhile, a large crowd rushed
to witness this, as the rumor spread and attracted everyone
immediately on account of the high status of the people involved.

Having requested and being granted a short time for 60
prayer, they entreated Christ for stability for the Church
and peace for all. The great Kyprianos did not fail to retain his wisdom and bravery, even when about to be killed.
Rather, suspecting the weakness of the female gender, he
requested that those entrusted with the killing execute
Ioustina first. When this happened, and she received her
blessed death, he gave many thanks to God for attaining the
noble and desirable title of martyr and, filled with joy, he too
was immediately killed by the sword and raised to heaven.

61 Οὕτως οὖν τῶν ἱερῶν κειμένων σωμάτων, καὶ μηδενὸς θαρροῦντος αὐτῶν τὴν ἀνάληψιν, διὰ τὸ πολὺ τῶν Ἑλληνιστῶν ἄγριον καὶ πρὸς τὰς τιμωρίας ὀξύρροπον. Σημεῖον δέ (καὶ γὰρ ἤδη κατὰ τῶν ἁγίων μαρτύρων δοθείσης τῆς ἀποφάσεως), παροδεύων τις ᾧ Θεόκτιστος ὄνομα, καὶ τὸν ἅγιον ἀπαγόμενον θεασάμενος, ὡς μόνον ἔφη, "Ἀδίκως ἀτίμῳ θανάτῳ ὅσιος ἀνὴρ παραδέδοται," μάρτυς ἦν παραχρῆμα σχέδιος· ἅμα γὰρ τῇ φωνῇ, τοῦ ἵππου κατενεγκὼν αὐτὸν Φέλβιος ὁ συγκάθεδρος, ᾧ καὶ τὰ περὶ τῶν ἁγίων ὁ βασιλεὺς προηγουμένως ἐπέσκηψε, τὸν ἴσον καὶ αὐτῷ τοῖς τοῦ Χριστοῦ μάρτυσιν ἐπήγαγε θάνατον.

62 Χρόνου οὖν οὐχὶ συχνοῦ διαγενομένου, καὶ τῶν τιμίων οὕτω λειψάνων κειμένων, διαπόντιον ἐκ τῆς Ῥώμης πορείαν τινὲς τῶν Χριστιανῶν στελλόμενοι, ἐπεὶ τὸν μὲν ἅγιον ἰδόντες εὐθὺς ἐγνώρισαν, οὐκ εἶχον δὲ τοὺς τῶν φυλάκων λαθεῖν ὀφθαλμούς, οἳ ἐπ' αὐτὸ τοῦτο παρέμενον, τὴν τῶν λειψάνων φυλακὴν ἐπιτετραμμένοι τοῦ μὴ παρά τινων ἀποκλαπῆναι ταῦτα ἕως ἂν φθάσωσι τροφὴ πετεινοῖς καὶ θηρίοις γινόμενα, οὐδὲ αὐτοὶ τῆς προσεδρείας ἠμέλουν, ἄχρις οὗ οἱ φύλακες μὲν ὕπνου ἡττήθησαν, αὐτοὶ δέ, τοὺς πολυτίμους ἀνελόμενοι θησαυρούς, ἐπὶ τὴν Ῥώμην ἀνέπλεον, ἐπιφερόμενοι καὶ τὰ τῆς ἀθλήσεως αὐτῶν ὑπομνήματα. Ἅ τινι τῶν περιφανεστάτων μετὰ καὶ τῶν ἱερῶν σωμάτων πιστεύουσι γυναικῶν, Ματρώνῃ μὲν τοὔνομα, Ῥουφίνῃ δὲ τὸ ἐπώνυμον, Κλαύδιον αὐχούσῃ τοῦ γένους αὐτῆς ἀρχηγόν. Ἥπερ, ἐν τῷ ἐπισημοτάτῳ λόφῳ τῆς πόλεως, τιμίως ἐν τιμίᾳ ταῦτα κατατίθησι θήκῃ, ἰάσεις

The sacred bodies were left lying there and no one dared 61
to retrieve them, because of the great cruelty of the heathens and their rapid recourse to punishment. A clear sign
of this was the following. After the verdict had been given
against the holy martyrs, a certain man by the name of
Theoktistos, who was passing by, had seen the holy man being led to death. As soon as he uttered, "Unjustly a holy man
is brought to a dishonorable death," he immediately became
a spontaneous martyr. For as soon as he spoke, Felvius, a
counselor with whom the emperor had previously consulted
about the saints, dismounted from his horse and inflicted
upon Theoktistos a death equal to that of the martyrs of
Christ.

A short time later, as the venerable bodies remained lying 62
there, certain Christians were sent from Rome traveling by
sea. They immediately recognized the holy man when they
saw him, but were unable to escape the notice of the guards
who stood firmly by their task: posted to guard the relics
lest anyone steal them before they were devoured by birds
and beasts. Like the guards, the Christians did not relax
their surveillance until the former were overcome by sleep,
and then the Christians took the precious treasures and
sailed to Rome, bringing with them also the documents narrating their martyrdom. Along with the holy bodies, they
entrusted these acts to a most renowned woman, named
Matrona, surnamed Rufina, and belonging to the proud lineage of Claudius. She placed the holy relics honorably in a
precious casket on the most distinguished hill of the city,

ἀφθόνους οὐ τοῖς ἐν τῇ Ῥώμῃ μόνον οἰκοῦσιν, ἀλλὰ καὶ τοῖς πανταχόθεν ἐκεῖσε φοιτῶσιν ὅσαι ἡμέραι παρέχοντα, εἰς δόξαν Θεοῦ Πατρὸς καὶ Κυρίου ἡμῶν Ἰησοῦ Χριστοῦ, ᾧ πρέπει τιμὴ πᾶσα, μεγαλωσύνη τε καὶ μεγαλοπρέπεια, νῦν καὶ ἀεὶ καὶ εἰς τοὺς αἰῶνας τῶν αἰώνων. Ἀμήν.

offering abundant healings not only to those living in Rome, but also to all those visiting from all places, almost every day, for the glory of God the Father and our Lord Jesus Christ, to whom belongs all honor, grandeur as well as magnificence, now and forever and unto the ages of ages. Amen.

LIFE AND CONDUCT OF SAINT PELAGIA OF ANTIOCH

Βίος καὶ πολιτεία τῆς ὁσίας Πελαγίας τῆς ἐν Ἀντιοχείᾳ

Κύριε, εὐλόγησον.

Γυναικείαν ἀρετήν, τῆς τῶν ἀνδρῶν οὐδὲν ἀπολειφθεῖσαν, πᾶσι διεξιέναι λυσιτελὲς καὶ ὠφέλιμον· καὶ τοσούτῳ μᾶλλον, ὅσωπερ ἀναλόγου πρότερον ἀντεισηνέχθη κακίας. Οὕτω γὰρ ἂν τὸ μὲν τῶν ἀρρένων γένος τὴν τοῦ θήλεος ὑπερβαλέσθαι φύσιν φιλοτιμήσαιτο· γυναῖκες δὲ τῆς τῶν συγγενῶν ἀρετῆς μὴ ἀπολειφθῆναι διὰ σπουδῆς ἂν ποιήσαιντο· ἑκατέρων δὲ ὑπεξαιρεθείη τὸ τῆς πονηρᾶς ἕξεως, ὡς τὰ πολλὰ δυσαπόνιπτον. Ὃ δὴ καὶ αὐτὸς πρὸ τῶν ἄλλων εἰδώς, τὰ κατὰ τὴν μακαρίαν ταύτην Πελαγίαν, ἣν τὸ τῆς Θεοῦ φιλανθρωπίας ἡμῖν ἐγνώρισε πέλαγος, ἄνωθεν εἴπω καὶ διηγήσομαι.

2 Αὕτη πατρίδα μὲν ἔσχε καὶ πόλιν τὴν Ἀντιόχου. Πλούτῳ δὲ γενομένη περιφανὴς καὶ κάλλει διαπρεπής, οὐκ εἰς καλὸν τῷ πλούτῳ ἐχρήσατο· οὐδὲ τοσοῦτον τῷ κάλλει τοῦ σώματος ἔνειμεν, ὅσον μὴ τὸ τῆς ψυχῆς παραβλάπτεσθαι. Ἀλλὰ τὸ μὲν ἐπήνθει ταύτῃ πολύ, πολλῷ μὲν κομώσῃ τῷ φυσικῷ, πλείονι δὲ χρωμένῃ τῷ τεχνητῷ· τὸ δὲ τῆς ψυχῆς ἀπήνθει καὶ ἐμαραίνετο. Χρυσὸς δὲ ἦν αὐτῇ, πολὺς μὲν ὁ τὸ σῶμα κοσμῶν, πολὺς δὲ καὶ ὁ ταῖς χρείαις ὑπηρετῶν· καὶ πλῆθος ἀκολούθων, τῶν μὲν προηγουμένων, τῶν δὲ καὶ ἐφεπομένων. Οἷς δὴ καὶ μάλιστα τὸ τῶν παθῶν ἔχουσα πῦρ ἀναπτόμενον, καὶ τοὺς ἐραστὰς ὑπαγομένη τε καὶ

Life and Conduct of Saint Pelagia of Antioch

Lord, give the blessing.

Recounting the virtue of women, since it is in no way outclassed by that of men, is advantageous and beneficial for all. And it is so much more advantageous, to the degree that this virtue has been introduced so as to balance a comparable vice. In this way, the male gender could be incited to surpass female nature, women could strive to not be outclassed by the virtue of their fellow women, and the evil habits of both, which are generally difficult to expunge, could be erased. I, more conscious of this than others, will tell and narrate from the beginning the story of that blessed Pelagia whom the sea of God's love made known to us.

Pelagia's fatherland and city was that of Antiochos. 2 Though she became prominent in wealth and acclaimed for her beauty, she did not apply her wealth to good causes, nor did she spend on the body's beauty only so much as would not be to the soul's detriment. Rather, while her body was blossoming fully as she prided herself on her abundant natural beauty, and applied even more abundant artificial adornments, her soul was losing its bloom and decaying. She had gold, much of which adorned her body, while the rest served her needs; she also had a large number of attendants, some preceding her, some following behind. With the fire of her passions blazing mightily because of all this, and with many lovers being seduced and inflamed by her, she worked (alas!)

ἐκκαίουσα, ἐν πόρναις (οἴμοι!) ἐτέλει· καὶ πρώτη τῶν ἐν τῇ πόλει μαινάδων ἐπεγινώσκετο.

3 Ἀλλὰ γὰρ οὐκ ἤνεγκε Κύριος φύσιν καὶ ψυχὴν γενναίαν τυραννουμένην ὑπὸ τοῦ Πονηροῦ, τό τε μέλλον ὁρῶν ὡς ἤδη παρόν, καὶ οἷα ἂν ἐξ οἵας γένοιτο προειδώς, καί τι καὶ δοῦναι θέλων τοῖς αὐτὸν σεβομένοις παράδειγμα, ὡς ἀρκεῖ τὸ θελῆσαι μόνον πρὸς τὸ γενέσθαι χρηστόν. Καὶ δή ποτε τοῦ ἐν Ἀντιοχείᾳ τότε τὸν ἱερατικὸν διέποντος θρόνον κατά τινα χρείαν τοὺς ὑπ' αὐτὸν ἐπισκόπους συναγαγόντος—ἐν οἷς ἄλλοι τε πολλοὶ προέχοντες τῶν πολλῶν ἦσαν, καὶ δὴ καὶ Νόννος, ἀνὴρ τἄλλα τε θαυμαστὸς καὶ τὸν τρόπον ἀγγελικός—, τούτων οὖν ἤδη συνειλεγμένων, καί τινος τῶν ἐν τῇ πόλει νεῶν—Ἰουλιανοῦ δὲ τοῦ μάρτυρος οὗτος ἦν—πρὸ τῶν πυλῶν καθεζομένων, καὶ φιλοσοφούντων τὰ θεοφιλῆ τε καὶ ἄνω φέροντα, καὶ τοῦ ἱεροῦ Νόννου ψυχωφελῆ τινα διδασκαλίαν πρὸς αὐτοὺς μετιόντος, παρῄει Πελαγία τῇ συνήθει χρωμένη καὶ σκευῇ καὶ στολῇ, ἐπί τινος ὀχήματος καθημένη, πολλοῖς δὲ παραπεμπομένη, καὶ τὸν πλησίον ἀέρα καταχρωννῦσά τε καὶ μυρίζουσα—τὸ μὲν τῇ τῶν μύρων ὀσμῇ, τὸ δὲ τῇ τῶν λίθων καὶ μαργάρων αὐγῇ.

4 Ταύτην οὖν παριοῦσαν ἀνερυθριάστως οὕτω καὶ ἰταμῶς ὁ τῶν ποιμένων ἰδόντες χορός, οἱ μὲν ἄλλοι, ἅτε δὴ μηδέν τι πλέον τῶν ὁρωμένων ἔχοντες ἐνορᾶν, θέαν αὐτῆς κατεγίνωσκον πορνικήν· καὶ οὐδὲ προσιδεῖν ὅλως ὑπέμενον, ἀλλ' ἠρυθρίων καὶ ἀπεστρέφοντο. Νόννος δὲ ἄρα ᾔδει καὶ τἀναντία πολλάκις ἐκ τῶν ἐναντίων καρποῦσθαι· καὶ δι' οὗ κέντρον ἡδονῆς ἄλλος ἂν ἴσως ἐδέξατο τῇ ψυχῇ, τοῦτο δὴ

among the prostitutes and was recognized as the first among the city's harlots.

Yet the Lord could not bear that a noble nature and soul ₃ continue under the tyranny of the Evil One, since He saw the future as already present, and foresaw what kind of person she would become from what she was before; moreover, He wished to offer to those who revered Him an example of the fact that one's will alone is sufficient for one to become good. Thus, when on one occasion the incumbent to the priestly throne in Antioch at that time summoned, on some pressing matter, all the bishops under his authority—among whom were many other prominent leaders, as well as that Nonnos, a man admirable in all respects and angelic in his ways—and when they had already gathered, and were sitting in front of the gates of a certain church in the city—this was the church of Ioulianos the martyr—discussing philosophically matters pleasing to God and uplifting, and as holy Nonnos presented to them some beneficial teaching, Pelagia was passing by in her usual attire and dress, sitting on a chariot, with a large escort, and filling the air around her with color and fragrance: the latter from the scent of her perfumes, the former from the luster of her gems and pearls.

When the chorus of bishops saw her parading so shame- ₄ lessly and impudently, everyone else, incapable of seeing anything beyond the visible things, condemned her lascivious appearance; they could not even bear to look at her, but blushed and turned their faces away. Yet Nonnos knew well how one can often gain the opposite benefit from opposite things; what might create in another person's soul an incentive for pleasure, this was for him an incentive for virtue.

οὗτος ἔσχεν ὑπέκκαυμά τι πρὸς ἀρετήν. Ἀνθ' ὧν καὶ τῆς πόρνης οὐκ ἀφίστη τὸν ὀφθαλμόν· ἀλλὰ καί, παρούσης, ἀτενὲς πρὸς αὐτὴν ἑώρα, καί, ἀπιούσης, αὐτὸς ἔτι τῆς θέας εἴχετο.

5 Εἶτα καὶ μέγα στενάξας καὶ δακρύων πλησθείς, ἑαυτὸν ὁ μακάριος ἀπεκλαίετο· καὶ τὸν ἐκείνης καλλωπισμὸν κατάκρισιν ἔλεγεν ἑαυτοῦ, εἴπερ "Ἐκείνη μέν, σωμάτων ἐρῶσα φθαρτῶν, καὶ ταῦτα ἐπὶ λύμῃ τῇ ἑαυτῆς, καί τοι γνήσιον ἔχουσα κάλλος τοῖς μέλεσιν ἐπανθοῦν, ὅμως οὐκ ἀποκνεῖ ἐπιδημιουργοῦσα τῷ φυσικῷ κάλλει καὶ ἐπιτεχνωμένη, καί τισι τοῦτο μηχαναῖς ἐπιλαμπρύνουσα καὶ ὑπογραφαῖς, ἵνα κλέψῃ δούλην πικρὰν ἡδονήν. Ἡμεῖς δέ, οἷς μὲν ἀθάνατος ὁ ἐρώμενος (προσθήσω δ' ὅτι καὶ ἐραστής), ἀθάνατος δὲ ὁ νυμφών, ἡ δὲ χάρις τοῖς ὄντως κεκαλλωπισμένοις μηδὲ γηράσκουσα, τοσοῦτον ἀπέχομεν τὴν ἀθάνατον καλλωπίζειν ψυχήν, ὥστε καὶ τὸ φυσικὸν αὐτῆς κάλλος αἰσχύνοντες οὐκ ἐπαισχυνόμεθα. Ἀλλ' ἐφυβρίζομεν ἑαυτούς· καὶ τῆς ἡδονῆς ἐκείνης τῆς ἀπορρήτου καὶ θαυμαστῆς ἐλεεινῶς ἀπειργόμεθα, καὶ ταῦτα μηδὲ τὴν ἐπηρτημένην ἡμῖν ἀγνοοῦντες κόλασιν καὶ τὰ ἐκεῖθεν δικαιωτήρια."

6 Οὕτως μὲν ἐκεῖνος, οὐ μόνον πρός γε τὸ παρὸν ἀποβλέπων (ὡς πείθομαι), ἀλλ' ἤδη καὶ τὸ μέλλον τῷ νῷ προορῶν, καὶ εἰδὼς ὡς οὐ μετὰ πολὺ καὶ τοῦ τῆς ψυχῆς αὐτῆς ἡττηθήσονται κάλλους, καὶ πόρνης φανοῦνται πρὸς ἀγῶνας πνευματικοὺς δεύτεροι. Ὁ δὴ καὶ ὀνειράτων ὄψις αὐτῷ προεδείκνυ· καὶ ἡ ὅρασις τοιάδε τις θεία καὶ θαυμαστή, καὶ παρὰ Θεοῦ. Ἐδόκει τῆς θείας λειτουργίας

For this reason, he did not turn his eyes away from the harlot; rather, when she drew near, he stared at her steadily, and,
when she began to leave, he continued to watch her.

Then the blessed man sighed deeply and, filled with tears,   5
started bemoaning his condition; the way she cultivated her
beauty, he said, was a rebuke to him, if indeed "she, who desires perishable bodies, moreover to her own destruction,
and though indeed she possesses genuine beauty blooming
on her body, nevertheless does not hesitate to apply creativ-
ity and artistry to her natural beauty; she increases its glam-
our with devices and cosmetics so as to purloin slavish, bitter pleasure. Yet we, whose beloved (and, let me add, also
lover) is immortal, whose bridal chamber is also eternal,
and for whom the grace of those truly made beautiful never
grows old, are so far from beautifying our immortal soul that
we are not ashamed to disgrace its natural beauty. Rather,
we debase ourselves and are pitifully excluded from that
ineffable and wondrous pleasure, even if we know well the
punishment that awaits us and the just retribution for our
behavior."

These were his words, as he observed not only the pres-   6
ent (as I am certain), but already foresaw with his mind the
future as well, knowing that, not much later, they would
be defeated also by the beauty of her soul, and would be
proven inferior to a prostitute in spiritual labors as well. A
dream vision also signaled this to him; and this was more or
less what he saw, in a divine and wondrous vision coming
from God: Nonnos dreamed that, during the celebration of

τελουμένης ὁ Νόννος, αὐτὸς μὲν τῷ λαιῷ κέρατι τοῦ θυ-
σιαστηρίου παρεστηκέναι, περιστερὰν δέ τινα βεβορβορω-
μένην αὐτὸν περιπέτεσθαι· καὶ μηδὲ ῥᾳδίως ἀφίστασθαι,
ἀλλὰ πλησίον ἵπτασθαι καὶ διοχλεῖν, καὶ μυρίαν ἐμποιεῖν
τῇ δυσωδίᾳ τὴν ἀηδίαν. Καὶ ταῦτα μέχρι τῆς τῶν κατηχουμένων παρὰ τοῦ ἱερέως προσκλήσεως.

7 Τὸ δὲ μετὰ ταῦτα, τί; Ἀφανὴς μὲν αὕτη, ὅσον ὁ τῶν
μυστηρίων καὶ πάσης τῆς λειτουργίας ἐπεῖχε καιρός. Ἤδη
δὲ ταύτης τελεσθείσης, ἐξερχομένῳ τοῦ ἱεροῦ καὶ γενομένῳ πρὸς τῇ φλιᾷ, πάλιν τὴν αὐτὴν φανῆναι περιστεράν,
οὕτω μὲν ἔχουσαν, οὕτω δὲ καὶ ποιοῦσαν, μέχρις οὗ τείνας
τὴν δεξιὰν καὶ ταύτης λαβόμενος τῇ χειρί, καθῆκεν ἐπὶ
τὸν λουτῆρα, ὕδατος ὄντα πεπληρωμένον. Κἀκείνη λοιπὸν
τῶν πτερῶν ἀποβαλοῦσα τὸν μολυσμόν, αἰθέριος ἵπτατο·
καὶ πρὸς τοσοῦτον ὕψος ἐφέρετο, πρὸς ὃ μηδὲ αὐτὸς οἷος
τε ἦν ἐξικνεῖσθαι τοὺς ὀφθαλμούς. Τοῦτο τὸ μέλλον προ-
εζωγράφει· καὶ τὸ γενόμενον ἐν νυκτὶ τοῦ μεθ' ἡμέραν ἦν
γενησομένου προτύπωσις.

8 Ἕωθεν οὖν ὁ ἱερὸς ἀνὴρ ἀναστάς, καί τισι τὴν ὅρασιν
κοινωσάμενος, ἀφικνεῖται μὲν ἐπὶ τὸν ναὸν ἅμα τοῖς ἄλλοις
ποιμέσι· τὴν δὲ Καινὴν ἐπὶ χεῖρας Διαθήκην, τὸ θεῖον φημὶ
λαβὼν Εὐαγγέλιον, τοῦ ἀρχιποίμενος αὐτῷ ἐπιτρέψαντος,
διὰ τῆς ἐν αὐτῷ τοῦ Πνεύματος χάριτος τοῖς λαοῖς ὡμίλει.

9 Γίνεται οὖν ὃ μὴ πρότερον, καὶ πρᾶγμα τῶν οὐκ ἐλπι-
ζομένων οὐδὲ συνήθων. Πελαγία τῶν ἱερῶν ἀκροατὴς λόγων, καὶ τί μὲν ἀκούσασα τὰ παρόντα, τί δὲ τὰ μέλλοντα,
καὶ τί μὲν ἡμῶν ἡ ψυχή, τίς δὲ ὁ ταύτης δεσμός, καὶ ὅπως
τοῦ σώματος διαζεύγνυται, καὶ πάλιν ἀνίσταταί τε καὶ

the divine liturgy, he himself was standing on the left side of the altar while a dove, smeared with filth, was flying around him; it would simply not leave him alone, but rather hovered close to him and annoyed him, causing unending disgust with its foul odor. And this went on until the priest invited the catechumens to leave.

And then, what happened? The dove disappeared, during the time of the sacraments and the entire liturgy. But when the liturgy was finished, and he went out of the sanctuary and approached the threshold, the same dove appeared again: it continued to be and do the same, until he stretched out his right hand and caught it, and then placed it on the font which was filled with water. Shedding the filth from its wings, it flew up into the air and rose to such a height as he himself could not reach with his eyes. This vision prefigured the future; what happened during the night foreshadowed what was going to happen during the day. 7

The holy man rose early in the morning, shared the vision with some men, and then arrived at the church, together with the rest of the clergy; taking the New Testament (I mean the divine Gospel) in his hands, with the archbishop's permission, he started speaking to the crowds through the grace of the Spirit in him. 8

At that moment, something that had never happened before, a thing unexpected and unusual, took place: Pelagia listened to the sacred words, and heard about the present world and the future life, what our soul is, what is its bond, how it is separated from the body, how it is resurrected and 9

κρίνεται, καὶ τίσιν αἰσχύνεται. Ὦ τοῦ θαύματος! Γινώσκει
τὰ ἑαυτῆς· καὶ πάντων καταγινώσκει τῶν πρίν· καὶ συστα-
λεῖσα πρὸς ἑαυτήν, ὅλη τοῦ καλοῦ καὶ τῆς μετανοίας γίνε-
ται· καὶ δάκρυα χέει τοῖς πρὶν γέλωσιν ἀντισούμενα.

10   Εἶτα καὶ τούτοις χρῆται πρὸς σωτηρίαν, οἷς ἐχρῆτο
πρότερον εἰς ἀπώλειαν. Καί τισιν ἐπιτρέπει τῶν ἑαυτῆς,
συνεξελθοῦσι τοῦ ἱεροῦ τῷ Νόννῳ καὶ συνακολουθήσασι,
καὶ δὴ καὶ θεασαμένοις οἷ τὴν κατοίκησιν ποιεῖται, τάχιστα ἀπαγγέλλειν αὐτῇ καὶ μὴ μέλλειν πρὸς τὴν ἐπίταξιν.

11   Τούτου δὴ γενομένου, καὶ τῶν ἐκπεμφθέντων ἐπανελ-
θόντων, καὶ τὸ προσταχθὲν ἀγγειλάντων, βουλὴν βουλεύεται γενναίαν καὶ ἀνδρικήν. Καὶ πρὸς τὸν ἱερὸν παρρησιά-
ζεται Νόννον· καὶ δὴ καὶ λαβοῦσα χάρτην, διεχάραξεν
οὕτως· "Ἤκουσα του τῶν Χριστιανῶν, Χριστοῦ μαθητά,
ὡς φησί που τῶν ἑαυτοῦ λόγων ὁ σὸς Δεσπότης, *Οὐκ
ἦλθον καλέσαι δικαίους, ἀλλὰ ἁμαρτωλοὺς εἰς μετάνοιαν·*
καὶ ὡς δὴ καὶ τελώναις συνανεκλίθη· καὶ πόρναις συνανε-
στράφη· καὶ Σαμαρείτιδι πρὸς τὸ φρέαρ ὡμίλησε, καὶ λόγου μετέσχε τε καὶ μετέδωκεν· ὃν τρέμει τὰ Χερουβίμ, καὶ
οὐδὲ βλέπειν στέγει τὰ Σεραφίμ. Ἀλλ᾽ εἴ τι σὺ τοιούτου
μὲν δοῦλος Δεσπότου, τοιούτου δὲ μαθητὴς Διδασκάλου,
δεῖξον τοῖς ἔργοις· καὶ μὴ βδελύξῃ πόρνην ὁμογενῆ καὶ
ὁμόδουλον. Ἀλλὰ καὶ δεομένην τῆς σῆς ἱερᾶς ἀξίωσον
θέας· καὶ ἐξομολογουμένην δέξαι· καὶ σῶσον ἀπολλυμέ-
νην, καὶ σοῦ μόνου ἐξεχομένην, καὶ σοὶ τὰς ἐλπίδας σαλεύ-
ουσαν."

12   Ταῦτα δεξάμενος, ὁ ἱερὸς ἠδέσθη ἀνήρ. Καὶ μόνῳ μὲν
ἀντεπιστέλλει μὴ προσελθεῖν, ἤδη δέ γε καὶ τῶν λοιπῶν

judged, and what behavior brings shame to it. What a miracle! She came to understand herself; she repudiated her past; having turned inwardly, she was won over completely to virtue and repentance; and she started pouring out tears, equal to her earlier laughter.

Then she even used for her salvation the very means that 10 she previously employed for her damnation. She thus ordered some of her servants to leave the church together with Nonnos, follow him, see where he lived, and then immediately, without delay, inform her.

This indeed happened, and when those who had been 11 dispatched returned and reported on their assignment, she came to a noble and manly resolution. She decided to speak openly to holy Nonnos and so, right away, she took a piece of paper and wrote the following: "I heard from some Christian, O disciple of Christ, that your Lord said somewhere in his speeches, *'I did not come to call the righteous, but sinners to repentance';* and that He dined with publicans, consorted with prostitutes, and spoke to the Samaritan woman at the well, engaging in a conversation with her, He at whom the Cherubim tremble, and at whom the Seraphim do not dare even to look. But if you are a servant to such a Master, and a disciple of such a Teacher, show it with your deeds; do not abhor me, a prostitute, though of the same kin as you and a fellow servant. Rather, as I implore you, allow me to see your holy face, and receive my confession, and save one who is ruined and depends on you alone, with my hopes resting in you."

When the holy man received this letter, he felt embar- 12 rassed. He wrote back that she should not come to him

συμπαρόντων ἀρχιερέων φανεροῦν ἑαυτήν, καὶ ὃ βούλοιτο λέγειν καὶ ἐκκαλύπτειν τὰ ἑαυτῆς. Ἡ δέ, τούτου
τυχοῦσα, τὸν καιρὸν ἁρπάζει· καὶ διώκει τὸν σῴζοντα. Καὶ
καταλαβοῦσα τὴν ἐκκλησίαν, πόρνη τις ἦν ἄλλη κατὰ γῆς
ἐρριμμένη, καὶ κλίνουσα καὶ γόνυ καὶ τὴν ψυχήν, καὶ πόδας βρέχουσα, κἂν μὴ δεσποτικούς, ἀλλ᾽ οὖν ἱερατικοὺς
καὶ ὡραίους, καὶ ψυχῆς εἰρήνην (ἀληθῶς εἰπεῖν) εὐαγγελι-
ζομένους. Καὶ οὐδ᾽ ἂν εἴ τι καὶ γένοιτο μεθήσειν πρότερον
ἔφασκε, πρὶν ἢ τὴν δι᾽ ὕδατος λάβοι καὶ Πνεύματος ἀνα-
γέννησιν. Καὶ ἦν ἀγὼν ἀμφοτέροις, τῷ μὲν πεῖσαι ταύτην
τῶν ποδῶν ἀφεμένην ἐξαναστῆναι, τῇ δὲ τούτων ἔχεσθαι
μᾶλλον· καὶ πρὸ τοῦ λουτροῦ, κάθαρσις ἦν ἄλλη καὶ δακρύων λουτρόν, τοῦ πνευματικωτέρου δηλαδὴ τὸ ἐπιπο-
νώτερον.

13   Ταῦτα καὶ παρὰ τῶν ὁρώντων δάκρυον ἐξεκαλεῖτο. Καὶ
ἦν αὐτοῖς λύπη τις ἐκπλήξει καὶ ἡδονῇ σύγκρατος, τῶν
δακρύων μὲν αὐτῇ κοινωνούντων καὶ συναλγούντων, καὶ
τὴν πίστιν ἐκπληττομένων, χαιρόντων δὲ καὶ ἡδομένων τῇ
σωτηρίᾳ.

14   Εἶτα μόλις πεισθείσης καὶ ἀναστάσης, καὶ τοῦ ἱεροῦ
Νόννου ἐγγύας ζητοῦντος καὶ ἀναβαλλομένου τὴν κάθαρ-
σιν, πάλιν ἐκείνη τῶν αὐτοῦ ποδῶν γίνεται· καὶ τὰς αὐτὰς
ἐκπέμπει φωνάς· "Καὶ σὺ λόγον ὧν ἔπραξα δώσεις," ἔλεγεν, "ἀρχιερεῦ τοῦ Θεοῦ· καὶ σοὶ τῶν ἐμῶν ἀνομιῶν ἐπι-
γραφήσεται ἡ πληθύς, ἐὰν ὑπερθῇ τὸν φωτισμόν, καὶ
ἀναβάλῃ τὸ βάπτισμα, καὶ μὴ σπεύσῃς μηδ᾽ ἐπειχθῇς πρὸς
τὴν ἐμὴν σωτηρίαν, καὶ πνευματικῶς ὠδινήσῃς καὶ

alone, but should present herself before the rest of the bishops as well, and say what she wanted to say, and reveal her story. When she received this response, she seized the opportunity; and she sought her savior. Reaching the church, like the Gospel's harlot she threw herself on the ground, genuflecting with body and soul, watering with tears feet that, though not of the Lord, were still priestly and *beautiful, proclaiming* (to use the true words) *the good tidings* of *peace* of soul. And she kept saying that, whatever might happen, she would not let go of his feet before receiving rebirth through both water and the Spirit. They both engaged in a struggle: his was to persuade her to let go of his feet and stand up, and hers was to cling to them even more; before her spiritual baptism, there was another purification, the more arduous baptism of tears.

This also provoked tears in those watching. And their 13 sorrow was mixed with astonishment and pleasure as they shared her tears and pain, astonished at her faith and rejoicing with pleasure in her salvation.

Then, when she was with difficulty persuaded to stand up 14 and holy Nonnos started asking for guarantees and delayed the purification, she again clasped his feet; and she voiced the same cries. "You too will answer for my deeds," she said, "archpriest of God; the multitude of my iniquities will be ascribed to you too, if you postpone my enlightenment, and delay my baptism, and neither rush nor hurry for my salvation, nor give birth, a new birth, to me spiritually, nor

ἀναγεννήσῃς, καὶ νύμφην με σήμερον καθαρὰν τῷ καθαρῷ προσαγάγῃς νυμφίῳ καὶ παραστήσῃς Χριστῷ."

15   Τέλος, πείθει. Καὶ ἀναστᾶσα ἐξομολογεῖται· καὶ τὴν θείαν ἐκκαλεῖται φιλανθρωπίαν. Καὶ τί αὐτῇ τὸ ἐκ νεότητος ὄνομα παρὰ τοῦ ἐπισκόπου ἐρωτηθεῖσα, Πελαγία μὲν ἔλεγεν ἐξ ὑπαρχῆς καλεῖσθαι πᾶσι καὶ ὀνομάζεσθαι, Ἀντιοχέας δέ, τό τε πλῆθος καὶ κάλλος τῶν ἐν αὐτῇ λίθων καὶ μαργάρων τεθαυμακότας, Μαργαριτὼ καλεῖν, οἷς ἐκοσμεῖτο, κλῆσιν προσεξευρόντας φερώνυμον.

16   Ἐνταῦθα τὴν πρώτην ἀναλαμβάνει κλῆσιν· καὶ Πελαγία καλεῖται· καὶ δέχεται τὸ λουτρόν· καὶ καθαίρεται· καὶ μύρῳ χρίεται· καὶ μέτοχος τῆς ἀχράντου καὶ ἀναιμάκτου θυσίας γίνεται. Καὶ ἦν τις Ἀντιοχεῦσιν εὐφροσύνη τότε πάνδημος καὶ κοινή, τοῦ μὲν κοινοῦ πολεμίου πεσόντος ἤδη καὶ ἡττηθέντος, τῶν δὲ πιστῶν ἀγαλλιωμένων, καὶ τὴν ἐκείνης σωτηρίαν ἰδίαν ἑκάστου καὶ λεγόντων καὶ νομιζόντων.

17   Ἀλλὰ γὰρ φιλεῖ πως ὁ Πονηρός, ἡττώμενος, ἀναιδέστερος γίνεσθαι· ὅθεν οὐκ ἤνεγκε τὴν ἑαυτοῦ τοσαύτην αἰσχύνην, οὐδὲ τὴν τοσαύτην τῶν πιστῶν πνευματικὴν ἡδονήν. Ἀλλὰ δὴ μετασχηματισθεὶς εἰς ἄνθρωπον ὁ μισάνθρωπος, καὶ μέσος πάντων φανεὶς τὰς χεῖρας ἔχων ἐπὶ τῆς κεφαλῆς, καὶ κόπτων ἑαυτὸν πάντων ὁρώντων, πρῶτον μὲν κατεβόα τοῦ ἱεροῦ Νόννου· καὶ ἀδικεῖσθαι διετείνετο τὰ μέγιστα παρ' αὐτοῦ, καὶ τὰς οὔσας αὐτῷ δυνάμεις ἀφαιρεῖσθαι καὶ περικόπτεσθαι. Εἶτα καὶ τῇ Πελαγίᾳ ὁ ἀναιδὴς προσελθών, προδότην αὐτὴν καὶ ἄπιστον ἀπεκάλει. Καί, "Ἵνα τί," φησί, "τὸν σὸν ἠρνήσω, καὶ τῷ ἀλλοτρίῳ

74

lead me today as a pure bride to the pure bridegroom, presenting me to Christ."

In the end, she persuaded him. And she stood up and 15
confessed and appealed to God's mercy. When the bishop
asked her what had been her name since childhood, she answered that, from the beginning, everyone had called and
named her Pelagia, yet the Antiochenes, admiring the multitude and beauty of her gems and pearls, used to call her
Pearly, devising a name appropriate to her adornments.

Thereupon, she received anew her first name and was 16
called Pelagia; she was baptized, purified, and anointed with
perfumed oil; and she partook of the undefiled and bloodless sacrifice. A shared and collective joy came upon the Antiochenes, since their common foe had already fallen defeated, and the faithful were rejoicing, saying and thinking
that her salvation was salvation for each and every one of
them.

However, the Evil One usually becomes more ruthless 17
when he is defeated. Hence, he could bear neither his great
humiliation, nor the great spiritual pleasure of the faithful.
This hater of mankind transformed himself into a man and
appeared in the midst of the crowd holding his hands to his
head; striking himself in sight of all, he first cried out
against holy Nonnos, claiming that he was terribly wronged
by Nonnos who had removed and cut off his powers. Then,
this shameless one approached Pelagia, calling her a faithless traitor. "Why," he said, "did you reject your own, and

συνέθου;" Ἡ δὲ τείνει τὴν χεῖρα· καὶ βάλλει τὸν Πονηρὸν τῷ σταυρῷ· καὶ παρευθὺ ὁ Πολέμιος ἀφανής.

18 Καὶ οὐδὲ οὕτω τῆς ἀναιδείας ἀφίσταται καὶ τοῦ ἐγχειρήματος, ἀλλὰ καὶ αὖθις ἐπιχειρεῖ καὶ πειρᾶται. Καὶ καθευδούσῃ περὶ μέσας νύκτας αὐτῇ προσελθών, ἐφίσταται καὶ διυπνίζει. Καὶ λέγει μὲν τὰ αὐτά· πάλιν δὲ βάλλεται τῷ σταυρῷ· καὶ ἀφανὴς εὐθὺς γίνεται. Ἡ δέ, διαναστᾶσα, γνωρίζει μὲν τῇ ἀπὸ τοῦ ἁγίου ταύτην ἀναδεξαμένῃ βαπτίσματος—ᾗ δὴ καὶ Ῥωμάνα τοὔνομα—τὴν πάλην τοῦ δυσμενοῦς. Ἐπιρρώνυται δὲ τοῖς ἐκείνης λόγοις· καὶ πρὸς παράταξιν ἀντιτάττεται· καὶ πλήττει τὸν Πονηρόν, δευτέρᾳ καὶ καιρίᾳ ταύτῃ πληγῇ· καλέσασα γὰρ τῶν ἑαυτῆς θεραπόντων τὸν εὐνούστατόν τε καὶ εὐπειθέστατον, πᾶσαν μὲν αὐτῇ τὴν ἐν τῷ οἴκῳ οὐσίαν ἀπογραφῆναι κελεύει, ὅση τε εἴη, καὶ οἴα, ἐν χρυσῷ, ἐν ἀργύρῳ, ἐν λίθοις, ἐν μαργάροις, ἐν σκεύεσιν, ἐν στολαῖς, καὶ μηδ' ὁτιοῦν ὅλως ὃ μὴ ἀπογραφείη παραλειφθῆναι, καὶ τὴν ἀπογραφὴν ὡς τάχος αὐτῇ κομισθῆναι.

19 Ὃ δὴ καὶ κατὰ γνώμην ἐκείνῃ χωρεῖ. Καὶ τὸν ἱερὸν προσκαλεσαμένη Νόννον, πάσης μὲν αὐτῷ τῆς οὐσίας παραχωρεῖ, ἀρκεῖν εἰποῦσα τὸν ἐξ ἀρετῆς αὐτῇ πλοῦτον, καὶ ὅσος ὁ τοῦ ταύτης νυμφίου καὶ δεσπότου Χριστοῦ. Τοὺς δὲ ἑαυτῆς οἰκέτας τοῦ τῆς δουλείας ἀνῆκε ζυγοῦ. Ἀλλ' ὅπως καὶ μὴ παρούσης ὡς ἔτι παρούσης προνοίας τῆς ἐξ αὐτῆς ἀπολαύοιεν, μηδ' ἐν στενῷ αὐτοῖς καταντήσῃ τὰ τῆς ζωῆς, καὶ χρήματα τούτοις ἡ φιλάνθρωπος ἐπιδίδωσιν.

20 Εἶθ' οὕτως πάντων αὐτῇ κατὰ νοῦν χωρησάντων, τῇ

join the opposition?" She stretched out her hand, struck the Evil One with the cross, and the Enemy immediately disappeared.

Yet, even treated in this way, he did not cease his shameless endeavor, but tried again to tempt her. He approached her, while she was asleep in the middle of the night, stood beside her and woke her up. He repeated the same words, but again was struck by the cross and disappeared immediately. Pelagia got up and revealed to her godmother—her name was Romana—this struggle against the malignant one. She was then strengthened by Romana's words, prepared herself for battle, and struck the Evil One with this second and fatal blow. She summoned her most loyal and trusted servant, and ordered him to inventory all her household property—how much it was and of what kind, in gold, silver, gems, pearls, vessels, garments—and she ordered him to leave nothing out, but to bring her the list as soon as possible. 18

This order was carried out exactly as she wished. She then summoned holy Nonnos, and offered him her entire property, saying that the wealth of virtue and the wealth that belonged to her bridegroom and master Christ were sufficient for her. She also liberated her servants from the yoke of slavery. Moreover, so that they might enjoy her benevolence just as if she were still present—even if she would no longer be there—and so that their lives might not end up straitened by need, this merciful woman also gave them money. 19

With everything carried out according to her wish, on 20

κυρίᾳ τῶν ἡμερῶν τὴν ἐμφώτειον ἀποδυσαμένη στολήν, καὶ τρύχινόν τε καὶ ῥακῶδες περιβαλλομένη χιτώνιον, ἐπείγεται πρὸς Ἱεροσόλυμα· καὶ τὸ Ὄρος καταλαμβάνει τῶν Ἐλαιῶν, ἅμα δὲ καὶ τῶν ἀρετῶν, μηδενὶ τὴν γνώμην κοινωσαμένη, μηδὲ μεταδοῦσα τοῦ μυστηρίου.

21 Καὶ τὰ μὲν ἐκείνης οὕτω κρυπτά, καὶ μόνῳ δῆλα τῷ τὰ ἀφανῆ βλέποντι. Ἤδη δὲ τῶν ἐν Ἀντιοχείᾳ συνειλεγμένων ἐπισκόπων (ἐν οἷς ἦν καὶ Νόννος) ταῖς αὐτῶν ἐκκλησίαις αὖθις ἀποδοθέντων, κἀκείνης ἀγνώστως οὕτω τοῖς Ἱεροῖς Τόποις προσεδρευούσης, καὶ χρόνου τριετοῦς αὐτῇ διαγενομένου, θεῖος αἱρεῖ τινα πόθος τῶν τῷ ἐπισκόπῳ Νόννῳ συνόντων—Ἰάκωβος οὗτος ἦν—, καὶ τῶν Ἱερῶν ἐρᾷ Τόπων, θεατὴς ἅμα καὶ προσκυνητὴς ἐκείνων γενέσθαι βουλόμενος. Καὶ δὴ προσελθὼν τῷ ἀρχιερεῖ, τὴν ἐπὶ τὰ Ἱεροσόλυμα ταύτην ὁδὸν ἐξαιτεῖ· καὶ δεῖται τοῦτο αὐτῷ χαρίσασθαι.

22 Ὁ δέ (ἦν γὰρ προφητικὸς ὁ ἀνὴρ καὶ Πνεύματος πλήρης, καὶ τὸ πόρρω καὶ μέλλον ἰδεῖν ἱκανός), "Ἀπελεύσῃ μέν," ἔφη· "εὑρήσεις δέ τινα ζητήσας εὐνοῦχον Πελάγιον μοναχόν" (τὴν μακαρίαν δηλαδὴ Πελαγίαν τοῦτο καλῶν)· "τούτῳ πρόσελθε, καὶ συναναστρέφου· καὶ πολλῆς ὠφελείας ὄντως, ἀδελφέ, μεθέξεις πνευματικῆς."

23 Ἰάκωβος μὲν οὖν, ὡς εἶχεν ἑτοίμως, πρὸς τοὺς Ἁγίους ἐπείγεται Τόπους· καὶ προσκυνητὴς ἐκείνων γενόμενος, ἐπὶ τὴν ζήτησιν ὁρμᾷ Πελαγίου δῆθεν. Καὶ δὴ Πελαγίας ἐπιστὰς τῇ κέλλῃ, κρούσας ἐκάλει· κἀκείνης ἐξελθούσης, ὁρᾷ Πελαγίαν—μήτε εἰδὼς ἥτις ἦν, μήτε κἄν τις προεῖπεν,

Sunday she took off her baptismal garment, put on a tattered and ragged garment, and hastened to Jerusalem. She arrived at the Mount of Olives, and forthwith at the mount of virtues, sharing with no one her intent, nor disclosing her secret.

In this way, her actions remained hidden, revealed only to the One who sees the invisible. Meanwhile, the bishops who had gathered in Antioch (among them Nonnos) had already returned to their churches, and she continued to dwell in the Holy Land hidden and unknown for three years. Then, a sacred longing overtook one of those who were together with the bishop Nonnos; this person was Iakobos, who desired to see the Holy Land as a visitor and pilgrim. So, he came to the bishop, and requested his permission for this journey to Jerusalem, and implored him to grant this favor. 21

Nonnos (a man of prophecy, filled with the Spirit, able to foresee what is distant and future) said to him: "You may go, and you will seek and find a certain eunuch monk Pelagios" (calling the blessed Pelagia thus). "Approach him, converse with him, and indeed, my brother, you will receive great spiritual benefit." 22

Iakobos, ready as he was, hastened to the Holy Land; after he had completed his pilgrimage there, he set about the search for this supposed Pelagios. He found Pelagia's cell, knocked at the door, and called out to her. When she came out, he saw Pelagia—and he knew neither who she was, nor, 23

ἔκ γε τῶν ὁρωμένων ἔχων τοῦτο συνιδεῖν ὅλως ἢ συμβα-
λεῖν· τό τε γὰρ χρῶμα ταύτῃ μετήλλακτο, καὶ οἱ ὀφθαλμοὶ
κεκοίλαντο, καὶ πάντα τῇ ἐγκρατείᾳ ἠλλοίωτό τε καὶ μετ-
εβέβλητο, ἀλλ᾽ οὐδὲ τῶν ἄλλων τῶν ἐν Ἱεροσολύμοις
οὐδείς, ταύτην βλέπων, γυναῖκα ᾤετο καθορᾶν.

24   Ὁ μὲν οὖν, ὡς παρὰ ἀνδρὸς τῆς εὐλογίας τυχών, εἱστή-
κει πρὸς τὴν ἐκ τῆς ἐγκρατείας θέαν ἐξεστηκώς. Ἡ δέ,
γνοῦσα οὗ τε ἦν καὶ ὅστις ἦν ὁ παρεστηκώς, εἰ τοῦ ἀρχι-
ερέως ἐστὶν ἐπυνθάνετο Νόννου, ἑκοῦσα δήπου πυνθανο-
μένη τὸ ταύτῃ καὶ πρὸ τῆς ἐρωτήσεως γνώριμον. Τοῦ δὲ
τοῦτο συνειπόντος, "Ἀπόστολος," φησίν, "ὁ ἀνήρ· καὶ
ὑπὲρ τῶν ἐμῶν εὐξάσθω ἀνομιῶν." Καὶ μέχρι τοῦδε τὸν
λόγον ἐκτείνασα, κλείει τὴν θύραν αὖθις· καὶ τὰς εἰωθυίας
ἤρξατο ψάλλειν ᾠδάς. Ἰάκωβος δέ, πολὺ τὸ κέρδος ἐν
βραχεῖ καιρῷ πορισάμενος, καὶ δὴ καὶ μέτρα διδαχθεὶς λόγου μονασταῖς ἀρκοῦντος καὶ πρέποντος, ἀναχωρήσας,
ἐπὶ τὰ ἑξῆς ἐχώρει σεμνεῖα καὶ φροντιστήρια, πολλήν τινα
καὶ παρὰ πολλῶν συλλέγων ὠφέλειαν ψυχικήν.

25   Οὐ πολὺ τὸ ἐν μέσῳ, καὶ φημίζεταί τις σημειοφόρος
ἀνὴρ Πελάγιος ἐκβιούς, πολλῇ τινι τῇ παρὰ τὸν βίον χρη-
σάμενος ἀσκήσει καὶ ἀρετῇ. Καὶ αὐτίκα, συνήθροιστο μὲν
πλῆθος μοναχῶν, συνήθροιστο δὲ τῶν ἄλλως εὐλαβῶν καὶ
ἐπιεικῶν, καὶ ὅσον μὲν παρῴκει τὸν Ἰορδάνην, ὅσον δὲ ἦν
Νικοπόλεως καὶ Ἱεριχοῦς καὶ τῶν πέριξ ἁπάντων, συνερ-
χομένων καὶ χαριζομένων τὰ προπεμπτήρια. Καὶ δὴ τῷ
σώματι προσελθόντες, καὶ χρῖσαι μύρῳ τὰς χεῖρας ἐπιβαλόντες, ὁρῶσι θέαμα ξένον, γυναῖκα, λαθοῦσαν τὴν φύσιν,

even if someone had forewarned him, would he have been able to recognize her at all or surmise who she was from her appearance; for her skin color had been transformed, her eyes had become hollow, and everything about her had been altered and changed because of her abstinence; indeed no one else in Jerusalem, when seeing her, suspected that he was looking at a woman.

Iakobos, as if receiving the blessing from a man, stood be- 24 wildered at the sight of her abstinence. Though she knew whom he served and who this visitor was, Pelagia asked whether he served the archpriest Nonnos, in appearance inquiring with genuine curiosity about what was known to her even before her question. When he replied "Yes," "The man is an apostle," she said; "may he pray also for my iniquities." With only so many words, she closed the door again and began to chant her hymns as usual. Having procured much profit in a short time, as he had been taught the appropriate limits of speaking that are sufficient and proper for monks, Iakobos departed and went on to visit other holy places and monasteries, collecting much spiritual benefit from many sources.

Not long after, the news spread that a certain Pelagios 25 who had worked miracles had departed from this life, during which he had practiced much ascetic discipline and virtue. Immediately, there gathered a multitude of monks as well as many pious and devout laymen, and whoever lived by the Jordan, or in Nikopolis, Jericho, and all the nearby places; all assembled together to offer the final farewell. When they approached the body and extended their hands to anoint it with perfumed oil, they saw a strange sight: a woman, who had been concealing her gender, and who like a

καὶ ἀνδρισαμένην τὰ τῶν ἀνδρῶν, καὶ τῶν γε πόνων πλεῖον ἀπενεγκαμένην τὸ κέρδος.

26   Τότε γίνεται πᾶσιν ἴσος ἀγών, ἄλλον ἄλλου προφθάσαι ζητοῦντος, καὶ πρὸς τὴν ἐκδημίαν ἁμιλλωμένων, καὶ μόνῳ πλησιάσαι τῷ σώματι φιλοτιμουμένων καί τι τούτου καὶ προσεφάψασθαι. Καὶ οὕτω πολλαῖς μὲν ταῖς λαμπάσι, πλείονι δὲ τῇ τιμῇ, τὸ τίμιον Πελαγίας ἐξεκομίσθη λείψανον, ὑπὸ ἀνδρῶν ἁγίων καὶ εὐλαβῶν παραπεμφθὲν ἅμα καὶ βασταχθέν.

27   Οὗτος ὁ τῆς πόρνης βίος· ταῦτα τῆς ἀπεγνωσμένης τὰ κατ᾽ Ἐχθροῦ στρατηγήματα· τοιαύτη ταύτης ἡ πρὸς τὸ βέλτιον μεταβολή· καὶ οὕτω ῥᾳδία ἡμῖν εἰς ὁδηγίαν τοῦ κρείττονος. Ἧι θαρρείτω τις, εἰ καὶ τὰ πρῶτα σύνοιδεν ἑαυτῷ μὴ καλά, μόνον εἰ τοῖς τελευταίοις προθυμηθείη τὰ πρότερον ἀπονίψασθαι. Μεθ᾽ ἧς δῴη Κύριος καὶ ἡμῖν τὴν ἐκεῖθεν ἄρρητον ἀπολαβεῖν ἡδονήν, καὶ τῶν ἐκεῖθεν ἀξιωθῆναι στεφάνων· ὅτι αὐτῷ ἡ δόξα σὺν τῷ Πατρὶ καὶ τῷ ἁγίῳ καὶ ζωοποιῷ Πνεύματι, νῦν καὶ ἀεὶ καὶ εἰς τοὺς αἰῶνας τῶν αἰώνων. Ἀμήν.

man had performed the deeds of men, and indeed obtained for her labors an even greater benefit than men.

Everyone began to strive equally, each trying to outdo the other, competing to attend the funeral, and vying just to come near the body and to even touch some part of it. In this way, with many candles, and even greater honor, the honorable body of Pelagia was buried, escorted and carried by holy and pious men. 26

This was the life of the harlot; these were the stratagems against the Enemy adopted by the woman who had lost all hope; such was her transformation into a better self; so easy a guide is she for us toward a superior life. Even if someone is aware that his early works were evil, let him take courage from her example, if he is only willing to wash away his earlier deeds by his later works. Together with her may the Lord grant to us also to receive that ineffable pleasure in the next life, and to be deemed worthy of the crowns in the next life; since to Him belongs the glory, together with the Father and the Holy and life-giving Spirit, now and forever, and unto the ages of ages. Amen. 27

LIFE, CONDUCT, AND PASSION OF THE HOLY AND GLORIOUS MARTYRS GALAKTION AND EPISTEME

Βίος καὶ πολιτεία καὶ μαρτύριον τῶν ἁγίων καὶ ἐνδόξων μαρτύρων Γαλακτίωνος καὶ Ἐπιστήμης

Εὐλόγησον, πάτερ.

Τῆς πρὸς τῷ Λιβάνῳ ὄρει Φοινίκης, πολλαὶ μὲν πόλεις καὶ ἕτεραι, νοτιώτεραι καὶ προσάρκτιοι· ταύτης δὲ καὶ ἡ τῶν ἄλλων πασῶν διαφέρουσα καὶ τοῖς ἀρκτίοις κειμένη μέρεσιν, Ἔμεσα. Ἣν ἐνεγκοῦσαν ἔσχε καὶ θρεψαμένην ἀνήρ, ὄνομα Κλειτοφῶν, γένος ἐπίσημος, πλοῦτον οὐδενὸς τῶν πολιτῶν δεύτερος, τὴν σύνεσιν πολλῷ τῶν ἄλλων ὀξύτερος. Τούτῳ τοίνυν συνῆπτο γυνὴ Λευκίππη τοὔνομα, τἆλλα μὲν δεξιὰ τοὺς τρόπους, καὶ ἀνδρὶ τοιούτῳ προσήκουσα, καὶ μηδὲ τῆς κατ᾽ ὄψιν ὥρας τῶν ἐν τούτῳ ἄκρων ἐλλείπουσα· τοῦτο δὲ μόνον στείρωσιν δυστυχοῦσα, δι᾽ ἣν πολλοῖς παρὰ τοῦ ἀνδρὸς ὀνείδεσι βαλλομένη, ἀθυμίᾳ συνείχετο, καὶ φροντίσιν ἐκόπτετο, καὶ παντοία ἦν, λύσιν τῶν δεσμῶν τούτων ἐπιζητοῦσα.

2   Ἀμφοτέρων οὖν δι᾽ αἰσχύνης τὸ πρᾶγμα τιθεμένων, τὸ μὴ παίδων ὀφθῆναι πατέρας, μηδέ τινα ἕξειν, ὃς τοῦ πλούτου τε κληρονόμος ἔσται καὶ δι᾽ οὗ τὸ γένος πάλιν αὐτοῖς σωθήσεται, ἐπεὶ συνέβαινε κατ᾽ ἐκεῖνο καιροῦ καὶ τὰ τῆς εἰδωλολατρείας ἐπικρατεῖν, Σεκοῦνδον τέ τινα τῆς πόλεως Ἐμέσης τὴν ἀρχὴν πεπιστεῦθαι—ἄνδρα Ἕλληνα μὲν τὴν θρησκείαν, τὴν δὲ γνώμην κομιδῇ βάρβαρον· ᾧ ἔργον ἦν ὡς οὐδὲν ἄλλο ἐπιμελές, Χριστιανοὺς ἅπαντας ἐκτρίψαι,

Life, Conduct, and Passion of the Holy and Glorious Martyrs Galaktion and Episteme

Father, give the blessing.

In Phoenicia, by Mount Lebanon, there are many cities, some of them in the south and some in the north; to this region, in its northern parts, belongs also that city which surpasses all others: Emesa. This was the fatherland that bore and raised a man of noble lineage by the name of Kleitophon, who was second to none among the citizens in wealth, and much sharper than all the others in sagacity. A woman named Leukippe was married to him, virtuous in her manners, appropriate for such a husband, and, furthermore, lacking in no way in external beauty, even if compared to the most beautiful women. This alone was her misfortune: infertility, for which she was subjected to many insults by her husband. She was thus overcome by desperation and was tormented with worry; and she did everything in her power to find deliverance from these fetters.

Both were thus ashamed by the fact that they would not 2 become parents nor have anyone to inherit their wealth and secure the continuation of their family line. Meanwhile, at that time, it also happened that idolatry was prevailing, and the governing of the city of Emesa was entrusted to a certain Sekoundos, a man who was Greek in his religion, but entirely barbarous in his character; his diligent work was nothing but the following: how to crush all the Christians and

καὶ τὴν εὐσέβειαν, εἴ τις δύναμις, ῥίζαις αὐταῖς ἐξελεῖν· ἐπεὶ οὖν οὕτως ἐν κινδύνῳ τὰ τῶν εὐσεβούντων ἦν, φυγῇ τὴν σωτηρίαν ἕκαστος ἐπορίζετο.

3   Εἷς δέ τις τὴν κλῆσιν Ὀνούφριος, τὸ σχῆμα μοναχός, τὸν τρόπον ἀγαθὸς καὶ φιλόθεος, τὸ μὲν παντάπασιν ἐκχωρῆσαι, καὶ καταλιπεῖν ἐν καιρῷ τοιούτῳ καὶ ζάλῃ τὰς τῶν ἀσθενεστέρων κινδυνεύειν ψυχάς, οὐκ ἔγνω θεοφιλοῦς ἀνδρὸς εἶναι καὶ ἅπαξ ἑαυτὸν τῷ χορῷ τῶν τοιούτων ἐγγράψαντος. Οὐ μὴν ἀλλὰ καὶ τὸ παρρησιάσασθαι τὴν εὐσέβειαν καὶ τοῖς κινδύνοις ἑαυτὸν ἐμβαλεῖν οὐκ ἄμεμπτον εἶναι δοκιμάσας, οὐδὲ τῶν νόμων τῆς εὐσεβείας ἐχόμενον, μέσος ἐχώρει. Καὶ κρύπτων ἑαυτὸν ἐσθῆτι λευκῇ, ἣν ἐπὶ τοῖς μοναχικοῖς ἐνεδύετο, μοναχὸς ἦν ἀληθῶς τὴν γνώμην· καὶ τὰ βίῳ προσήκοντα τοιούτῳ μετῄει· καὶ οὕτω κατεσοφίζετο τὴν ἀσέβειαν.

4   Εἰς πρόφασιν οὖν εὐσεβείας τὴν πενίαν ὑποκριθείς, προσαίτης ἦν ἐθελούσιος. Καὶ τὰς οἰκίας περιϊὼν κατὰ χρείαν τῶν ἀναγκαίων, αὐτὸς ἄρτον ἐδίδου μᾶλλον, τὸν ψυχὰς στηρίζειν δυνάμενον, λόγοις ὑπαλείφων, οἷς ἐντύχοι, τῆς εὐσεβείας καὶ φεύγειν, ὅση δύναμις, παραινῶν ἀπὸ τῶν μακρὰν ποιούντων ἑαυτοὺς τῆς ζωῆς καὶ χωριζόντων τοῦ Πλάσαντος.

5   Παρελθὼν οὖν ποτε καὶ ἐπὶ τὴν τοῦ Κλειτοφῶντος οἰκίαν, ᾔτει τὰ πρὸς τροφήν, χεῖράς τε προτείνων καὶ φωνὰς ἀφιείς, ἐπάγεσθαι ψυχὴν πρὸς ἔλεον δυναμένας. Ἔτυχε δὲ τότε τὴν Λευκίππην διατεταραγμένην εἶναι καὶ λύπης μεστήν, ἅτε δὴ παρὰ τοῦ ἀνδρὸς ὀνείδη διὰ τὴν στείρωσιν ὑπομείνασαν· ὡς τοίνυν ὀχληρῷ φανέντι τῷ Ὀνουφρίῳ, ἐπικλεισθῆναι τούτῳ τὰς θύρας προστάττει.

how to remove, if he could, Christianity root and branch. Since Christians were in such danger, each sought his survival by fleeing.

There was a man called Onouphrios, a monk by vocation, virtuous and pious in his manners, who thought that it would not be appropriate for a devout man, once he had registered himself in the chorus of monks, to leave the city altogether and to abandon weaker souls to danger in such tumultuous circumstances. But then again he also found speaking out on behalf of piety and endangering himself to be equally reprehensible, and not in accordance with Christian law. He thus took a middle course. Disguising himself in a white garment, which he wore over his monastic habit, he was in reality a monk and led a life appropriate to monks, but he also fabricated the appearance of impiety.

As a pretext for his pious life, he pretended to be poor, a beggar by his own volition. He wandered from house to house seeking means of sustenance, yet he was actually the one who offered that bread which can sustain souls, exhorting whomever he met with words of faith, urging them to avoid, as much as possible, anything that would keep them away from true life and separate them from their Creator.

One day, he came by Kleitophon's house too and asked for food, stretching out his hands and voicing such cries as could compel any soul to pity. That day Leukippe happened to be distressed, in complete desolation, having endured many insults from her husband because of her infertility; since Onouphrios appeared rather annoying, she ordered that the doors be shut in his face. But he did not give up,

Ὁ δὲ οὐδὲν μᾶλλον ἀνίει, εἰδὼς ὃ βούλεται, καὶ ὅτι δώσων αὐτὸς μᾶλλον ἢ ληψόμενος παραγένοιτο· καὶ διὰ τοῦτο ἐνέκειτο ἐπαιτῶν, ἕως, διὰ τὴν ἐπαινετὴν ταύτην ἀναίδειαν, καὶ εἰσεκλήθη καὶ δὴ δεξιᾶς ἔτυχε τῆς φιλοφροσύνης.

6   Λόγων οὖν κινηθέντων, καὶ τῆς ὁμιλίας οὕτω παραταθείσης, διηγεῖτο μὲν ἡ Λευκίππη τὰ καθ᾽ ἑαυτήν· καὶ ὡς πεπήρωται αὐτῇ τὰ τῆς μήτρας, καὶ ὡς οὐδεὶς εὑρεθείη θεῶν ἄχρι καὶ τήμερον, τῶν δεσμῶν τούτων ἀνεῖναι αὐτὴν καὶ τοῦ τῆς ἀτεκνίας αἴσχους ἀπαλλάξαι δυνάμενος.

7   "Ἀλλ᾽ εἰκότως," ἔφησεν ὁ Ὀνούφριος, "οὐδὲν ἀπέλαυσας τῆς σπουδῆς, βοηθοὺς τοιούτους αἰτησαμένη λαβεῖν τῆς στειρώσεως· οἷς γὰρ αἰσχύνης ἔργα ἐπιτετήδευται, πῶς ἂν αἰσχύνης οὗτοι ἀπαλλάττειν ἑτέρους δύναιντο; Ἀλλ᾽ εἴ μοι πειθομένην παράσχῃς σαυτήν, καὶ Θεὸν ἐπιγνῶναι τὸν ἀληθῆ βουληθῇς, ὃς δύναται καὶ ἐκ λίθων ἐγεῖραι τέκνα καὶ δεσμὰ στειρώσεως διαλῦσαι, οὐκ εἰς σὲ μόνην τὰ τῆς ὠφελείας ὄψει περιερχόμενα, ἀλλὰ καὶ τὸ γένος ἕξεις εὐεργετεῖν, ὥς τινα κλῆρον εἰς αὐτοὺς παραπέμπουσα τὴν εὐσέβειαν."

8   Τούτοις ἡ Λευκίππη προσεῖχε τὸν νοῦν· καὶ ὥς τινα γῆν ἀγαθὴν παρεῖχε τοῖς τῶν λόγων ἐκείνου σπέρμασιν. Ὁ δέ γε θεῖος οὗτος ἀνήρ, πρῶτα μέν, αὐτῇ τὴν τῆς ὑψηλῆς Τριάδος εἰσηγεῖτο θεογνωσίαν· ἔπειτα δέ, πρὸς τὴν τῶν ἀρετῶν ἐπιμέλειαν παρεκάλει· ἐπὶ τούτοις, καὶ τὸν ἐκ τοῦ σωτηριώδους βαπτίσματος ἁγιασμὸν ἀνεδίδασκε, δι᾽ οὗ ἔσται καὶ τῶν προτέρων αὐτῇ μολυσμῶν κάθαρσις. Ὑπέδειξε δὲ καὶ τὸ τῶν μοναχῶν σχῆμα, ὃ περιεβέβλητο μέν,

knowing what he was after and that he had come to give, rather than to receive. For this reason, he continued to beg, until, because of this admirable lack of manners, he was allowed to enter; indeed, he was given a warm welcome.

They started talking, and their conversation became pro- 6 longed. Leukippe told her story: how her womb was defective; and how, until that day, no one among the gods was to be found who could free her from these bonds and release her from the shame of childlessness.

"It is to be expected," Onouphrios said, "that you re- 7 ceived no benefit from your zealous effort, if you requested such helpers for your infertility; for how could those engaged in shameful deeds release others from what brings them shame? If you listen to me, however, and choose to recognize the true God, who *can raise up children* even *from stones* and dissolve the bonds of infertility, then you will benefit not only yourself, but you will also be able to benefit your entire bloodline, offering them true faith as their heritage."

Leukippe paid attention to these words and offered her 8 mind as fertile ground for the seeds of his instruction. First, that divine man introduced her to the lofty theology of the Trinity. Then, he exhorted her to cultivate the virtues and taught her about the sanctification that derives from the baptism of salvation, from which she could also obtain purification from her earlier defilements. He also showed her the monastic habit which he wore, but had concealed in

ὑπέκρυπτε δέ, τῶν πονηρῶν ἐκκλίνων θηρατῶν τὴν ἐπίθε-
σιν καί, ὡς ἐπὶ τῇ αὐτῆς παραγένοιτο σωτηρίᾳ, τὴν τοῦ
ἐλέου προσποιηθεὶς αἴτησιν.

9 Ἡ δὲ πρὸς ταῦτα δυσὶν ἐναντιώμασιν ἔφη δεδοικέναι
περιπεσεῖν· "Ἑνὶ μέν, ὅτι, τοῖς οὕτως ἔχουσι πίστεως καὶ
τὴν προσηγορίαν Χριστιανοῖς, μεγάλαι μὲν παρὰ τοῦ νῦν
κρατοῦντος αἱ ἀπειλαί, δεινότερα δὲ τὰ ἐπ' αὐταῖς κολα-
στήρια· ἑτέρῳ δέ, ὅτι, ἐμοῦ μεταχωρούσης πρὸς τὴν εὐσέβειαν καὶ προγονικῶν δογμάτων ἀφισταμένης, εἰ μὴ καὶ
τὸν συνοικοῦντα ἔξω τὴν ἴσην ὑποστάντα μεταβολήν, ἀλλ'
ἧς ἔχει νῦν θρησκείας καὶ εἰς τὸ ἑξῆς ἐχόμενον, πῶς ἂν ἓν
καὶ τὸ αὐτὸ συμφρονήσαιμεν οἱ καὶ ἓν εἶναι ὀφείλοντες,
τῷ μεγίστῳ μέρει διῃρημένοι; Τοῦτό μοι λῦσον διαπορού-
μενον, καὶ περὶ τῶν ἄλλων ἀφρόντιδα θήσεις."

10 Ὁ δέ, πολλά τε ἄλλα εἰπών, καὶ προσθεὶς ὅτι "Καὶ ὁ
ἀνὴρ ὅσον οὔπω πρὸς τὸ αὐτό σοι σέβας μεταβληθήσεται," τοσοῦτον ἔσχε πειθομένην αὐτήν, ὥστε καὶ ταῖς θε-
ραπαινίσιν εὐθὺς ἐπιτάττειν, ὅπερ ἂν αὐτὸς λέγοι ποιεῖν.
Ἕνα τοιγαροῦν τῶν πίθων αὐτοῦ, ποῦ παρὰ τῷ κήπῳ τυγ-
χάνοντα, Ὀνουφρίου κελεύσαντος, ὕδατος ἐκεῖναι πλη-
ροῦσιν. Ἐφ' ᾧ, κατηχηθεῖσα πρότερον ἡ Λευκίππη, καὶ
τῶν ἄλλων ὅσα θέμις Χριστιανοῖς ὑπ' αὐτοῦ τελεσθέντων,
εἶτα καὶ τοῦ θείου βαπτίσματος ἀξιοῦται.

11 Ὀλίγῳ δὲ ὕστερον ἐκεῖθεν μὲν ὁ Ὀνούφριος ἀπηλλάττετο, πολλὰ αὐτῇ ἐντειλάμενος, πρός τε φυλακὴν τῆς πίστεως καὶ τῶν τοῦ Χριστοῦ ἐντολῶν. Ἡ Λευκίππη δὲ καὶ
νοσεῖν σκηψαμένη, ἰδιάζουσά που ἐτύγχανε, τὴν τοῦ ἀνδρὸς φεύγουσα κοινωνίαν· οὐδὲ γὰρ ἠβούλετο, ἁγνισθεῖσα

order to avoid the attack of the evil pursuers and, by pretending to be a beggar, come to her salvation.

Leukippe replied that she was afraid of stumbling against 9
two obstacles with respect to his instructions: "The first is
that the threats of the present ruler are considerable for
those who follow your faith and are called Christians, and
even more harsh are the punishments that follow those
threats. The second is that if I convert to Christianity and
abandon my ancestral faith, and if my husband does not follow my conversion, but continues to maintain his current
beliefs, how might we, who must stay united, remain of the
same mind if we are divided with respect to the most important matter? Solve this quandary for me, and you will find
me worrying about none of the other matters."

He said many things in response and added: "Your hus- 10
band too will quickly convert to the same faith as you." He
was thus able to persuade her in such a way that she immediately ordered her servants to do exactly as he might say.
Following Onouphrios's orders, they found a large jar lying
somewhere in the garden and filled it with water. In it, after
having been first initiated into the faith and after every
other appropriate Christian rite was performed by Onouphrios, Leukippe was then blessed also with the holy baptism.

A little later Onouphrios left, after having instructed her 11
in many matters, so that she might preserve both her faith
and Christ's commandments. As for Leukippe, she began
pretending to be ill, and would stay by herself, avoiding intercourse with her husband. Having already been cleansed

ἤδη τῷ Πνεύματι καὶ τὸ θεῖον λουτρὸν δεξαμένη, ἀνά-
γνοις μολῦναι τοῦτο τοῦ ἀνδρὸς συνελεύσεσιν.

12 Ἡμερῶν δὲ διαγενομένων, ἐπέγνω ἑαυτὴν κατὰ
γαστρὸς ἔχουσαν· ὃ καὶ τῷ Κλειτοφῶντι δῆλον οὐκ εἰς
μακρὰν γίνεται. Καὶ οὗτος, ἀγνοῶν τὴν ἀλήθειαν, "Νῦν
μοι ἔοικας," ἔφη, "γύναι, τοῖς ἀθανάτοις εὐαρεστῆσαι θε-
οῖς· καί, διὰ τοῦτο, καὶ προνοίας ἄρτι τῆς παρ' αὐτῶν ἀξία
κατέστης." Ἡ δέ, μικρὸν ἐπισχοῦσα, "Μή μοι θεούς, ἄνερ,
ὀνόμαζε," ἔφη, "οὐ βούλομαι γάρ· ἀλλὰ Θεὸν ἕνα, τὸν τοῦ
παντὸς Κύριόν τε καὶ Ποιητήν· ὃς σοῦ τε καὶ ἡμῶν κηδό-
μενός ἐστι, καὶ δυνάμενος, οὐ στείρωσιν μόνην λύειν, ἀλλὰ
καὶ πάντα ὅσα ἐκείνῳ θέλησις εὐκόλως ποιεῖν."

13 Ὁ δέ, "Καὶ τίς οὗτος," ἔφη, "τῶν ἄλλων τε ἰσχυρότατος
καὶ πρὸς ἡμᾶς οὕτως ὁρῶν εὐμενές;" Καὶ ἡ Λευκίππη,
"Ὄναρ μοι," ἔφη, "γλυκύτατε ἄνερ, ἐφάνη οὗτος, ἀνθρω-
πείαν μὲν τὴν μορφὴν ἔχων, τὰς χεῖρας δὲ ἄρα ἡπλωμένας
ἐπὶ σταυροῦ. Ὃς εὐθέως καὶ δεσμά μοι τῆς γαστρὸς ἀνῆκε·
καὶ πρὸς ὠδῖνα ταύτην παραδόξως διήγειρεν. Ἵνα τί οὖν
μὴ καὶ ἡμεῖς αὐτῷ μᾶλλον ἐσόμεθα προσανέχοντες, καὶ
πάντα δὴ τὰ καθ' ἡμᾶς τῆς αὐτοῦ χρηστότητος ἀπαρ-
τῶντες;"

14 Καὶ ὁ Κλειτοφῶν, ὀλίγον ἐφησυχάσας ὥστε δοῦναι λογισμῷ τὴν διάσκεψιν, "Οἶδα ὃν λέγεις," ἔφη. "Καὶ γὰρ
οὗτος ὁ ὑπὸ τῶν Γαλιλαίων ἐστὶ τιμώμενος· καί, ταῖς ἀληθείαις, πολλὴν ἔχει καὶ ἄμαχον τὴν ἰσχύν. Ἀλλὰ τίς οἴσει
τὴν τοῦ κρατοῦντος ἀπήνειαν;"

15 Καὶ ἡ Λευκίππη, ἡδέως ἁρπάσασα τὸ λεχθέν, "Τέως
μέν," ἔφη, "τιμία μοι κεφαλή, ἐν τῷ ἀφανεῖ τὸ πρὸς αὐτὸν

94

by the Spirit and having received the holy baptism, she did not want to defile it with impure intercourse with her husband.

Several days passed, and she realized that she was pregnant. Not long afterward, this became obvious to Kleitophon as well. As he did not know the truth, he said: "You seem to me, O wife, to have now pleased the immortal gods and, because of this, you were now deemed worthy of their providence." Leukippe hesitated for a moment and then said: "Do not speak of gods, O husband—I do not want that. Rather, name the one and only God, the Lord and Creator of everything. He is the one who cares about you and us, and He is able not only to end infertility, but also to easily do whatever He wills." 12

"Who is this god," Kleitophon said, "who is much more powerful than all the others and who looks upon us so benevolently?" Leukippe replied: "He appeared to me in a dream, O sweetest husband, with a human form and with His hands stretched out on a cross. He immediately released the bonds of my womb and inexplicably caused this pregnancy of mine. Why are we not devoting ourselves more to Him, relying on His goodness in every respect?" 13

For a moment, Kleitophon remained silent, so that he might think about all this, and then said: "I know whom you mean. This is the God whom the Galileans honor. Indeed, he possesses great and invincible power. But who can bear the ruler's cruelty?" 14

Leukippe gladly seized the opportunity and said: "My dear, let us keep our faith in Him as a secret for now. In this 15

σέβας ἡμῖν κείσθω· οὕτω γὰρ ἂν τὸ τῶν ἀνοσίων φιλοπό-
νηρον διαφύγοιμεν. Ἐξέσται δέ ποτε, τῆς αὐτοῦ δυνάμεως
συναιρομένης ἡμῖν, καὶ ἐν ἡμέρᾳ εὐσχημόνως περιπατεῖν,
καὶ τὰ τοῦ φωτὸς ἔργα κατὰ τὸ φανερὸν δρᾶν."

16   Ταῦτα λέγουσα, ἐπεὶ πρὸς πάντα εἶχε τὸν ἄνδρα καταπειθῆ (ἔδει γὰρ καὶ τὸ τοῦ Χριστοῦ φανῆναι φιλάνθρωπον,
καὶ ὅπερ αὐτῇ προεῖπεν Ὀνούφριος περὶ τοῦ ἀνδρὸς μὴ
διαπεσεῖν), τὸ λοιπόν, οὐ μετά τινος τῆς ὑποστολῆς, ἀλλὰ
πεπαρρησιασμένως, πάντα αὐτῷ τὰ κατὰ τὸν μοναχὸν ἐξε-
κάλυπτε· καὶ ὅτι καὶ βεβάπτισται παρ' αὐτοῦ, καὶ ὡς τοῦτό
ἐστι τὸ τῆς μήτρας αὐτῆς τὰ δυσχερῆ ἄμματα λῦσαν. Εἶτα
καὶ προσετίθει, ὡς οὐδὲν ἔσται τὸ ἐμποδίζον καὶ αὐτὸν τοῦ
ἴσου καταξιωθῆναι βαπτίσματος· "Καὶ γάρ μοι μετὰ τῶν
ἄλλων," φησί, "καὶ τοῦτο προεῖπεν ὁ θεῖος ἀνὴρ ἐκεῖνος,
ὅτι καὶ σὲ τὸν φίλτατον ὅσον οὔπω τῆς αὐτῆς ἔξω κοινω-
νοῦντά μοι πίστεως." Ταῦτα ἐκείνη τε εἴρηκε· καὶ μετ' ὀλίγον εἰς ἔργον τὰ λεχθέντα ἐξέβη. Καὶ τοῦ θείου καὶ αὐτὸς
λουτροῦ ἠξιοῦτο· καὶ τὰ τῆς εὐσεβείας ἀπόρρητα ἐδιδά-
σκετο, Ὀνουφρίου πάλιν πρὸς ταῦτα τοῦ θαυμασίου ὑπη-
ρετήσαντος.

17   Ἤδη δὲ ὥραν τόκου τῆς Λευκίππης ἐχούσης, παῖδά τε
γειναμένης ἄρρενα, εἰσκαλεῖται καὶ αὖθις Ὀνούφριος, ἡ
συνήθης ὠφέλεια, τὸ θεόπεμπτον ἀγαθόν. Καὶ τὸ γεν-
νηθὲν ἀνεγεννᾶτο δι' αὐτοῦ πάλιν τῷ μακαρίῳ βαπτίσματι·
καὶ τὴν κλῆσιν ἐλάμβανε παρ' αὐτοῦ· καὶ Γαλακτίων κατω-
νομάζετο. Καὶ ἦν ἡ κλῆσις τῶν ἐσομένων ἀσφαλὴς προα-
γόρευσις· ἐκ καθαρῶν γὰρ καθαρὸς καὶ οὗτος ἀπέβη, καὶ
ἐξ εὐγενῶν ὄντως εὐγενὲς βλάστημα. Προϊόντος δὲ τοῦ

way, we might be able to avoid the wickedness of the impious. It will be possible for us some day, with the succor of His power, *to walk honestly in day* and to perform the deeds of light openly."

After her words, her husband was fully persuaded (since 16 also Christ's love of mankind needed to manifest itself and what Onouphrios had foretold her about him needed to be fulfilled). From that point on, openly and without any caution, she revealed to him everything about the monk: both that she was baptized by him and that this baptism was what released the restraining bonds of her womb. And then she also added that nothing prevented him too from being honored with the same baptism. "Indeed, that divine man foretold this too, along with other things," she said, "that I will also quickly attain your conversion, my dearest, into the same faith." These were her words and shortly thereafter what she had said came to pass. He too was blessed with the divine baptism and was taught the mysteries of Christianity by the admirable Onouphrios who again provided this service.

As the time quickly arrived for Leukippe to be in labor, 17 she gave birth to a boy, and Onouphrios, the benefit for all, the divine-sent good, was again summoned. The newborn was reborn with the blessed baptism by Onouphrios, received his name from him, and was called Galaktion. It was a name that securely predicted his future: for coming out of pure parents, Galaktion too became pure, a truly noble offspring of noble origins. As the time passed, Galaktion

χρόνου, κατὰ μικρὸν ὁ Γαλακτίων, ἐπὶ τῇ προσθήκῃ τῆς ἡλικίας, καὶ σύνεσιν προσετίθει· μᾶλλον δὲ καὶ ὑπὲρ τὴν ἡλικίαν τὸ φρονοῦν εἶχε. Διδασκαλείοις δὲ ἐκδοθείς, καὶ τοῖς τελεωτέροις ἐκπονηθεὶς μαθήμασι, τῷ φιλοτίμῳ τῆς φύσεως, καὶ αὐτοὺς ὀπίσω τοὺς διδασκάλους ἐποίει.

18 Εἰκοστὸν δὲ καὶ τέταρτον ἐνιαυτὸν ἄγοντος, φροντὶς ἦν τῷ πατρὶ κοινωνὸν αὐτῷ βίου τὴν προσήκουσαν συναρμόσαι, τῆς μητρὸς ἤδη Λευκίππης τὸν βίον ἀπολιπούσης. Ἐτύγχανε δέ τις τὸ τηνικαῦτα παρθένος, κάλλει τε καὶ ἤθει κοσμίῳ τῶν πασῶν διαφέρουσα, Ἐπιστήμη ταύτῃ τὸ ὄνομα, κλέος εὐγενείας καὶ δόξης αὐτὸ τὸ πρῶτον ἐν γυναιξὶν ἔχουσα. Ταύτην ἡρμόσατο Γαλακτίων· νῦν μὲν εἰς πρόσχημα τοῦ γάμου, μετὰ ταῦτα δὲ καὶ τῆς ψυχῆς ἔνωσιν.

19 Ἐπεὶ δὲ τὴν συμβίωσιν ταύτης ἐδυσχέραινε Γαλακτίων καὶ φανερὸς ἦν τὰς συμπλοκάς τε καὶ δεξιώσεις οὐ προσιέμενος, διὰ τὸ περὶ τὸ σέβας ἀνόμοιον καὶ τὸ τοῦ θείου βαπτίσματος ἀμέτοχον εἶναι ταύτην, πολλοὺς παρὰ τῶν οἰκείων ἐπράττετο λόγους, καὶ βαρεῖς αὐτοὺς εἶχε τοῦ πράγματος λογιστάς. Μόνος δέ ποτε πρὸς μόνην τὴν Ἐπιστήμην γενόμενος, εἶτα παρ' αὐτῆς τοῦ μίσους ἐρωτώμενος τὴν αἰτίαν, φάναι τὸν Γαλακτίωνα, μὴ ἂν ἄλλως ἀνασχέσθαι τὴν μετ' αὐτῆς κοινωνίαν, εἰ μὴ καὶ κατὰ τὸ σέβας ἴδοι κοινωνοῦσαν αὐτῷ· ἀνόσιον γὰρ ἄντικρυς ἔλεγεν εἶναι τὸν κεκαθαρμένον ἀκαθάρτῳ συνάπτεσθαι. "Εἴπερ οὖν, ὦ γύναι, τὴν μεθ' ἡμῶν ἀσπάζῃ συμβίωσιν, πείθου μοι τὰ βέλτιστα συμβουλεύοντι. Καὶ ἐπεὶ κατὰ τὸ νῦν ἔχον ἱερέων ἐστὶν ἀπορία τῶν πρὸς τὸ βάπτισμα τεταγμένων

gradually added wisdom to his growth in age; or, rather, his wisdom surpassed his age. Sent to schools, and instructed in the most advanced studies, he surpassed even the teachers themselves by his assiduous nature.

He was now in his twenty-fourth year and his father was   18
concerned to find for him the right companion in life, as his mother Leukippe had already left this life. At that time there happened to be a virgin who surpassed all others in beauty and well-mannered character. Her name was Episteme, and she was first among all women in reputable nobility and eminence. Galaktion was wedded to her, first under the pretense of marriage, but later also for the sake of the union of their souls.

Galaktion found it difficult to live with his wife and   19
clearly avoided her embraces and invitations, as she did not share the same faith and had not participated in holy baptism. Because of this, he received much abuse from her family who insistently scrutinized him about it. One day, when they were alone, Episteme asked him why he rejected her and Galaktion responded that he could not accept union with her, unless they were united also in their faith; for it would be simply sacrilegious, he said, if a purified person were joined with an impure one. "So, my wife, if you wish to live as a couple with me, follow my advice toward what is best. Since right now there is a shortage of priests whose task is to celebrate baptism, and since there is no other way

ὑπηρετεῖν, ἀδύνατον δὲ ἄλλως καθαρόν τινα καὶ εἶναι καὶ ὀνομάζεσθαι, τὰ τοῦ χαρίσματος ἡμεῖς, καθὼς ὁ καιρὸς δίδωσι, σχεδιάσωμεν."

20 Ἐπεὶ δὲ πρὸς τοῦτο πειθομένην εἶδε καὶ οὐδ' ὁτιοῦν ἀνανεύουσαν, μίαν τῶν τοῦ κήπου δεξαμενῶν ὕδατος πληρωθῆναι κελεύει· καὶ οὕτω, πάντας διαλαθών, βαπτίζει τὴν Ἐπιστήμην. Αὕτη γοῦν, καὶ μετὰ τὸ βάπτισμα ἡμερῶν ὀκτὼ διαγενομένων, καινήν τινα καὶ ἀσυνήθη κατὰ τοὺς ὕπνους ὄψιν ὁρᾷ. Ἐδόκει γὰρ περί τινας οἴκους βασιλικοὺς ἀναστρέφεσθαι, κάλλει ἀμυθήτῳ διαπρεπεῖς, ἐφ' οἷς ἑκατέρωθεν χοροὺς περὶ τοὺς τοίχους ἵστασθαι τρεῖς· ὧν ὁ μὲν ἄνδρας εἶχε, σεμνούς τε ἰδεῖν καὶ στολῇ μελαίνῃ κεκοσμημένους· ὁ δεύτερος δὲ γυναῖκας ὁμοίως ἐχούσας· ὁ δὲ τρίτος παρθένων ἦν, αἷς ἐπήνθει φαιδρότης ἐπιτερπὴς καὶ χάρις προσεμειδία ταῖς ὄψεσιν ἐλευθέριος. Αἱ μέντοι γυναῖκες, αἱ τὴν μέλαιναν στολὴν περιβεβλημέναι, καὶ πτέρυγάς τινας ἐῴκεσαν ἔχειν καὶ πῦρ ἀφιέναι, ὑφ' οὗ πᾶν τὸ παραπίπτον ἐδόκει φλέγεσθαι.

21 Ἀκούσας τοίνυν ὁ Γαλακτίων τὸ ὁραθέν, τοιαύτην ἔλεγε τὴν δύναμιν ἔχειν· εἴρηκε γὰρ καὶ τοὺς τρεῖς τούτους χοροὺς τῶν χωριζόντων ἑαυτοὺς κόσμου καὶ τῶν τοῦ κόσμου πάντων εἶναι, παρθενίαν τε φυλαττόντων, καὶ ζῆν κατὰ Χριστὸν ἐπανελομένων· τῶν δὲ τὰ μέλαινα περιβεβλημένων, καὶ αὐτοὺς εἶπεν ἐοικέναι τοῖς ἀγγέλοις· ἐκείνων γὰρ αἱ πτέρυγες καὶ τὸ πῦρ, τάχος ἅμα καὶ ἰσχὺν ἄμαχον εἰκονίζοντα.

22 Ἡ Ἐπιστήμη δὲ τούτων ἀκούσασα, εὐθὺς τὴν εὐγένειάν τε καὶ τὸ φιλόκαλον τῆς οἰκείας ἐδήλου ψυχῆς, ἐν

for someone to be and be called pure, let us improvise this gift as the current circumstances allow."

As she was persuaded by this and made no objection 20 whatsoever, he ordered that one of the pools in the garden be filled with water; in this way, without anyone noticing, he baptized Episteme. Eight days later, she saw a strange and extraordinary vision while asleep. She dreamed that she was wandering around some royal palace that gleamed with indescribable beauty. Three choruses were standing within its walls on either side: the first included men, solemn in countenance and dressed in black garments; the second included women with a similar appearance as the first group; and the third belonged to virgins on whom joyful radiance and grace of a liberal sort blossomed. The women dressed in black appeared to also have some kind of wings and to issue fire which seemed to set aflame everything that crossed their path.

When Galaktion heard about this vision, he explained its 21 meaning in the following way: he said that all three choruses belonged to those who separate themselves from the world and all worldly things, preserve their virginity, and enter a way of life according to Christ. As for those dressed in black, he said that they were like angels—for their wings and fire signify speed and indomitable power.

Upon hearing these words, Episteme immediately dis- 22 played her soul's nobility and love of what is good, expressing

CHRISTIAN NOVELS FROM THE *MENOLOGION*

ἐπιθυμίᾳ τε τῆς τῶν ὁραθέντων γενομένη μεγαλειότητος. "Ἄρα δέ," εἶπεν, "εἰ διασταίημεν ἀπ᾽ ἀλλήλων, ἄνερ, καὶ Θεῷ προσχωρήσαιμεν, δυνησόμεθα καὶ τὴν εἰς ἀλλήλους διάθεσιν ἀχώριστον συντηρεῖν; Τούτου μοι δίδου βεβαίω-σιν ἀσφαλῆ· καὶ οὐκ ἐκστήσομαι πώποτε τοῦ μὴ κοινωνεῖν σοι τῆσδε τῆς προαιρέσεως."

23   Ἐπεὶ δὲ ἀλλήλοις ἰσχυρὰς δεδώκασι πίστεις, μὴ ἀπ᾽ ἀλλήλων κατὰ γνώμην ποτὲ διαστῆναι, ὁ Γαλακτίων τὰ συνήθη δι᾽ ἱκετηρίας ἐντυχὼν τῷ Θεῷ, τῇ Ἐπιστήμῃ τὰ συνοίσοντα ὑπετίθει, "Σὺ μὲν ἄπιθι," λέγων, "καὶ τοῖς δε-ομένοις ἐλευθερίως τὰ προσόντα διάνειμε, οὐκ ἀναλίσκειν, ἀλλὰ θησαυρίζειν μᾶλλον αὐτὰ ἐν ἀσύλοις πιστεύουσα. Ἐγὼ δέ σοι καὶ τούτου τύπος ἔσομαι· καὶ πρῶτος τῶν ἐμῶν ποιήσομαι τὴν διανομήν, οὐκ ὀλίγῃ καὶ φειδομένῃ χειρί, ἀλλὰ φιλοτίμως ἐξαντλῶν καὶ πλουσίως. Εἰς τὴν τρίτην δὲ ἡμῖν ἀφίξῃ, καὶ κατά γε τὸ ἀμφοτέροις δόξαν οἰκονομήσο-μεν."

24   Ἐπεὶ οὖν τὰ ὄντα τε διενείμαντο καὶ ἀλλήλοις συνῆλθον, Εὐτόλμιόν τινα πάντων ὧν εἶχον εὐνούστατον ὑπάρχοντα θεραπόντων ἀκολουθεῖν ἐντειλάμενοι, ἐξήρχοντο τῆς οἰ-κίας, τὸν τῶν μονοτρόπων μέλλοντες ὑπελθεῖν βίον. Δέκα δὲ ὅλας ἡμέρας ὁδοιπορήσαντες, ὄρος φθάνουσι, Πού-πλιον μὲν ὑπὸ τῶν προσοικούντων καλούμενον, ἐγγὺς δέ που τοῦ Σινᾶ κείμενον Ὄρους, ἔνθα δυοκαίδεκα μοναχοῖς ἐντυχόντες ἀσκητικὴν πολιτείαν μετερχομένοις, τὰ τοῦ σκοποῦ τε αὐτοῖς διηγόρευον· καὶ προσληφθῆναι καὶ τῷ καταλόγῳ τούτων ἐγγραφῆναι ἠξίουν. Ὃ δὴ καὶ οὐ πολ-λαῖς ἡμέραις ὕστερον γίνεται. Καὶ Γαλακτίων μὲν τῷ

her desire for the magnificence of the things she saw. "Could it be, my husband," she said, "that, if we were to separate from each other and enlist with God, we would still be able to preserve our affection for each other undivided? Offer me this firm pledge and I will always stand by you, sharing in this decision."

After offering each other firm vows to never stand apart in their intent, Galaktion first prayed his usual entreaties to God and then suggested to Episteme an expedient course of action. "You should go," he said, "and freely distribute your possessions to those in need, with the confidence that you are not expending them, but rather storing them in unassailable treasuries. I will become your model also in this respect, as I first will distribute my possessions, not with an exiguous and ungenerous hand, but will get rid of them all unsparingly and abundantly. On the third day come to me, and we will arrange our affairs according to our mutual decision." 23

They thus distributed their possessions and then met with each other. Having ordered a certain Eutolmios, the most well-disposed among all their servants, to follow them, they left their house with the intention to undertake the life of solitaries. They walked for ten whole days until they reached a mountain which is called Pouplion by those living nearby and is located somewhere near Mount Sinai. There, they came across twelve monks leading an ascetic life, told them about their goal, and asked permission to join them and be enlisted among them. This indeed happened not many days later. Galaktion joined the ranks of these men 24

τάγματι τῶν ἀνδρῶν τούτων συναριθμεῖται· ἡ Ἐπιστήμη
δὲ πρός τι τῶν ἀπῳκισμένων σεμνείων ὑπ᾽ αὐτοῦ στέλλεται, παρ᾽ ᾧ τέσσαρες ἠσκοῦντο παρθένοι.

25 Τὴν οὖν ἀγωγὴν ταύτην ὁ Γαλακτίων ἑλόμενος, ποίαν
μὲν οὐκ ἐπῆλθεν ὁδὸν διδάξαι τὸ μέτριον δυναμένην; Τίνα
δὲ τῶν αἰσθήσεων οὐκ ἐπαιδαγώγησε, πάσαις ὅρους ἐπι-
θεὶς καὶ μέτρα, καὶ πειθηνίους αὐτὰς λογισμῷ τῷ σώφρονι
καταστήσας; Οὕτω δὲ αὐτῷ καὶ νηστείας ἐμέλησεν, ὡς ἐπὶ
δυσὶν ἔτεσιν ἅπαξ τῆς ἑβδομάδος ἄρτου μόνου μεταλαμ-
βάνειν, καὶ τούτου βραχέος καὶ ὅσον ἀποζῆν δύνασθαι.
Συνησκεῖτο δὲ αὐτῷ τῇ ἀσιτίᾳ, καὶ τὸ φιλάγρυπνον, καὶ ἡ
περὶ τὰς εὐχὰς διηνεκὴς ἐπιμέλεια. Σωφροσύνης δὲ οὕτως
ἐφρόντισεν, ὡς μηδὲ πρὸς ὄψιν ἐλθεῖν γυναικὶ μηδέποτε
ἀνασχέσθαι, ἀφ᾽ οὗ δὴ καὶ τῷ τῶν μοναχῶν ἐνεγράφη βίῳ.
Τεκμήριον ἀκριβές, ὅτι δύο τῶν μοναχῶν μητέρα ἐχόντων,
οὐ μόνον ἀρετῆς ἐπιμελομένην, ἀλλὰ καὶ ἔξωρον ἤδη καὶ
τῷ ἀσκητικῷ καταγηράσασαν βίῳ, ἀξιούντων τε θεάσα-
σθαι ταύτην καὶ μητρικῶν εὐχῶν μετασχεῖν, οὐκ ἠνέσχετο.

26 Οὕτω τοιγαροῦν ἔχοντος καὶ πρὸς ἀρετὴν πᾶσαν εὐθυ-
ποροῦντος, οὐκ ἀνεκτὸν ἐδόκει τῷ Πονηρῷ, ἀλλὰ τὸν τὴν
αὐτοκράτορα τότε μετιόντα ἀρχὴν ὑπελθών, ἠρέθισέ τε
κατὰ Χριστιανῶν πάντων, καὶ διωγμὸν φανερὸν κινῆσαι
κατ᾽ αὐτῶν παρεσκεύασε· καὶ γὰρ ἐπῆλθεν αὐτοῖς βαρύτα-
τος, τὰ μὲν δι᾽ ἑαυτοῦ, τὰ δὲ διὰ τῶν ὁμοίως αὐτῷ ἐχόντων
ὑπασπιστῶν τιμωρούμενος.

27 Τούτῳ δὲ προσελθόντες οἱ τὰ τοῦ καιροῦ θεραπεύειν
σπουδάζοντες, τοὺς ἀνὰ τὸ Σίναιον Ὄρος οἰκοῦντας τὰ
μὲν τῶν θεῶν ἀτιμοῦν ἔλεγον, ἕνα δὲ μόνον Θεόν, καὶ

and Episteme was sent by him to some remote convent where four virgins lived as ascetics.

After adopting this way of life, what path that could 25 teach moderation did Galaktion not traverse? Which of the senses did he not train, imposing limits and restraint on all of them, and rendering them submissive to his chaste mind? He devoted himself to fasting to such an extent that for two years he ate only once a week and only bread, and that in small quantities, just barely able to sustain him. Along with refraining from food, he also renounced sleep, and he also gave constant heed to prayer. And his adherence to chastity was such that, after he enlisted into the life of monks, he could not bear to ever even come into the sight of a woman. A precise proof of this is that he did not allow it when two monks requested to see their mother and receive her blessings, even though she was not only virtuous, but also quite old, aged by her ascetic life.

That Galaktion lived this way, moving unswervingly to- 26 ward every virtue, was unbearable to the Evil One. He thus possessed the man holding imperial authority at that time, incited him against all Christians, and prompted him to start an open persecution against them. And, indeed, he launched a severe attack upon them, enforcing punishments either himself or through his henchmen who held the same beliefs as he did.

Opportunist men came to him and reported that those 27 living on Mount Sinai disrespected the gods and honored

τοῦτον ἐσταυρωμένον, τιμᾶν, καὶ πᾶσαν αὐτῷ προσάγειν λατρείαν. Εὐθὺς οὖν ἐκεῖνος, ὥσπερ μύωπι τῷ λόγῳ πληγείς, στρατιωτῶν ἐπέτατte φάλαγγα ταχέως τε τὸ ὄρος καταλαβεῖν, καὶ δεσμίους πρὸς αὐτὸν τοὺς ὅσοι Χριστιανῶν οἰκοῦσι τοῦτο τὸ ὄρος ἀγαγεῖν.

28   Ἐν ᾧ οὖν οἱ πεμφθέντες ἀνὰ τὸν τόπον γενόμενοι τοὺς θείους ἔμελλον ἄνδρας συλλαβεῖν, ἡ Ἐπιστήμη κατὰ τὸ ῥηθὲν ἀσκητήριον τὰ τῶν ἀσκουμένων μετερχομένη, περὶ μέσας νύκτας, ὄναρ ὁρᾷ· ἐδόκει γὰρ εἴ τι ἀνάκτορον συνειστρέχειν ἅμα τῷ Γαλακτίωνι, στεφάνοις τε ὑπὸ βασιλέως κοσμηθῆναι τὰς κεφαλάς. Ἕωθεν δὲ τῷ οἰκονόμῳ τῶν τῆς μονῆς περὶ ὧν τεθέαται κοινολογουμένη, ὅπῃ τείνει τὸ ὄναρ σαφῶς ἐδιδάσκετο· ἀνάκτορα μὲν τὰ τῶν οὐρανῶν εἰπόντος βασίλεια· βασιλέα δὲ αὐτὸν εἶναι τὸν ἀληθῶς καὶ μόνως φυσικῶς βασιλεύοντα· τοὺς στεφάνους δὲ τοῦτο δηλοῦν, ὅτι πρὸς ἀγῶνας ἄρτι χωρήσουσι, καὶ κρείττους τῶν ἀντιπάλων ἀτεχνῶς ἔσονται.

29   Οἱ στρατιῶται τοίνυν, κατὰ τὸ προστεταγμένον αὐτοῖς ἐπελθόντες, τῶν ἄλλων πάντων φυγῇ χρησαμένων, δύο μόνους τῶν μοναχῶν εὑρίσκουσιν, ὧν εἷς ἐτύγχανε Γαλακτίων. Ἐπεὶ οὖν κἀκεῖνος ὑπ' αὐτῶν ἤγετο, μαθοῦσα τοῦτο ἡ Ἐπιστήμη καὶ ἐν ἀπόπτῳ τοῦ ὄρους καθίσασα, ὅθεν ἦν ὁρῶσαν αὐτὴν μὴ ὁρᾶσθαι, ἐκεῖνα ἐθεᾶτο τοῖς ὀφθαλμοῖς, ἃ μηδὲ ἀκοῇ παραδέξασθαι δυνατῶς εἶχε, δέσμιον ἀγόμενον Γαλακτίωνα, καὶ χαλεπὰ πείσεσθαι προσδοκώμενον.

30   Προσκαταβαλοῦσα γοῦν εἰς ἔδαφος ἑαυτήν, πολλή τις ἦν δεομένη τῆς διακόνου ἀφεθῆναι ταύτην ἐπειχθῆναι πρὸς Γαλακτίωνα· καί, εἴπερ ἐγχωροῦν εἴη, τοῖς αὐτοῖς

only the one crucified God, addressing all worship to Him alone. Immediately, stung by these words as if by a gadfly, the emperor ordered a corps of soldiers to occupy the mountain at once, and to bring him in chains all Christian inhabitants of that mountain.

While those dispatched arrived at the place and were about to arrest the divine men, Episteme—who was living as an ascetic in the aforementioned convent—saw a dream in the middle of the night: she dreamed that she was running into some royal dwelling together with Galaktion and that both were adorned with crowns by an emperor. Early in the morning she shared what she had seen with the steward of the monastery and learned with clarity the intended meaning of the dream. He said that the royal dwelling signified the heavenly palace, the emperor was the true and single ruler of nature himself, and the crowns indicated that they were soon to enter into a contest and would be absolutely victorious against their opponents. 28

The soldiers thus attacked as they were ordered and, since all the rest fled away, found only two monks, one of whom was Galaktion. While they were carrying him off, Episteme found out about it and sat out of sight, at a spot on the mountain where she could see, but remain unseen, and witnessed with her eyes things unbearable to even hear: Galaktion was led off in chains and was expected to suffer the worst. 29

She thus fell down on the ground and fervently begged the deaconess that she be permitted to rush to Galaktion and, if she was allowed, be subjected to the same chains; and 30

ὑποβληθῆναι δεσμοῖς· εἰ δὲ καὶ τὸν βίον δέοι ἐκεῖνον ἀπολιπεῖν, τὸν ἴσον καὶ αὐτὴν τότε θάνατον ὑποστῆναι· εἶναι
γὰρ ἀμφοτέροις τοῦτο ἐκ πλείονος αὐτοῖς συμπεφωνημέ-
νον, μὴ τῆς ἀπ᾽ ἀλλήλων διαστῆναί ποτε γνώμης καὶ δια-
θέσεως. Δεινὸν οὖν ἔλεγεν εἶναι, τοῦ καιροῦ καλοῦντος,
φανῆναι ταύτην τῶν συνθηκῶν ἐπιλήσμονα.

31   Ἡ διάκονος δὲ λόγοις μὲν ἐπειρᾶτο πρότερον τῆς
ὁρμῆς ἀπάγειν αὐτήν· ὡς δὲ οὐκ ἔπειθεν, ἀφῆκε ποιεῖν ὃ
καὶ βούλοιτο. Ἀσμένως οὖν ἐκείνη τὰ τελευταῖα τὰς συν-
ούσας προσαγορεύσασα, τῶν ἰχνῶν κατόπιν τοῦ Γαλακτίωνος εἴχετο. Ἐπεὶ δὲ καὶ ἐγγίζουσα ἦν, "Κύριέ μου," ἐβόα,
"καὶ τῆς ἐμῆς ὁδηγὲ σωτηρίας, μὴ παραιτήσῃ με τὴν σήν,
μηδὲ ὧν συνεθέμεθα πρὸς ἀλλήλους ἀμνημονήσῃς." Ὧν
οἱ ὀξεῖς ὑπηρέται τῆς ἀσεβείας ἀκούσαντες, ἐκ μέσης ἀνέ-
στρεφον τῆς ὁδοῦ· καὶ κατασχόντες, δεσμοῖς αὐτὴν περι-
βάλλουσιν, οὐδ᾽ ὁτιοῦν εἰπόντες, ἀλλὰ καὶ πρὸς αὐτὴν
ὑπερηφανευσάμενοι τὴν ἐρώτησιν.

32   Ὁ δὲ Γαλακτίων, οὐδὲ οὕτως ἔχων καιροῦ, τῶν θείων
ἀπείχετο παραινέσεων. Ἀλλά, καὶ βαδίζων καὶ δεσμὰ περι-
κείμενος, ἐνουθέτει τὰ δέοντα, "Μή σε," λέγων, "ὦ γύναι,
ἀπάτη περιέλθοιεν οἱ ἐχθροί, ἢ δεινὰ πρὸς φόβον ἐπάγον-
τες, ἢ τοῖς ἡδίστοις τοῦ κόσμου παρακαλοῦντες πρὸς τὴν
ἀσέβειαν." Ἐν ᾧ δὲ ταῦτα ἐλέγοντο, ἧκέ τις ἐσπουδασμέ-
νως καὶ πολὺν τῷ προσώπῳ διασημαίνων τὸν θόρυβον, εἰς
τὴν αὔριον λέγων τὴν περὶ τῶν ἁγίων ταμιευθῆναι ἐξέτασιν, οὕτως τῷ ἄρχοντι δόξαν.

33   Ἕωθεν οὖν ὁ δικάζων, ἐπὶ τὸν τόπον ἔνθα τοὺς κρινο-
μένους ἔθος, ἀχθῆναι αὐτοὺς προσέταττε. Καὶ σπουδῇ

if he had to depart from this life, that she too would then suffer the same death. For this had been their reciprocal agreement of long standing: to never stand apart from each other in intent and frame of mind. It would be terrible, she said, if the moment arrived and she appeared forgetful of their mutual pact.

At first, the deaconess tried to dissuade her with words 31 from her impulse. As she could not persuade her, however, she let her do what she wanted. Thus, after eagerly bidding her last farewell to her fellow nuns, Episteme followed the footsteps of Galaktion. When she came near, she cried to him, "My master, you who led me to salvation, do not abandon me, your own, nor forget our pact." As soon as the keen servants of impiety heard this, they stopped in midcourse and turned around. They then captured and chained her, without saying a single word, not even deigning to question her.

Even in such circumstances, Galaktion did not refrain 32 from his exhortations toward piety; though walking in chains, he gave proper advice, saying: "Do not let our enemies deceive you, O wife, either by creating fear in you with their harsh words, or by urging you toward impiety through promises of worldly pleasures." While these words were being spoken, someone arrived hurriedly, his face indicating his turmoil, and said that the interrogation of the saints had been arranged for the following day, according to the ruler's decision.

The interrogator had ordered that they be brought early 33 in the morning to the place where the accused were usually

πολλῇ παραστάντων, ὁ ἄρχων εὐθὺς οὐ τύχην, οὐ τὴν ἐνεγκοῦσαν, οὐκ ἄλλο τι τῶν συνήθων αὐτοὺς ἐπηρώτα· οὐδὲ πρὸς λόγους ἐχώρει τὸ πείθειν ἔχοντας. Ἀλλὰ δριμὺ καὶ ἀπειλητικὸν ἐμβλέψας τῷ Γαλακτίωνι, "Τίς οὗτος ὁ ἐπὶ συννοίᾳ καὶ σκυθρωπότητι;" τῷ περιόντι τοῦ θυμοῦ παρεφθέγγετο, "Καὶ τίνι ἄλλῳ τὸ σέβας ἀποδιδοὺς ἀτιμάζει θεούς;"

34 Ὁ Γαλακτίων δέ, μηδὲν ὑποπτήξας, μήτε τῆς συνήθους μεταβαλὼν καταστάσεως, "Τὸν μὲν βίον," εἶπε, "μοναχός, ἀπὸ Χριστοῦ δὲ τὸ καλεῖσθαι Χριστιανὸς ἔχων· ᾧ καὶ τὸ σέβας, εὖ φρονῶν, ἀποδίδωμι." Ὡς δὲ καὶ πολὺς ἦν ὁ ἅγιος βάλλων αὐτὸν τοῖς ὀνείδεσι, καὶ τὰ τῶν θεῶν αὐτοῦ κωμῳδῶν, καὶ ἐπίσης ἀνοήτους ἀποκαλῶν τοὺς τὰ ἄψυχα ταυτὶ σεβομένους, τὰς χεῖρας ὀπίσω δεθέντα, βουνεύροις ἐπέταττεν ὁ κατάρατος ἀνηλεῶς αὐτὸν τύπτεσθαι.

35 Μαστιγουμένου δὲ τούτου, ἡ Ἐπιστήμη βλέπουσα καὶ ἀρρήτως τὴν ψυχὴν πάσχουσα, "Φεῦ τῆς ἀκορέστου πρὸς τὸ κολάζειν," ἔφη, "ψυχῆς! Ἵνα τί τοιαύτας ἐνετείνατε μάστιγας νεαροῖς οὕτω μέλεσι καὶ πολλοῖς ἀσκήσεως πόνοις συντετηγμένοις; Πῶς δὲ καὶ ἡ χεὶρ τῶν ὑπηρετουμένων ταῖς μάστιξιν οὐκ ἐνάρκησε;"

36 Τούτοις ὁ ἄρχων ἐπὶ μᾶλλον εἰς ὀργὴν ἐξαφθείς, "Τὴν ἀναιδῆ ταύτην," ἔφη, "καὶ προπετῆ, τῶν περικειμένων μέχρις ὀθόνης γυμνώσαντες, ἰσχυρῶς ταῖς μάστιξι τιμωρεῖσθε, ἵνα πεφυλαγμένως φθέγγεσθαι μάθοι, καὶ μὴ πρὸς τὸ ὑπερέχον οὕτως ἀπαυθαδίζεσθαι."

37 Τούτου δὲ πολλῷ τῷ τάχει τελεσθέντος, καὶ εἰς μακρὸν

questioned. After they were set before him in great haste, the ruler immediately began his questioning, though he inquired nothing about their background or their motherland nor asked any of the usual questions, nor did he proceed to words aiming at persuasion. Rather, casting a harsh and menacing look at Galaktion, he muttered with excessive anger, "Who is this sullen and morose man? And to which other god does he offer his devotion and thus dishonor our gods?"

Showing no fear, nor altering his usual resolve, Galaktion 34 replied: "In my way of life, I am a monk, bearing the name Christian because of Christ; to Him, and rightly so, I offer my devotion." As the saint zealously offended him with insults, mocking his gods, and calling equally stupid those who worship what is lifeless, that abominable man ordered that Galaktion be flogged with rawhide whips, with his hands tied behind him.

As Episteme saw him being flogged, suffering indescrib- 35 able pain in her soul, she said: "Alas! How eager to inflict torture is this man! Why do you flog in this way such young limbs, worn out by the many labors of ascetic discipline? How is it that the hand of the floggers has not become numb?"

This provoked more anger in the ruler who said: "Strip 36 this rude and audacious woman down to her linen undergarment and punish her with strong whippings so that she may learn to speak guardedly and not show such impudence to superiors."

His command was executed with great swiftness and the 37

ἤδη παραταθείσης τῆς τιμωρίας, περὶ πᾶσαν μὲν ἐπα-
γωγὴν τῶν δεινῶν ἡ μάρτυς ὑπερφυῶς ἀπεμάχετο. Οὐδέν
δὲ ἀνίει καταβοῶσα τοῦ δικαστοῦ καὶ τὸ τοῦ πράγματος
ἄσεμνον ὀνειδίζουσα, ὅτι φύσιν, ἣν ἔδει διαμένειν ἀθέατον,
οὐ μόνον ἁπλῶς ἐκκαλύπτειν ἠνέσχετο, ἀλλὰ καὶ πολλῶν
ἐνώπιον ἐπέτρεψε τιμωρεῖσθαι. "Διὰ τοῦτο μένουσί σε,"
φησί, "τὰ ἐκεῖθεν δικαιωτήρια· πλὴν ἀλλὰ κἀνταῦθα, οὐκ
εἰς μακρὰν ὑμᾶς ἡ δικαία κρίσις τοῦ Θεοῦ μετελεύσεται."

38   Εἶπε· καὶ ἡ δίκη κατὰ πόδας εὐθὺς εἵπετο· καὶ πεπηρω-
μένοι τὰς ὄψεις οἱ περὶ τὸν ἄρχοντα καθωρῶντο. Τοῦτο δὲ
τῇ μὲν ἁγίᾳ δόξης, τοῖς κολάζουσι δὲ πρόξενον ἐγένετο
σωτηρίας· ἡ γὰρ τῶν ὀφθαλμῶν πήρωσις τὸ τῆς ψυχῆς
διέλυσε νέφος· καὶ φῶς αὐτοῖς θεογνωσίας ἐπηύγασε. Διὰ
τοῦτο καὶ πιστεύειν ὡμολόγησαν τῷ Χριστῷ· καὶ ἀντι-
στρόφως πάλιν, σὺν τῷ φωτὶ τῆς ψυχῆς, καὶ τὸ τῶν
ὀφθαλμῶν τοῦ σώματος ἐλάμβανον φῶς, ἄνδρες, οὐ δύο
καὶ τρεῖς ὄντες, ἀλλὰ καὶ τρεῖς καὶ πεντήκοντα ἀριθμού-
μενοι.

39   Πλὴν καὶ τούτων γενομένων, ὁ ἄρχων ἔτι τυφλώττων
τὸν νοῦν, ἅτε διὰ βάθους αὐτῷ τῆς κακίας ἐνσημανθείσης,
καλάμους εἰς ἄκρον ὀξυνθῆναι κελεύει, καὶ τοῖς τῶν ἁγίων
ὄνυξιν ἐμπαρῆναι. Οὗ καὶ ταχύτατα γενομένου, οἱ ἅγιοι τὸ
καρτερικὸν μᾶλλον ἐν τοῖς ἀλγεινοῖς ἐπεδείκνυντο, τῷ δι᾽
οὗ ταῦτα ὑπέμεινον πολλὴν τὴν χάριν ὁμολογοῦντες, καὶ
τὰ τῶν ψευδωνύμων θεῶν ἐξυβρίζοντες.

40   Ὁ δικαστὴς οὖν αὖθις χειρῶν αὐτοὺς καὶ ποδῶν ἅμα,
προσέτι δὲ καὶ γλώττης, ἀποστερεῖσθαι προσέταττεν,
ἡδονὴν ὥσπερ οἰκείαν ἐν ἀνθρώπων ὁμογενῶν τιμωρίαις

torture was extended for a long time, yet the martyr fended off every infliction of pain with strength that exceeded human nature. She did not cease to rebuke the judge and to reprimand him for the indignity of his decision, since he had not simply sanctioned the exposure of her sex, which should remain unseen, but also allowed her torture in front of many. "On account of this," she said, "just punishments await you in the next world. Even here and very soon, the just judgment of God will fall upon you."

She had hardly spoken and the punishment followed straight away. All those in the ruler's entourage were deprived of their sight. This brought glory to the saint and salvation to her torturers; for the loss of their sight dissolved the cloud covering their soul and the light of the knowledge of God shone upon them. Because of this, they confessed their belief in Christ and now, in reverse, they regained their bodily eyesight along with vision in their souls—and these were not just two or three men, but fifty-three altogether. 38

Even so, the ruler remained blind in his mind, since evil had been imprinted deeply inside him, and he ordered that reeds be sharpened to the finest point and inserted under the saints' nails. His order was carried out most swiftly, yet the saints showed their endurance toward pain even more, thanking the man that caused this suffering and inveighing against his false gods. 39

Then, the judge ordered that their hands, legs, and also their tongues be cut off, as if this bloodthirsty soul found personal pleasure in torturing fellow human beings. After 40

ἡ αἱμοβόρος ψυχὴ λαμβάνουσα. Ὡς δὲ καὶ ταῦτα θᾶττον ἐγένετο, τῶν μαρτύρων οὐδὲν ἧττον ἐπὶ τοῖς ἴσοις διαμενόντων, ὁ δεινὸς μὲν δικάζειν, ὠμότατος δὲ κολάζειν, τὴν τελευταίαν τοῖς μάρτυσι ψῆφον ἐπάγει, τὸν διὰ ξίφους αὐτοὺς κελεύσας ὑπελθεῖν θάνατον.

41   Οὗτοι μὲν οὖν τὴν ἐντεῦθεν ἀποδημίαν ἐστείλαντο, τὰς ἱερὰς κεφαλὰς κατὰ τὴν πέμπτην τοῦ Νοεμβρίου ἀποτμηθέντες. Τὰ δὲ τούτων τίμια σώματα τιμίῳ τινὶ ἐνθέμενος σκεύει ὁ δηλωθεὶς Εὐτόλμιος, ᾧ καὶ πρὸς τοῦ μάρτυρος ἀκολουθεῖν ἐπιτέτακτο, διὰ τιμῆς αὐτὰ καὶ τοῖς ἄλλοις ἄγεσθαι παρεσκεύασεν, εἰς δόξαν Πατρός, Υἱοῦ καὶ ἁγίου Πνεύματος, τοῦ ἐν Τριάδι μόνου Θεοῦ, ᾧ πρέπει τιμὴ πᾶσα, μεγαλωσύνη τε καὶ μεγαλοπρέπεια, νῦν καὶ ἀεὶ καὶ εἰς τοὺς αἰῶνας τῶν αἰώνων. Ἀμήν.

this order too was carried out swiftly, and the martyrs remained equally unwavering, that terrible judge and cruelest torturer proclaimed his last verdict against the martyrs and ordered that they undergo death by sword.

This then is how the saints departed from this life, as 41 their holy heads were cut off on the fifth of November. The aforementioned Eutolmios, who had been instructed by the martyr to follow them, placed their sacred bodies in a sacred casket and thus also prepared for their veneration by others, for the glory of the Father, the Son, and the Holy Spirit, the one God in Trinity, to whom all honor, majesty, and magnificence are appropriate, now and forever, and unto the ages of ages. Amen.

MIRACLE CONCERNING EUPHEMIA THE YOUNG MAIDEN

Θαῦμα εἰς Εὐφημίαν τὴν κόρην

Τοιοῦτον μὲν δὴ καὶ ὁ μάρτυς Ἄβιβος ἐπὶ τῶν Λικινίου καιρῶν εὗρε τὸ τέλος· καὶ τοιαύτης τῆς μετὰ τῶν ἁγίων ἔτυχε καταθέσεως· καὶ οὕτω κατάπαυσιν τῶν διωγμῶν τοῖς εὐσεβέσι διέθετο. Τὸ γὰρ ἀπὸ τοῦδε, Λικίνιος μὲν ἐλικμᾶτο τὴν ἐξουσίαν, Κωνσταντίνῳ δὲ τὸ κράτος ἐπήνθει, καὶ τὰ Ῥωμαίων αὐτῷ σκῆπτρα ηὐξάνετο, ὃς πρῶτος ἐν βασιλεῦσιν ἐπαρρησιάσατο τὴν εὐσέβειαν, καὶ Χριστιανοῖς τὸ ζῆν, ὡς Χριστιανός, ἐχαρίσατο. Ἀλλ' ὅπως ἂν ἔχοιτε γνῶναι οἵας τῆς χάριτος οἱ μάρτυρες παρὰ Θεοῦ ἔτυχον, διεξελθεῖν ἄνωθεν ἀναγκαῖον.

2   Οὖννοι μὲν οἱ Ἐφθαλῖται, Περσῶν ὅμοροι καὶ πρὸς ἀνίσχοντα ἥλιον οἰκοῦντες, τὸ σκαιὸν ἔθνος τουτὶ καὶ βάρβαρον, χρόνοις οὐκ ὀλίγοις ὕστερον μετὰ τὴν τῶν μαρτύρων τελείωσιν, εἰς τοσοῦτον ἐπέθεντο Ῥωμαίοις, ὡς καὶ μέχρις αὐτῆς Ἐδέσης ἐλάσαι καὶ τὰ πέριξ ληΐσασθαι. Οἱ δὲ Ῥωμαίων βασιλεῖς σφόδρα τε ἤμυνον τῇ πόλει, καὶ τὴν στρατιὰν ἐν βραχεῖ πᾶσαν συνέλεξαν, ὥστε ὑπερμαχέσασθαι τῆς Ἐδέσης, ἀνάλωτον αὐτὴν φυλάξαι βουλόμενοι, καὶ μάλιστα τοῖς τοῦ Χριστοῦ λόγοις θαρροῦντες οἷς ἐπέστειλεν Αὐγάρῳ, ὡς οὐδὲ ἡ πόλις ποτὲ βαρβάροις ἔσται ἁλώσιμος, καὶ τῷ ἐν αὐτῇ πρώτῃ τὸ τοῦ Κυρίου ἡμῶν καὶ Χριστοῦ ἐκμαγεῖον τῷ Αὐγάρῳ πεμφθῆναι.

Miracle Concerning Euphemia the Young Maiden

Such was thus also the death of Abibos the martyr at the time of Licinius, such was his burial together with the saints, and such was the end of the persecutions of the Christians. From that point on, as Licinius's power was destroyed, Constantine's rule blossomed and his imperial power over the Romans grew, and he was the first among the emperors to openly accept Christianity and, as a Christian, grant pardon to the Christians. So that you may know, however, what sort of grace the martyrs obtained from God, it is important to tell the following story from the beginning.

Long after the death of the martyrs, the Ephthalite Huns, 2 that wicked and barbarian nation, neighbors of the Persians, living toward the East, launched such an attack against the Romans that they even reached Edessa and plundered its hinterland. The emperors of the Romans defended the city forcefully, and, in a short time, assembled the entire army for Edessa's defense, wishing to keep the city impregnable, and having faith especially in the words of Christ which he had sent to Abgar—namely that the city would never be conquered by barbarians—, and also in the fact that the image of our Lord and Christ was sent to Abgar first in Edessa.

3 Ἤλασαν μὲν οὖν παρὰ τὴν πόλιν τὸ Οὐννικόν, ἑλεῖν αὐτὴν ῥᾳδίως οἰόμενοι. Ῥωμαῖοι δὲ συμμαχίαν Ἐδεσηνοῖς πέμπουσιν, ὡς μὴ ὑπὸ Οὔννων χειρωθῆναι τὴν πόλιν. Ἐπεὶ δὲ οἱ πρὸς Ῥωμαίων σταλέντες τὴν Ἔδεσαν ἤδη κατέλαβον, ἔτυχέ τινα Γότθον ἐν αὐτοῖς, βάρβαρόν τε τὸν τρόπον καὶ τὴν γνώμην ὀλέθριον, ἔν τινος οἴκῳ καταλῦσαι Σοφίας ὄνομα γυναικός. Τῇ δὲ ἦν θυγάτηρ μονογενὴς Εὐφημία, χηρείᾳ τε συζώσῃ καὶ ἐπὶ μόνῃ τῇ θυγατρὶ σαλευούσῃ. Ἀνήγετο οὖν ὥς τι νεοθαλὲς ἔρνος ἡ παῖς τῇ μητρί, σωφροσύνην τε ἀσκοῦσα καὶ παρθενίαν, καὶ τὸ μὴ ἀρρένων ὄμμασι θεαθῆναι διὰ σπουδῆς ἔχουσα. Ἦν δὲ ἡ παῖς ἄρα τὴν ὄψιν εὐπρεπὴς καὶ τὸ κάλλος ἀμήχανος.

4 Ἐπειδὴ τοίνυν συχνὸς ἐν τῇ καταγωγῇ τῷ Γότθῳ χρόνος ἐτρίβετο, (οὐκ οἶδ' ὅπως) θεᾶται τὴν κόρην· καὶ οὕτως αὐτῆς ἑάλω τῷ ἔρωτι, ὡς μηδὲν κατὰ νοῦν ἕτερον στρέφειν ἢ τὴν παρθένον. Προσωπεῖον τοιγαροῦν χρηστότητος ὑπελθών, καὶ φίλος εἶναι ὑποκρινάμενος, ἄπεισι παρὰ τὴν μητέρα, κολακείαις τε αὐτὴν ἐπιχειρῶν πεῖσαι καὶ ἀγαθῶν ἐπαγγελίαις, πρὸς γάμον αὐτῷ ἐκδοῦναι τὴν θυγατέρα. Ἡ δὲ βαρέως τε ἔφερε, καὶ τοῖς παρ' αὐτοῦ λεγομένοις ἥκιστα προσεῖχε τὸν νοῦν. Τοῦ δὲ θρασυνομένου καὶ μεγάλα διαπειλοῦντος, ἐκείνη, "Τὴν μόνην ἐμοὶ θυγατέρα," ἔφη, "βαρβάρῳ συζεῦξαι ἀνδρὶ οὐκ ἂν ἀνασχοίμην ποτέ. Μὴ κολάκευε τοίνυν μηδὲ ἀπείλει· οὔτε γὰρ χαυνώσεις ταῖς κολακείαις οὔτε φοβήσεις ταῖς ἀπειλαῖς."

5 Ὁ δὲ τῶν ὁμοίων καὶ πάλιν εἴχετο· καὶ πάλιν τὸ ἀναιδὲς ἐπεδείκνυτο· καὶ περὶ τῶν αὐτῶν, ὁπόσαι ὧραι, τῇ μητρὶ διελέγετο. Εἶτα καὶ κόσμους αὐτῇ πολυτελεῖς προσεκόμιζε· καὶ πολλῶν ἄλλων ἔσεσθαι κυρίαν διεβεβαίου. Ἡ δὲ

The Huns marched against the city, thinking that they 3
would easily capture it, but the Romans sent reinforcements
to the Edessenes, so that the city could not be conquered by
the Huns. When those sent by the Romans reached Edessa,
a certain Goth of barbarian manners and baleful character,
who happened to be among them, took up residence in the
house of a woman called Sophia. She had an only daughter, Euphemia, and was a widow, depending entirely on her
daughter. The girl was brought up by her mother like some
newly-sprouted scion, practicing chastity and preserving her
virginity, studiously avoiding the eyes of men. The girl was
moreover of fair countenance and extraordinary beauty.

The Goth spent much time in his lodgings and, I do not 4
know how, saw the girl and fell so much in love with her that
he could think of nothing else except this virgin. He thus
put on the mask of virtuousness, pretended to be a friend,
went to the mother, and with flatteries and promises of
good things attempted to persuade her to offer her daughter
to him in marriage. Sophia was rather vexed by this and paid
little attention to his words. As he, however, became bolder
and uttered many threats, she said, "I could never bear to
marry my only daughter to a barbarian. So stop flattering
and threatening; you will neither weaken my resolve with
your flatteries, nor scare me with your threats."

Yet he continued with the same behavior, repeating his 5
display of impudence and talking with the mother for hours
about these same things. Then he would also bring her ex-
pensive jewelry and would assure her that she would acquire

τῆς παιδὸς μήτηρ οὐδὲ οὕτω τοῖς παρ' αὐτοῦ λεγομένοις παρεῖχε τὸ οὖς.

6   Εἶτα ἐκείνου τοῖς προτέροις ἐμμένοντος, αὖθις ἡ Σοφία (οὐδ' οἶδ' ὅθεν μαθοῦσα), "Ἔστι σοι καὶ τέκνα καὶ γυνή," πρὸς αὐτὸν ἀπεκρίνατο, "καὶ οὐκ ἂν ἐγώ σοι πρὸς γάμον τὴν ἐμὴν παῖδα ἐκδοίην." Ὁ δέ, τοῦτο μὲν τῷ ἔρωτι τῆς κόρης νικώμενος, τοῦτο δὲ καὶ θείου φόβου μὴ φροντίδα ποιούμενος, ἐμαρτύρετο τὸν Θεὸν μηδέποτε γυναῖκα μηδὲ τέκνα σχεῖν, ἀλλὰ καὶ εἰς σύζυγον ἀγαγέσθαι τὴν κόρην βούλεσθαι, καὶ τῶν αὐτοῦ πάντων κυρίαν αὐτὴν ποιήσασθαι. Ἡττᾶται τοιγαροῦν ἡ τῆς παιδὸς μήτηρ τῶν τοῦ Γότθου ῥημάτων· καὶ τί γὰρ ἔμελλε δρᾶν, καὶ γυνὴ οὖσα τὸ εὔκολον εἰς ἀπάτην, καὶ ὅρκων ἐσμοὺς ἀκούουσα, καὶ φόβῳ τὴν ψυχὴν βαλλομένη;

7   Τὰς χεῖρας οὖν εἰς οὐρανοὺς ἀνατείνασα, "Ὁ πατὴρ τῶν ὀρφανῶν καὶ προστάτης τῶν χηρῶν, Δέσποτα καὶ Θεέ," ἔφη, "μὴ τὴν ὀρφανὴν τήνδε περιΐδῃς, ἀγνώστῳ συζευγνυμένην ἀνδρί· σὲ γὰρ τῶν αὐτοῦ ὑποσχέσεων ἔφορον δέχομαι καί, σοὶ πεποιθυῖα, τὴν μόνην ἐμοὶ παῖδα τῷ ξένῳ τούτῳ ἐκδίδωμι." Οὕτως ἔφη· καὶ μεταξύ, γαμικὰ συμβόλαια γράφονται. Καὶ δή τινα χρόνον τοῖς παρὰ τὴν Ἔδεσαν τόποις τῶν Οὔννων στρατοπεδευσαμένων, καὶ τῶν συμμάχων τῇ πόλει προσεδρευόντων, καὶ τὴν τῶν πολεμίων ἔφοδον ἀποκρουομένων, ἐγκύμων ἡ κόρη τῇ τοῦ Γότθου γίνεται συναφείᾳ.

8   Οὔπω οὖν ὁ καιρὸς αὐτῇ τῶν ὠδίνων ἐπέστη, καὶ τὸ μὲν Οὐννικόν, οὐδὲν ὧν ἤλπισεν ἐργάσασθαι δυνηθέν, ἀπαίρειν ἤδη πρὸς τὴν οἰκείαν διενοοῦντο· οἱ σύμμαχοι δὲ

much more. Even so, the girl's mother would pay no heed to his words.

Still, he insisted as before and thus Sophia in turn re- 6 sponded to him: "You have both children and a wife" (I do not know how she had found out) "and I would never give my girl in marriage to you." Overwhelmed by his desire for the girl, and caring little about the fear of God, the Goth called God as his witness that he had neither a wife nor children, but wanted to make the maiden his lawful wife and mistress of his entire household. The girl's mother was thus swayed by the words of the Goth. What else could she have done, being a woman, the gender that is easily deceived, hearing such a stream of oaths, and also being stricken with fear in her heart?

She raised her hands to the heavens and said: "Father of 7 orphans and protector of widows, Master and God, do not abandon this orphan girl, who is being married off to a stranger. You should be the overseer of his promises, and only by placing my trust in You do I give my only child to this foreigner." This is what she said and, immediately, a nuptial agreement was signed. As the Huns camped outside Edessa for some time, and the allies stayed on guarding the city and repelling the enemy's onslaught, the young maiden became pregnant after sleeping with the Goth.

The time of her labor pains had not yet arrived, and the 8 Huns decided to return home, since they had been unable to achieve any of their plans; the allies too wished to return

ἀπιέναι πάλιν πρὸς Ῥώμην ἐβούλοντο. Ἐπεὶ οὖν καὶ ὁ
Γότθος συναπιέναι Ῥωμαίοις ἡτοίμαστο, ἠνιᾶτό τε ἡ μήτηρ τῷ τῆς παιδὸς χωρισμῷ, καὶ τὰ σπλάγχνα ἐκόπτετο.
Ἐντεῦθεν εἴχετο τῆς παιδός· καὶ συναποδημεῖν τῷ Γότθῳ
οὐκ εἴα, κἂν οὐχὶ καὶ κατασχεῖν αὐτὴν ἠδυνήθη, νόμῳ γάμου καὶ φύσεως τῷ ἀνδρὶ ἕπεσθαι τῆς γυναικὸς βουλομέ-
νης.

9   Ἄρτι τοίνυν ἀποδημοῦντας ἡ μήτηρ παραλαβοῦσα,
τὴν τῶν ὁμολογητῶν καταλαμβάνει σορόν· καὶ πρὸς τὸν
Γότθον, "Οὐκ ἂν ἐγώ σοι τὴν ἐμὴν παῖδα πιστεύσω," φησί,
"εἰ μή, τῆς τιμίας σοροῦ τῆσδε τῶν ὑπὲρ Χριστοῦ παθόντων ἁψάμενος, ἐγγυητάς μοι τούτους παράσχῃς, μὴ μόνον
μηδέν τι πρὸς τὴν παῖδα λυπηρὸν διαπράξασθαι, ἀλλὰ καὶ
πάσης αὐτὴν ἀξιῶσαι τῆς θεραπείας."

10   Καὶ ὁ Γότθος εὐθύς, ὥσπερ τὸ πάντων εὐκολώτατόν τε
καὶ ἀφοβώτατον δράσειν ἐπιτραπείς, "Ἐκ τῶν χειρῶν
ὑμῶν, ἅγιοι, τὴν κόρην," εἶπε, "παραλαμβάνω· καὶ τῇ μητρὶ
ἐγγυητὰς ὑμᾶς δίδωμι, ὡς οὐδ' ὁτιοῦν αὐτῇ παρ' ἐμοῦ γενήσεται λυπηρόν, ἀλλὰ μᾶλλον καὶ πρὸς πᾶν ὅτι βούλοιτο
ἕτοιμον ἕξει με πληροῦντα ταύτῃ τὰ καταθύμια." Οὐ
ταῦτα μόνον ὁ ἀλιτήριος, ἀλλὰ καὶ εἰς τὴν μεγάλην τοῦ
Θεοῦ δύναμιν ὄμνυσι τὰς ὑποσχέσεις ἐπὶ τῶν ἔργων φυλάξαι.

11   Δεξαμένη τοίνυν ἡ μήτηρ τὸν ὅρκον, "Ὑμῖν, ἅγιοι, τὴν
παῖδα μετὰ Θεὸν ἀνατίθεμαι καὶ δι' ὑμῶν τῷ Γότθῳ," τοῖς
μάρτυσιν ἐπεβόησεν. Ἐπὶ τούτοις εὐξάμενοι τῷ Θεῷ καὶ ἡ

back to Rome. As the Goth prepared to depart together with the Romans, the mother was very upset to be separated from her child and stricken in her heart. Therefore she clung to the girl and would not let her leave with the Goth, even though she was unable to prevent her from going, since both the law of marriage and her nature as woman demanded that she follow her husband.

As they were departing, the mother took them to the caskets of the confessors. And she said to the Goth: "I will not entrust my girl to you, unless you touch this holy casket of those who suffered on behalf of Christ and provide them to me as guarantors, not only that you will not harm my child, but also that you will treat her with every respect and care." 9

As if urged to do the simplest and most undaunting thing, the Goth immediately said: "I accept the maiden from your hands, O saints, and I invoke you as her mother's guarantors not only that I will do to her no harm whatsoever, but also that I will be ready to fulfill her every wish." This was not the rogue's only commitment, but he also swore on God's great power that he would indeed keep his promises. 10

Upon hearing this oath, the mother exclaimed to the martyrs: "After God, I refer my child to you and then, through you, to the Goth." Prayers to God followed, the 11

μήτηρ τὴν παῖδα περιβαλοῦσα καὶ περιπτυξαμένη τὰ ποθεινότατα, αὐτὴ μὲν οἴκαδε ἐπανῄει, ὁ δὲ Γότθος τῆς ὁδοῦ μετὰ τῆς παιδὸς εἴχετο.

12   Εἶτα τὴν χώραν ἧς ὁ Γότθος ὥρμητο καταλαβόντες, ἐπεὶ ἤδη πρὸς τὴν τοῦ ἀνδρὸς ἤγγιζον οἰκίαν, ἐπιλαθόμενος μὲν ὁ δεινὸς ἐκεῖνος τῆς πρὸς τὴν γυναῖκα στοργῆς, καταφρονήσας δὲ ὅρκων καὶ συνθηκῶν, τὸν τοῦ Θεοῦ τε φόβον ἀφ' ἑαυτοῦ ποιησάμενος (ὦ μέχρι πόσου προήκει κακία!), ἀφαιρεῖ μὲν αὐτῆς τὰ ἱμάτια, προσαφαιρεῖται δὲ καὶ τὸν χρυσόν. Ῥάκος τε αὐτὴν οἷα δούλην ἀτίμως περιβαλών, "Ἐμοί," εἶπεν, "ὦ γύναι, καὶ τέκνα εἰσὶ καὶ γυνή. Διὸ καὶ δούλην αἰχμάλωτον σεαυτὴν κάλει· καὶ πρὸς τὴν ἐμὴν γυναῖκα πᾶσαν ἔσο φυλάττουσα τὴν ὑποταγήν, ὡς κυρίαν αὐτὴν καὶ τιμῶσα καὶ ὀνομάζουσα. Εἰ γὰρ ἔκφορα τὰ ἡμέτερα θήσεις ἢ καὶ τῷ τῆς ἐμῆς συζύγου θελήματι ἀπειθήσεις, θάνατον ἕξεις τὴν τιμωρίαν."

13   Τί πρὸς ταῦτα παθεῖν οἴεσθε γυναῖκα, γυμνωθεῖσαν μὲν μητρός, γυμνωθεῖσαν δὲ πατρίδος, φίλων πάντων καὶ συγγενῶν, καὶ πρὸς μόνην τὴν ἐκείνου ψυχὴν βλέπουσαν, τοιοῦτόν τε τὸ πέρας τῶν μακρῶν ἐκείνων ἐλπίδων ἰδοῦσαν; Πάντως εἰ μὴ λίθος ἦν, εἰ μὴ σίδηρος, ἢ ἄλλο τι τῶν ἀψύχων, πληγεῖσαν τῷ ἀνελπίστῳ τῆς ἀκοῆς, εὐθὺς τὴν ψυχὴν ἀφεῖναι. Ἀλλ' οἱ τῆς μητρὸς ἐγγυηταὶ ταύτην ἔσωζον, οὓς εἴληφεν ἐκείνη παρὰ τοῦ Γότθου, ἐπὶ κακῷ μὲν τῆς μιαρᾶς αὐτοῦ κεφαλῆς, δείγματι δὲ τῆς μεγίστης αὐτῶν χάριτος.

14   Μέγα τοίνυν στενάξασα καὶ βύθιον ἀπὸ τῆς ψυχῆς, "Σοί, Κύριε," εἶπε, "καὶ τῷ σῷ ἀφάτῳ ἐλέει ἐπὶ πᾶσι τούτοις εὐχαριστῶ." Εἶτα καὶ πρὸς τὸν Γότθον ἐπιστραφεῖσα,

mother embraced and kissed her child dearly, and she returned home, while the Goth set forth with the maiden.

When they reached the land of the Goth's origins, and 12 they began to approach his house, that wicked man forgot all about his affection for his new wife, disregarded oaths and agreements, abandoned any fear of God (oh, how far can wickedness go!), and removed her clothes as well as her golden jewelry. He dressed her shamefully as a slave in rags and said: "O woman, I have both children and a wife. You should thus call yourself a captive slave and obey all of my wife's commands, honoring and addressing her as your mistress. If you defy these orders of mine or disobey my wife's wishes, you will be punished with death."

What do you think a woman would feel upon hearing 13 these words, when deprived of her mother and fatherland, of all friends and relatives, depending entirely on that man, and encountering such an end to her high hopes? Surely she would breathe her last, when wounded by these unexpected words, unless she were made of stone or iron, or some other inanimate substance. Yet her mother's guarantors saved her, the ones whom she had received from the Goth, with bad consequences for his abominable head, and as proof of their great grace.

She gave out a loud and deep moan from her soul, and 14 said: "I thank You, Lord, and Your ineffable mercy for all this." Then she turned to the Goth and said: "My best wishes

"Εὖγέ σοι," φησί, "γένοιτο, ὅτι, καὶ δυνάμενος ἡμᾶς ἀνελεῖν, ἠρκέσθης τούτῳ μόνῳ τῷ δούλην ἀντ' ἐλευθέρας ποιήσασθαι. Τὰς ἐπαγγελίας ἐπὶ τῶν ἔργων ἐξήνεγκας· τοὺς ὅρκους ἐπιστώσω τοῖς πράγμασι. Τί δῆτα λοιπὸν ἐμοὶ ἢ ἐκείνους πάντως ἐφόρους τοῖς πραττομένοις ἐπικαλεῖν, οὓς τότε μάρτυρας αὐτὸς τοῖς παρὰ σοῦ λεγομένοις ἐπῆγες; Αὐτοῖς γὰρ καὶ οὐκ ἄλλῳ θαρρήσασα, τῆς τεκούσης διαζυγῆναι, τὴν ἐνεγκαμένην ἀπολιπεῖν, καὶ σοὶ μόνῳ εἱλόμην ἀκολουθεῖν."

15   Ταῦτα εἰποῦσα, τοὺς τῆς ψυχῆς ὀφθαλμοὺς ἅμα τοῖς αἰσθητοῖς πρὸς οὐρανὸν ἄρασα, "Ὁ Θεὸς τῶν πατέρων μου," σὺν οἰμωγαῖς καὶ δάκρυσιν ἔλεγε, "παράστηθί μοι τῇ ἀθλίᾳ καὶ ἴδε, τί μὲν οὗτος ὑπὸ σοὶ μάρτυρι καὶ τοῖς σοῖς ἁγίοις καὶ ὁμολογηταῖς ἐπηγγείλατο, τί δὲ νῦν ἐπὶ τῶν ἔργων ποιεῖ. Καὶ τῶν δεινῶν τούτων ἡμᾶς ἐξελοῦ, πρέσβεις ὑπὲρ ἡμῶν τοὺς μάρτυράς σου δεχόμενος, ὅτι τούτοις θαρρήσασα μετὰ σὲ τὰ παρόντα ὑφίσταμαι."

16   Τοιαῦτα τῆς κόρης ἡσυχῇ τοῦ Θεοῦ δεηθείσης, ἐπειδὴ τὸν τοῦ Γότθου οἶκον εἰσῄεσαν, ἡ τοῦ ἀνδρὸς σύζυγος τὴν κόρην θεασαμένη, καὶ τὸ κάλλος οἷον ἐν ταύτῃ κατανοήσασα, ζήλου καὶ ὑπονοίας πίμπλαται τὴν ψυχήν. Ὅθεν καὶ ἐπυνθάνετο τοῦ ἀνδρός, τίς τε αὕτη εἴη, καὶ ὅθεν ὁρμᾶται, καὶ ἐφ' ὅτῳ μεθ' ἑαυτοῦ ταύτην ἀγάγοι. Ὁ δὲ αἰχμάλωτόν τε εἶναι καὶ τῆς Ἐδέσης ἀχθῆναι, ἀχθῆναι δέ, ἐφ' ᾧ δουλεύσειεν αὐτῇ, ἀπεκρίνατο. Ἡ δέ, τῇ μορφῇ μᾶλλον ἢ τοῖς αὐτοῦ λόγοις προσέχουσα, "Ὁ τῆς ὄψεώς," φησι, "χαρακτὴρ οὐ δουλείαν κατηγορεῖ τῆς γυναικός." Καὶ ὁ Γότθος, "Σὺ δὲ ἀλλὰ χρῆσαι αὐτῇ ὅσα καὶ οἰκέτιδι."

to you, since you were satisfied by this outrage alone, turning me, a free woman, into a slave, although you could have killed me. You brought your promises to completion and confirmed your oaths with deeds. What else is left for me to do other than to appeal to those martyrs as overseers of your actions, those whom you yourself had summoned as witnesses to your words? I placed my trust in them alone and in no one else, when I was separated from my mother, abandoned my home country, and chose to follow you alone."

This is what she said. She then raised the eyes of her soul 15 together with her bodily eyes toward heaven and began saying with wailing and tears, "God of my fathers, stand by me in my misery and see what this man had promised before You as witness and Your saints and confessors and how he is acting now. Deliver me from this calamity, accepting Your martyrs as intercessors on my behalf, since, having faith in them after You, I am now suffering this affliction."

Such was the maiden's quiet entreaty to God. When they 16 entered the Goth's house and the man's wife saw the maiden and realized how beautiful she was, her soul was filled with jealousy and suspicion. Hence she began to ask her husband, who this maiden might be, where she came from, and why he had brought her along with him. He replied that she was a captive, brought from Edessa to work as her slave. But his wife focused more on her face than his words and said: "Her appearance does not indicate that she is a slave." "Still," the Goth said, "you should treat her like your servant."

17   Ἐντεῦθεν ἡ κόρη σιωπήν τε ἤσκει τῷ φόβῳ, καὶ κατὰ τάχος ἐποίει τὰ προστάττόμενα· οὐ γὰρ εἶχεν ὅ τι καὶ δράσειε, τῶν παρόντων αὐτὴν κακῶν δυνάμενον ἀπαλλάξαι. Πρὸς δὲ τοὺς ἁγίους διαπαντὸς ἐν τῇ καρδίᾳ αὐτῆς ἔλεγε· "Σπεύσατε πρὸς τὴν βοήθειαν τῆς δούλης ὑμῶν, ἅγιοι, σπεύσατε! Μηδὲ τὸν κατ' ἐμοῦ παρίδητε δόλον!"

18   Ἡ δὲ τῆς κόρης μὴ κατὰ νόμους κυρία, ζηλοτύπως ἔχουσα πρὸς αὐτήν, βαρέως τε τῇ κόρῃ ἐχρῆτο καὶ βαρυτέρας αὐτῇ τὰς ἐργασίας ἐπέταττεν, ὥσπερ τοὺς ἐκείνης πόνους τοῦ ταύτην διακαίοντος φθόνου ἴδιον αὐτῇ παραμύθιον ἔχουσα. Τὸ δέ γε μεῖζον δεινόν, ὅτι μηδὲ λόγου αὐτῇ κοινωνεῖν ἠξίου. Ἐπεὶ δὲ καὶ ἐγκυμονεῖν τῷ χρόνῳ τὴν κόρην ἐμάνθανε, τὴν τῆς ζηλοτυπίας φλόγα ἐπὶ πλέον ἐκκαύσασα, βαρυτάτην ἐξ αὐτῆς ἀπῄτει τὴν ἐργασίαν. Τί τοῦτο; Σπουδάζουσα θάνατον τῆς κόρης ἰδεῖν, ἐκτρωθέντος αὐτῇ μὴ κατὰ καιρὸν τοῦ ἐμβρύου. Ἀλλ' ἡ τοῦ Χριστοῦ καὶ τῶν διὰ Χριστὸν παθόντων ἰσχὺς ἄμαχος ἦν, δι' ἧς κρείττων τε ἡ κόρη τῶν ἀλγεινῶν, καὶ ἀπαθὴς κακῶν ἔμενεν.

19   Ἐπεὶ δὲ ὁ τῶν ὠδίνων αὐτῇ ἐπέστη καιρός, τίκτει παιδίον ἄρρεν, τὸν χαρακτῆρά τε τοῦ πατρὸς ἐφ' ἑαυτοῦ διασῶζον, καὶ τῷ Γότθῳ τὰ πάντα προσεοικός. Τοῦτο ἡ τοῦ Γότθου σύζυγος θεασαμένη, καὶ αὐτὴν ἐννοήσασα τῆς ὁμοιότητος τὴν ἀκρίβειαν, οὐδὲν ἦν ἕτερον στρέφουσα κατὰ νοῦν, ἢ ὅπως τὸ παιδίον ἀνέλῃ. Πρὸς δὲ τὸν ἄνδρα, "Οὐκ ἂν ἐγώ σοι πιστεύσαιμι," ἔφη, "τῇ κόρῃ μὴ συνελθεῖν· τὸ γὰρ ἐξ αὐτῆς τεχθὲν σαφῶς διομολογεῖ τὸν πατέρα, καθάπερ γλώττῃ τῇ μορφῇ χρώμενον." Ὁ δὲ μὴ

From that point on, the maiden kept silent in fear, and 17
would quickly do as she was ordered; for there was nothing she might do that could release her from her present
misfortunes. Yet in her heart she would ceaselessly say to
the saints, "Hurry to the succor of your slave, saints, hurry!
Do not disregard his treachery against me!"

The girl's unlawful mistress was jealous of her and would 18
abuse her, ordering her to perform the most onerous tasks,
as if the girl's labors could provide relief from the jealousy
that burned within her. And the worst evil was that she
would not even deign to speak to her. When with time she
found out that the maiden was also pregnant, the flame of
her jealousy was kindled even more, and she would demand
that she do the heaviest work. Why did she do that? She was
striving to bring about the maiden's death by a premature
abortion of the fetus. But the power of Christ and those
who had suffered on behalf of Christ was invincible and,
with it, the girl withstood this ordeal and remained unaf-
fected by her tribulations.

When the time of her labor pains arrived, she gave birth 19
to a male child, who resembled his father and looked like
the Goth in every respect. When his wife saw this and realized their exact resemblance, she thought about nothing
else except how she might kill the baby. "I cannot believe,"
she said to her husband, "that you did not sleep with the girl;
with its face like a tongue, her newborn baby gives away its
father clearly." He, however, kept claiming that what she

ἀληθῆ λέγειν αὐτὴν ἰσχυρίζετο· προετρέπετο δὲ ὡς δούλῃ κεχρῆσθαι, "Τοῦτο σε πιστώσεται," λέγων, "μηδέποτε ταύτῃ συνελθεῖν ἐμέ· οὐδὲ γὰρ ἄν σοι πάντως εἰς ἐξουσίαν οὕτως ἐδέδοτο· κιρνῶσι γὰρ φιλίας, οὐ διϊστῶσιν οἱ ἔρωτες."

20   Τότε τοίνυν ὁ ἐκ πολλοῦ τῷ ἀνθρωπείῳ γένει Πολέμιος, τὴν τοῦ Γότθου σύζυγον ὑπελθών, ἐξέμηνε κατὰ τοῦ παιδός. Καὶ διὰ τοῦτο πόνον τε συνελάμβανε, καὶ ἀνομίαν ἀπέτικτε. Καί τι δηλητήριον ὑπὸ κόλπον αὐτῆς ἐνθεμένη, τὴν μὲν τοῦ παιδὸς μητέρα κατά τινα δῆθεν χρείαν τῆς οἰκίας ἐκπέμπει. Καὶ ἡ μὲν ἔξεισιν ἀνῦσαι τὸ προσταχθέν· ἡ δὲ τῷ τοῦ παιδὸς στόματι ἐμβάλλει τὸ δηλητήριον, καὶ τῷ δηλητηρίῳ θάνατος εὐθὺς ἠκολούθει.

21   Ἐπανελθοῦσα τοίνυν μετ' ὀλίγον ἡ μήτηρ, καὶ νεκρὸν μὲν τὸ παιδίον εὑροῦσα, περικεχυμένον δὲ τοῖς χείλεσιν ἐκείνου τὸ δηλητήριον, πλήττεται μὲν τὴν καρδίαν καὶ πάσχει τὴν ψυχὴν ἰσχυρῶς. Κρύπτει δὲ ὅμως τὸ πάθος ἐν ἀπορρήτῳ, τὸ μὲν ὡς μήτηρ παθοῦσα, τὸ δὲ ὡς νουνεχὴς φυλάξασα. Εἶτα κώδιον ἐρέας λαβοῦσα καὶ τὸ στόμα τοῦ βρέφους ἐκμάξασα παρ' ἑαυτῇ κατεῖχε τὸ ἔριον, γνῶναι διὰ τῆς πείρας τἀληθὲς βουλομένη.

22   Μετὰ γοῦν ἡμέρας ὀλίγας, τῶν φίλων καὶ συγγενῶν τινας ἐπὶ δεῖπνον τοῦ Γότθου παραλαβόντος, ἁρπάζει τὸν καιρὸν ἡ κόρη· καὶ τῇ κύλικι ἐναποπλύνει τὸ ἔριον, τοῦ Γότθου τε τῇ γυναικὶ ἀναδίδωσι, τἀληθές, ὥσπερ ἔφην, μαθεῖν βουλομένη, εἴτε φαρμάκῳ τὸν παῖδα ἐζημιώθη, εἴτε καὶ κοινῷ θανάτῳ τοῦτον ἀπέβαλεν. Ὤιετο μὲν γὰρ ὡς, εἰ πιοῦσα τοῦ φαρμάκου ζήσοι, εὔδηλον ὅτι μηδὲ ὁ παῖς

said was not true and urged her to use the girl as a slave: "This will prove to you," he said, "that I never slept with her. Otherwise, I would never have given you such authority over her; for erotic desire strikes up friendship, it does not create separation."

At that point, the ancient Enemy of the human race took 20 possession of the Goth's wife and enraged her against the child. *She conceived mischief* because of this *and gave birth to iniquity.* She thus placed some poison in the folds of her robe, and sent the child's mother on some supposed errand for the house. The maiden left to carry out her order; and the wife put the poison into the child's mouth, and death immediately followed his poisoning.

When the mother returned a little later and found her 21 baby dead and his lips covered with the poison, she was stricken in her heart and suffered fiercely in her soul. Yet she hid her pain in silence: the pain she felt as a mother, the silence she kept as a prudent woman. Then she took a piece of wool cloth, wiped the baby's mouth, and kept the cloth, wishing to find out the truth by an experiment.

A few days later, when the Goth received some friends 22 and relatives as guests for dinner, the maiden seized the opportunity. She wiped a cup with the cloth and gave it to the Goth's wife, wishing, as I said, to find out the truth, namely whether she had been deprived of her child by poisoning, or whether she lost him by ordinary death. For Euphemia thought that, if the wife were to drink the poison and live, it would be clear that neither did Euphemia's child die by

φαρμάκῳ ἀνῄρητο, εἰ δὲ καὶ τοῦτο αὐτὴν ἀνέλοι, ἐκεῖνο πείσεται πάντως, ὅπερ αὐτὴ δέδρακεν.

23 Ἐπεὶ οὖν ἡ τοῦ Γότθου γυνὴ μηδὲν πονηρὸν ὑφεώρα μηδὲ ὑπώπτευε, δεξαμένη, πίνει τὴν κύλικα. Καὶ εὐθὺς ἐπέστρεφεν ὁ πόνος εἰς κεφαλήν· καὶ ἐπὶ κορυφὴν ἡ ἀδικία αὐτῆς κατέβαινεν, εἰς βόθρον τε ἐνέπιπτεν ὃν εἰργάσατο· καὶ ἐν παγίδι ᾗ ἔκρυψε, δικαίως συνελαμβάνετο. Ἔκειτο μὲν οὖν ἐκτάδην νεκρά, τοὺς καρποὺς ἀξίους τῶν πόνων κομισαμένη. Ἀθυμία δὲ τὸν Γότθον, τοὺς προσήκοντας, τοὺς ἐπιτηδείους κατεῖχεν· ὅλον ἐπλήρου τὸν οἶκον ἀηδία, στυγνότης, κατήφεια, ἐπὶ τῇ ἀώρῳ ταύτῃ τῆς γυναικὸς τελευτῇ. Ἀλλ᾿ ὅμως καὶ θρηνεῖται παρ᾿ αὐτῶν τὰ εἰκότα, ταφῆς τε λαμπρᾶς ἀξιοῦται, καὶ πολυτελῶς κατατίθεται.

24 Ἐπεὶ δὲ μετὰ τὴν ταφὴν ἑπτὰ παρῆλθον ἡμέραι, καὶ ἱκανῶς περὶ τὸ πάθος ἠσχόληντο, ἔννοιά τις αὐτοῖς γίνεται τῇ τῆς αἰχμαλωτίδος ἐπιβουλῇ τεθνάναι τούτοις τὴν συγγενῆ. Ἐντεῦθεν ἐβούλοντο μὲν αὐτὴν παραδοῦναι τῷ ἡγεμόνι, ὅπως ὑπ᾿ ἐκείνου ἀναιρεθείη· οὐ γὰρ ἐξῆν αὐτοῖς ἀνθρώπῳ σίδηρον ἐπιφέρειν. Ἐπεὶ δὲ ἀποδημῶν οὗτος ἔτυχεν, αὐτοὶ καθ᾿ ἑαυτοὺς συνδιασκεψάμενοι, ἐν ᾧπερ ἡ τοῦ Γότθου σύζυγος ἐτέθαπτο μνήματι, τό γε νῦν ἔχον, αὐτὴν κατακλείουσι, λίθῳ τε τραχεῖ τὸν τάφον διασφαλίζονται, καὶ φύλακας αὐτῷ ἐφιστᾶσι.

25 Προσβαλούσης δὲ αὐτῇ τῆς τοῦ νεκροῦ δυσωδίας, πολλῆς ἀναπλησθεῖσα τῆς ἀηδίας, "Κύριε ὁ Θεὸς τῶν δυνάμεων," ἡ παῖς ἔλεγεν, "ὁ τὰ τῶν σῶν μαρτύρων καὶ ὁμολογητῶν ὑπὲρ σοῦ αἵματα ὡς ζῶσαν προσδεξάμενος θυσίαν, ἐπίβλεψον ἐπ᾿ ἐμέ, τὴν ἐπὶ τῷ σῷ τε καὶ τῷ τῶν διὰ

poison; but if this poison were to kill the wife too, then she would in any case suffer exactly what she had caused.

Since the Goth's wife neither presumed nor suspected 23 anything evil, she took the cup and drank. Immediately, *her mischief returned upon her own head; and her violent dealing came down upon her own pate; she fell into the ditch she made,* and *she was* justly *captured in the net in which she hid.* She thus lay stretched out dead, having received the fruits she deserved for her labors. Sorrow overwhelmed the Goth, his relatives, and his friends. Abhorrence, distress, desolation filled the entire house upon this untimely death of his wife. She was then appropriately lamented and given a splendid burial and a sumptuous tomb.

Seven days passed after the burial and they had suffi- 24 ciently dealt with their grief, when the thought occurred to them that their relative had died because of the captive's evil ploy. They thus wanted to deliver her to the ruler, so that he might execute her; for they themselves could not kill someone by the sword. Since, however, he happened to be away, they discussed this among themselves and then shut her, for the time being, in the tomb where the Goth's wife had been buried, sealing the tomb with an unhewn rock and stationing guards upon it.

As the stench of the corpse struck her, the girl was filled 25 with great disgust and began to say: "Lord, the God of powers, the one who received the blood of Your martyrs and confessors as a living sacrifice on Your behalf, look down upon me as well, who, having faith in Your name and the

σὲ παθόντων ἁγίων ὀνόματι ἀγνώστῳ ἀνδρὶ καὶ ἀλλο-
φύλῳ ἑαυτὴν ἐμπιστεύσασαν, καὶ διὰ τοῦτο ταύτην κατα-
κριθεῖσαν τὴν βάσανον. Αὐτός μοι τὴν ἀπὸ σοῦ παράσχου
βοήθειαν· καὶ τοῦ παρόντος ἐξελοῦ κινδύνου. Καὶ ὑμεῖς δὲ
ἅγιοι τοῦ Χριστοῦ, οἱ τοὺς μυρίους ἐκείνους ἄθλους δι᾽
αὐτὸν ὑποστάντες, καὶ τοῦτον ζῶντα Θεὸν ἐναντίον βασιλέων ὁμολογήσαντες, οὓς τῇ ἐμῇ μητρὶ παρέσχεν ὁ
Γότθος ἐγγυητὰς ἐπ᾽ ἐμοί, αὐτοί μοι νῦν πρὸς τὰ δεινὰ
παράστητε βοηθοί, μηδὲ τὴν ὑμῖν ἀναθεμένην τὰ κατ᾽
αὐτὴν περιόψεσθε."

26   Ταῦτα προσευξαμένης, οὐκ ἔμελλον οἱ ἐγγυηταί, οὐδὲ
πρὸς τὴν αὐτῆς βοήθειαν ἀνεβάλλοντο. Ἀλλὰ τρεῖς ἄνδρας
φῶς ἀπρόσιτον περικειμένους ὁρᾷ· καὶ τὰ τῆς δυσωδίας
εὐθὺς εἰς εὐωδίαν μετέβαλεν, ὥστε θαυμαστήν τινα καὶ
ἡδεῖαν προσβάλλειν αὐτῇ τὴν ὀσμήν. Καὶ "Θάρσει, γύναι," φασὶ πρὸς αὐτὴν ἐκεῖνοι, "καὶ μὴ φοβοῦ· ταχείας γὰρ
τεύξῃ τῆς σωτηρίας, δεινὸν οὐδὲν οὐδὲ ἄχαρι ὑπομείνασα·
οὔτε γὰρ τὴν ἐγγύην ψευσόμεθα, οὔτε ἀναβολῇ περὶ τὴν
σωτηρίαν χρησόμεθα."

27   Ταῦτα τοίνυν αὐτῇ τῶν ἁγίων διαλεχθέντων, αὐτίκα,
ὥσπερ ἐν ἐκστάσει γενομένη, ὑπνοῖ τῇ τοῦ Θεοῦ τε ἀμάχῳ
καὶ τῶν αὐτὸν ὁμολογησάντων δυνάμει. Ὦ θαύματος
ἀξίου τῆς τοῦ Θεοῦ χρηστότητος καὶ δυνάμεως! Καθάπερ
τις ἄλλος Ἀμβακοὺμ προφήτης, ἐν μιᾷ καιροῦ ῥοπῇ, ἀπὸ
τῶν Ἱεροσολύμων πρὸς τὴν Βαβυλῶνα μετετέθη, ἢ ὡς ὁ
μαθητὴς Φίλιππος ἀπὸ προσώπου τοῦ εὐνούχου Αἰθίοπος
ἡρπάγη ὑπὸ τοῦ Πνεύματος, τὸν αὐτὸν δήπου καὶ αὕτη

name of the saints who had suffered for You, entrusted myself to an unknown foreigner and, because of this, has been condemned to this torment. Give me Your help and release me from this danger. You too, saints of Christ, who suffered myriad trials for Him, and who professed Him to be the living God in front of emperors, and whom the Goth offered as guarantors to my mother for my sake, stand by me as helpers in my present misfortunes, and do not abandon me who dedicated myself to you."

This was her prayer and the guarantors did not delay, nor did they postpone helping her. Rather, she saw three men surrounded by unapproachable light and, immediately, the stench was turned into fragrance and a marvelous and pleasant smell reached her. "Have courage, O woman," they said to her, "and do not be afraid. You will quickly attain deliverance, suffering nothing terrible or disagreeable, as we will neither fail in our pledge, nor delay your deliverance." 26

After this exchange between her and the saints, at once, as if going into rapture, she fell asleep by the indomitable power of God and His confessors. What a miracle commensurate with God's goodness and power! Exactly like another prophet Habakkuk who, in a single instant, was transported from Jerusalem to Babylon, or like Philip the disciple who was taken away from the Ethiopian eunuch by the Spirit, in 27

τρόπον τοῦ μνήματος καθεύδουσα μετατίθεται· καὶ τῷ
ναῷ τῶν ὁμολογητῶν ὁμοῦ καὶ μαρτύρων ἀποκαθίσταται.

28   Τῷ τοιῷδε οὖν ἀποκαταστᾶσα τῶν μαρτύρων νεῷ, κατὰ
τὸ περίορθρον τοῦ ὕπνου αὐτὴν ὑπανέντος, παρεστῶτας
αὐτῇ τοὺς τοῦ Χριστοῦ ὁμολογητὰς καὶ αὖθις ὁρᾷ καὶ
"Οἶσθα ποῦ ἄρτι εἶ;" λέγοντας. Περιβλεψαμένη οὖν τῇδε
κἀκεῖσε, καὶ ὥσπερ ἐν ἑαυτῇ γενομένη, καὶ τὸν εὐκτήριον
τῶν μαρτύρων οἶκον ἀναγνωρίσασα, πάσης τε ἡδονῆς πε-
πλήρωτο· καὶ πολλῷ τῷ θαύματι κατεπλήττετο. Ἔχαιρεν
ὁρῶσα· ἐξίστατο ἐννοοῦσα· ἑαυτῇ διηπίστει· οὐκ εἶχεν ὅ τι
καὶ γένοιτο. Τέλος, τοῖς τῶν ἁγίων προσπίπτει ποσί· καὶ
τὰς εὐχαριστηρίους εὐχὰς ἀποδίδωσιν.

29   Οἱ δὲ πρὸς αὐτήν, "Τὰ τῆς ἡμετέρας ἰδού," φασιν,
"ἐγγύης πεπλήρωται. Πορεύου παρὰ τὴν μητέρα τὴν σὴν
ἐν εἰρήνῃ." Καὶ οἱ μὲν εὐθὺς τῶν ὀφθαλμῶν ἐκείνης δι-
έστησαν. Ἡ δὲ τῇ τούτων προσελθοῦσα σορῷ, θερμῶς τε
περιπτυξαμένη, καὶ δάκρυα ἡδονῆς ὁμοῦ καὶ φόβου συμ-
μιγῆ καταχέασα, "Ὁ Θεὸς ἡμῶν," ἔλεγεν, "ἐν τῷ οὐρανῷ καὶ
ἐν τῇ γῇ πάντα ὅσα ἠθέλησεν ἐποίησεν· ἐξαπέστειλεν ἐξ
οὐρανοῦ καὶ ἔσωσέ με. Εὐλογητὸς εἶ, Κύριε, ὁ σώζων τοὺς
ἐλπίζοντας ἐπὶ σοί. Τὸ ἑσπέρας ηὐλίσθη μοι κλαυθμός, καὶ
εἰς τὸ πρωῒ ἀγαλλίασις."

30   Ἐφ᾽ ἱκανὸν οὖν τῆς ὥρας τὰς εὐχὰς σὺν δάκρυσι παρα-
τείνασαν, ὁ ἐν τῷ ναῷ ἱερεὺς τὴν κόρην ὁρῶν, καὶ τῶν
εὐχαριστηρίων ἀκούων, διαπορῶν ἦν. Εἶτα ἤρετο προσελθὼν τὴν αἰτίαν, δι᾽ ἣν οὕτω τε προσευχομένη ὀδύραιτο,
καὶ τοσαῦτα ἐκχέοι τὰ δάκρυα, καὶ ὑπὲρ ὅτου τὰς εὐχαρι-
στίας προσφέροι. Ἡ δὲ αὐτῷ πάντα διεξῄει τὰ κατ᾽ αὐτήν·

the same manner she too was transported away from the tomb while asleep, and was restored back to the church of the confessors and martyrs.

Restored in this way to the church of the martyrs, when 28 sleep left her early in the morning, she saw again by her side the confessors of Christ, asking her, "Do you know where you are?" She looked all around and, as if coming back to her senses, recognized the shrine of the martyrs. She was filled with every happiness and stunned. She rejoiced at the sight; she was astounded at the realization; she disbelieved her eyes; she was beside herself. In the end, she fell at the saints' feet and offered in return prayers of gratitude.

They said to her, "Our pledge has been, as you see, ful- 29 filled. Go to your mother in peace," and immediately disappeared from her sight. She then came to their casket, embraced it with fervor, and, shedding tears that mixed fear with joy, said, "*Our God in heaven and upon earth has done whatsoever He has pleased; He sent from heaven and saved me.* Blessed are You, O Lord, *who saves those who put their hopes in You.* My *weeping may have endured for a night, but joy came in the morning.*"

As the maiden continued her tearful prayers for a long 30 time, the priest in the church saw her and was baffled when he heard her prayers of thanks. He approached and asked her what was the reason for her wailing in prayer and the shedding of so many tears, and what was the cause of her prayers of thanks. She narrated her entire story to him: how

ὅπως τε τῷ Γότθῳ παρὰ τῆς μητρὸς συναφθείη, καὶ ὡς τούτῳ συναποδημήσοι τοῖς ὅρκοις πιστεύσασα, ὅπως τε τὸ τεχθὲν αὐτῇ ὑπὸ τῷ Γότθῳ φαρμάκῳ ζημιωθείη, καὶ ὅπως τῷ τάφῳ κατακλεισθείη, καὶ οἵας τῆς τύχης πειράσαιτο, καὶ οἵας τῆς ἀπαλλαγῆς παρὰ τῶν ἁγίων τύχοι.

31 Τούτων ὁ ἱερεὺς ἀκούσας, ἐξίστατο ἑαυτοῦ· διηπορεῖτο τῷ μεγέθει τοῦ διηγήματος· πρὸς ἀπιστίαν καὶ πίστιν τὴν ψυχὴν ἐμερίζετο. Ὅθεν καὶ τελεώτερον τὰ κατ' αὐτὴν πιστωθῆναι βουλόμενος, τίς τε ἡ μήτηρ τῆς κόρης ἐπυνθάνετο, καὶ ἧστινος ὥρμηται τῆς οἰκίας. Τῆς δὲ ταῦτα τῷ ἱερεῖ ἀποκριναμένης, τὴν μὲν κόρην οὗτος ἐν τῷ ναῷ κατέχει, μεταστέλλεται δὲ τὴν μητέρα πρὸς ἑαυτόν.

32 Ἡ δέ, τὸν εὐκτήριον οἶκον καταλαβοῦσα, καὶ τὴν θυγατέρα τῷ ἱερεῖ παρεστῶσαν ἐξαίφνης θεασαμένη, πρῶτα μὲν περιβάλλει ταύτην καὶ θερμῶς περιπτύσσεται, τοῦ φίλτρου πάντως ἁπλῶς ποιοῦντος τὸ ἴδιον. Εἶτα ἐπὶ πολὺ ἀλλήλαις ἐφησυχάζουσι, τῆς οἰμωγῆς αὐταῖς τὴν φωνὴν ἐπεχούσης, καὶ τῶν δακρύων τὴν ὁμιλίαν διακοπτόντων· τῆς μὲν γὰρ ὑπέθραττε τὴν ψυχὴν ἡ παῖς, ὁρωμένη ἐν δουλικοῖς ἐνδύμασι καὶ προσχήμασι· ἡ θυγάτηρ δὲ πάλιν ἐπλήττετο τὴν καρδίαν, ὅτι, ἐπὶ χρησταῖς ἐλπίσι τῆς μητρὸς διαζυγεῖσα, οὕτως ἐπανῆκεν ἀτίμως, ὡς ἐκκαλεῖσθαι καὶ ἀπὸ μόνης τῆς θέας τὸν ἔλεον.

33 Μόλις γοῦν ἡ μήτηρ, τῆς πικρᾶς ἐκείνης ἀνενεγκοῦσα συγχύσεως, ἀνεπυνθάνετο τῆς παιδός, τίνα τε αὐτῇ τὰ συμβεβηκότα, καὶ ὅπως ἐπανῆκε, καὶ τί τὸ δουλικῶς αὐτὴν οὕτω περιβεβλῆσθαι ποιῆσαν. Ἡ δὲ πάντα τὰ κατ' αὐτήν,

her mother gave her in marriage to the Goth, how she departed with him trusting his oaths, how her child was poisoned by the Goth, how she was shut into the tomb, the misfortune that befell her, and the deliverance that she received from the saints.

When the priest heard all this, he was amazed; he was 31 perplexed by the greatness of the story; his soul was divided between disbelief and belief. Wishing therefore to confirm her story, he asked the maiden who her mother was and from which household she came. When she told him, the priest kept her in the church and sent for her mother to come to him.

When she reached the shrine and suddenly saw her 32 daughter standing by the priest, the first thing she did was to take her in her arms and embrace her fervently—motherly love was simply acting according to its nature. Then, for a long time, they tried to calm each other down, as wailing overwhelmed their voices and tears interrupted their words. The mother's soul was perturbed when she saw her girl looking like a slave in her clothes and appearance; and the daughter was stricken in her heart because she had been separated from her mother in hopes of a better future, but had returned in this dishonored state that elicited one's mercy simply by her appearance.

When the mother managed to recover from this bitter 33 turmoil, she asked her girl about what had happened to her, how she had returned, and what made her wear the garb of a slave. The maiden recounted to her mother in detail her

ὡς εἶχε, τῇ μητρὶ διεξήει, ἡδέα μετὰ τὴν ἀπαλλαγὴν ὄντα καὶ λέγεσθαι καὶ ἀκούεσθαι.

34 Ἐπεὶ οὖν καὶ ἡ μήτηρ τὰ τοῦ Θεοῦ τε καὶ τῶν ὁμολογητῶν αὐτοῦ καὶ μαρτύρων εἰς τὴν θυγατέρα γεγονότα τεράστια ἐπύθετο παρ᾽ αὐτῆς, πᾶσαν ἐκείνην τὴν ἡμέραν ὁ εὐκτήριος τῶν μαρτύρων οἶκος ἀμφοτέρας εἶχε μεγαλυνούσας τὸν Κύριον. Ἑσπέρας δὲ ἄρτι καταλαβούσης, ἐξίασι τοῦ νεὼ καὶ τῷ οἴκῳ μὲν ἑαυτῶν ἀποδίδονται. Τῇ ἐπιούσῃ δέ, πανταχῇ τε τὸ γεγονὸς διεδίδοτο· καὶ τὸ πλῆθος ἐπὶ τὴν κόρην καὶ τῶν ἄλλως προσηκόντων συνέρρεον, τὸν Θεόν τε ἅμα αὐτῇ καὶ τοὺς δι᾽ αὐτὸν παθόντας ἁγίους ἐδόξαζον.

35 Χρόνῳ δὲ ὕστερον, *Θεὸς ὁ τῶν ἐκδικήσεων Κύριος ἐπαρρησιάσατο· ὑψώθη ὁ κρίνων τὴν γῆν· ἀπέδωκεν ἀνταπόδοσιν τοῖς ὑπερηφάνοις.* Πέρσαις γὰρ Οὔννων προσθεμένων, καὶ τοὺς περὶ τὴν Ἔδεσαν τόπους ἔτι κατατρεχόντων, στέλλεται μὲν καὶ αὖθις Ἐδεσηνοῖς εἰς συμμαχίαν παρὰ Ῥωμαίων στρατός, ἐφ᾽ ᾧ τὴν πόλιν φυλάξουσι. Τῶν δέ, εἷς ἦν καὶ ὁ πολὺς τὴν μοχθηρίαν Γότθος· καὶ τῇ τῆς γυναικὸς οἰκίᾳ πάλιν ἐπιδημεῖ. Ἐπιδημεῖ δὲ πεποιθότως, ἅτε γαμβρὸς ἑστίᾳ πενθερικῇ, καὶ μηδέν, ὧν ἐν τῷ ἀφανεῖ ἐπεβούλευσε, φανερὸν γενέσθαι ὑπονοῶν.

36 Γνοῦσα τοίνυν ἡ τῆς παιδὸς μήτηρ τὴν τοῦ ἀνδρὸς παρουσίαν, τὴν μὲν θυγατέρα τῇ ἐνδοτέρᾳ οἰκίᾳ ἐγκατακλείει, σοφώτερον ἢ κατὰ γυναῖκα πρᾶγμα δρᾶσαι διανοησαμένη. Ἡ δὲ μετὰ περιχαρείας αὐτὸν ὑποδέχεται, ὅπως μὲν οὗτος ἔχοι διερωτῶσα, ὅπως δὲ τὴν ἐπὶ τὰ οἰκεῖα τούτου ὁδὸν ἡ θυγάτηρ διήνυσεν, ὅπως τε διεσώθη, ὅπως τε

whole story that gave pleasure both to the speaker and to
her listener, now that she had been released.

Once the mother learned from her about the wonders 34
that God and His confessors and martyrs did for her daughter, for the rest of that day the entire shrine of the martyrs
was filled with their eulogies of the Lord. When evening
came, they left the church and went back to their home. On
the next day, the news spread everywhere. Crowds of friends
and relatives streamed to the maiden and, together with her,
glorified God and the saints that had suffered on His behalf.

Some time later, *Lord God, to whom vengeance belongs,* 35
showed Himself; the judge of the earth lifted Himself up; He ren-
dered a reward to the proud. The Huns joined the Persians and
ravaged the countryside around Edessa. Thus once more an
army was sent by the Romans as allies to the Edessenes, so
that they might protect the city. Among them was also the
Goth, that very wicked man, who came to stay again in his
wife's house. He came with confidence, as a son-in-law to
the house of his mother-in-law, without suspecting that any
of his secret schemes had been revealed.

When the girl's mother realized that the man was com- 36
ing, she shut up her daughter in the inner part of the house,
devising a course of action that was wiser than one would
expect of a woman. She received him with expressions of
joy, asking him how he was, how her daughter made the
journey to his homeland, how she held up, how she gave

ἐγκύμων οὖσα τέτοκε, καὶ ὅ τι τὸ τεχθέν, ἄρρεν ἢ θῆλύ ἐστιν. "Ἐγὼ γάρ," φησι, "πολλὴν τὴν περὶ ὑμῶν ἐποιούμην φροντίδα, μή πού τι κατὰ τὴν ὁδοιπορίαν ὑμῖν, καὶ μάλιστα τῇ ἐμῇ θυγατρί, συνενεχθῇ δυσχερές, ἐγκύμονί τε καὶ ἤδη πρὸς τὸ τίκτειν καθισταμένη."

37 Καὶ ὁ Γότθος ὥσπερ οὐκ ἀφ' ὧν αὐτὸς ἔδρασεν, ἀλλ' ἀφ' ὧν ἡ ἄρρητος ᾠκονόμησεν ἀγαθότης τὰς ἀποκρίσεις ποιούμενος, "Ἐν καλοῖς," ἔλεγε, "πάντα ταῖς σαῖς προῆλθον εὐχαῖς. Ἀλύπως δὲ καὶ τὴν ὁδὸν ἅμα τῇ σῇ θυγατρὶ διηνύσαμεν· καὶ τοῖς ἐμοῖς εὐθύμως ἀπεσώθη· καὶ ὅτι τέκοι παιδίον ἄρρεν, καὶ νῦν ἐν ὑγείᾳ οὖσα καὶ εὐθυμίᾳ, πολλά σε δι' ἐμοῦ προσαγορεύει τε καὶ ἀσπάζεται. Εἰ δὲ μὴ ἐκ τοῦ αἰφνιδίου πρὸς συμμαχίαν ἐστάλημεν, ἐπανῆκεν ἄν σοι καὶ αὐτὴ σὺν ἐμοί."

38 Τούτων ἡ μήτηρ ἀκούσασα, ὀργῆς τε ἐπληροῦτο, καὶ τὰ σπλάγχνα ἐστρέφετο, ἔργων ἀδίκων ἐπίπλαστον μυσαττομένη χρηστολογίαν. Εἶτα μηκέτι δυναμένη διενεγκεῖν θυμὸν δίκαιον εἰς φανερὰν ᾄττοντα παρανομίαν, ἐνεβριμήσατό τε τῷ τὰ πάντα ἀδίκῳ ἀνδρί· καί, "Δόλιε," φησι, "καὶ φονεῦ, τί μετὰ τῆς ἐμῆς πεποίηκας θυγατρός; Τοιαῦτά μοι μεθ' ὅρκων ἐπηγγείλω; Ἐπὶ τοιούτοις ἐγγυητὰς ἐμοὶ καὶ μάρτυρας τοὺς διὰ Χριστὸν παθόντας παρέσχες; Ἀλλ' αὐτοί σε πάντως, οὓς ἐγγυητὰς δέδωκας, αὐτοί σε τῆς πονηρᾶς τιμωρήσονται γνώμης· καὶ τῆς ἀδίκου ταύτης ἐπιβουλῆς εἰσπράξονται δίκας. Αὐτοὺς εἰς ἄμυναν ἐγὼ καλέσω, οὓς εἰς ἐγγύην σὺ τότε παρείληφας."

39 Ταῦτα ἡ μήτηρ εἰποῦσα, ἐξάγει τῆς οἰκίας τὴν θυγατέρα· καί, "Οἶδας τίς αὕτη," φησίν, "ἀνόσιε;" τῷ Γότθῳ

birth, as she was pregnant, and what the newborn was, a boy or a girl. "I worried," she said, "much about you two, lest some harm befall you during your journey, and especially my daughter, who was pregnant and already about to give birth."

As if describing not what he himself had done, but what the ineffable goodness had intended, the Goth replied, "All your wishes came to a good end. Your daughter and I journeyed together without any trouble. She arrived happily in my house and gave birth to a baby boy. Now, healthy and cheerful, she sends you many greetings and kisses through me. And if we had not been sent suddenly as allies here, she too would have returned to you together with me." 37

When the mother heard this, she was filled with rage and her innards churned with revulsion at his false niceties covering up wrongful deeds. Then, unable to restrain her righteous anger any longer as it dashed against an obvious wrongdoing, she railed against the man who was wicked in every way. "You rogue," she said, "and murderer, what have you done to my daughter? These are the promises you made with oaths to me? For such deeds you evoked as guarantors and witnesses those who died for Christ? Yet these same ones, whom you offered as guarantors, will punish you for your wicked intent and will demand retribution for your wrongful plot. I will summon to my defense those whom you then appropriated for a guarantee." 38

After saying this, the mother brought out her daughter. Showing her to the Goth, she said, "Do you know who this 39

δείξασα, "Οἶδας τίς αὕτη καὶ ὅπου ταύτην κατέκλεισας, καὶ οἵῳ παραδοῦναι ἠβουλήθης θανάτῳ, μὴ φύσιν, μὴ νόμους, μὴ ὅρκους τοὺς μακροὺς ἐκείνους εὐλαβηθείς; Ἀλλ' οἱ τοῦ Χριστοῦ ὁμολογηταὶ καὶ μάρτυρες, Σαμωνᾶς, Γουρίας καὶ Ἄβιβος, ἐφ' οἷς ἐγὼ θαρρήσασα τῇ βαρβάρῳ σου ταύτην ἐπίστευον δεξιᾷ, ἐκεῖνοί μοι παρ' ἐλπίδα πᾶσαν αὐτὴν διεσώσαντο, καὶ τοῖς ἐμοῖς ἀπέδωκαν κόλποις."

40   Τούτων ἐπειδὴ ὁ Γότθος ἤκουσε, καὶ παρεστῶσαν εἶδε τὴν κόρην, ὑπό τε τῆς αἰσχύνης αὐτῷ καὶ τοῦ φόβου τὸ φθέγμα ἐσβέσθη, καὶ ἄφωνος ἦν, μηδὲ ἀναπτύξαι τὸ στόμα δυνάμενος. Εἶτα ἐπειδὴ ἔλεγχος ἦν ἀκριβής, καὶ φανερὸς ὑπῆρχε τοιαῦτα κατὰ τῆς κόρης διαπραξάμενος, μηδὲ λόγου μεταδόντες αὐτῷ οἱ παρόντες, ἀσφαλῶς κατακλείουσιν. Ἡ δὲ μήτηρ σὺν τῇ θυγατρὶ τὸν ὑπογραφέα παραστησάμεναι καὶ τὰ συμβεβηκότα πάντα διαχαράξασαι, τῷ τὰ πάντα ὁσίῳ τῆς Ἐδέσης ἐπισκόπῳ—Εὐλόγιος δὲ οὗτος ἦν—ἐγχειρίζουσι. Καὶ ὅς, ταῦτα διεξελθών, συνάμα τῷ κλήρῳ παντί, παρὰ τὸν τῆς πόλεως ἄπεισι στρατηλάτην· καὶ τὸ γραμματεῖον αὐτῷ ἀναδίδωσιν. Ὁ δὲ καὶ αὐτὸς τὰ γεγραμμένα ἐπιλεξάμενος, πρῶτα μὲν ἐν θαύματος λόγῳ τὰ τοῦ πράγματος ἐποιεῖτο· καὶ τὸν ἐπὶ πάντων ὕμνει Θεόν, ὃς διὰ τῶν αὐτοῦ μαρτύρων τὸ καινὸν τοῦτο καὶ πᾶσαν ὑπερεκπλῆττον ἀκοὴν θαῦμα πεποίηκεν. Ἔπειτα, πολὺς ἦν κατὰ τοῦ Γότθου φερόμενος, τοιούτῳ ἑαυτὸν τολμήματι ἐπιδόντος. Χαλεπήνας τοίνυν ὁ στρατηλάτης, συγκάθεδρον μὲν ἑαυτῷ τὸν ἐπίσκοπον ποιεῖται, ἔπειτα τὸν Γότθον καὶ τὴν κόρην παρίστησι· καὶ εἰς

is, you unholy man? Do you know who this is and where you enclosed her and to which death you wished to deliver her, fearing neither nature, nor laws, nor those lengthy oaths? It is the confessors and martyrs of Christ, Samonas, Gourias, and Abibos, in whom I placed my faith, and, when I entrusted her to your barbarous right hand, it is they who saved her against all hope and brought her back to my bosom."

When the Goth heard all this and saw the maiden stand- 40
ing there, his voice failed out of shame and fear and he was speechless, unable to even open his mouth. A thorough examination followed and he was found clearly guilty of having committed such crimes against the maiden. Without even addressing a word to him, those present put him in a secure jail. Together with her daughter, the mother brought in a notary and had everything that had happened written down. They then presented this document to the all-holy bishop of Edessa—this was Eulogios. He read it and, together with all the clergy, went to the military commander of the city and gave him the written report. He too read the document and, at first, was amazed by what had taken place and began praising God who watches over everyone and who, through His martyrs, performed this novel miracle that astounded all ears. Then, he turned with much indignation against the Goth who committed such a brazen act. Enraged, the commander had the bishop join him as judge, and then summoned the Goth and the maiden. He ordered that the

ἐπήκοον τοῦ ὄχλου παντός—πολὺς δὲ ἄρα συνδεδραμή-
κει—τὰ κατὰ τοῦ Γότθου ἀναγνωσθῆναι διακελεύεται.

41   Ἀναγνωσθέντων οὖν, εἰ ἀληθῆ ταῦτα εἶεν, τοῦ Γότθου
ἀνεπυνθάνετο. Ὁ δὲ (τί γὰρ ἂν καὶ δράσειέ τις ὑφ' ἑαυτοῦ
καὶ τῆς ἀληθείας φανερῶς ἐλεγχόμενος;) μηδὲν τούτων
ψευδὲς εἶναι διωμολόγει· καὶ τὴν ὑπὲρ αὐτῶν ᾔτει συμπά-
θειαν. Καὶ ὁ στρατηλάτης, "Ἄδικέ," φησι, "καὶ φονεῦ, τί
δῆτα μηδὲ τὴν κρίσιν ἔδεισας τοῦ Θεοῦ, μηδὲ τὸν ἀλάθη-
τον αὐτοῦ ὀφθαλμόν; Εἴγε καὶ ἀνθρώπους λανθάνειν ἐξῆν,
τί μὴ τοὺς ὅρκους ἐδυσωπήθης; Τί μὴ τοὺς Ῥωμαίων ἠδέ-
σθης νόμους, οὕτως ἀνοσιωτάτῳ ἐπιχειρήσας τολμήματι;
Ἐπεὶ οὖν πάντων τούτων ἠλέγχθης καταφρονῶν, βαρυτέ-
ραν καὶ τὴν κόλασιν εἰσπραχθήσῃ." Εἶπε· καὶ ξίφει τὴν
αὐτοῦ κεφαλὴν ἀποκοπῆναι προστάττει, καὶ κατὰ πυρὸς
αὐτοῦ τὸ σῶμα ῥιφῆναι, ὡς ἂν μηδὲ ὁ χοῦς αὐτοῦ κοινω-
νήσοι χοός, μηδὲ τῇ κοινῇ πάντων δοθείη μητρί, τοιαῦτα
περὶ τὸ συγγενὲς ἐνδειξάμενος.

42   Ἐν ὅσῳ δὲ οἱ στρατιῶται τοῦ προστάγματος εἴχοντο, ὁ
τῷ Θεῷ φίλος ἐπίσκοπος ἐδεῖτο τοῦ στρατηλάτου φιλανθρωπίας, ὅσον εἰκός, τὸν ἄνδρα τυχεῖν, μηδὲ τῇ ἑαυτοῦ
ἀπονοίᾳ συναπολέσθαι. Ὁ δέ, "τοὺς τοῦ Χριστοῦ," φησι,
"δέδοικα μάρτυρας, οὓς οὗτος ἐγγυητὰς ἑαυτοῦ δέδωκε.
Οὗτοι γάρ, οἷα παρ' αὐτοῦ ψευσθέντες, εἰ μὴ δίκας ὑπ'
ἐμοῦ τῶν τετολμημένων οὗτος ἐκτίσει δικαίας, ἐμοὶ πάντως οὐκ αὐτῷ τὴν ὀφειλομένην ἐπάξουσι τιμωρίαν. Ἄλλως
τε, καὶ πολλοὺς ἑτέρους ὁμοίους γενέσθαι παρασκευάσει,
μὴ δικαίαν τὴν δίκην ἐπὶ τοῖς φθάσασι δεδωκώς."

43   Ἐπεὶ δὲ ὁ ἐπίσκοπος προσέκειτο πλέον, καὶ θερμοτέραν

accusations against the Goth be read aloud so that the entire crowd (indeed a large crowd had gathered) could hear.

When these were read aloud, he asked the Goth if the accusations were true. And he (what else could he have done, as both he himself and the truth proved him clearly guilty?) confessed that none of them were false and he asked for compassion for his crimes. "Wicked murderer," the commander said, "how did you not fear God's judgment, nor His all-seeing eye? Even if you could perhaps escape the notice of men, how did you not feel shame in breaking your oaths? How could you not respect the laws of the Romans, and dare to commit such an unholy crime? Since you were proven to disregard all of that, your sentence too will be heavier." He spoke thus and ordered that his head be cut off with a sword and his body thrown into the flames, so that neither his dust touch dust, nor be given to the earth, the common mother of all, since he had committed such offenses against his fellow humans. 41

While the soldiers were about to follow his orders, the bishop, a friend of God, pleaded with the commander that the man obtain some mercy, as much as might be fair, and not perish along with his mad folly. "I fear," the commander responded, "the martyrs of Christ, whom he presented as his guarantors. He deceived them in such a way that, unless this man pays a just penalty for his brazen deeds, they will surely exact their obligatory punishment upon me, and not upon him. In any case, if he is not punished fairly in accordance with his crimes, he will make many others act like him." 42

As the bishop, however, insisted and petitioned more 43

τὴν ὑπὲρ τοῦ ἀνδρὸς ἐποιεῖτο πρεσβείαν, ἀφαιρεῖ μὲν τῆς τιμωρίας ὁ στρατηλάτης τὸ πῦρ, τὴν δὲ διὰ τοῦ ξίφους ἐκκοπὴν τῆς κεφαλῆς ἐπιτείνει. Παραλαβόντες οὖν τὸν Γότθον οἱ στρατιῶται, καὶ τῆς πόλεως ἐξαγαγόντες, ξίφει κατὰ τὸ κελευσθὲν αὐτοῖς ἀφαιροῦσι τούτου τὴν κεφαλήν· ἐφ' ᾧ παρὰ πάντων αἶνος τῷ Σωτῆρι Χριστῷ καὶ τοῖς δι' αὐτὸν παθοῦσιν ὡς τὸ εἰκὸς ἀνεπέμπετο μάρτυσιν, ὅτι *τοῖς ὑπερηφάνοις ἀπέδωκεν ἀνταπόδοσιν,* εἰς δόξαν Πατρός, Υἱοῦ καὶ ἁγίου Πνεύματος, νῦν καὶ ἀεὶ καὶ εἰς τοὺς αἰῶνας τῶν αἰώνων. Ἀμήν.

fervently for the man, the commander removed the burning by fire from the sentence, but demanded the beheading by sword. The soldiers thus took the Goth, led him outside the city, and, as they were ordered, cut his head off with a sword; for this, as expected, everyone praised Christ the Savior and the martyrs who had suffered for Him, that *He rendered retribution to the arrogant ones,* for the glory of the Father, Son, and Holy Spirit, now and forever, and unto the ages of ages. Amen.

PASSION OF THE HOLY AND TRIUMPHANT MARTYR OF CHRIST BARBARA

Ἄθλησις τῆς ἁγίας καὶ καλλινίκου μάρτυρος τοῦ Χριστοῦ Βαρβάρας

Κύριε, εὐλόγησον.

Μαξιμιανῷ τῷ δυσσεβεῖ βασιλεῖ, πολλὴν περὶ τὴν τῶν εἰδώλων πλάνην εἰσφέροντι τὴν σπουδήν, ἔργον ἦν τοῦτο τῶν ἄλλων ἐπιμελέστατόν τε καὶ φροντίδος διηνεκοῦς ἄξιον, τὸ δαίμονας μὲν θεραπεύειν καὶ τὴν ἀσέβειαν κρατύνειν, ὁπόση δύναμις· τοὺς δὲ τὸ θεῖον ὄνομα τοῦ Χριστοῦ σεβομένους, ἢ τὴν εὐσεβῆ ταύτην ἐξόμνυσθαι πίστιν, ἤ, ποικίλαις παραδοθέντας κολάσεσιν, μετὰ τῶν προσόντων πάντων βιαίως ἐκπίπτειν καὶ τῆς ζωῆς.

2   Χώρα δέ τις κατ᾽ ἐκεῖνο καιροῦ, Ἡλιούπολις καλουμένη, ἄνδρα ἐκ τῶν ἐπισήμων ἔχουσα ἦν, Ἕλληνα μὲν τὴν θρησκείαν, πλούσιον δὲ κομιδῇ, καὶ τῇ κατὰ κόσμον περιφανείᾳ λαμπρότατον. Οὗτος Διόσκορος μὲν ἐκαλεῖτο, μιᾶς δὲ παιδὸς πατὴρ ἐγνωρίζετο (Βαρβάρα ταύτῃ τὸ ὄνομα)· καὶ τὸ φίλτρον οἷον, ἐπεὶ καὶ ἐπ᾽ αὐτῇ μόνῃ ἐσάλευε τὰς ἐλπίδας.

3   Ταύτην, ὡς λίαν εὐπρόσωπον οὖσαν καὶ τὸ κάλλος ἐξαίσιον, ἄμωμον περισώζειν βουλόμενος, καὶ διὰ τοῦτο μηδὲ θεατὴν εἶναι τοῖς ἔξω παραχωρῶν, πύργον δειμάμενος ὑψηλόν, ἐν αὐτῷ τε οἰκίαν φιλοτεχνήσας, ἐκεῖ τὴν Βαρβάραν ἔθετο κατοικεῖν, ἀπρόϊτόν τε οὖσαν, καὶ ὀφθαλμοῖς ἀνδρῶν πᾶσιν ἄψαυστον. Τὸ δὲ ἄρα θείας οἰκονομίας

154

Passion of the Holy and Triumphant Martyr of Christ Barbara

Lord, give the blessing.

Maximian, the impious emperor, exerted much effort in support of the fallacy of idolatry. This among all things was his most assiduous effort and constant concern: to serve the demons and strengthen impiety, as much as possible; and also that those who revered the divine name of Christ either renounce this true faith or be submitted to various tortures and violently lose, along with all their possessions, their very lives.

At that time, a certain place called Helioupolis had as one of its dignitaries a man who was pagan by religion, amply wealthy, and most illustrious in his worldly status. This man was called Dioskoros and was the father of a single child— her name was Barbara; very deep was his affection for her, as his hopes rested on her alone.

As she was very fair in appearance and of extraordinary beauty, and he wanted to preserve her unblemished, and would not even allow her to be seen by people outside, he built a high tower, fashioned chambers inside, and placed Barbara to live there, where she was restrained from going out and remained untouched by the eyes of all men. In fact, this was the work of divine dispensation, perceiving the fu-

ἔργον ἦν, ἄνωθεν σκοπουμένης τὸ μέλλον· ἐν αὐτῷ γὰρ ἡ
τοῦ Παρακλήτου χάρις τῶν ἀφανῶν αὐτῆς ὀφθαλμῶν
ἀφανῶς ἁψαμένη, φωτί τε θεογνωσίας ἐφώτισε, καὶ τὸν
ἀψευδῆ Θεὸν γνώριμον αὐτῇ παραδόξως κατέστησεν.

4   Εἶχεν οὖν τὴν παρθένον ὁ πύργος ἐπὶ τῷ θεμελίῳ ἤδη
τῆς πίστεως ᾠκοδομημένην, καὶ εἰς πολλῶν γενέσθαι σωτηρίαν συντηρουμένην. Ἐπεὶ δὲ γάμου ἦν ἤδη ὡραία, μέ-
ριμνα πολλὴ τῷ πατρί, τίς ὁ ληψόμενος αὐτὴν εἰς γυναῖκα.
Καὶ πολλοὶ μὲν τῶν εὐγενείᾳ καὶ πλούτῳ διαφερόντων εἰς
λόγους αὐτῷ περὶ συζυγίας συνῆλθον· πᾶσι γὰρ τὸ κάλλος, εἰ καὶ μὴ θεατόν, ἀλλ᾽ ὅμως ἀκουστὸν ὄν, περιμάχη-
τον αὐτῆς ἐποίει τὸν γάμον. Πλὴν ἀλλὰ τῷ πατρὶ σκαιὸν
ἐδόκει καὶ προφανῶς ἀνελεύθερον, εἰ μὴ καὶ τῇ θυγατρὶ
πρὸς γνῶσιν ἔλθοι τὸ σπουδαζόμενον, καὶ συναιροῦσα δὴ
καὶ αὐτὴ τῷ σκοπῷ γένοιτο. Ἀμέλει καὶ πρὸς αὐτὴν ἀφικόμενος, κοινολογεῖται περὶ τοῦ γάμου καί, ὅπως ἦν αὐτῷ
μελετώμενον, ἀπαγγέλλει.

5   Ἡ δέ, μηδὲ ἄκροις ὠσὶ τὸ πρᾶγμα μή τι γε εἰς καρδίαν
πεσεῖν βουλομένη, ἀλλ᾽ ὥσπερ ἀπηχές τι καὶ ἄτοπον ἀπο-
σεισαμένη, αὐτόν τε διώσατο μετ᾽ ὀργῆς τὸν πατέρα· καί,
"Ἦ μὴν μὴ δεύτερον," ἔφη, "περὶ τούτου λόγον μοι προσαγάγῃς, ἐπεὶ καὶ σὺ πατὴρ τὸ λοιπὸν οὐ κληθήσῃ, κἀμὲ
ἀναιρέτιν ἐμαυτῆς γενέσθαι παρασκευάσεις."

6   Ὁ δὲ πατήρ, τὸ πείθειν εὐγενὲς μᾶλλον οὐ τὸ βιάζεσθαι
κρίνας, αὐτῆς τε τὴν ἔνστασιν οὐ ῥοπὴν αὐθέκαστον, οὐδ᾽
ἀπείθειαν, ἀλλὰ πόθον ἁγνείας ἰσχυρὸν ἡγησάμενος,
ἄλλως τε δὲ καὶ διασκέψεως αὐτῇ παρέχων καιρόν, εἴπως
μεταβαλεῖ καὶ πειθήνιος αὐτῷ γένηται, πλέον οὐδὲν ἐπει-
πών, κάτεισι μὲν εὐθέως τοῦ πύργου. Πρὸς δὲ τὸ λουτρὸν

ture from on high; for in the tower, the grace of the Paraclete invisibly touched her inner invisible eyes, enlightened
her with the light of the knowledge of God, and miraculously made the true God known to her.

Thus the tower housed a virgin already edified upon the   4
foundation of faith and being preserved so as to offer salvation to many. As she quickly reached the age for marriage,
her father worried greatly about who would take her as his
wife. Many men, exceptional in their nobility and wealth,
met with him to discuss marriage; for even if her beauty had
remained unseen, its reputation had spread to all and made
marrying her a great prize. Nevertheless, her father thought
that it would be unwise and plainly uncivilized, if his daughter should not become aware of his plan and give her assent
to this objective. Indeed, he went to her, shared with her the
discussions about her marriage, and announced to her his
plans about it.

She, however, did not wish to even hear about the matter,   5
lest some of it taint her heart. She thus rejected it as something discordant and absurd and angrily pushed her father
away. "Don't ever say a word to me about this again," she
said, "for then you will not be called 'father' any more as you
will drive me to suicide."

Her father judged persuasion more noble than force, and   6
considered her refusal neither stubborn spite nor disobedience, but rather vehement desire for chastity. In any case, in
order to give her also time for reflection, so that she might
perhaps change her mind and acquiesce to him, he said
nothing more and forthwith descended from the tower. He

ὃ κατασκευάζων ἔτυχε νεωστὶ γενόμενος, ὅλον ἑαυτὸν ἀπησχόλει. Οὗ καὶ τὴν οἰκοδομὴν ἐπισπεύδων, πλῆθός τε τεχνιτῶν ἐφίστησι, καὶ ὅπως ἂν ἐργάσαιντο τὴν οἰκοδομὴν ἐπισκήψας, ἐντελῆ τε τὸν μισθὸν αὐτοῖς παρασχόμενος, εἰς μακροτέραν αὐτὸς ἀπεδήμει χώραν.

7 Ἐμβραδύνοντος δὲ τῇ ἀποδημίᾳ, ἡ τοῦ Θεοῦ δούλη Βαρβάρα κατῄει τοῦ πύργου, τὸ λουτρὸν ὅπως γίνοιτο ἐπισκεψομένη. Ἔπειτα ἐκεῖ γενομένη, καὶ δυσὶ φωτιζόμενον θυρίσι τὸ πρὸς μεσημβρίαν μέρος θεασαμένη, μέμψιν ἐπῆγε τοῖς τεχνίταις, "Ὅτου χάριν," λέγουσα, "ταῖς δυσὶ θυρίσι μὴ καὶ τὴν τρίτην προσέθεσθε, πλείονος οὕτω τῆς φωταυγείας μετὰ καὶ τοῦ εὐπρεποῦς ἐγγίνεσθαι δυναμένης;"

8 Τῶν δέ, "Οὕτω τὸν πατέρα τὸν σὸν ἐπιτάξαι," φαμένων, ἡ Βαρβάρα καὶ τὴν ἑτέραν αὐτοῖς ἰσχυρίζετο προσθεῖναι. Ὡς δὲ ὤκνουν αὐτοὶ τὴν προσθήκην, τοῦ πατρὸς τὸν φόβον ἀπολογίαν ὥσπερ εὐπρόσωπον προβαλλόμενοι, ἡ μακαρία τοὺς τρεῖς ἅμα τῶν δακτύλων παραδεικνῦσα, "Τὰς τρεῖς," ἔφη, "τὰς τρεῖς θυρίδας ὑμῖν κατασκευαστέον. Εἴ τι δὲ ὑπὲρ τούτου δυσχεραίνοι ἂν ὁ πατήρ, αὐτὴ τὸν λόγον ὑφέξω." Εἴκουσιν οἱ τεχνῖται, καὶ πληροῦσι τὸ κελευσθέν.

9 Ὡς οὖν ὁ τοῦ λουτροῦ ἅπας κόσμος ἐξείργαστο, πυκνότερον ἡ ἁγία παραβάλλουσα πρὸς τὴν θέαν, ἐπεὶ καὶ ἡ καρδία ταύτης τῇ τοῦ ἀγαθοῦ Πνεύματος χάριτι κάτοχος ἦν, πίστει τε τῆς πρὸς τὸν Χριστὸν παρρησίας ἐμπέπληστο, πρὸς τῷ κολύμβῳ στᾶσα, καὶ εἰς Ἀνατολὰς βλέψασα, τοῖς ἐν αὐτῷ μαρμάροις τὸν θεῖον τοῦ σταυροῦ τύπον διεχάραξε τῷ δακτύλῳ. Καὶ ἵνα καὶ τοῖς μετέπειτα τὸ γενόμενον τοῦτο γνώριμον ᾖ καὶ ἡ τοῦ Χριστοῦ κηρύττηται

then went to the bath, whose construction he had recently started, and became fully absorbed there. In order to expedite its completion, he appointed a large number of craftsmen and, after giving them instructions as to how they should complete the construction, he paid them in full, and left for a distant land.

As his absence was extended, Barbara, the servant of 7 God, went down from the tower in order to see how the bath was being built. When she came there and saw that the southern side was lit with two windows, she criticized the craftsmen, saying, "Why did you not add also a third window to the other two? In that way, there would be more illumination and it would look better as well."

And when they said, "Your father ordered it this way," 8 Barbara insisted that they add one more window. As they hesitated to make the addition and presented their fear of her father as a reasonable excuse, the blessed maiden showed them three of her fingers, and said: "You should build three, three windows. And if my father should be displeased about it, I will take the responsibility." The workmen yielded and fulfilled her command.

While, then, every aspect of the bath's decoration was 9 being worked on, the holy woman came to observe quite often. As her heart was possessed by the grace of the good Spirit and in faith she was filled with boldness on behalf of Christ, she stood by the pool, looked toward the East, and carved on the marbles with her finger the divine sign of the cross. And so that this deed might be known also to posterity and the power of Christ be proclaimed, until this very

δύναμις, ὁ σημειωθεὶς δακτύλῳ τοῦ σταυροῦ τύπος, οἷα
σιδήρῳ ἐγκολαφθείς, ἄχρι τῆς δεῦρο δείκνυται τῷ μαρ-
μάρῳ σεσημασμένος, οὐκ εἰς θαῦμα μόνον ἁπλῶς, ἀλλὰ
καὶ εἰς μείζονα πίστιν ἐνάγων τοὺς θεωμένους. Οὐ μὴν
ἀλλὰ καὶ αὐτὸ μέχρι καὶ νῦν τὸ λουτρὸν διασώζεται, ἴαμα
παντὸς πάθους τοῖς φιλοχρίστοις γινόμενον. Ὅπερ εἴ τις
τοῖς Ἰορδάνου ῥείθροις, ἢ τῇ τοῦ Σιλοὰμ πηγῇ, ἢ καὶ τῇ
προβατικῇ κολυμβήθρᾳ παραβαλεῖν ἐθελήσειεν, οὐκ ἂν
ἁμάρτοι τῆς ἀληθείας· καὶ δι' ἐκείνου γὰρ ὁμοίως ἡ τοῦ
Χριστοῦ δύναμις πολλὰ τῶν παραδόξων διενεργοῦσα δείκνυται.

10 Διὰ τούτου ποτὲ τοῦ λουτροῦ ἡ μάρτυς παρερχομένη,
τὸν ὀφθαλμόν τε τοῖς εἰδώλοις ἐπιβαλοῦσα, ἃ τῷ πατρὶ
ταύτης ἐτιμῶντο καὶ θεοὶ κακῶς ἐνομίζοντο, ἀηδῶς μὲν
ἤνεγκε πρὸς τὴν ὄψιν· βαρὺ δὲ καὶ τῆς ἀναισθήτου κατα-
στενάξασα τοῦ σεβομένου ταῦτα ψυχῆς, εἶτα καὶ εἰς τὰ
ἐκείνων ἐμπτύει πρόσωπα, ἐπειποῦσα, "Ὅμοιοι ὑμῖν γέ-
νοιντο οἱ προσκυνοῦντες ὑμᾶς, καὶ πάντες ὅσοι δὴ βοηθείας τῆς παρ' ὑμῶν δέονται." Οὕτως ἔφη. Καὶ εἰς τὸν
πύργον αὖθις ἀνελθοῦσα, προσευχαῖς ἐσχόλαζε καὶ νηστείαις, ὅλην τε ἑαυτὴν τῶν ἀγαθῶν ἐξήρτα τῶν οὐρανίων.

11 Οὐ πολὺ τὸ ἐν μέσῳ, καὶ ὁ πατὴρ ἤδη ταύτης ἐπανελ-
θών, τά ἐν τῷ οἴκῳ τε πάντα περισκοπῶν, ἐπεὶ καὶ τῷ
λουτρῷ τὴν ὄψιν ἐπιβεβλήκει, θεασάμενος πρὸς ταῖς δυσὶ
θυρίσι καὶ τρίτην ἐξειργασμένην, ἐπυνθάνετο πῶς ἄρα
τοῦτο παρὰ τὴν αὐτοῦ διάταξιν γένοιτο. Ὡς δὲ ἐκεῖνοι τῇ
θυγατρὶ παρέπεμψαν τὴν καινοτομίαν, μεταστειλάμενος

day the sign of the cross, engraved by her finger, can be seen etched in the marble, as if inscribed by iron, leading its viewers not simply into wonder, but also into greater faith. Not only that, but also the bath itself survives until now, offering cures for every affliction to the lovers of Christ. If someone should wish to compare it with the streams of the Jordan, or the spring of Shiloh, or even with the pool of Bethesda, he would not be far from the truth as, similarly to those, through this bath too the power of Christ is shown to accomplish many miracles.

Once, when passing through the bath, the martyr cast 10 her eyes upon the pagan idols which her father honored and wrongly esteemed as gods, and she felt displeasure at the sight. She thus sighed deeply against the senseless soul of her father who revered them and then also spat on their faces, saying, *"Let them become like you,* those who worship you and all those who seek your help." Thus she spoke. And she went back up to her tower again, where she passed her time in prayers and fasting, affixing her whole self to the heavenly blessings.

Not much time had passed when her father returned. 11 While examining everything in the house, he cast his eye also upon the bath. When he saw a third window made next to the other two, he asked how this could have happened against his orders. When they attributed the responsibility for this innovation to his daughter, he summoned her and

αὐτὴν ἀνηρώτα. Ἡ δὲ οὐχ ὅπως ἔξαρνος ἦν, ἀλλὰ καὶ οὕτως ἔδει πραχθῆναι, καὶ ὡς καλῶς πέπρακται διετείνετο.

12 Καὶ ὅς, πρὸς ὀργὴν εὐθὺς κινηθείς, "Καὶ λέγε μοι," ἔφη, "τὸν τρόπον, καὶ παρὰ τί βέλτιον οὕτως ἔχει." Ἡ δὲ παρ' ὃ πολὺ διαφέρειν τῶν δύο τὰς τρεῖς ἔλεγεν· "αἱ γὰρ τρεῖς," ἔφη, "θυρίδες φωτίζουσι πάντα ἄνθρωπον ἐρχόμενον εἰς τὸν κόσμον"· τοῦτο δὲ εἶπε πάντως τὴν τῆς Ἁγίας Τριάδος παραδηλοῦσα μεγαλειότητα.

13 Εἶτα πρὸς τὸ τοῦ λόγου ξενικὸν καὶ ἀσύνηθες ὁ πατὴρ διαταραχθείς, ἰδίᾳ ταύτην παραλαβών, καὶ πρὸς αὐτῷ τῷ κολύμβῳ τοῦ λουτροῦ γενόμενος, "Πῶς," ἔφη, "τὸ τῶν τριῶν θυρίδων φῶς παντὸς ἀνθρώπου φωτιστικὸν γίνεται;" Ἡ δέ, "Πρόσχες," ἔφη, "πάτερ, καὶ συνήσεις τὸ εἰρημένον." Καὶ ἅμα, τὸ τοῦ σταυροῦ ὑπεδήλου σημεῖον· εἶτα καὶ τοῖς δακτύλοις ὑποδεικνῦσα, "Ὅρα," ἔφη, "Πατήρ, Υἱός, καὶ τὸ ἅγιον Πνεῦμα· ὑπὸ τῷ φωτὶ τούτῳ κτίσις πᾶσα νοερῶς καταλάμπεται." Τοῦτον ἄρα τὸν ἀληθῆ λόγον ἡ φαύλη ἀκοὴ καὶ πρὸς ψεῦδος γεγυμνασμένη μὴ ἐνεγκοῦσα, θυμοῦ καὶ ὀργῆς ἐπληροῦτο. Καὶ ὁ πατὴρ τοῦ εἶναι πατὴρ ἐκλαθόμενος, τύραννος καὶ φονεὺς ἀπήει γενέσθαι· καὶ τὸ ξίφος ὃ παρήρτητο τῶν ὤμων διασπασάμενος, αὐτοχειρίᾳ τὴν Βαρβάραν ἔσπευδεν ἀνελεῖν.

14 Ἐκείνη δὲ χεῖρας ἅμα καὶ ὀφθαλμοὺς καὶ διάνοιαν εἰς οὐρανὸν ἄρασα, τὸν σώζειν δυνάμενον ἐκάλει πρὸς ἀρωγήν. Καὶ ὃς οὐκ ἠμέλει τὰ συνήθη ποιῶν· ἀλλ' ὥσπερ Θέκλαν τὴν πρωτομάρτυρα τῶν διωκόντων διέσωσε, πέτρᾳ τῇ προστυχούσῃ διαρραγῆναι καὶ αὐτὴν ἐγκολπώσασθαι διακελευσάμενος, οὕτω καὶ τὴν ἀοίδιμον ταύτην ὁμοίῳ

asked her about it. Not only did she not deny it, but also insisted that it should have been built this way and that it was good that it was done so.

Immediately moved to anger, he said, "Tell me how and 12 why it is better this way." And she responded that the three differ greatly from two; "For the three windows," she said, "*illuminate every man coming into this world*"; with these words she evidently alluded to the magnificence of the Holy Trinity.

Then her father, confused by her strange and unusual assertion, took her away in private; when they came to the pool of the bath, he said, "How does the light of the three windows illuminate every man?" "Pay attention, father," she said, "and you will understand my words." At once, she pointed to the sign of the cross and then, showing it also with her fingers, said, "Look, this is the Father, the Son, and the Holy Spirit; all of creation is spiritually illuminated by this light." Unable to bear these words of truth, the wicked listener, trained in falsehood, was filled with anger and rage. The father forgot that he was a father and was on his way to becoming a tyrant and murderer; he drew the sword that hung from his shoulders and rushed to kill Barbara with his own hands.

She raised her hands as well as her eyes and her mind to- 14 ward heaven and called for help to the one able to save her. And He did not neglect what He usually does; just as He had saved Thekla, the first female martyr, from her persecutors, by ordering the rocks in her way to split open and envelop her, by a similar and equal miracle He also saved this

καὶ ἴσῳ τῷ θαύματι διασώζει. Ὡς γὰρ ἐκεῖνος ὁ δήμιος (οὐδὲ γὰρ ὅσιον πατέρα τὸν μιαιφόνον καλεῖν) τὸ ξίφος ἄρας ἐχώρει κατὰ τῆς θυγατρός, πέτρα διχῇ τμηθεῖσα θείῳ καὶ παντουργῷ νεύματι ταύτην τε εἰσεδέξατο, καὶ χερσὶ φονώσαις ἄληπτον διεσώσατο, τόποις παραπέμψασα τοῖς ὀρεινοτέροις.

15   Ἀλλ' οὐκ ἦν οὐδὲ οὕτως συνιέναι τὸν καὶ λίθων αὐτῶν ἀπαθέστερον καὶ ἀναισθητότερον· ἔτι γὰρ εἴχετο τῆς ὁρμῆς, καὶ λαβεῖν ἐπόθει τὴν θυγατέρα, οὐχ ὡς πατὴρ ὢν ἐκεῖνος, ἀλλ' ὡς υἱὸς μᾶλλον τοῦ ἐξ ἀρχῆς ἀνθρωποκτόνου (κατὰ τὴν θείαν φάναι φωνήν), ἵν' εὑρὼν ἅμα καὶ θύσῃ καὶ ἀπολέσῃ. Ποιμέσι δὲ δύο περιτυχών, εἴ τι καὶ ἴσασι περὶ ταύτης ἀνεπυνθάνετο. Τούτων δέ, ἅτερος μέν, γνώμης ὢν συμπαθοῦς καὶ τὸ προδοῦναι τὴν διωκομένην οὐκ ἐπαινῶν, ἔξαρνος ἦν παραχρῆμα καὶ τὴν ἄγνοιαν ὑπεκρίνετο, ψεῦδος (εἶπεν ἄν τις) σωτήριον, ἀντὶ βλαπτούσης ἀληθείας ἑλόμενος—πλὴν ἀλλ' αἰσχυνέσθω φανερῶς ἐνταῦθα Ἡρώδης οὐ καλῶς εὐορκῶν (ἵνα τι καὶ παρενείρω τῷ διηγήματι) καὶ ἡδονῆς ἐκδίκησιν πονηρᾶς τοῦ ὅρκου τὴν φυλακὴν ποιούμενος. Ὁ δὲ ἄλλος, γλώττῃ μὲν οὐδαμῶς, τῷ δακτύλῳ δὲ κακουργότερον ὑποφαίνων, τὴν ὡς αὐτὴν ἀπάγουσαν ὑπεδείκνυ. Τοιγαροῦν οὐκ ἤνεγκε τὸ πραχθὲν ἡ δίκη, ἀλλὰ τιμωρίαν ἐπῆγε παραχρῆμα τοῦ κακουργήματος. Καὶ τὰ αὐτοῦ θρέμματα τῆς μάρτυρος ἐπαρασαμένης, οὐκ ἔτι θρέμματα ἦν· ἀλλ' εἰς κανθάρων ὁμοιότητα μετεβλήθη, στήλη κατήγορος ἄχρι τέλους, τὸν τῆς ἁγίας τάφον περιϊπτάμενα.

16   Τούτοις οὖν τοῖς ὑποδείγμασι τοῦ δολίου Διόσκορος

celebrated maiden. When that executioner (for it would not be proper to call this bloodthirsty man a father) moved against his daughter with his sword raised, a rock was split in two by a divine and all-powerful signal and took her in, saving her from his murderous hands and bringing her to a mountainous place.

Still he was incapable of understanding, as he was more 15 unfeeling and more insensitive than stones. He continued to follow his impulse, yearning to seize his daughter, in order to find, kill, and slaughter her, not as a father, but rather as the son of the *original murderer of humankind* (to use the words of the divine voice). He chanced upon two shepherds and asked them whether they perhaps knew anything about her. Of them, the one was compassionate and did not approve the betrayal of her who was pursued. He thus immediately denied knowing anything and feigned ignorance, choosing a saving lie (one might say) instead of the harmful truth—in comparison to him (if I may introduce a digression from my narrative), Herod should be ashamed that he took an oath, yet not for a good purpose, and used his keeping of that oath as vindication for evil pleasure. The second man, however, did not reveal anything with words, but indicated rather more cruelly with his finger the road leading to her. Yet justice could not bear his action and exacted vengeance for the crime straightaway. The martyr put a curse on his sheep and they were sheep no more; turned into scarab beetles, they are a perpetual reminder of the crime, flying around the saint's tomb.

Still, following the directions of that wicked man, the 16

ἀκολουθήσας ὁ παραπλήξ, καὶ τὴν ἁγίαν ἐπ' ὄρους κατα-
λαβών, πρῶτα μὲν οὕτως ὡς εἶχε θυμοῦ πληγαῖς κατα-
κόπτει. Ἔπειτα τῆς κόμης αὐτὴν λαβόμενος, καὶ πρὸς
βίαν ἕλκων, τότε μὲν οἰκίσκῳ βραχεῖ κατακλείει, φύλακας
ἐπιστήσας, καὶ τὴν θύραν σφραγῖσιν ἀσφαλισάμενος.
Εἶτα, καὶ πολλῷ τῷ τάχει πρὸς τὸν ἡγεμόνα Μαρκιανὸν
ἀφικόμενος, ὃς τὴν ἀρχὴν τότε τῶν ἐκεῖσε διεῖπεν, αὐτῷ
πάντα τὰ τοῦ πράγματος καταλέγει, καὶ τὸ κεφάλαιον ὅτι
θεοὺς μὲν τὸ θυγάτριον ἀρνηθείη, τὰ δὲ Χριστιανῶν
ἕλοιτο παρ' ἐλπίδα τιμᾶν. Ταῦτά τε ἔφη· καὶ ἀγαγών, χερσὶν αὐτὴν ἔκδοτον ταῖς ἐκείνου ποιεῖ, κατὰ τῶν ἰδίων ὅρ-
κώσας θεῶν μὴ φείσασθαι τούτου τῆς θυγατρός (ὦ σπλάγ-
χνων πατρικῶν ὁ πατήρ!), ἀλλὰ καὶ βιαιότατα μετελθεῖν,
καὶ βασάνοις ἀναλῶσαι χαλεπωτάταις.

17   Ὁ τοίνυν Μαρκιανὸς δικαστήριον καθίσας εὐθύς, καὶ
τὴν ἁγίαν παραστησάμενος, τό τε τοῦ ἤθους ὁμοῦ κό-
σμιον, καὶ τὸ τῆς μορφῆς πάγκαλον θεασάμενος, τῶν τοῦ
πατρὸς ὅρκων ἐπιλαθόμενος, θαυμάζειν τότε μᾶλλον ἢ
κολάζειν ἕτοιμος ἦν. Ταύτῃ γοῦν καὶ ῥήμασι χρηστοτέ-
ροις, "Οἴκτειρον σεαυτήν," ἔλεγεν, "ὦ Βαρβάρα· καὶ μεθ'
ἡμῶν θῦσαι τοῖς θεοῖς προθυμήθητι. Ὡς ἔγωγε κήδομαί
σου καὶ βασάνοις κάλλος τοσοῦτον ὑποβαλεῖν φείδομαι!
Εἰ δὲ μὴ πεισθείης, ἀλλ' ἐμὲ χρήσασθαί σοι καταναγκάσεις
τὸ λοιπὸν ὡς οὐ βούλομαι."

18   Ἡ δὲ μάρτυς, "*Ἐγὼ θυσίαν αἰνέσεως τῷ ἐμῷ*," ἔφη,
"*προσάγω Θεῷ, ὃς οὐρανόν τε καὶ γῆν ἔκτισε, καὶ τὰ ἐν
αὐτοῖς ἅπαντα*. Περὶ δὲ τῶν ματαίων, φημί, θεῶν σου, προ-
είρηται μὲν ἐν θείῳ Πνεύματι τῷ Δαυίδ, ὅτι *τὰ εἴδωλα τῶν*

deranged Dioskoros caught up with the saint on the mountain. At first, he started beating her angrily with heavy blows. Then, grabbing her by the hair and dragging her by force, he imprisoned her in a small hut, establishing guards, and securing the door with seals. Then with great speed, Dioskoros went to the governor Markianos, who at that time held power there, and told him everything about the matter; most importantly, he told him that his little daughter had disowned the gods and had unexpectedly chosen to honor the faith of the Christians. That is what he said. He then brought her in, and handed her over to the governor, making him swear by his own gods that he would not spare his daughter (oh, what a paternal heart this father had!), but would treat her with the utmost violence and kill her with the most grievous tortures.

Markianos set up a trial at once and had the saint appear before the court. But when he saw the elegance of her comportment as well as the exceptional beauty of her appearance, he forgot his oaths to her father and was ready to marvel rather than punish. Using kind words, he said: "Have mercy on yourself, O Barbara. Join us willingly and sacrifice to the gods. How much indeed I care about you and how I hesitate to subject such great beauty to tortures! If you do not change your mind, however, you will then force me to deal with you in a way which I do not want." 17

The martyr said, "I offer *my sacrifice of thanksgiving* to my God, who created *heaven and earth,* and *all that is therein.* As for your empty gods, I say, it has been already spoken by David in the divine Spirit that *the idols of the heathen are silver* 18

ἐθνῶν ἀργύριον καὶ χρυσίον, ἔργα χειρῶν ἀνθρώπων, καὶ ὅτι πάντες οἱ θεοὶ τῶν ἐθνῶν δαιμόνια. Σύμφημι δὲ κἀγώ· καὶ τὴν πρὸς αὐτοὺς ἐλπίδα κενὴν εἶναι καὶ ματαίαν διαρρήδην ὁμολογῶ."

19   Ταῦτα τῆς μάρτυρος εἰπούσης, ὁ δικαστὴς πρὸς ὀργὴν ἐξαφθείς, περιδυθεῖσαν αὐτὴν κελεύει βοείοις νεύροις ὠμοῖς ἀνηλεῶς καταξαίνεσθαι. Εἶτα δριμυτέραν αὐτῇ τὴν αἴσθησιν ἐνθεῖναι βουλόμενος, καὶ τριχίνοις ὑφάσμασιν ἐπιτάττει προστρίβεσθαι τὰς πληγάς. Οὕτως οὖν ἀπανθρώπως αἰκιζομένης, χαλεπαὶ τῷ σώματι καὶ ἀνήκεστοι ἀνεστομοῦντο πληγαί, ὡς τὸ ὅλον ἔδαφος τῆς παρθένου περιερράνθαι τοῖς αἵμασιν. Ἔπειτα μετὰ τὰς πληγάς, τὸ δεσμωτήριον αὐτὴν διαδέχεται, τοῦ ἡγεμόνος πρὸς διάσκεψιν ἐνασχολουμένου, τίνι τὸ μετὰ ταῦτα τιμωρίᾳ τὴν μάρτυρα παραδώσει.

20   Ἤδη δὲ μεσούσης νυκτός, φῶς τε αὐτὴν φαιδρὸν ἄνωθεν περιλάμπει· καὶ Χριστὸς ἐπιφαίνεται, θάρσος τε αὐτῇ ἐντιθείς, καὶ τὰ ἐξ ἀνθρώπων κακὰ μὴ δεδιέναι ὅλως ἐγκελευόμενος. "Ἐγὼ γάρ εἰμι μετὰ σοῦ," ἔφη, "καὶ ὑπὸ τῇ σκιᾷ τῶν ἐμῶν πτερύγων ἔσῃ φυλαττομένη." Οὔπω τέλος εἶχον οἱ πρὸς τὴν μάρτυρα τοῦ Χριστοῦ λόγοι, καὶ τὸ τοῦ Ἡσαΐου ἐπ᾽ αὐτῇ πέρας εἶχε, ταχὺ τῶν ἰαμάτων ἀνατειλάντων αὐτῇ, καὶ τῶν πληγῶν, ὥσπερ ἐξ ἀρχῆς μηδὲ γενομένων, ἀπελαθέντων τοῦ σώματος. Χαρὰ δὲ τὴν ἁγίαν εἶχε καὶ ἀγαλλίασις, εὐφροσύνη τε αἰώνιος ὑπὲρ κεφαλῆς αὐτῆς, τὸ τοῦ Ἡσαΐου πάλιν εἰπεῖν.

21   Γυνὴ δέ τις θεοσεβὴς καὶ φοβουμένη τὸν Κύριον, Ἰουλιανὴ ὄνομα, τῇ μάρτυρι τότε συνοῦσα, ἐπεὶ τῶν εἰς αὐτὴν

and gold, the work of men's hands, and that *all the gods of the nations are demons.* I too agree; and I loudly declare that believing in them is futile and in vain."

When the martyr spoke thus, the judge became enraged 19 and ordered that she be stripped naked and scourged mercilessly and savagely by rawhide whips. Then, wishing to impose an even more bitter pain on her, he ordered that her wounds be also rubbed with haircloth. While she was being tortured in this inhumane manner, awful and fatal wounds opened on her body and the whole ground was spattered with the virgin's blood. Then, after the lashes, the prison received her, as the governor was busy thinking about the punishment to which he would next subject the martyr.

It was already the middle of the night, when a beaming 20 heavenly light illuminated her. And Christ appeared, instilling courage in her, and urging her not to fear at all afflictions imposed by humankind. *"For I am with you,"* He said, "and you will be protected under *the shade of my wings."* Christ was still speaking to the martyr, when Isaiah's words were fulfilled for her, for *His healings sprang forth speedily* upon her, and her wounds disappeared from her body as if they had never even been there before. *Joy and exultation* overcame the saint, and *everlasting gladness was upon* her *head* (to use again the words of Isaiah).

A certain pious and Lord-fearing woman, whose name 21 was Iouliane, who happened then to be with the martyr,

παραδόξων θεατὴς γέγονε, καὶ ὅπως ἀφανεῖς ἐκ τοῦ παραχρῆμα κατέστησαν αἱ πληγαί, δοῦσά τε δόξαν τῷ Θεῷ, καὶ
ἀδελφὰ τῇ μάρτυρι συμφρονήσασα, πρὸς πληγὰς ἑαυτὴν
καὶ μάστιγας παρεσκεύαζεν.

22   Εἶτα πρὸς δευτέραν καθίσας ὁ ἡγεμὼν τὴν ἐξέτασιν, καὶ
τῆς ἁγίας προσαχθείσης αὐτῷ καὶ φρικτὸν θέαμα πᾶσιν
ὀφθείσης, ὅτι μηδὲ τὸ τυχὸν σπάραγμα τῷ σώματι αὐτῆς
ἐδηλοῦτο, μηδὲ μώλωψ μηδείς, ὁ δικαστὴς (φεῦ!) φανερῶς
τυφλώττων πρὸς τὴν ἀλήθειαν, ἀπολιπὼν τῇ μεγάλῃ τοῦ
Θεοῦ δυνάμει τὸ γεγονὸς ἐπιγράφειν, μετάμελον τε λαβεῖν τοῦ προτέρου βίου καὶ τῆς ἀπάτης, ὁ δὲ καὶ μᾶλλον
ἀπηναισχύντει· καὶ τοῖς αὑτοῦ θεοῖς τὴν ἴασιν ἐλογίζετο·
καί, "Ὁρᾷς," ἔλεγε, "πῶς ἀντιποιοῦνταί σου οἱ θεοί, Βαρβάρα, καὶ κηδόμενοί σου τὰς πληγὰς ἐθεράπευσαν;"

23   Πρὸς ὃν ἡ τοῦ Χριστοῦ μάρτυς, "Οἱ ὁμοίως σοι τυ-
φλώττοντες," ἔφη, "καὶ ἀνθρωπίνης χειρὸς δεόμενοι πρὸς
τὴν τοῦ εἶναι παραγωγήν, πῶς ἄρα τοιοῦτον ἠδύναντο
δρᾶν; Ἀλλ' εἰ τὸν ἐμὲ ἰασάμενον ὅστις εἴη βούλει μαθεῖν,
Ἰησοῦς Χριστός ἐστιν ὁ Θεοῦ τοῦ ζῶντος Υἱός· ὃν σὲ
καθορᾶν ἀμήχανον, βαθεῖ σκότῳ πηρωθέντα τῆς ἀσεβείας
τοὺς τῆς ψυχῆς ὀφθαλμούς."

24   Τοῖς λόγοις τούτοις ὁ ἡγεμὼν εἰς μείζονα τὸν θυμὸν
ἐκκαυθείς, καὶ μηδὲ κατέχειν ἑαυτὸν οἷός τε ὤν, τοῖς παρ-
εστῶσι διακελεύεται, σιδηροῖς ὄνυξι τὰς πλευρὰς τῆς μάρτυρος ἀποξέειν, πρὸς δὲ καὶ λαμπάσι πυρὸς τὰ ἤδη ξαν-
θέντα τῶν μελῶν ἐπικαίειν, εἶτα καὶ σφύρᾳ παίειν τὴν
τιμίαν αὐτῆς κεφαλήν. Ὧν δὴ καὶ ὡς τάχιστα πραττομένων, ἡ θεοσεβὴς Ἰουλιανὴ καθορῶσα, καὶ τὴν ψυχὴν

became a witness to the wonders performed on Barbara's body and saw how Barbara's wounds suddenly disappeared. She thus gave glory to God, assumed the same attitude as the martyr, and prepared herself also for wounds and lashes.

When the governor sat down for the second interrogation and the saint was led to him, it was an awesome sight for everyone's eyes, as neither a single cut nor a single bruise was visible on her body; the judge (alas!) remained clearly blind to the truth, and failed to ascribe what had happened to the great power of God and thus to repent for his prior life and treachery. Instead, he acted even more shamelessly and reckoned his own gods responsible for the healing. "Do you see, O Barbara," he said, "how the gods lay claim on you, and, caring for you, have healed your wounds?" 22

The martyr of Christ responded to him: "How could those who are blind just like you, and need human hands so as to come into being, how could they perform something like this? Rather—if you wish to learn who is the one who cured me—it *was* Jesus *Christ, Son of the living God,* whom it is impossible for you to see, since the eyes of your soul are incapacitated by the deep darkness of impiety." 23

Inflamed to greater anger by these words, and unable to restrain himself, the governor ordered those present to scrape the martyr's sides with iron claws, and, in addition, to burn her already scraped limbs with lit torches, and then to also strike her honorable head with a hammer. These tortures were performed most speedily and the pious Iouliane, looking on, suffered severely in her soul and, since she was 24

ἰσχυρῶς ἀλγοῦσα, ἐπεὶ μὴ βοηθεῖν ἐδύνατο, ὅπερ ἦν αὐτῇ δυνατὸν ἐποίει· καὶ τὸ φίλτρον ὡς εἶχεν ἐδείκνυ, μηδὲν τῶν παρόντων καὶ τοῦ ἄρχοντος ἐπιστρεφομένη, ἀλλ᾽ ἀστακτὶ τὸ δάκρυον τῶν ὀμμάτων προϊεμένη. Ὁ Μαρκιανὸς οὖν εἰς αὐτὴν ἀποβλέψας καὶ ἥτις εἴη μαθών, ἐπεὶ καὶ αὐτὴν εἶναι Χριστιανὴν ἤκουε καὶ τῇ πρὸς τὴν Βαρβάραν συμπαθείᾳ παθαίνεσθαι τὴν ψυχήν, συλληφθῆναι καὶ ταύτην κελεύει, καὶ τῷ ξύλῳ προσαναρτᾶσθαι, καὶ τῇ μάρτυρι παραπλησίως σιδηροῖς ξυστῆρσι τὰς πλευρὰς ἀποξέεσθαι.

25 Ἡ μὲν οὖν πολύαθλος Βαρβάρα, δεινῶς ξεομένη, ὑψοῦ τὸ ὄμμα διάρασα, "Σύ γινώσκεις," ἔφη, "*καρδιογνῶστα Θεέ, ὅτι, σὲ ποθοῦσα καὶ τοὺς σοὺς στέργουσα νόμους, ὅλην ἐμαυτήν σοι προσήγαγον, καὶ τῆς σῆς ἀπήρτησα δεξιᾶς. Αὐτὸς οὖν Δέσποτα, μὴ ἐγκαταλίπῃς ἡμᾶς, ἀλλ᾽ ἀντιλαβοῦ κατὰ τὸ ἔλεός σου· καὶ τελειῶσαι τὸν παρόντα δρόμον ἀμφοτέρας ἐνίσχυσον.*"

26 Ἀλλ᾽ οὕτω μὲν ἡ τοῦ Χριστοῦ μάρτυς τὸν δι᾽ ὃν ταῦτα ὑπέμενε Δεσπότην ἠξίου, τὴν φυσικὴν ἀσθένειαν ῥωσθῆναι τῇ παρ᾽ αὐτοῦ ῥοπῇ δεομένη· ἤδει γὰρ τίς ὁ ἀψευδῶς εἰρηκώς, ὡς *τὸ μὲν πνεῦμα πρόθυμον, ἡ δὲ σὰρξ ἀσθενής*. Ὁ τύραννος δέ, καθάπερ ἀντίπαλον ἑαυτὸν τοῖς ὅλοις ἀντιτιθείς, ἵνα ψυχῆς ἀνδρείαν ἀλγεινῶν ἡττήσῃ περιουσίᾳ, πρὸς ἑτέραν ἅμα τρέπεται τιμωρίαν· καὶ σμίλῃ τοὺς μασθοὺς αὐτῶν ἐκκοπῆναι κελεύει.

27 Οἶδ᾽ ὅτι καὶ πρὸς τὴν ἀκοὴν μόνην τοῦ πάθους ἰλιγγιάσατε. Τί οὖν ἔμελλεν αὐτὸ τὸ πάσχειν ποιεῖν, καὶ ταῦτα γυναῖκας, εἰ μὴ φίλτρον ἦν τὸ συνέχον (φίλτρον ἄμαχον τοῦ Χριστοῦ), μηδὲ πίστις ἐνεύρου τὰς ἐκείνων ψυχάς;

unable to help, did what she could do: she showed all her affection, paying attention neither to those who were present nor to the governor, and pouring floods of tears from her eyes. Markianos turned his gaze toward her and asked who she was. As soon as he learned that she too was a Christian who felt compassion in her soul for Barbara, he ordered that she too be arrested, that she be hung on a wooden cross, and, just like the martyr, that her sides be torn by iron scrapers.

While being cruelly scraped, Barbara, the sufferer of 25 many trials, raised her eyes toward the sky and said: "You know, O God, *knower of hearts,* that desiring You and loving Your laws, I offered my whole self to You and fixed my hopes on Your right hand. *Do not forsake us,* therefore, O Lord, but help us according to Your mercy. Give us both the strength to complete this present course."

This is how the martyr of Christ beseeched the Lord, for 26 whom she endured these torments, asking that their natural weakness be fortified with His might; she after all knew who had spoken the unadulterated truth that *the spirit is willing, but the flesh is weak.* The tyrant, however, as if setting himself up as an absolute rival, so that he might defeat the valor of her soul with an abundance of sufferings, turned to another punishment: he ordered that the breasts of both women be cut off with a knife.

I know that you felt dizzy only hearing about this torture. 27 What, then, would the actual suffering cause—to women no less—unless intense love, the indomitable love for Christ, held them together and unless faith invigorated their souls?

Πλὴν ἀλλὰ καὶ τὴν τοῦ Χριστοῦ δούλην Βαρβάραν, τί φάρμακον αὐταῖς ἔσται πρὸς τοσαύτην ὀδύνης ἀκμήν, ἐλάνθανεν οὐδαμῶς. Διὰ ταῦτα καὶ τὴν ἐξ ὕψους πάλιν ἐκάλει βοήθειαν, "Μὴ ἀποστρέψῃς ἀφ' ἡμῶν," λέγουσα, "τὸ πρόσωπόν σου, Χριστέ· καὶ τὸ πανάγιόν σου Πνεῦμα μὴ ἀντανέλῃς. Ἀπόδος ἡμῖν, Κύριε, τὴν ἀγαλλίασιν τοῦ σωτηρίου σου· καὶ Πνεύματι ἡγεμονικῷ στήριξον ἡμᾶς ἐν τῷ φόβῳ σου."

28   Ὡς δὲ καὶ πρὸς ταύτην τὴν τιμωρίαν μία καὶ ἡ αὐτὴ ἀμφοτέραις ὑπῆρχε γνώμη καὶ καρτερία, ὁ ἡγεμὼν σοφώτερόν τι, μᾶλλον δὲ κακουργότερον, ἐννοήσας, διΐστησιν αὐτὰς ἀπ' ἀλλήλων. Καὶ Ἰουλιανὴν μὲν τῇ εἰρκτῇ παραδοθῆναι, Βαρβάραν δὲ γυμνωθεῖσαν, κελεύει διὰ πάσης θριαμβευθῆναι τῆς χώρας, καὶ προσέτι πληγαῖς μαστίζεσθαι.

29   Ἡ μάρτυς οὖν τῇ ἀσχήμονι ταύτῃ περιαγωγῇ θεατριζομένη, τὰ συνήθη πάλιν ἐποίει. Καὶ πρὸς οὐρανὸν ἀτενίσασα, "ὁ τὸν οὐρανόν," εἶπεν, "περιβάλλων τοῖς νέφεσιν, καὶ τὴν γῆν σπαργανῶν ὁμίχλῃ, αὐτὸς καὶ τὴν ἐμὴν γύμνωσιν σκέπασον, βασιλεῦ· καὶ τὰ ἐμὰ μέλη ἀθέατα γενέσθαι ὀφθαλμοῖς ἀσεβῶν παρασκεύασον, ἵνα μὴ ἡ σὴ δούλη, Χριστέ, μυκτηρισμός τε καὶ χλευασμὸς γένωμαι τοῖς κύκλῳ ἡμῶν." Ἤκουσεν ἐκ ναοῦ ἁγίου αὐτοῦ ὁ ταχὺς Θεὸς εἰς ἀντίληψιν· καὶ παραυτίκα ἐπιφανείς, χαρᾶς μὲν αὐτῆς πληροῖ τὴν καρδίαν, ἀόρατον δὲ στολὴν αὐτῇ περιτίθησι· καὶ οὕτω τὴν πομπὴν διανύσασαν, Μαρκιανῷ καὶ αὖθις παριστῶσι τῷ μιαρῷ.

In any case, Christ's servant, Barbara, knew perfectly well what would be the cure for the agony of such pain. She thus started invoking again help from on high, saying: "*Hide not Your face from us,* O Christ; *and take not Your all-holy spirit from us. Restore unto us,* Lord, *the joy of Your salvation; and uphold us with Your directing Spirit* in the fear of You."

Since the spirit and endurance of both these women was one and the same even toward this punishment, the governor thought of something shrewder, or rather more cruel, and separated them from each other. He ordered that Iouliane be delivered into prison, and that Barbara be stripped naked and be paraded through the entire land, and that she be flogged with even more whippings. 28

While exposed in such shameful public spectacle, the martyr followed again her customary course of action. Gazing toward heaven, she said: "You, *who cover the heaven with clouds* and *swathe* the earth *in mist,* now, O king, cover my nakedness too; make my limbs invisible to the eyes of impious men, lest I, Your servant, O Christ, be mocked and ridiculed by those against us round about." God, who is swift in succor, *heard out of His holy temple.* He appeared at once, filled her heart with joy, and placed an invisible garment around her. She walked the procession in this way before being brought to the vile Markianos yet again. 29

30 Ἐπεὶ οὖν ἔγνω ταύτην τε καὶ τὴν τὰ ἴσα φρονοῦσαν
πάγκαλον Ἰουλιανὴν μήτε ἀγαθῶν ἐπαγγελίαις μήτε
κακῶν ἐπινοίαις μηδὲ βραχὺ πειθομένας, τὸ πλείονα τὴν
αἰσχύνην ὄφλειν ἀδυνάτοις ἐπιχειρῶν ὡς φανερὰν ἄνοιαν
ἐκτρεπόμενος, τὴν ἀπόφασιν ἐπάγει κατ' ἀμφοτέρων, ξίφει τὰς κεφαλὰς αὐτῶν ἐκκοπῆναι κελεύσας.

31 Παρὼν οὖν ὁ παιδοκτόνος ταύτης πατήρ, καὶ θεατὴς
ὑπάρχων τῶν πραττομένων, οὐκ ἠγάπησε τοῦτο μόνον,
οὐδὲ ἠρκέσθη τῷ μεγέθει τῆς συμφορᾶς, τῷ πατρικοῖς
ὀφθαλμοῖς θυγατέρα ἰδεῖν, καὶ θυγατέρα οὕτω καλήν,
χερσὶ δημίων ἀναιρουμένην. Ἀλλ' εἰ μὴ καὶ αὐτόχειρ
ἐκεῖνος τῆς πληγῆς γένοιτο, ἀσθένειαν ἔκρινε τοῦτο καὶ
μαλακίαν ψυχῆς, ὥσπερ τὸ μὴ καινὸς ὀφθῆναι κακὸς
αἰσχύνην εἶναι φανερὰν λογιζόμενος. Διὰ ταῦτα γοῦν καὶ
τῆς ἀποφάσεως ἤδη ἐξενεχθείσης, παραλαμβάνει τὴν μάρτυρα, χερσὶν οἰκείαις τὴν σφαγὴν ἐργασόμενος.

32 Ἐν τῷ ὄρει τοίνυν ἀπαγομένη, καὶ Ἰουλιανῆς ταύτῃ
συνεπομένης, ἡ Βαρβάρα καὶ πρὸς τῷ τέλει οὖσα, τῆς φίλης ἐφρόντισε προσευχῆς. Καὶ εἰς γόνυ κλιθεῖσα, "Ἄναρχε,"
ἔφη, "Θεέ, ὁ τὸν οὐρανὸν τείνας ὡσεὶ καμάραν, τὴν δὲ γῆν
ἐφ' ὑδάτων ἑδράσας, ὁ νεφέλαις ὕειν προστάττων, ἥλιον τε
φωταγωγὸν πᾶσι παραστησάμενος, καὶ τὰς κοινὰς ταύτας
ἀπολαύσεις δικαίοις τε καὶ ἀδίκοις, ἀγαθοῖς ἅμα καὶ πονη-
ροῖς χορηγῶν, αὐτὸς καὶ νῦν ἐμοῦ δεομένης εἰσάκουσον,
βασιλεῦ. Καὶ ὃς ἂν τοῦ σοῦ ὀνόματος καὶ τῆς ἐμῆς ἀθλήσεως διαμνημονεύσει, μὴ λοιμώδης νόσος τῷ οἴκῳ αὐτοῦ
ἐπισκήψειε, μὴ ἄλλο τι μηδὲν τῶν λωβᾶσθαι σώματα καὶ

When he realized that both Barbara and Iouliane—a 30 woman most beautiful and of equal resolve—would not be persuaded, not even a little bit, neither by promises of blessings, nor by threats of torments, and as he wanted to avoid the clear folly of incurring greater shame for attempting what is impossible, he passed the final sentence against both of them; he ordered that they be decapitated by the sword.

Barbara's father, the child-murderer, happened to be present as a spectator of the events, and neither was it enough for him to simply watch, nor was he satisfied by the magnitude of this misfortune, that paternal eyes would witness the death of a daughter, such a beautiful daughter, at the hands of executioners. Rather, he judged that it would be a sign of weakness and soft-heartedness, if he himself did not inflict the fatal blow with his own hands, as if he reckoned it a clear disgrace not to become an innovator in wickedness. Therefore, indeed, when the sentence was already issued, he seized the martyr in order to perform the slaughter with his own hands.

Led up to the mountain, with Iouliane accompanying her, 32 Barbara, even as she was nearing her end, devoted herself to her beloved prayer. Going down on her knees, she said: "O God, You without beginning, who stretched out *the heavens as a curtain,* established *the earth above the waters,* and commanded the clouds to rain, who set the sun as the light for all, and who grants these joys to everyone, whether just or unjust, good or evil, hear me too, now as I implore You, O king. Let no pestilence, nor anything else that can injure and harm one's body, befall the house of whoever will mention Your name and remember my martyrdom. For You know,

λυπεῖν δυναμένων· οἶδας γάρ, Κύριε, ὅτι σάρκες ἡμεῖς καὶ αἷμα, ποίημα τῶν σῶν ἀχράντων χειρῶν, καὶ εἰκόνι σῇ καὶ ὁμοιώσει τετιμημένοι."

33 Ἔφη· καὶ φωνή τις παραδόξως οὐρανόθεν ἡκούετο, αὐτήν τε καὶ Ἰουλιανὴν τὴν σύναθλον ἐκκαλουμένη πρὸς οὐρανόν, καὶ τῶν αἰτηθέντων ἅμα τὴν ἐκπλήρωσιν ἐπαγγελλομένη. Ταύτης δὴ τῆς γλυκείας φωνῆς ἐνωτισθεῖσα Βαρβάρα, ὁδοῦ τε εἴχετο, καὶ πρὸς τὸν τοῦ τέλους τόπον ἡπείγετο. Ἐπεὶ δὲ καὶ φθάσασα ἥν, τὴν κεφαλὴν κλίνασα, πατρικαῖς χερσὶ τῷ πατρικῷ ξίφει τὴν τελείωσιν δέχεται, καρπὸς ἀγαθὸς ἐκ πονηροῦ δένδρου παραδόξως ἀναφανεῖσα, καὶ Ἰουλιανῆς αὐτῇ πρός τινος τῶν ἐκεῖσε στρατιωτῶν συνάμα τελειωθείσης.

34 Ἐν ᾧ δὲ ταῦτα γέγονε, καὶ τὸν ἀσεβῆ πατέρα ἡ θεία μέτεισι δίκη, μηδὲ βραχὺ τῆς ἀγαθότητος ἐνταῦθα περιμεινάσης, διὰ κακίας πάντως ὑπερβολὴν καὶ ἰάσεως ἀπαγόρευσιν· ἐπανιὼν γὰρ ἀπὸ τοῦ ὄρους, κεραυνῷ βάλλεται· καὶ τῆς ζωῆς ὅλως ἐκβάλλεται, οὐ τῆς ῥευστῆς μόνον, ἀλλὰ καὶ τῆς μενούσης, ὁ ἄθλιος ὄντως ἐκεῖνος καὶ ἀμφοτέρων ἀνάξιος. Διέβη δὲ καὶ εἰς τὸν ἡγεμόνα Μαρκιανὸν τὸ τοῦ θηλάτου τοῦδε πυρὸς ὅρμημα, προοίμιον δήπου καὶ σύμβολον ἀψευδὲς τοῦ ἀΰλου πυρὸς ἐκείνου, καὶ αἰωνίως αὐτὸν τιμωρήσοντος.

35 Οὐαλεντῖνος δέ τις εὐσεβὴς ἀνὴρ καὶ φιλόθεος, ἀνελόμενος τὰ τῶν μαρτύρων ἱερὰ σώματα, καὶ ἱεροῖς ᾄσμασιν ὡς ἔδει τιμήσας, ἐν χωρίῳ Γελασσὸν καλουμένῳ, δώδεκα μιλίοις Εὐχαΐτων ἀπέχοντι, σεμνῶς τε καὶ θεοφιλῶς κατα-

Lord, that we are flesh and blood, a creation of Your immaculate hands, honored by Your image and likeness."

She spoke and a voice was miraculously heard from 33 heaven, calling to heaven Barbara as well as Iouliane, her companion in martyrdom, and, simultaneously, promising the fulfillment of her request. Upon hearing this sweet voice, Barbara took to the road, and hurried to the place of her death. When she arrived there, she bowed her head and received her death by paternal blade in paternal hands, she, a good fruit that miraculously appeared from a wicked tree. Together with her, Iouliane too was also killed by one of the soldiers there.

While this happened, divine justice was exacted on the 34 impious father as well, as in this case the divine benevolence could not wait for even a moment, because of the total excess of his evil and the hopelessness of a cure: as he was returning from the mountain, he was struck by a thunderbolt and was completely cast out of life, not only from this fleeting one, but also from the eternal one, he who was truly wretched and unworthy of both lives. The force of that God-sent fire was also transmitted to the governor Markianos, a forerunner, it seems, and unerring sign of that immaterial fire which will also punish him eternally.

A certain pious and god-fearing man, Valentinos, col- 35 lected the sacred bodies of the martyrs. After honoring them with sacred hymns, as was fitting, he solemnly and piously laid them in a village called Gelassos, which lies twelve

τίθησι, νόσων ἴαμα, ψυχῶν ἀγαλλίαμα, φιλοθέων ἀνδρῶν ἐντρύφημα πολυέραστον, εἰς δόξαν Χριστοῦ τοῦ ἀληθινοῦ Θεοῦ ἡμῶν, ᾧ πρέπει τιμή, κράτος, μεγαλωσύνη τε καὶ μεγαλοπρέπεια, νῦν καὶ ἀεὶ καὶ εἰς τοὺς αἰῶνας τῶν αἰώνων. Ἀμήν.

miles from Euchaita, as a cure for illnesses, exultation for souls, a much-desired pleasure for pious men, for the glory of Christ our true God, to whom befits honor, power, greatness, as well as magnificence, now and forever unto the ages of ages. Amen.

LIFE, CONDUCT, AND PASSION OF THE HOLY MARTYR OF CHRIST SAINT EUGENIA AND HER PARENTS

Βίος καὶ πολιτεία καὶ ἄθλησις τῆς ἁγίας ὁσιομάρτυρος τοῦ Χριστοῦ Εὐγενίας καὶ τῶν ταύτης γονέων

Εὐλόγησον.

Κομόδου μετὰ Μάρκον τὸν αὐτοῦ πατέρα τὸ Ῥωμαϊκὸν σκῆπτρον ἔχοντος, καὶ ἕβδομον ἔτος ἤδη τῇ ἀρχῇ διανύοντος, Φίλιππος, ἀνήρ τις τῶν ἐπιφανῶν, ἔπαρχος Αἰγύπτου καθίσταται· ὅς, ἅμα γυναικὶ Κλαυδίᾳ καὶ τέκνοις, ἀνὰ τὴν Αἴγυπτον στέλλεται. Τούτῳ παῖδες μὲν ἄρρενες δύο, Ἀβίτας τε καὶ Σέργιος· θυγάτηρ δέ, Εὐγενία μὲν ὄνομα, εὐγενὴς δὲ καὶ ψυχήν, ὥσπερ ἄρα καὶ σῶμα, καὶ τὸ κάλλος ἀοίδιμος. Ἧς καὶ τὸν βίον ὁ λόγος ἄρτι τοῖς φιλαρέτοις ὑπόθεσιν προεστήσατο.

2   Ὁ μὲν οὖν Φίλιππος, ὡς ἤδη τὴν Ἀλεξάνδρου πόλιν τὴν μεγάλην κατέλαβε, νόμοις τὰ ἐκεῖ πάντα διώκει Ῥωμαϊκοῖς. Καὶ τοῖς πατρῴοις ἀκολουθῶν ἔθεσι, χαλεπὸς μὲν ἦν τοῖς τὴν μάγον τέχνην μεταχειρίζουσι, χαλεπὸς δὲ τοῖς Ἰουδαΐζουσι· τῶν μὲν καὶ πολλοὺς ἀναιρῶν, Ἰουδαίους δὲ μηδὲ ὀνομάζεσθαι συγχωρῶν. Χριστιανοῖς γε μὴν ἐπιεικέστερον προσεφέρετο· τῆς μὲν πόλεως καὶ αὐτοὺς ἐξωθῶν, πλησίον δέ που πρὸ τῶν τειχῶν, βασιλέως οὕτω κελεύσαντος, ἐφιεὶς διάγειν καὶ κατοικεῖν.

3   Δῆλος δὲ ἦν, Χριστιανοὺς μὲν διὰ τὴν ἀκριβῆ τοῦ βίου φιλοσοφίαν αἰδούμενος, καὶ παρὰ τοῦτο καὶ πρὸ τῶν εἰδωλολατρῶν τιθέμενος· αὐτὸς δὲ πάλιν, ὑπὸ τῆς πατροπαρα-

184

Life, Conduct, and Passion of the Holy Martyr of Christ
Saint Eugenia and Her Parents

Give the blessing.

While Commodus wielded the Roman scepter after his father Marcus, and while he was already in the seventh year of his rule, Philip—one of the eminent men—was appointed eparch of Egypt; he was sent to Egypt together with his wife Claudia and their children. He had two sons, Abitas and Sergios. He also had a daughter; Eugenia was her name, noble was her soul as well as her body, and celebrated was her beauty. It is her life which the present narrative offers as a subject for lovers of virtue.

Once Philip arrived at the great city of Alexander, he 2 managed all the affairs there according to Roman laws. Following ancestral customs, he was harsh with practitioners of magic, and he was harsh with the Jews; he killed many of the former, and did not permit the latter even to call themselves Jews. Toward the Christians, however, he showed more tolerance; although he forced them too out of the city, he allowed them to live and dwell somewhere near the city walls—for these were the emperor's orders.

Evidently, he respected Christians for their exacting phi- 3 losophy of life and, because of this, even favored them over idol worshippers. Still, in the tradition of his ancestors, he

δότου δεισιδαιμονίας ἐχόμενος. Παιδείας δὲ καὶ λόγων γενόμενος ἐραστής, καὶ Εὐγενίαν τὴν αὐτοῦ θυγατέρα παιδεύμασιν ἐλευθερίως ἀνέτρεφε, διδάσκων ἄμφω τὸν Ῥωμαϊκόν τε καὶ Ἕλληνα λόγον, καὶ φιλοσοφίας ἐπὶ μέγα ἤκουσαν σπουδάζων ἰδεῖν. Ἐκείνη δέ, τῇ τῆς φύσεως εὐμαθείᾳ προσθεῖσα καὶ ἄσκησιν, ὀξέως πάνυ τοῖς λόγοις ἵπτατο· πᾶσι μὲν τοῖς ὠφελίμοις προσέχουσα, πάντα δὲ οἷς προσεῖχεν εὐχερῶς παραδιδοῦσα τῇ διανοίᾳ· ἃ δὲ μάθοι, οὕτω τῇ μνήμῃ διακατέχουσα, ὡς ἐν χαλκαῖς δοκεῖν πίναξιν ἐγγεγράφθαι αὐτῆς τῇ καρδίᾳ.

4   Οὕτω περὶ λόγους ἔχουσα, οὐδὲν ἧττον καὶ τὴν ψυχὴν πρὸς ἀρετὴν εὖ ἐπεφύκει. Καὶ ἦν ἰδεῖν μὲν ἀξιοθέατος, εἰπεῖν δὲ ἀξιάκουστος, ζηλῶσαι δὲ πᾶσιν ὠφέλιμος καὶ σωτήριος· καὶ τό γε πάντων θαυμασιώτερον ὅτι, μήπω τὸ πέμπτον ἔτος καὶ δέκατον ὑπερβᾶσα τῆς ἡλικίας, εἰς εὐκοσμίαν ἤθους καὶ ἀρετῆς ἐπιμέλειαν τῶν πολλῷ τὴν ἡλικίαν πρεσβυτέρων ἐκράτει.

5   Ἐπεὶ δὲ μὴ εἶχε λαθεῖν, τῆς φήμης διὰ πάντων χωρούσης, τὴν ἐνδοξοτάτην κατ᾽ ἀρετὴν ὁ ἐνδοξότατος τὴν πολιτικὴν ἀρχὴν ἐμνηστεύετο Ἀκυλῖνος, ὕπατος ὢν τηνικαῦτα, καὶ ἄλλως τὰ πρῶτα τῶν παρὰ Ῥωμαίοις ἔχων εὐπατριδῶν. Ἐπεὶ γοῦν οἱ γονεῖς προσιόντες ἠρώτων, εἰ κατὰ νοῦν ὁ γάμος αὐτῇ καὶ ἀρεστὸς ὁ νυμφίος, ἐνταῦθα δὴ καὶ μάλιστα Εὐγενία τῆς ψυχικῆς εὐγενείας ἐδείκνυ τὸ σύμβολον· πάντα γὰρ μᾶλλον παθεῖν ὑπομένουσα, ἢ τὴν φίλην αὐτῇ παρθενίαν ἀπώσασθαι καὶ τὴν ἁγνείαν ἀποβαλεῖν, σοφίζεται τοὺς τεκόντας. Καὶ τὸ μὲν γένος ἐπῄνει τοῦ ἀνδρός, τὸν τρόπον δὲ ᾐτιᾶτο· καὶ "Ὅτι," φησίν, "ἐκείνους

himself remained a follower of their superstitious religion. A lover of learning and discourse, he also raised his daughter Eugenia in liberal learning, teaching her both Latin and Greek rhetoric, and was eager to see her excel in philosophy. Adding discipline to her teachable nature, she flew swiftly over her studies, attending to everything useful, and readily committing to her mind everything to which she had paid attention; whatever she learned, she then preserved in her memory so thoroughly that it seemed to have been engraved on her heart as if on bronze tablets.

While such was her disposition toward education, no less   4 was her soul naturally inclined toward virtue. She was a worthy sight to behold, a worthy speaker to hear, and beneficial and salutary for everyone to emulate; and what caused the most amazement was this: though she had not yet exceeded the fifteenth year of her age, she surpassed in propriety of character and cultivation of virtue those who were significantly older.

Unable to escape notice, as her fame traveled everywhere,   5 the maiden most acclaimed in virtue was sought in marriage by a man most acclaimed in civic authority, Aquilinus, a consul at that time, who also ranked among the first of Roman nobles. When her parents approached her with the question of whether this marriage was agreeable to her and the bridegroom was to her liking, it was above all then that Eugenia gave proof of the nobility of her soul; ready to suffer anything rather than spurn the virginity that was dear to her and cast aside her purity, she deceived her parents cleverly. She praised the man's lineage, but found fault with his character, "because," she said, "generally, one must choose from

δεῖ ὡς τὰ πολλὰ ἐκλέγεσθαι τῶν νυμφίων, οἳ τὸ γένος κοσμοῦσι μᾶλλον, οὐχ οἳ διὰ τοῦ γένους κοσμεῖσθαι βούλονται."

6   Πολλῶν δὲ καὶ ἄλλων ἐξαιτουμένων αὐτὴν παρὰ τῶν τεκόντων, πλούτῳ τε λαμπρῶν καὶ τῷ γένει περιφανῶν, οὐδ᾽ ὅλως ἐπὶ πᾶσιν ἐκείνη εὐπροσώπου ἠπόρησεν ἀφορμῆς. Ἀλλὰ τῷ μὲν δοκεῖν τὸν γῆμαι νῦν βουλόμενον ἀπωθεῖτο· τῇ δὲ ἀληθείᾳ τὸν γάμον ὅλως ἐξώμνυτο, καὶ τοῦτο μόνον αὐτῇ διὰ τέλους ἦν, ἁγνεῦσαι, τὸ σπουδαζόμενον. Οὕτω τὸ σκεῦος εὐπρεπῶς τε καὶ καθαρῶς ἔχον, ἕτοιμον ἦν εἰς ὑποδοχὴν τοῦ θείου δηλαδὴ μύρου. Διὰ τοῦτο καὶ ὅσον οὔπω τοῖς καλοῖς ἔργοις καὶ ἡ καλῶς ἔχουσα πίστις ἐπηκολούθει· καὶ ἡ καθαρὰ τῷ καθαρῷ τῆς εὐσεβείας προσῄει φωτί.

7   Πρόφασις δὲ τοῦ πράγματος· ἧκεν εἰς χεῖρας αὐτῇ Παύλου τοῦ θείου κήρυκος ἡ θεία τῶν ἐπιστολῶν βίβλος· καὶ τῇ διανοίᾳ τῶν λόγων ἐρείσασα τὴν ψυχήν, καὶ γνοῦσα ὅτι εἷς ἐστι Θεὸς ἀληθὴς ὁ τὸ πᾶν τοῦτο πεποιηκώς, περιλάμπεται μὲν αὐτίκα τὸν νοῦν, ἅτε καὶ ἐκ πολλοῦ τοῦτον καθηραμένη καὶ πρὸς ὑποδοχὴν οὖσα ηὐτρεπισμένη τοῦ θείου Πνεύματος. Κατὰ ψυχὴν δὲ τό γε νῦν ἔχον τῷ Χριστῷ πιστεύσασα, ἐν τῷ φανερῷ τὴν τῶν τεκόντων λύσσαν ὑποβλέπουσα ἦν.

8   Ἐπεὶ δὲ καὶ βασιλέως ἐφοίτα πρόσταγμα, ἔξω τειχῶν τοὺς Χριστιανοὺς ἐξωθοῦν, καὶ ὁ ἔπαρχος ἤδη ἔργου εἴχετο, αὐτή, γλιχομένη κατὰ πολλὴν ἄδειαν Χριστιανῶν τε καὶ τῆς ἐκείνων ἀπολαῦσαι διδασκαλίας, σκήπτεται μέν, τῶν ἐν ἀγροῖς χάριν χαρίτων καὶ τῆς ἐκεῖθεν εὐαερίας,

those bridegrooms who adorn a lineage rather than those who want to be adorned by it."

As many other men, illustrious with wealth and prominent in lineage, were also asking her parents for her hand, in no case did she ever lack a decent excuse. While she gave the appearance of spurning each new suitor, in truth she forswore marriage completely; and this alone, to the end, was her aspiration: to remain chaste. Thus proper and pure, the vessel was prepared to receive indeed the divine perfumed oil. Because of this, good faith also soon followed her good works and the pure Eugenia approached the pure light of piety. 6

The occasion for this was as follows. The divine book of the letters of Paul, the divine herald, came into her hands; fixing her soul firmly on the meaning of his words and understanding that the true God who made everything around us is one, she was immediately illumined in her mind, since she had been purifying it for a long time and was prepared to receive the divine Spirit. Believing in Christ for now only in her soul, she began to openly cast a defiant eye toward the insanity of her parents. 7

When then also the imperial decree arrived, expelling Christians outside the city walls, and the eparch already began to carry out this order, Eugenia, longing to enjoy with greater freedom the presence of Christians and their teachings, pretended to leave the city for the delights of rural 8

ἐκχωρῆσαι τῆς πόλεως, καὶ τὴν ψυχὴν μετρίως τῶν τῆς παιδείας φροντίδων ἀνεῖναι. Ἐπεὶ δὲ οἱ τεκόντες οὐδὲν ὑποπτεύοντες ἑτοίμως ἐφῆκαν, ἔξεισιν εἰς τὰς κώμας. Χωρίον δέ τι καταλαβοῦσα καὶ μοναχοῖς ἔν γε τούτῳ περιτυχοῦσα, πολλοῖς τε καὶ κοσμίοις καὶ λίαν εὐτάκτως ᾄδουσι, τῆς ἱερᾶς ἐκείνης ἀκούει φωνῆς, "Πάντες οἱ θεοὶ τῶν ἐθνῶν δαιμόνια· ὁ δὲ Κύριος τοὺς οὐρανοὺς ἐποίησε."

9 Τοῦτο ἐκείνη ἀκούσασα, καὶ ὥσπερ ἐπὶ τῇ πατρικῇ πλάνῃ βαθείας αἰσχύνης ὑποπλησθεῖσα, στενάζει μὲν ἐκ καρδίας περιπαθές τι καὶ βύθιον. Στραφεῖσα δὲ πρὸς τοὺς ἐφεπομένους εὐνούχους, ὧν ὁ μὲν Πρωτέας, ὁ δὲ Ὑάκινθος ἐκαλεῖτο, λόγων δὲ καὶ οὗτοι σοφῶν καὶ φιλοσοφίας ἐπήκοοι, "Οἶδα μὲν ὑμᾶς," ἔφη, "καὶ παιδείας ἀπολαύσαντας ἱκανῶς, καὶ δόγμασι περιτυχόντας σοφῶν, ὅσα τε Σωκράτης, καὶ Ἀριστοτέλης, καὶ Πλάτων, καὶ ἡ περιώνυμος διεξῆλθε Στοά, ἥ τε τῶν Ἐπικουρείων δόξα παρέδωκεν, ὁμοίως δὲ καὶ ποιητῶν τῶν ἄλλων καὶ σοφιστῶν, καὶ ὅσοι τὴν τῶν ὄντων αὐχοῦσι γνῶσιν, οὐκ ἀμαθῶς ἔχοντας.

10 "Ἴστε γοῦν, ὡς ταῦτα πάντα μυθολογία σαφής, καὶ πιθανότης, παρακρούεσθαι τοὺς πολλοὺς δυναμένη· ἀλλὰ καὶ τῶν μέγα περὶ τὴν γνῶσιν αὐχούντων Ἑλλήνων, οἱ μὲν οὐδ' ὅλως εἶναι Θεόν, οἱ δὲ πολλοὺς εἶναι μείζονας καὶ ἐλάττονας ἐδοκίμασαν. Οὗτοι γοῦν ἑνὶ τούτῳ πάντες ἐκκρούονται ῥήματι, τῷ Πάντες οἱ θεοὶ τῶν ἐθνῶν δαιμόνια· ἔστι γὰρ τῆς πολυθεΐας παντελὴς ἀναίρεσις. Τὸ δὲ Κύριος τοὺς οὐρανοὺς ἐποίησε, τοῦτο δὴ μοναρχίαν ἀκριβῶς ἀντεισάγει· καὶ τὸν κοινὸν ἡμῖν Δεσπότην γνώριμον καθιστᾷ. Συνῳδὰ δὲ τούτοις καὶ ὁ ἀπόστολος εἰσηγεῖται Παῦλος·

life and its good quality of air and to give her soul some rest from the strains of learning. Suspecting nothing, her parents allowed her to go without any hesitation, and she set out for the countryside. Arriving at a certain village and chancing upon monks there, who were numerous and virtuous and were chanting in a quite orderly fashion, she heard that sacred voice, *"All the gods of the nations are demons; but the Lord made the heavens."*

Having heard this, Eugenia was so flooded with profound shame for the erroneous beliefs of her parents that she let out an intense and deep moan from her heart. Then she turned to her attendant eunuchs—the one named Proteas and the other Hyacinth, both of them also devotees of the words of the wise and of philosophy—and said: "I know that you have acquired considerable education and have read the teachings of wise men, such as those of Socrates, Aristotle, Plato, and the famous Stoics, and what the Epicurean school taught; neither are you ignorant of the rest, of poets and sophists and others who boast in their knowledge of being. 9

"Know therefore that all these are clearly myths and persuasive words capable of deceiving the multitude. Yet even among the Greeks who boasted greatly of their knowledge some contended that there is no God at all, others that there are many gods, superior and inferior. All of these are proved wrong by this one saying: *All the gods of the nations are demons;* for this indicates the complete abolition of the belief in many gods. As for the words *The Lord made the heavens,* these introduce in the stead of many gods precisely the rule of one God and make our common Master known to us. The apostle Paul too introduces similar notions; for his 10

ἐπάγεται γάρ με καὶ τούτου τὰ ῥήματα, ἃ χθὲς καὶ πρῴην ἐπῆλθον αὐτή, ἕνα τῶν πάντων εἶναι διασαφοῦντα Θεόν. Οἷς καὶ ἡμεῖς πειθώμεθα, πολὺ τὸ περιφανὲς καὶ ἀξιόπιστον ἔχουσιν, ἅτε ἀπὸ τῶν ἔργων τὰς ἑαυτῶν πίστεις παρεχομένοις.

11   "Βουλομένοις οὖν ὑμῖν, ἕτοιμος τῆς σωτηρίας ὁ τρόπος καὶ εὐτρεπής. Ἐγὼ δὲ ὑμῖν οὐχ ὡς δέσποινα ἔτι προσενεχθήσομαι, ἀλλ᾽ ὁμόδουλος ἔσομαί τε καὶ ἀδελφή, ἐπεὶ καὶ κοινὸν Δεσπότην καὶ Πατέρα ἕξομεν τὸν Θεόν. Ἅτε γοῦν ποιμένος ἑνὸς ὄντες, καὶ ὡς ἀδελφοὶ τὸ ἓν πνέοντες, κοινῇ γνώμῃ πρὸς Χριστιανοὺς ἐλευσόμεθα. Ἀκούω γὰρ καὶ Ἐλένῳ τινὶ φροντιστήριον ἐνταυθοῖ γενόμενον, κἀκεῖνον μὲν διὰ μέγεθος ἀρετῆς τὸν τῆς ἐπισκοπῆς ἀναβῆναι θρόνον, Θεόδωρον δέ τινα εἰς τὸν ἐκείνου κλῆρον ἐγκαταστῆναι, καὶ τῆς μάνδρας ἐγχειρισθῆναι τὴν προστασίαν· ὃν οὕτω δὴ φιλαρέτως τοῦ ποιμνίου προστῆναι, εἰς τοῦτό τε προβῆναι θεϊκῆς χάριτος, ὡς καὶ δαιμονῶσι καὶ ἀσθενοῦσι, τοῖς μὲν τὸ ἐνοχλοῦν πνεῦμα, τοῖς δὲ τὴν νόσον, εὐχερῶς ἀπελαύνειν, οὐ μὴν ἀλλὰ καὶ τυφλοῖς ὄμμασι τὸν ποθούμενον ἥλιον παρέχειν ὁρᾶν, καὶ τοῖς ὑπ᾽ αὐτὸν δὲ μοναχοῖς οὕτω τὴν ἄσκησιν ἐπιτείνειν, ὡς μικροῦ μηδὲν αὐτοὺς ἀπολείπειν μέρος ἡμέρας τε καὶ νυκτός, ὃ μὴ εὐχαῖς καὶ ᾠδαῖς ἀπαύστοις ἀναλωθείη.

12   "Τούτων οὐδέποτε γυναιξὶ βάσιμος ἡ μονή, οὔτε ὀφθῆναι γυναῖκα θεμιτὸν ἐκείνοις. Ὑμεῖς δὲ ἀλλὰ τὴν κόμην γοῦν τῆς κεφαλῆς ἀποκείρατε τῆς ἐμῆς· καὶ πλοκάμους δὴ περιέλετε τούτους. Ἔπειτα καὶ ἀνδρικήν μοι περιθέντες στολήν, νυκτὸς ἀγάγετε παρ᾽ αὐτούς, ὑμῶν μὲν

words too, which I myself read yesterday and the day before, lead me to the clear conclusion that there is one God above all. May we too believe in these words, since they are self-evident and trustworthy, verified as they are by deeds.

"Therefore, if you are willing, the means of salvation is 11 readily available to you. As for me, I will no longer behave toward you as a mistress, but rather I will be a fellow slave and sister, since we will have God as our common Master and Father. Therefore, since we belong to one shepherd, and since we breathe as one like brothers, we shall go to the Christians with common purpose. For I hear that a certain Helenos founded a monastery in this place, but he rose to the bishop's throne on account of the magnitude of his virtue, and a certain Theodoros took his place and the shepherding of the monastery was entrusted to him. This Theodoros leads his flock with such love of virtue and has reached such a level of divine grace that he can easily drive away vexatious spirits from the possessed and diseases from the sick, not to mention that he can grant to blind eyes the power to see the desired sun. He also intensified the ascetic practice of the monks under him so much that there is scarcely a part of the day or night left to them that they do not spend in their incessant prayers and chants.

"Women are never allowed to set foot in their monastery, 12 nor is it permissible for them to set their eyes on women. You, then, cut the hair from my head and remove these plaits. Then, dress me in man's garb and lead me to them by

πλησίον μοι τοῦ ὀχήματος παρεπομένων, τῶν δὲ λοιπῶν παίδων προαγόντων ὁμοῦ καὶ ἐφεπομένων, ἵν᾽, ὅταν καὶ πρὸς αὐτῷ γενώμεθα τῷ τόπῳ, αἴσθησιν αὐτοῖς τὸ παράπαν μηδὲ μίαν δῶμεν τοῦ πεπραγμένου. Τὸ λοιπὸν μέλον ὑμῖν ἔστω, ὅπως, ἔσω τῶν θυρῶν γενόμενοι, τῆς σωτηρίας ὡς προσῆκον ἐπιλαβώμεθα."

13   Ἤρεσε τοῖς εὐνούχοις τὰ λαληθέντα· καὶ εἰς ἔργον ἔσπευδον ταῦτα προαγαγεῖν. Τυγχάνουσι δὲ καί τινος αἰσίου συμβόλου· οὔπω γὰρ ἔφθασαν ἐπιβῆναι καλῶς τοῦ φροντιστηρίου, καὶ ὁ μέγας ἐν ἐπισκόποις Ἔλενος ἐξ Ἡλιουπόλεως ἧκε, καὶ συνάμα πλήθη ἀνδρῶν ὥσπερ ἐκ συνθήματος ταῦτα ψαλλόντων, "Ἡ ὁδὸς τῶν δικαίων κατηυθύνθη· ἡ ὁδὸς τῶν ἁγίων ἡτοιμάσθη." Τοῦτο καὶ τοῖς περὶ τὴν Εὐγενίαν τὴν πίστιν ηὔξησε, κἀκείνην ἡσθῆναι διαφερόντως πεποίηκεν.

14   Ἀμέλει καὶ ὥσπερ καιροῦ δραξαμένη, μᾶλλον ἔτι τοὺς περὶ αὐτὴν πρὸς τὴν εὐσέβειαν ἀνεθέρμηνεν, ἄλλα τε πολλὰ καὶ τῷ καιρῷ καὶ τῷ τόπῳ συντείνοντα φθεγξαμένη, καὶ ὡς οὐ κατά τινα συντυχίαν, ἀλλ᾽ ἐκ θείας προνοίας καὶ ταῦτα καὶ τὰ τοῦ Δαυὶδ πρότερον ἀκοῦσαι ψαλλόμενα· ἀλλ᾽ ἐκεῖνα μὲν εἶναι πρὸς εὐσέβειαν ἐνάγοντα ταύτην· τὰ δὲ νῦν ὑπᾳδόμενα πρὸς τὴν τῆς ἀρετῆς τρίβον παρακαλοῦντα.

15   Ταῦτα εἰποῦσα καὶ τοῖς ψάλλουσιν αὐτήν τε καὶ τοὺς περὶ αὐτὴν μίξασα, τὴν ὁδὸν ἤνυε σὺν ἐκείνοις. Ὅτε δὴ καὶ τῶν ὄχλων ἄλλα τε θαυμαστὰ περὶ τοῦ Ἐλένου διεξιόντων ἤκουσεν, ὅσος ἦν τοῖς θαύμασιν ὁ ἀνήρ, καὶ ὅτι καί, πυρὸς αὐτῷ πολλάκις δεῆσαν, ἄνθρακας ἐπὶ τῶν ἱματίων

night, following close by my carriage, while the rest of the slaves lead or follow, so that, when we arrive at the place, we do not allow them to perceive anything at all of what we have done. Then, once we get through the door, let your only care be how we are to attain salvation, as is right."

The eunuchs were pleased by her words and eager to put them into effect. And they also chanced upon a good omen: they had scarcely reached the monastery, when Helenos, great among bishops, arrived from Helioupolis, and with him were a multitude of men chanting (as though it had been prearranged) the following: "The path of the righteous has been made straight; the path of the holy has been made ready." This both increased the faith of Eugenia's companions and made Eugenia herself exceedingly happy. 13

Seizing the occasion, as it were, she excited her attendants yet more toward piety; in addition to many other things appropriate to the time and place, she asserted that it was not by chance, but through divine providence that she heard these words as well as those of David which were being chanted earlier. The latter, she said, had induced her to piety; the ones that they were hearing now were exhorting her to the path of virtue. 14

With these words, she had herself and those with her join the company of those chanting and continued along the road with them. It was then that she also heard the crowd narrating many marvelous tales concerning Helenos: what a miracle worker he was; and that often, when he was in need of fire, he would be seen carrying coals in his robes which 15

ἑωρᾶτο κομίζων, οὐδὲν ἐκείνων ἀπὸ τοῦ πυρὸς βλαπτομέ-
νων· πρὸς τούτοις καὶ ἄλλα ὅσα τερατουργῶν αὐτὸς διε-
τέλει· ὁποῖον δὴ καὶ τόδε, λόγου καὶ μνήμης ἄξιον.

16   Φασί τινα μάγον, Ζαρέαν καλούμενον, αὐτὸ τῆς κακο-
τεχνίας φθάσαντα τὸ ἀκρότατον, τοῖς ἐκεῖθι τόποις ἐπὶ
λύμῃ πολλῶν ἐπιχωριάσαι, δεινῇ τῇ ἀπάτῃ καὶ πολλῇ χρώ-
μενον· ὃν μετὰ τῶν ἄλλων καὶ τοιοῦτόν τι τολμῆσαι θεο-
μισέστατον· φήμῃ τινὶ σπουδάσαι περιλαβεῖν τοὺς ἐπιχω-
ρίους, ὡς αὐτὸς μὲν εἴη ἀπεσταλμένος ὑπὸ Χριστοῦ,
εὐεργέτης ἀνθρώπων καὶ διδάσκαλος ἀγαθός, ψευδὴς δὲ
Ἕλενος, μάτην αὐτῷ τὸ διδασκαλικὸν ἀξίωμα περιάπτων·
ἐνόμιζε γὰρ ὡς εἰ τὸν ποιμένα τῷ ποιμνίῳ ἐκπολεμώσοι,
τοῦ λοιποῦ ῥᾳδίως αὐτοῖς ὥσπερ ἀφυλάκτοις ἐπελθὼν
θρέμμασι, θήραμα οὐκ εὐκαταφρόνητον τῷ πατρὶ αὐτοῦ
τῷ Διαβόλῳ προσενεγκεῖν.

17   Ταῦτα λέγων ἐκεῖνος, καὶ πιθανὸς ἦν ἐκ κακουργίας—
ἴστε γὰρ ὅπως ἀνυσιμώτατον ἡ κακία, καὶ τοὺς πολλοὺς
ἑλκύσαι πάνυ ῥᾳδία—ὥστε καὶ τῷ Ἑλένῳ τὸν ὄχλον προσελθόντας εἰπεῖν, ἢ κοινωνὸν καὶ αὐτὸν τῆς διδασκαλίας
λαβεῖν, ἢ γοῦν πρὸς ἀλλήλους διὰ λόγων ἁμιλληθῆναι, ἵνα
τῷ νικῶντι καὶ αὐτοὶ πρόσθοιντο. Ἄσμενος οὖν ὁ Ἕλενος
τὴν τῆς ἁμίλλης καταδέχεται πεῖραν· ἐπεθάρρει γὰρ τῷ
Χριστῷ. Τὸ δὲ κοινωνὸν Ζαρέαν παραλαβεῖν, ἄνθρωπον
τερατείαις δαιμόνων ἐπικαυχώμενον, τοῦτο καὶ ἀκοῇ μόνῃ
λαβεῖν ἀπευκτὸν ἡγεῖτο.

18   Ὡς οὖν καὶ ἡ κυρία παρῆν, πρὸς τοὺς λόγους ἐχώρει καὶ
τὴν διάλεξιν. Καὶ πρῶτα μὲν ἰσχυρῶς ἐπετίθετο· καὶ πυ-
κνοῖς ἄγαν τὸν μάγον ἔβαλλε τοῖς ἐλέγχοις. Ἐπεὶ δὲ ἑώρα

remained completely unharmed by the fire; in addition to these, they spoke about the many other wonders which he accomplished; one such miracle is also the following, which is worth both telling and remembering.

They say that a certain magician named Zareas, who had 16 reached the very pinnacle of his evil artistry, took up residence in those regions to the detriment of many, exercising much dire treachery. Among other things, he dared the following deed most hateful to God: he tried assiduously to take in the locals by spreading a rumor that supposedly he himself had been sent by Christ as a benefactor of mankind and a true teacher, while Helenos was a liar, falsely attributing to himself the rank of teacher. For Zareas believed that if he could estrange the shepherd from his flock, he would then easily, by attacking them as if they were unguarded lambs, be able to present a magnificent catch to his father, the Devil.

With these rumors, he was so persuasive, a result of his 17 wicked ways—you know how efficacious evil is and how easily it attracts the many—that the crowd approached Helenos and said that he must either accept Zareas as an associate in his teaching or else engage in debate with him, so that they then might side with the victor. Helenos gladly accepted the challenge to compete with him, for he had confidence in Christ. He detested even hearing the idea of taking Zareas, a man who exulted in the bogus nonsense of the demons, as a fellow teacher.

When the agreed-upon day arrived, Helenos entered into 18 the discussion and the debate. At first, he accosted Zareas forcefully and amply refuted the magician with argument

τῇ αὐθαδείᾳ ὡς ὅπλῳ χρώμενον, καὶ τὸ νικᾶν οὐκ ἐκ τῆς
ἀληθείας ἀλλ' ἐκ τῆς ἀναιδείας μᾶλλον ἑαυτῷ περιθέσθαι
φιλονεικοῦντα, ἔργῳ τὴν κρίσιν ἐπέτρεπε. Καὶ πῦρ πολὺ
κατὰ μέσου τῆς πόλεως ἀναφθῆναι κελεύει, ἐπιβῆναι δὲ
τῆς φλογὸς ἀμφοτέρους, καὶ ὃς ἂν αὐτῶν ἀπαθὴς μείνοι
καὶ τοῦ πυρὸς ἰσχυρότερος, τοῦτον εἶναι σαφῶς τὸν καὶ
ὑπὸ Χριστοῦ πεμφθέντα, καὶ τὸν ἐκείνου κλῆρον διδά-
σκειν ἄξιον.

19   Ὡς οὖν ὁ λόγος ἔργου εἴχετο, καὶ ἡ φλὸξ ἤδη πρὸς ὕψος
ἤρετο, δειλίᾳ μὲν εὐθὺς ὁ Ζαρέας συνείχετο· καὶ τὸν Ἕλενον ἐπιβῆναι πρῶτον διεκελεύετο, τοῦτο καθ' ἑαυτόν, ὡς
ἔοικε, διανοηθεὶς ὡς ἤ, μὴ θαρρήσας, Ἕλενος αἰσχύνην
ὀφλήσοι, ἢ γοῦν καὶ τολμήσας ἀπορρήξειε τὴν ψυχήν, καὶ
οὕτως ἂν αὐτῷ ῥᾷον τὸ κρατεῖν περιγένοιτο, ἀνταγω-
νιστὴν ἀποβαλόντι μάλα στερρόν, καὶ παρὰ τοῦτο πάντας
ὑφ' ἑαυτὸν ἑλκύσαι δυνατὸς γένηται.

20   Ἐπεὶ δὲ καὶ τὴν πεῖραν πρῶτος ὁ θεῖος ἀνὴρ ὑποστῆναι
διωμολόγησε, καὶ προσευξάμενος ἐπέβαινε τῆς πυρᾶς, τὴν
δὲ οὐκ ἐλάνθανεν ὅστις εἴη, καὶ οὐδὲ τριχὸς ἐκείνου ψαύ-
ειν ἐτόλμα, τότε δὴ τὸν μάγον, φόβου καὶ δειλίας ὑποπλη-
σθέντα, μάλιστα μὲν ἐκποδὼν γενέσθαι καὶ διαδρᾶναι τὴν
πεῖραν φανερὸν καταστῆναι, ἢ τὴν Ἅιδου κυνῆν ὑπελ-
θόντα λαθεῖν· ὑπὸ δὲ τοῦ πλήθους εἰς τὸ πῦρ καὶ ἄκοντα
συνωθούμενον, ἀναγκαίως τὴν κάμινον εἰσελθεῖν. Ἥτις
αὐτὸν οὕτω θᾶττον περιελάμβανεν ἤδη καὶ κατεβόσκετο,
ὡς οὐδὲ μίαν ὕλην ἑτέραν καυθῆναι ῥᾳδίαν. Καὶ εἴγε μὴ
φθάσας ὁ μέγας Ἕλενος, οἰκτείρων ὥσπερ τῆς συμφορᾶς
τὸν ἄθλιον, ἡμίφλεκτον εὐθὺς γενόμενον τοῦ πυρὸς

after argument. But when he realized that Zareas was using his churlishness as a weapon, and was striving to win not by means of the truth but rather through his shamelessness, he entrusted the judgment to action. He ordered a large fire to be lit in the middle of the city and that both should enter the flames; whoever of them should remain unharmed and prevail over the fire would clearly be the one sent by Christ and worthy to teach His flock.

When word turned into deed and the flames were already 19 reaching for the sky, Zareas was immediately seized with cowardice; and he urged Helenos to enter first, with these thoughts, it seems, in his mind: that either Helenos would not dare and would thus incur shame, or else, if he did make the bold bid, he would breathe his last, and so it would be easier for Zareas to win the victory, having thrown off his very resolute antagonist, and then he could bring everyone under his control.

Since the divine man had agreed to undertake the ordeal 20 first, after praying, he stepped into the pyre. Aware of the sort of man he was, the fire did not dare to touch even one of his hairs. Thereupon, the magician was filled with fear and cowardice. Indeed, he could not conceal that he was trying to either run away and avoid the ordeal, or become invisible, putting on the helmet of Hades. But despite his reluctance the crowd pushed him into the fire, so that he had no choice but to enter the furnace. The fire enveloped him and began to consume him so quickly that no other fuel could have burned more easily. If the great Helenos had not intervened out of pity for the wretch's misfortune and re-covered him already half-burned from the fire, Zareas would

ἀνεσώσατο, κἂν εἰς τέλος αὐτῇ μαγείᾳ καὶ τοῖς σοφίσμασι διεφθάρη, καλῶς οὕτω τοῦ πυρὸς τὴν ἀπάτην σὺν ἀληθείᾳ κολάσαντος.

21 Ταῦτα ἐκείνων λεγόντων, ἡ μακαρία παντοία τις ὑπὸ περιχαρείας ἐγίνετο· ᾔδετο· ἐξεπλήττετο· τῶν ἀπαγγελλόντων ἐδέετο, προσαχθῆναί τε δι᾽ αὐτῶν καὶ συστῆναι τῷ ἐπισκόπῳ, αὐτή τε καὶ οὓς ἐπάγεται ἀδελφούς, καὶ οὕτως ὑπὸ τῇ μονῇ τῇδε ζῆσαι κοινῇ συνδιάγοντας. Οὕτω μετὰ πολλῆς δεομένη τῆς προσεδρίας, πείθει δὴ τῶν παρόντων ἕνα τινά, Εὐτρόπιον οὕτω καλούμενον, πάντα ταύτῃ γενέσθαι καὶ τῷ ἐπισκόπῳ τὴν δέησιν προσαγγεῖλαι. "Ὁπηνίκα δὴ καταλύσας," φησίν, "εἶτα μικρὸν διαναπαυσάμενος, εὐκαίρως καὶ κατὰ σχολὴν ἐκεῖνος ὑπέχει τὴν ἀκοὴν τῷ λέγοντι." Ἐν ᾧ δὲ ταῦτα πρὸς ἀλλήλους ὡμίλουν, ἤγγισαν τῷ μοναστηρίῳ. Καὶ αὐτοί τε μετὰ τοῦ ἐπισκόπου εἰσῄεσαν· καὶ τὴν Εὐγενίαν εἶχον συνεισιοῦσαν, νεανίσκῳ πρὸς ἀκρίβειαν ἐοικυῖαν τῇ τε κόμῃ καὶ τῇ στολῇ.

22 Ἤδη δὲ ὡρμημένου τοῦ Εὐτροπίου γνωρίσαι τῷ ἐπισκόπῳ τὰ κατ᾽ αὐτήν, ὄνειρός τις ἐφίπταται τῷ Ἐλένῳ, μετὰ τὴν θείαν μυσταγωγίαν πρὸς ὕπνον κλίναντι. Καὶ ὁ ὄνειρος· γλυπτόν τι ἐδόκει γυναικὸς εἴδωλον ὑπ᾽ ἀνδρῶν ἐντίμως διαβαστάζεσθαι, καὶ τοῦτο νομίζεσθαι παρ᾽ αὐτοῖς ὡς θεόν· τὸν δέ, τῇ ἀπάτῃ τῶν ἀνθρώπων περιαλγήσαντα, φάναι πρὸς τὴν παρ᾽ αὐτοῖς θεόν, "Εἶτα, σὺ δὲ ἀνέχῃ κτίσμα οὖσα Θεοῦ, καὶ ἡμῖν ὁμόδουλος, ὑπ᾽ αὐτῶν προσκυνεῖσθαι καὶ ἴσα Θεῷ νομίζεσθαι;"· τοῦτο ἐκείνην ἀκούσασαν, εὐθὺς ἔτι βασταζομένην, ἀποστῆναι μὲν τῶν ἀνδρῶν,

have been utterly destroyed, magic, sophistries, and all—in that way the fire, together with truth, would have rightly punished deceit.

While the people were saying these things, blessed Eu- 21 genia experienced and expressed every emotion in her joy: she was delighted; she was amazed; and she beseeched those narrating the tale to escort and introduce to the bishop both her and the brethren whom she was bringing along, so that they might live and spend their time together in the monastery. By pleading so assiduously, she persuaded one of those present, a man by the name of Eutropios, to help her fulfill her wish and present her request to the bishop. "Normally," he said, "after the bishop has gone to his chamber and rested a little, he gives audience to his visitors at the appropriate time, at his leisure." While discussing these things, they arrived at the monastery. The people entered with the bishop; with them, Eugenia entered too, looking exactly like a young man both in her hair and in her garb.

Eutropios was already setting out to inform the bishop 22 about her, when a dream alighted on Helenos as he was falling asleep after celebrating the divine mysteries. The dream was as follows: he saw a sculpted idol of a woman carried reverently by men who thought she was a god. Exceedingly pained at their deception, he said to their goddess, "How do you, created by God and being our fellow slave, permit yourself to be worshipped by them and reckoned equal to God?" Upon hearing this, she immediately, while still being carried, moved away from the men and followed him, making

ἀκολουθεῖν δὲ αὐτῷ, τοιαύτας ἀφιεῖσαν φωνάς· "Ἀλλ᾽ ἔγωγε οὐδαμῶς ἀποστήσομαί σου, ἕως ἂν τῷ Κτίστῃ με προσαγάγῃς!"

23   Ταῦτα μὲν ὁ Ἔλενος ἑώρα κατὰ τοὺς ὕπνους. Διεγερθεὶς δέ, διηπόρει καθ᾽ ἑαυτὸν εἰς τί ἂν καὶ ἀποβαίη τὸ ὁραθέν. Καὶ αὐτίκα παρέστη καὶ ὁ Εὐτρόπιος ὃς ἄρα καὶ ὡς περὶ ἀνδρὸς τῆς Εὐγενίας τὸν λόγον διεξιών, "Ἄνδρες," ἔφη πρὸς τὸν ἐπίσκοπον, "τρεῖς, ἀδελφοὶ τὰς ψυχάς, ἀδελφοὶ τὰ σώματα, ὁμοφρόνως ἄρτι τὰ Ἑλλήνων ἐξομοσάμενοι, ἀνὰ τὴν σὴν διατρίβουσι ποίμνην, Χριστῷ προσελθόντες, τοῦ τε θείου βαπτίσματος ἀξιοῦντες τυχεῖν, εἶτα κείρασθαι τὰς κόμας, καὶ τοῖς ὧδε μοναχοῖς ἐγκριθῆναι. Νέοι δὲ ὄντες καὶ ἀλλήλων ὑπερφυῶς ἠρτημένοι, καὶ τοῦτο πρὸς τοῖς ἄλλοις αἰτοῦνται· μηδεμίαν αὐτῶν ἐν μηδενὶ γενέσθαι διάστασιν, μὴ κατὰ τὴν ἐργασίαν, μὴ κατὰ τὴν οἴκησιν, μήτε μὴν περί τινα ἄλλην ἀναστροφήν· ἀλλ᾽ οὕτως ἀδιαιρέτους εἶναι, Χριστοῦ τῷ ὀνόματι συνηγμένους. Ταῦτα πρός με εἰρήκασι, δακρύων αὐτῶν τοῖς προσώποις ὑπορρεόντων· καὶ πάντα πρὸς σὲ διασαφῆσαι θερμῶς ἠξίωσαν."

24   Πρὸς ταῦτα τὸν ὄνειρον ὁ μακάριος Ἔλενος συμβαλών, καί, ὅπερ ἔδει, Θεῷ χάριν ὑπὲρ πάντων ὁμολογήσας, ὑπ᾽ ὄψιν αὐτῷ τοὺς τρεῖς ἅμα παραστῆναι κελεύει. Ὡς δὲ παρέστησαν, λαβόμενος Εὐγενίας εὐθὺς ἐκ τῆς δεξιᾶς, καὶ ἱλαρώτερος αὐτῇ ἐντυχών, ἤθει τε εὐπροσίτῳ καὶ προσώπῳ φαιδρῷ, ὀνόματα τούτων, καὶ γένος, καὶ πατρίδα διεπυνθάνετο. Ἡ δέ, μετὰ τῆς φίλης αἰδοῦς καὶ τοῦ παρθένῳ μάλιστα προσήκοντος ἐρυθήματος, "Πατρὶς μὲν ἡμῖν,"

exclamations such as: "In no way will I ever separate myself from you, until you lead me to the Creator!"

This is what Helenos saw in his sleep. When he woke up, 23 he wondered how his vision would come to pass. At that very moment, Eutropios arrived and began to give a thorough account of Eugenia's story, speaking about her as if she were a man. "There are three men," he said to the bishop, "brothers in soul, brothers in the flesh. Having recently of one accord forsworn the beliefs of the Greeks and having come to Christ, they are dwelling among your flock and are requesting to receive holy baptism, and afterward to be tonsured, and enrolled among the monks here. Being young and exceedingly attached to each other, they also ask this: that they never be separated, neither in work nor in living space nor in any other activity, but that they be bound together without separation in the name of Christ. They told me these things with tears streaming down their faces, and they fervently beseeched me to explain everything to you."

The blessed Helenos recognized his dream in all this and, 24 as was appropriate, gave thanks to God for everything. He then ordered that the three together be brought into his presence. When they appeared before him, he immediately took Eugenia by her right hand and, speaking to her most cordially, with a welcoming demeanor and a beaming countenance, inquired as to their names, family, and fatherland. She responded with the modesty that was dear to her and a blush that was particularly fitting for a virgin: "Our

ἔφη, "ὦ θεία μοι κεφαλή, καὶ γένος ἡ μεγαλόδοξος Ῥώμη. Ἀδελφοὶ ἀλλήλων ἡμεῖς· ὀνόματα δέ, τῷ μὲν πρώτῳ Πρωτᾶς, τῷ δὲ μετὰ τοῦτον Ὑάκινθος, ἐμοὶ δὲ Εὐγένιος."

25   Ἡδὺ δὲ αὐτὴν προσβλέψας ὁ μακάριος Ἕλενος, "Εὐλό-γως," ἔφη, "Εὐγένιον σεαυτήν, ὦ Εὐγενία, μετακαλεῖς, ἵνα δή σοι καὶ τὸ ὄνομα πρὸς τὸ φρόνημα ᾖ, ἀνδρείαν τε ψυχὴν ἐχούσῃ, καὶ πολὺ τὸ ἀρρενωπὸν ἐν ἅπασιν ἐπιδει-κνυμένῃ. Ἀλλὰ νικῴης καὶ ἔτι τῇ προθέσει τὴν φύσιν· καὶ κατισχύσειας ἐν Χριστῷ, δι' ὃν καὶ νῦν τὰ τῶν ἀνδρῶν ὑποκρίνῃ, γυνὴ οὖσα, καὶ μεταβαλοῦσα διὰ τὸν πρὸς αὐτὸν ἔρωτα, καὶ σχῆμα καὶ ὄνομα. Καὶ ταῦτα, οὔτε τὴν γυναικείαν σοι φύσιν δι' ὀνείδους τιθείς, οὔτε θριαμβεύειν τὰ σὰ βουλόμενος, ἀλλ' ἵνα γνῷς ὅσα μέλει περὶ σοῦ τῷ Θεῷ, καὶ ὅπως μοι ταῦτα πάντα μηδὲν ἀποκρύψας τῶν σῶν ἔδειξεν, ὅστις τε εἴης, καὶ ὅπως ἥκες, καὶ τίνες οἱ περὶ σέ, καὶ οἵας δόξης ἐν τῷ βίῳ καὶ γένους ἔτυχες.

26   "Σπεῦσον οὖν, Εὐγενία, μὴ ἔλαττον τὸ τῆς ψυχῆς εὐγενὲς ἢ τὸ τοῦ σώματος ἐπιδείξασθαι. Καὶ γὰρ δή μοι καὶ τοῦτο τῶν ἄλλων οὐχ ἧττον ἐγνώρισεν ὁ Θεός, ὅπως αὐτῷ καθαρὸν δοχεῖον σεαυτὴν προητοίμασας· τὴν μὲν παρθενίαν ἄσπιλον, τὴν δὲ καρδίαν ἄμωμον τηροῦσα· καὶ τὴν μὲν τοῦ βίου δόξαν ἀδοξίαν νομίζουσα, τὸν δὲ πλοῦτον πενίαν, λύπας δὲ τὰς ἡδονάς· καὶ οὐδὲν ἔχουσα μέγα τὴν παρὰ ἀνθρώποις εὐγένειαν· ἐκείνης δὲ μόνης ἐρῶσα, ἧς ἔκπτωτοι διὰ τὸν πρῶτον, καὶ κληρονόμοι διὰ τὸν δεύτε-ρον Ἀδὰμ γεγόναμεν."

27   Καὶ ταῦτα μὲν πρὸς Εὐγενίαν ὁ Ἕλενος. Πρὸς δὲ τὸν Πρωτᾶν καὶ Ὑάκινθον, "Ὑμεῖς δέ," φησίν, "—οὐδὲ γὰρ

fatherland, O my divine head, and lineage is the greatly-reputed Rome; we are brothers; and these are our names: the first one is called Protas, the next Hyacinth, and my name is Eugenios."

Looking upon her sweetly, the blessed Helenos said: "O 25 Eugenia, with good reason you have changed your name to Eugenios, so that your name matches your spirit, since you have a manly soul and show great manliness in all respects. May you defeat your nature even more with your will; and may you prevail in Christ, for whom, also now, while a woman, you pretend to be a man and, because of your intense desire for Him, you changed both your dress and your name. And I am saying these things, neither to disgrace your female gender, nor wishing to make a spectacle of your affairs, but so that you may learn God's great concern for you and how He did not conceal anything about you from me, but showed me who you are, how you came here, who your attendants are, and what sort of glory and lineage you were allotted in life.

"Now you should hasten, Eugenia, to prove that the no- 26 bility of your soul is no less than that of your body. For God made this known to me no less than the other things, namely, that you prepared yourself for Him as a pure vessel: preserving your virginity immaculate and your heart blameless; considering the honor of this life as dishonor, wealth as poverty, pleasure as pain; setting at naught the nobility highly prized by men; and desiring only that nobility from which we were banished on account of the first Adam, and which we have inherited on account of the second Adam."

This is what Helenos said to Eugenia. And turning to- 27 ward Protas and Hyacinth, he said, "As for you,—as Christ

οὐδὲ τὰ ὑμῶν εὐδόκησε διαλαθεῖν ὁ Χριστός—, οἵ γε τὴν
μὲν τύχην δοῦλοι, τὴν δὲ γνώμην ἐλεύθεροι τυγχάνετε
ὄντες, καὶ τὸ τῆς ψυχῆς ἀδέσποτον διατηρεῖτε ἀξίωμα,
σεμνύνοντες ἀρετῇ, πρὸς οὓς καὶ ὁ Χριστός, Οὐκέτι ὑμᾶς
καλῶ δούλους, ἀλλὰ φίλους, φησί, μακάριοι τῆς ἐλευθε-
ρίας, μᾶλλον δὲ τῆς πρὸς Χριστὸν φιλίας καὶ οἰκειώσεως,
διότι, τὸν ἐκείνου ζυγὸν ὑπελθεῖν ἑλόμενοι ἐν μιᾷ τῇ πρὸς
ἀλλήλους συμπνοίᾳ, οὐδὲν ἐμποδὼν οὐδὲ τῇ μακαρίᾳ
ταύτῃ τοῦ ἀγαθοῦ κατέστητε ἐγχειρήματος. Ἀλλὰ νῦν τε
αὐτῇ προθύμως συμπάρεστε· καί, ἀπιούσῃ τοῦ βίου, κἀκεῖ
συμπαρέσεσθε· καὶ τῶν ἴσων αὐτῇ στεφάνων καὶ γερῶν
τεύξεσθε."

28 Ταῦτα μηδενὸς ἄλλου παρόντος ὁ ἐπίσκοπος εἰρηκώς,
τὴν μὲν Εὐγενίαν ἐφίησι τῷ ἀνδρικῷ σχήματι προσμένειν,
οὐδενὶ τοῦτο γνωσθέν—οὔτε τὸ πρῶτον, οὔτε μὴν μετὰ
τὴν τοῦ ἐπισκόπου διάλεξιν. Ἥτις, συνάμα καὶ τοῖς εὐνούχοις, οὐ πρότερον αὐτὸν ἀνῆκεν, ἕως, ἐκείνου χερσὶ τοῦ
θείου καταξιωθέντες βαπτίσματος, τὸ σχῆμά τε ἤμειψαν,
καὶ τῇ τῶν μοναχῶν χορείᾳ συγκατελέγησαν.

29 Τοιαῦτα μὲν ὅσα τὸ μέχρι τοῦδε διὰ Χριστὸν Εὐγενία
διεσκέψατό τε καὶ θεοφιλῶς διεπράξατο. Τὰ δὲ ἐντεῦθεν—
ὅπως τε οἱ τεκόντες ἐπ᾽ αὐτῇ διετέθησαν, καὶ οἷα μὲν περὶ
αὐτῆς ἐλογίζοντο, οἷα δὲ μετὰ ταῦτα, τῶν ἐλπίδων διαμαρ-
τόντες, ἤλγησαν (διψᾶτε γάρ, οἶδα, καὶ ταῦτα μαθεῖν)—
ἄξιον παρελθεῖν οὐδαμῶς.

30 Ἐπεὶ γὰρ ἀωρὶ τῶν νυκτῶν, μηδενὸς αὐτοῖς τὸ πραχθὲν
αἰσθομένου, ἡ Εὐγενία μὲν τοῦ ὀχήματος ἀψοφητὶ
κατῆλθεν, Ὑάκινθος δὲ καὶ Πρωτᾶς τῶν ἄλλων ὁμοίως

did not see fit to hide anything, anything about you either—you who happen to be slaves by fortune, but are free in your mind, you who maintain the dignity of your soul unfettered, exalting it through your virtue, you to whom also Christ says, I call *you slaves no more,* but *friends,* you are blessed for your freedom and even more so on account of your friendship and affinity in respect to Christ, since by choosing to submit to His yoke in union with each other, you in no way impeded the good undertaking of this blessed girl. Now you stand eagerly here by her side; and, at her departure from this life, you will also be standing by her and will receive crowns and rewards equal to hers."

Having spoken thus with no one else present, the bishop 28 allowed Eugenia to remain in men's clothes, something that no one knew, neither from before, nor indeed after the bishop's speech. She and the eunuchs did not allow Helenos to leave, until they were dignified with the holy baptism from his own hands, and had donned the monastic habit and joined the company of monks.

Such are the deeds that Eugenia conceived and devoutly 29 accomplished for Christ up to this point. What followed—namely her parents' actions with regard to her, what they thought had happened to her, and how they grieved after their hopes were frustrated (for you thirst, I know, to learn these things too!)—would in no way deserve to be passed over.

In the dead of night, with nobody perceiving what they 30 were doing, Eugenia descended noiselessly from the chariot, Hyacinth and Protas likewise separated themselves from the

ἐξεχωρίσθησαν, κενὸν δὲ καὶ τὸ ὄχημα τοῖς προπορευομένοις ἐπηκολούθησεν, οἱ προάγοντες παῖδες, τοῦτο μὲν διὰ
τὸν καιρόν, τοῦτο δὲ καὶ διὰ τὴν τοῦ πραττομένου ἐπίκρυ-
ψιν, μηδὲν τῶν ὄπισθεν γενομένων αἰσθόμενοι, ἐπεὶ καὶ τὸ
ζῷον ἀκολουθοῦν εἶχον, ἄλλως τε δὲ καὶ τοῦ Θεοῦ συλ-
λαμβανομένου τῇ περὶ τοῦτο οἰκονομίᾳ, εὐθὺ τῆς Ἀλεξαν-
δρείας, ὡς εἶχον, ᾔεσαν.

31   Ἐπεὶ δὲ ἤδη τῇ πόλει προσέσχον, οἱ μὲν τῆς οἰκίας
γνόντες ἐξῄεσαν, μεθ᾽ (ὅσης ἂν εἴποις) τῆς ἡδονῆς, Εὐγενίαν δῆθεν ἀποληψόμενοι, τῶν τε προπομπῶν τὸ πλῆθος
ὁρῶντες, καὶ τὴν ἄλλην τῶν παίδων ἐφεξῆς συνοδίαν. Ὡς
δὲ καὶ πλησίον γενόμενοι πάντες ἐκθύμως προσέδραμον
τῷ ὀχήματι, καὶ τὴν μὲν καθέδραν κενὴν οὕτως ἑώρων,
τὴν Εὐγενίαν δὲ οὐδαμοῦ, στερρῶς τῷ ἀδοκήτῳ πληγέν-
τες, καὶ ᾧ μήποτε ἤλπισαν, εἰς δάκρυα τὸ λοιπὸν ἐχώρουν
καὶ οἰμωγάς. Καὶ κοινῇ τὸ κοινὸν ἀγαθὸν ἐδάκρυον, "Τί
γέγονε; Τί πέπρακται; Τί τὸ συμβὰν ἡμῖν ἄμαχον κακόν;"
λέγοντες. Εἶτα καὶ πρὸς ὄνομα τὴν Εὐγενίαν ἀνεκαλοῦντο,
ὄψιν χερσὶ παίοντες, χεῖρας ἀλλήλαις πατάσσοντες, περιφανῶς τῷ πάθει μεθύοντες.

32   Ἀλλὰ ταῦτα μὲν τὰ τῶν ἔξω, φίλων φημὶ καὶ γνωρίμων
καὶ μηδὲν κοινὸν ἐχόντων ἐξ αἵματος. Τῶν ἔνδον δέ, τίς
ἂν ἐκτραγῳδοίη τὴν συμφοράν; Οἱ γὰρ τεκόντες μικροῦ
καὶ ἐπὶ βρόχον ἦλθον· μικροῦ καὶ ξίφος καθ᾽ ἑαυτῶν ἐπ-
εσπάσαντο· τί μὴ φωνοῦντες ἐλεεινόν, τί μὴ δρῶντες δακρύων ἄξιον; Ἔξαινον παρειάς· κόνιν τῆς κεφαλῆς κατ-
έχεον· αἰσχρῶς ἑαυτοὺς τῇ γῇ κατέβαλλον· ἐπεβοῶντο

others, and an empty chariot followed the advance escort; the servants who were leading the procession, either because of the time of night or the stealthy nature of the deed, noticed nothing of what was happening behind them; and as also the horse drawing the chariot continued to follow them and, in any case, as God intervened and arranged this matter, they went straight to Alexandria in this very way.

When they were already close to the city, the people from 31 her household, recognizing them, came out to receive the one whom they thought was Eugenia with what great (would you say) joy, for they saw the multitude of attendants and the rest of the retinue of servants. As they approached, however, and everyone rushed excitedly to the chariot, but saw the seat empty and Eugenia nowhere to be seen, they were harshly stricken by the unexpected turn of events, one which they had never anticipated; they thus turned to tears and wailing. They all wept together at the loss of the blessing they had in common, saying, "What has happened? What has been done? What is this overwhelming evil that has befallen us?" Then, they also called out for Eugenia by name, striking their faces with their hands, beating their hands against each other, plainly inebriated by grief.

These were the reactions of people who did not belong to 32 the family, I mean friends and acquaintances with no blood relationship. But who could express the tragic suffering of her household? Her parents all but put a noose around their necks, all but drew the sword upon themselves. What pitiable expression did they not utter? What did they not do that was worthy of tears? They scratched their cheeks; poured dust on their heads; they threw themselves shamefully on the ground, and lamented bitterly, the parents for

πικρῶς, οἱ πατέρες τὴν θυγατέρα, οἱ ἀδελφοὶ τὴν γνησίαν, οἱ δοῦλοι τὴν δέσποιναν. Οὐδεὶς ἄτρωτος, οὐδεὶς τοῦ πάθους ἐλεύθερος· ἀλλ' οὕτω κομιδῇ κατειλήφει τὸν οἶκον, χωρὶς πυρός, ἐμπρησμός.

33   Ἐπεὶ δὲ ἄπρακτον τὸ δακρύειν ἑώρων, ἐπὶ τὴν ζήτησιν τῆς φιλτάτης ἐχώρουν. Ἡρωτῶντο οὖν ἔμποροι· περιειργάζοντο γεωργοί, χωρίων οἰκήτορες, ὁδῶν φύλακες· ἐπηρωτῶντο μάντεις, ἐγγαστρίμυθοι· πάντα τὰ τῶν δαιμόνων ἠρευνῶντο μαντεῖα καὶ θυσίαις ἐθεραπεύοντο. Ὡς δὲ οὐκ ἦν τῆς ζητουμένης ἡ εὕρεσις, ἐν τοῖς πατράσιν ἐπινοοῦσιν οἵ γε παρηγορεῖν δοκοῦντες τοῦ δεινοῦ παραμύθιον. Μῦθόν τινα πλάττουσι, τοῖς ᾀδομένοις παρ' Ἕλλησιν οὐδὲν ἀνόμοιον· ὅτιπερ Εὐγενίας οἱ θεοὶ ἔρωτα σχόντες, εἰς οὐρανὸν αὐτὴν ἀνηρπάσαντο. Ὅπερ τῷ μὲν πατρί, ἅτε πολλοῖς τοιούτοις ἐνειθισμένῳ τὴν ἀκοήν, εὐπαράδεκτον ἦν. Τιμαῖς τε τὴν θυγατέρα διαφερόντως ἐτίμα· καὶ ἄγαλμα ταύτῃ χρυσοῦν ἀνεστήσατο· καὶ ὡς καινῇ θεᾷ θύειν ἤρξατο. Ἡ μήτηρ δὲ καὶ οἱ ἀδελφοί, Ἀβίτας τε καὶ Σέργιος, οὐκ εἶχον ὁμοίως. Ἀλλὰ πιστεύειν οὕτω τοῖς λεγομένοις ὀκνήσαντες, ἰσχυρῶς ἐπένθουν. Πλὴν ἀλλὰ τὰ μὲν μετὰ τὴν φυγὴν Εὐγενίας, καὶ ὅπως οὐ γονέων αὐτῇ μόνον ἀλλὰ καὶ τῶν ἄλλως πρὸς αὐτὴν φιλίως διακειμένων καθίκετο, οὕτως ἔχει.

34   Τῇ Εὐγενίᾳ δέ, πολλὴ μὲν ἡ περὶ τὴν μελέτην τῶν θείων Γραφῶν προσεδρεία, πολλὴ δὲ ἡ περὶ τὴν κτῆσιν τῆς ἀρετῆς ἐπιμέλεια. Παρ' ὅ, καὶ μὴ πλεῖον ἢ δύο ἔτη τῇ μονῇ συνδιενεγκοῦσα, τῶν πάντων ἐκράτει (γυνὴ φημὶ τῶν ἀνδρῶν· ὥστε κοινὸν ἡ ἀρετή, καὶ οὐδὲν ἀπὸ τοῦ γένους

their daughter, the brothers for their sister, the slaves for their mistress. Nobody was unscathed, nobody was free from pain. A conflagration, only without fire, engulfed the house.

When they realized that tears were futile, they began 33 searching for their beloved girl. Merchants were questioned; farmers were interrogated, as were the inhabitants of villages and guards of the roads; seers and ventriloquists were consulted; all the oracles of the demons were sought out and had sacrifices offered to them. As she who was sought was nowhere to be found, those men who seemingly offer consolation devised a way to assuage the disaster for the parents. They fabricated a false story, not at all dissimilar to those sung by the pagan Greeks: namely that the gods had fallen in love with Eugenia and snatched her up to the heavens. The father readily accepted this story, as he was quite accustomed to hear many such tales. He thus honored his daughter with preeminent honors; he set up a golden statue in her likeness and began to sacrifice to her as if she were some new goddess. Her mother and brothers, Abitas and Sergios, did not, however, feel the same way. Reluctant to believe the story, they grieved profoundly. In any case, that is what happened after Eugenia's flight, and that is how it affected not only her parents but also others who considered her dear to them.

Meanwhile, Eugenia greatly exerted herself in the study 34 of the holy Scriptures, and to the same degree practiced due diligence in the acquisition of virtue. The result was that, though she had lived in the monastery for no more than two years, she surpassed everyone (a woman, I mean, surpassed the men; hence virtue is common to all, and gender poses no

κώλυμα τῷ κατορθοῦν βουλομένῳ). Ἦν οὖν ἡ Εὐγενία
κατ᾽ ἀρετὴν πρωτεύουσα· ἴδιον δὲ μάλιστα ταύτης, τὸ
ἐπιεικές τε καὶ μέτριον, καὶ τό, πρώτην οὖσαν ἐν τοῖς καλοῖς, οὐδὲν ἧττον καὶ πρώτην εἶναι τῷ μετρίῳ δηλαδὴ τοῦ
φρονήματος. Εὐγενίας καὶ ταῦτα γνωρίσματα, τὸ πρώτην
πάντων ἐν ταῖς συνάξεσιν ἀπαντῶσαν, ἐσχάτην αὖθις τῶν
ἄλλων ἀναχωρεῖν· πρὸς δὲ καὶ τῷ λυπουμένῳ παντὶ συμ-
πάσχειν, συγχαίρειν δὲ γνησίως καὶ τοῖς εὖ πάσχουσιν—
ὅπερ ἄρα καὶ πρὸς τὸ κατορθοῦν δυσχερέστερον διὰ τὰς
ἐκ τοῦ φθόνου κακοηθείας· τὸ λόγον ἔχειν παντὸς ὀργιζο-
μένου στορέσαι καρδίαν ἀνυσιμώτατον, ὥστε τὸν ἴσα καὶ
θηρσὶν ἀγριαίνοντα προβάτῳ δεῖξαι τὴν ἡμερότητα παρα-
πλήσιον.

35 Τὸ τελευταῖον τοῦτο καὶ πρῶτον καὶ πάντων ἀτεχνῶς
περιεκτικώτατον, ἡ πρὸς πάντας ἀψευδὴς ἀγάπη, καὶ μὴ
μέχρι χειλέων ἱστῶσα τὸ φίλτρον, ἀλλὰ καὶ ἀπὸ μέσης
ψυχῆς συνάπτουσα. Οὐ πολὺ τὸ ἐν μέσῳ, καὶ χάρις αὐτῇ
τῶν ἰαμάτων ἐπιφοιτᾷ (μεθ᾽ ὅσης τῆς ἀφθονίας!)· καὶ διὰ
τοῦτο ὅσοις ἂν καὶ κατ᾽ ἐπίσκεψιν νόσου παραβεβλήκοι,
οὐκ ἐκ τοῦ λέγειν μόνον αὐτοῖς ἐδίδου τὰς παρακλήσεις,
ἀλλὰ καὶ τοῦ λυποῦντος ἠφίει νοσήματος. Μιμοῦνται δὲ
αὐτὴν ὅσα πρὸς δύναμιν Πρωτᾶς καὶ Ὑάκινθος οὓς καὶ ὁ
λόγος ἤδη φθάσας ἐγνώρισεν.

36 Οὕτως Εὐγενίας βιούσης, ὁ τῆς μονῆς προεστὼς μετὰ
τρίτον ἔτος ἀπολείπει τὸν βίον. Ἐκάλει δὲ αὐτὴν ἡ κοινὴ
τῶν ἀδελφῶν ψῆφος εἰς προστασίαν, ὡς ἀνδρὶ προσέχον-
τες, καὶ τὸ μὲν περιὸν τῆς ἀρετῆς εἰδότες, ἀγνοοῦντες δὲ
τὸ παρ᾽ αὐτῇ κρυπτόμενον. Λαμβάνει γοῦν φόβος ἐκείνην

hindrance to one wishing to achieve virtue). Eugenia was thus first in virtue; and her most distinctive feature was this: her clemency and modesty, and the fact that, while she was first in virtue, she was no less first also in modesty of spirit. The following qualities too characterized Eugenia: she arrived first before everyone at the services, but was last to depart; she suffered with whomever was grieving, and genuinely rejoiced with those faring well—which is of course more difficult to achieve because of the malignity of jealousy; she always had a word most effective at mollifying the heart of anyone who was angry, so much so that she could make someone as wild as a savage animal act almost as mildly as a sheep.

Finally there was this, the first of all things, and that 35 which simply encompasses all: her unfeigned love for everyone, which did not show affection only so far as the lips, but rather extended from the depths of her soul. After not much time had passed, the grace of healing came upon her (with what abundance!). Because of this, whenever she would visit someone who was ill, she not only provided consolation with words, but would also release them from the afflicting illness. Protas and Hyacinth, who have already been mentioned, imitated her as much as they could.

Three years after Eugenia began to live in this way, the ab- 36 bot of the monastery departed from this life. The common vote of the brethren called Eugenia to the abbacy, as if offering it to a man, since they saw the profusion of her virtue but were ignorant of that which she concealed. She was overwhelmed by fear and perplexity; for she did not consider

καὶ ἀπορία· οὔτε γὰρ γυναῖκα οὖσαν προεστάναι ἀνδρῶν
ἐδικαίου, καὶ τὸ παριδεῖν ἀδελφότητα κοινῶς ἀξιοῦσαν
ἰσχυρογνώμονος εἶναι καὶ ἀπειθοῦς ἔκρινεν. Ἔδοξε τοίνυν
ἐκ τοῦ Εὐαγγελίου τί ποιητέον μαθεῖν, Θεῷ τὸ ἄδηλον
ἐπιτρέψασα. Ἐπεὶ δὲ ἀνεπτύσσετο, ἡ δεσποτικὴ αὕτη θαυ-
μασίως ὑπηχεῖτο φωνή, "Εἴ τις θέλει ἐν ὑμῖν εἶναι πρῶτος,
ἔστω πάντων ἔσχατος, καὶ πάντων διάκονος." Τούτου ῥηθέν-
τος, τὴν μὲν προστασίαν ὑπέρχεται, καὶ μὴ βουλομένη,
τῆς διακονίας δὲ ὅλη καὶ οὕτως ἑκοῦσα γίνεται (τί μὴ
ποιοῦσα τῶν εὐτελῶν καὶ ὑπ᾽ αὐτῶν ὅλως τῶν μικρῶν
ἀπαξιουμένων; ὕδωρ ἐξαντλοῦσα τοῦ φρέατος· οἰκίαν σα-
ροῦσα· ξύλα διακλῶσα χερσί· καὶ τἆλλα πάντα ὅσα μᾶλλον
τῶν ἐλαχίστων ἐστὶ κατὰ σπουδὴν πράττουσα) ὥστε καὶ
θυρωρὸς εἶναι διὰ τὸ πρὸς τὴν ἐντολὴν εὐπειθέστατον
ἡδέως ἀνέχεσθαι.

37   Οὕτω τὸ μέτριον διαφερόντως ἀσκήσασα, καὶ οὕτω κἂν
τῇ προστασίᾳ πάλιν περιφανῶς διαλάμψασα, εἴχετο καὶ ἔτι
τῆς πρὸς Θεὸν φερούσης, τοῖς μὲν ἔμπροσθεν, ἥπερ ὁ θεῖος
Παῦλός φησιν, ἐπεκτεινομένη, λήθην δὲ τῶν ὄπισθεν
ποιουμένη τῷ προθύμῳ τῆς ἐργασίας. Ὅσων μὲν οὖν θαυμάτων αὐτουργὸς γέγονεν, ἑτέρου διηγεῖσθαι καιροῦ
σχολῆς τε ἰδίας τοῦ πράγματος δεομένου, καὶ ἄλλως φεύ-
γοντος τοῦ λόγου τὸ μῆκος διὰ τὸν κόρον, ὃ δὲ καὶ λίαν
ἀναγκαῖον εἰπεῖν, καὶ ᾧ μαρτυρίου τέλος ἀκολουθεῖ, καὶ
τὸν εἱρμὸν ἀκόλουθον ἔχει τοῖς ἐφεξῆς, τοῦτο δὴ καὶ
λεχθήσεται.

38   Ἦν τις ἐν Ἀλεξανδρείᾳ γυνή, τοὔνομα Μελανθία, πο-
λυτάλαντος μὲν τὴν οὐσίαν, φόβου δὲ θείου καὶ ἀρετῆς

it right that as a woman she should rule over men, but she thought it would be obstinate and disobedient to disregard the common will of the brotherhood. Therefore she decided to learn from the Gospel what should be done, entrusting the problem to God. When the book was opened at random, these words of the Lord marvelously resounded, "*If anyone* among you *wants to be first, let him be last of all, and the servant of all.*" On account of these words, she assumed the abbacy against her will, but also assumed a position of servitude fully and so willingly (which of the humble duties spurned by even the lesser brethren did she not perform? She drew water from the well; swept the building; chopped wood; and zealously accomplished all the other things which are the domain of the lowest) that she even cheerfully accepted to become a doorkeeper because of her utter obedience to the commandment.

By exercising her modesty so outstandingly, and distin- 37 guishing herself also in her abbacy so strikingly, she continued to follow the way leading to God, while "*reaching forth,*" as divine Paul says, "*unto those things which lie ahead,*" and, in her zeal for labor, forgetting what lies behind. Now we would need another occasion and appropriate leisure to speak about how many miracles she performed, and, besides, storytelling avoids length so as to prevent excess; thus, this narration will present that which is obligatory to recount and those events which were followed by the martyrdom, and anticipated in sequence what was to come.

In Alexandria lived a woman by name of Melanthia, well 38 endowed with property, but lacking in the fear of God and

ἐνδεῶς ἔχουσα. Αὕτη ποτὲ χρονίῳ νοσήματι καὶ βαρεῖ λη-
φθεῖσα (ῥῖγος γὰρ ἦν τὸ διὰ τετάρτης ἐπισημαῖνον), ἐπειδὴ
δὲ καὶ αὐτὴν ἡ φήμη συμπεριέλαβεν ἄνδρα τινὰ εἶναι, τὴν
μὲν κλῆσιν Εὐγένιον, τὸν βίον δὲ πᾶσιν ἀξιοθαύμαστον,
τὰ δυσχερῆ τῶν νοσημάτων εὐχερῶς λύοντα, παραυτίκα
τἄλλα πάντα σχολάζειν ἀφεῖσα, τῷ μοναστηρίῳ πρὸς τάχος ἐπιφοιτᾷ· καὶ θερμῶς αἰτεῖται τῆς πιεζούσης μάστιγος
τὴν ἐλευθερίαν. Οἶκτος οὖν λαμβάνει τὴν Εὐγενίαν· καὶ
τῷ ἁγίῳ ταύτην ἐλαίῳ ἁγίαις χερσὶ περιχρίσασα, παραχρῆμα τὴν νοσοποιὸν ὕλην ἐξεμέσαι ποιεῖ. Καὶ οὕτως ἡ
Μελανθία καθαρᾶς τυχοῦσα τῆς ὑγιείας, ἐπάνεισι μὲν
ἐρρωμένη. Πρός τινα δὲ τῶν ταύτης ἀγρῶν, ὃς καὶ τῇ
μονῇ ἐν γειτόνων ἦν, παραγίνεται.

39 Καὶ μετ᾽ οὐ πολὺ ἀργύρου φαιδροῦ τρία σκεύη φιλοκά-
λως ἀσκήσασα, πέμπει τῇ Εὐγενίᾳ, τῷ εὐκτηρίῳ δῆθεν τῆς
μονῆς οἴκῳ δῶρα καθοσιοῦσα εὐχαριστήρια. Μὴ προσιε-
μένης δὲ τὴν προσαγωγήν—ἔφασκε γὰρ οὐ λυσιτελῆ μοναχοῖς εἶναι οὐδ᾽ οἰκείαν τὴν τοῦ ἀργύρου κτῆσιν, ἀλλὰ
πωλεῖν δεῖ καὶ πένησι διανέμειν, ἢ χρεῶν ἄλλως βάρει πι-
εζομένοις—, αὐτὴ πρὸς τὴν Εὐγενίαν φοιτήσασα, καὶ τί
πρὸς πειθὼ μὴ εἰποῦσα ἢ δράσασα, πείθει λαβεῖν καὶ ἀνα-
θεῖναι τὸν ἄργυρον τῷ ναῷ.

40 Ἦν δὲ ἄρα τῆς ἀσεβείας ὑπόθεσις ἡ εὐσέβεια. Καὶ
ἀληθὲς τὸ πάλαι ῥηθέν, ὅτι οὐδὲν ἐγγίζον οὕτως ἄλλο
πρὸς ἕτερον ὡς ἀρετὴ πρὸς κακίαν, καὶ πολλάκις τις παρὰ
ταύτην βαδίζων, τῆς ἐναντίας λαθὼν εἴσω γέγονεν. Ὁ δὴ
καὶ Μελανθίᾳ συμπέπτωκεν· ἀρετῆς γὰρ ἴσως μετρίως

virtue. Once when she was afflicted by a long-lasting and grievous disease (its distinguishing symptom was shivering on every fourth day) and as the rumor reached her too that there was a man, named Eugenios, whose life was worthy of wonder in every respect, as he could easily heal the most recalcitrant diseases, Melanthia abandoned all her other affairs straightaway, went to the monastery without delay, and fervently begged to be liberated from the oppressive scourge. Compassion overtook Eugenia; and so with her own holy hands she anointed the woman with the holy oil, causing her to vomit forth the pathogenic matter immediately. Thus Melanthia, fully recuperated, departed in good health. And she went to one of her estates near the monastery.

A short time later, she had three elegant vessels beautifully fashioned from gleaming silver which she sent to Eugenia, ostensibly dedicating them as thank-offerings to the chapel in the monastery. But as Eugenia did not accept the gift—saying that the acquisition of silver is neither useful nor fitting for monks and that, instead, she should sell them and distribute the money among the poor or people otherwise oppressed by the burden of debts—Melanthia came to Eugenia in person; doing and saying everything to convince her, she persuaded her to take the silver and dedicate it to the church. 39

Yet piety in this case was a pretext for impiety. Indeed, the old saying is true that nothing is as close to another as virtue is to evil and that, often, someone walking the path toward virtue finds himself, without even noticing, walking in the opposite direction. This is exactly what happened to Melanthia; perhaps because she did not care for virtue 40

φροντίζουσα, λέληθε τῷ μὴ προσέχειν τὸν νοῦν εἰς ἄκρον
μοχθηρίας παρενεχθεῖσα. Ἤδη γὰρ συνήθης γεγονυῖα,
καὶ συνεχῶς παρὰ ταύτην ἰοῦσα, ἄνδρα τε ὁρῶσα τῷ φαι-
νομένῳ νεάζοντα καὶ τὴν ὄψιν περικαλλῆ, ἔρως αὐτὴν
εἰσέρχεται, οὔμενουν ἀγεννής, καὶ κατὰ μικρὸν ἐθέλγετο
τὴν ψυχήν. Εἶτα καὶ ἰσχυρῶς ἀνεφλέγετο, νομίζουσα μηδ᾽
ἂν Εὐγενίαν ἁγνεύειν ποτὲ δύνασθαι, ἀλλὰ μηδὲ τὴν τῆς
νόσου φυγὴν θεϊκῆς εἶναι χάριτος, τέχνης δὲ μᾶλλον μαγικῆς καὶ ἀντιθέτου δυνάμεως.

41   Ταῦτα τὴν καρδίαν αὐτῆς ἐπισχόντα, φλόξ τε τοῦ ἔρω-
τος χαλεπή, καὶ ἀπιστία δεινὴ πείθουσι καὶ αὐτῷ τῷ ἔργῳ
ἐπιτολμῆσαι καὶ τὰ τοῦ σκότους παρρησιάσασθαι· δεινὸν
γὰρ καὶ ἰταμώτατον ἔρως, καὶ οὐχ οὕτως οὐδὲν τῶν ἀνε-
φίκτων ὃ μὴ ἐφικτὸν ἐκείνῳ δοκεῖ καὶ ἀνύσιμον. Διαιτω-
μένη γοῦν ἐν ἀγροῖς ὥσπερ εἴρηται γείτοσι τῆς μονῆς, καὶ
τὴν ψυχὴν σφόδρα παθαινομένη, σώματος ἀσθένειαν ὑπο-
κρίνεται· καὶ ἀπίστῳ τάχει μετεκαλεῖτο τὴν Εὐγενίαν, οὐ
τὴν προσποίητον ταύτην νόσον ἰασομένην, ἀλλὰ τῆς
ἀψευδοῦς καὶ κρυφίας ἐλεεινῶς κοινωνήσουσαν.

42   Ἐπεὶ δὲ καὶ τὸ ποθούμενον πρόσωπον εἴσω θυρῶν ἦν,
ἡ Μελανθία, τὸ πάθος ἔνδον φλεγμαῖνον οὐκ ἐνεγκοῦσα,
εὐθὺς ἐκ τοῦ πονηροῦ θησαυροῦ πονηροὺς προΐησι λόγους. Καὶ πρῶτα μὲν πρὸς ἄθεσμον ἠπείγετο μίξιν· "Εἰ δὲ
μὴ βούλοιο," φησίν, "ἀλλὰ καὶ νόμῳ γάμου λήψομαί σε
φανερῶς εἰς ἄνδρα· καὶ πλούτου κύριος ἔσῃ πολλοῦ, χρυσοῦ, ἀργύρου, ἐσθῆτος πολυτελοῦς, ἀγρῶν, κτηνῶν,
ἀνδραπόδων, μεθ᾽ ὧν ἕξεις κἀμὲ δούλην, ἀντ᾽ ἐλευθέρας

enough, she was carried unawares to the height of licentiousness by failing to safeguard her mind. As she became friendly with Eugenia and continually visited her, upon seeing a man, youthful in appearance and beautiful in his face, desire (albeit not a degenerate sort) entered her, and, little by little, her soul was seduced. Soon, she was burning intensely, thinking that Eugenia could not remain chaste forever, and in fact that her own earlier escape from the disease was not due to divine grace, but rather to witchcraft and a hostile power.

These thoughts that overpowered her heart, the disastrous flame of desire, and a terrible lack of faith persuaded her to venture upon the very deed and to express boldly her dark intent; for love is reckless and has a terrible force, and there is nothing impossible which it does not consider possible and attainable. Spending her time on an estate that was, as has been mentioned, next to the monastery and suffering greatly in her soul, she feigned an illness of the body; and with astonishing swiftness she summoned Eugenia, not so that she might cure her feigned disease, but so that she too might be pitiably infected with the real but hidden illness. 41

Once the person she desired was inside her doors Melanthia was unable to bear the passion burning inside her and instantly uttered wicked words from the treasury of evil. First, she urged eagerly for an illicit union; "And if you do not want this," she said, "then I shall take you openly as my husband by law; and you will be the lord of great wealth, gold, silver, fine clothing, fields, herds, and slaves, and, together with these things, you will also have me as your slave rather than a woman who is free and of equal worth. And 42

καὶ ὁμοτίμου. Καὶ τούτων ἀπολαύσεις πάντως αὐτός, ἐπεὶ
καὶ ἀνδρὸς ἔρημος ἐγὼ καὶ παίδων καὶ συγγενῶν· εἰς τί
γὰρ καὶ ἄνθος σώματος οὕτω καλὸν καὶ ὥρα πάγκαλος
ἀσκήσει καὶ πόνοις τηκόμενα διαμείνοι;"

43   Ταῦτα τῆς Μελανθίας θερμῷ καὶ συνεχεῖ πνεύματι δι-
εξιούσης, ἡ μακαρία καὶ καθ᾽ ἕκαστον μὲν τῶν λεγομένων
ἔστενε, καὶ τῆς διαλέξεως σφόδρα τὸ ἐμπαθὲς ἐμυσάττετο.
Τέλος δὲ πρὸς τὴν πολλὴν αὐτῆς ἀδολεσχίαν ἰλιγγιάσασα,
κηρῷ (τὸ τοῦ λόγου) φραξαμένη τὰ ὦτα, καὶ μηδὲ ἀκούειν
εἰσέτι ἀνεχομένη, "Ἐπίσχες," ἐξεβόησε, "γύναι, ἐπίσχες,
καὶ μακρὰν ταῦτ᾽ ἄγε ἀφ᾽ ἡμῶν· αὐτὸν γὰρ ἡμῖν τὸν ἰὸν
τοῦ παλαιοῦ δράκοντος ἀποπτύεις. Οὐ προησόμεθα τὴν
ἁγνείαν· οὐ φθεροῦμεν τὴν παρθενίαν· οὐ, Θεοῦ Μῆτερ
ἐφ᾽ ἣν ἐγὼ πέποιθα καὶ Παρθένε, οὐ ψεύσομαι τὰς ἐμὰς
συνθήκας. Εἷς ἡμῖν γάμος, ὁ πρὸς Χριστὸν πόθος· εἷς
πλοῦτος, τὰ ἐν οὐρανοῖς ἀγαθά· μία κτῆσις, ἡ γνῶσις τῆς
ἀληθείας."

44   Τούτων ἡ ἄσεμνος ἀκούσασα Μελανθία, θυμῷ τε ἀπορρήτῳ διακαυθεῖσα (βαρὺς γὰρ ἔρως, καὶ οὐδὲ καθεκτὸς
ὅλως), πρὸς τὴν Ἀλεξανδρέων ἐχώρει, δεινὰ λίαν κατὰ
Εὐγενίας ὠδίνουσα. Εἶτα καὶ χαλεπὴν αὐτῇ συρράψασα
τὴν διαβολήν, ἐφίσταται τῷ ἐπάρχῳ Φιλίππῳ, μηδὲν εἰδυῖα
τῶν κατ᾽ αὐτήν, μήθ᾽ ὅτι πατὴρ οὗτος Εὐγενίας, μήθ᾽
ὅπως ἐκείνη ἐκ γυναικὸς εἰς ἄνδρα τὸ σχῆμα μεταβεβλή-
κοι.

45   Τούτῳ τοιγαροῦν ἐπιστᾶσα, μέτεισιν ἐξ ἀκολασίας πρὸς
τὴν συκοφαντίαν· καὶ κατηγορεῖν ἄρχεται λίαν κακοήθως
καὶ πονηρῶς, "Νεανίας τις," λέγουσα, "τὴν μὲν ὄψιν

you alone will take pleasure in these things in every way, for I am without husband, children or relatives. Why should such a fine blossoming body and this fairest beauty continue to wither away in asceticism and toil?"

While Melanthia said these things in one continuous, fe- 43
verish breath, the blessed Eugenia sighed at every word, and felt strong disgust at the vile discourse. Finally, becoming dizzy with Melanthia's excessive prattling, she plugged her ears with wax, as the saying goes, unable to tolerate even the sound of another word. "Stop," she yelled, "woman, stop, and keep these things far from me; you are spewing at me the very venom of the ancient serpent. I will not abandon my chastity, nor destroy my virginity; I will not, O Mother of God and Virgin in whom I have placed my faith, renege on my vows. For me the only wedlock is yearning for Christ; my only wealth is heavenly goods; my only possession is knowledge of the truth."

When the indecent Melanthia heard these words, she be- 44
gan to burn with unspeakable rage (for desire is hard to bear and cannot be restrained); bursting with terrible fury against Eugenia, she left for Alexandria. Then, she also devised a terrible and false accusation against her and went to the eparch Philip, since she knew nothing about Eugenia, neither that Philip was Eugenia's father, nor that she had changed her appearance from that of a woman to that of a man.

And so when she came before him, she switched from 45
licentiousness to calumny, and began to make abominable and evil accusations. "There is a young man," she said, "who

περικαλλής, τὸν δὲ τρόπον καὶ λίαν ἐναγής, Χριστιανῶν ὑποκριθεὶς εὐλάβειαν, εἰσῆλθε πρός με. Μίαν δὲ κἀμὲ νομίσας τῶν ἀσέμνων εἶναι, πρῶτον μὲν ῥήμασιν ἀπατηλοῖς εἶτα καὶ χερσὶν ὁ πάντολμος πρὸς βίαν ἐχρῆτο. Καὶ εἴ γε μὴ γεγωνότερον ἐξεβόησα, καὶ ἐπιστῆναι τὴν θεράπαιναν παρεσκεύασα δρομαίαν, ὡς μία ἂν καὶ αὐτὴ τῶν ἐξηνδραποδισμένων ἐμιαινόμην." Οὕτως ἡ ἀναιδὴς τὸ ἐκείνης μῦσος τῇ καθαρᾷ περιάπτειν ἐτόλμα· καὶ ἅπερ αὐτὴ δράσειε παθεῖν μᾶλλον προσεποιεῖτο.

46   Ταῦτα οὕτω ῥηθέντα ἐξέμηνεν ἰσχυρῶς τὸν ἔπαρχον· καὶ δεσμίους ἄγεσθαι παρ' αὐτὸν ἐκέλευσεν, οὐκ Εὐγενίαν μόνην, ἀλλὰ καὶ πάντας ἅμα τοὺς σὺν αὐτῇ. Τούτους μὲν οὖν, κατὰ τὸ κελευσθὲν ἀχθέντας, αἱ φρουραὶ ἄλλον ἄλλη διεμερίζοντο· ᾠήθη γὰρ ὁ ἔπαρχος, μὴ ἄν ποτε τοιαῦτα διαψεύσασθαι Μελανθίαν, γυναῖκα οὕτω τε εὐγενῆ, καὶ πλούτῳ καὶ δόξῃ περιφανῶς ἔχουσαν, οὐκ εἰδὼς ὅτι πλούτου καὶ περιφανείας ἰσχυρότερον ψυχῆς πάθος, καὶ δυνάμενον πεῖσαι μικρὰ μὲν ἐκεῖνα λογίσασθαι, διὰ δὲ τὸ δοκοῦν ἐν τῷ παρόντι φίλον ἑλέσθαι τὸ ψεῦδος. Τοιγαροῦν ἐρήμην οἱ δικάζοντες πάντες μικροῦ τῶν ἁγίων κατεψηφίζοντο· καὶ τούτων, οἱ μὲν ὀδοῦσι θηρῶν ὑποβληθῆναι αὐτοὺς ἐδικαίουν, οἱ δὲ ἀναρτήσει ξύλων, οἱ δὲ ἑτέροις πικροτέροις τρόποις τιμωριῶν, κολάζοντες ἅμα τῇ συκοφαντίᾳ καὶ τὴν εὐσέβειαν.

47   Ἐπεὶ οὖν ἡ κυρία παρέστη, τὸ μὲν πλῆθος ἅπαν τῶν πέριξ συνήγετο πόλεων· παρῆν δὲ καὶ ὁ ἔπαρχος. Καὶ ἡ Εὐγενία εἰς μέσον ἤγετο, βαρυτάταις ἁλύσεσιν ἑλκομένη· κραυγαὶ δὲ τοῦ θεάτρου πάντοθεν ἀνερρήγνυντο· καὶ

has a beautiful appearance but is very wicked in his conduct; feigning the piety of Christians, he approached me. Thinking that I was one of those indecent women, that brazen man first used deceitful words and then assaulted me with his hands. If I had not called out loudly, causing my handmaid to come running, I too would now be defiled as if I were a slave woman." Thus the shameless Melanthia dared to attribute her own loathsome behavior to the pure Eugenia, and pretended that she had suffered the very fate she herself had intended to inflict.

These words fiercely enraged the eparch; he ordered that 46 not only Eugenia but also all her companions be brought to him in chains. When they had been brought as commanded, the guards separated them from one another; for the eparch thought that a woman of such nobility and so distinguished in wealth and fame as Melanthia would never make up such tales; he did not know that a soul's passion is stronger than wealth and prestige, and that it can persuade one to consider wealth and prestige to be a small matter and to choose falsehood for the sake of what seems dear at the present moment. The judges, almost to a man, condemned the saints by default; some of them passed judgment that they be thrown to the jaws of wild beasts, some that they be hung up on wooden gibbets, others thought of still more bitter forms of retribution, punishing piety together with the falsely reported crime.

When the appointed day arrived, whole multitudes gath- 47 ered from the surrounding cities and the eparch came too. Eugenia was led into their midst, dragged along with the heaviest of chains; shouts erupted from every corner of the

πάντες θανατοῦσθαι τὴν Εὐγενίαν κοινῶς ἀπεφαίνοντο. Ἡτοιμάζοντο θῆρες, ἡτοιμάζοντο στρέβλαι, τροχοί, πῦρ, ἕτερα εἴδη κολαστηρίων, καὶ διὰ πάντων οἱ πικροὶ κολασταὶ καὶ πρὸς τὰς τιμωρίας ἐπίσης ὠμότατοι καὶ ὀξύτατοι. Ἄγεσθαι τοιγαροῦν εἰς ὄψιν αὐτῷ τὴν Εὐγενίαν ἐπέταττεν ὁ δικάζων. Καὶ παραστάσης, "Τοῦτο ὑμῖν," ἔφη, "πάντων ἀνθρώπων ἀνοσιώτατε, ὁ ὑμέτερος ἐπιτρέπει Χριστός, τὸ μηδὲ κρυφῇ τὰ αἴσχιστα πράττειν, ἀλλ᾽ ἀναιδῶς οὕτω καὶ βιαίως τοῖς ἀθεμίτοις ἐπιχειρεῖν; Ἐπεὶ τίνα εἶχες σὺ τὴν ψυχήν, ὁπόταν ὡς ἰατρὸς εἰσιών, καὶ οὐχ ἁπλῶς ἰατρός, ἀλλὰ καὶ αὐτουργὸς θαυμάτων εἶναι δυνάμενος, τὰ τῶν λοιμῶν ἐποίεις καὶ τῶν μοιχῶν; Καὶ γυναῖκα, οὕτω μὲν γένους, οὕτω δὲ πλούτου, οὕτω δὲ καὶ τρόπου σώφρονος ἔχουσαν, οἷά τινα τῶν ἐπὶ τῆς σκηνῆς, ἢ δούλην ἐκ πολεμίας λαβών, αἰσχῦναι προείλου; Τοιγαροῦν τοῦ τολμήματος ἀξίαν ὑφέξεις τὴν δίκην, κακὸς κακῶς ἀπολλύμενος."

48   Οὕτω τοῦ ἐπάρχου πρὸς αὐτὴν ὀργίλως διαπειλησαμένου, ἡ Εὐγενία, τὸ πρόσωπον εἰς γῆν κλίνασα, ἵνα μὴ τό γε νῦν ἔχον ὄψις οὕτως οἰκεία δήλη τῷ πατρὶ γένοιτο, "Ὁ μὲν ἐμός," ἔφη, "Θεὸς οὐ ταῦτα μόνον ἃ νῦν κατηγόρημαι παρ᾽ ὑμῶν ἀπαγορεύει, ἀλλὰ καὶ ὑψηλότερα πολλῷ τούτων νομοθετεῖ. Ὅς, κἀμὲ νῦν ἀγνεύειν διὰ παντὸς βουλόμενος, τοῖς ἀσκητικοῖς ἀνδράσι τούτοις συμβιοῦν ᾠκονόμησεν, ὥσπερ δὴ καὶ εἰσέτι νῦν με διατετήρηκεν, ὡς αὐτῷ τε δῆλόν ἐστι, καὶ ὑμῖν ὅσον οὔπω γενήσεται. Ὅτι δέ μοι καὶ βασάνους καὶ θάνατον ἀπειλεῖς, λέληθας, τὸ τοῦ λόγου, ἀδεὲς δέος μοι ἐπισείων· αἰσχυναίμην γὰρ ἄν, εἰ φόβῳ τούτων ζητοίην ἀπολογεῖσθαι, ἀλλὰ μὴ φόβῳ τοῦ δόξαι τὰ

amphitheater; all with one accord declared that Eugenia must die. Wild beasts were readied; instruments of torture were prepared, wheels, fire, other types of punishment, and above all, the harsh torturers, most savage and quick in the exacting of vengeance. Then the judge ordered Eugenia to be led into his presence. When she had appeared, he said: "O most impious of all men, does your Christ enjoin this on you people: not even to hide your most despicable actions, but to undertake unlawful deeds in such shameless and violent manner? For what sort of soul did you have, that when you entered the building as a doctor, and not simply a doctor, but one able to perform miracles, you acted like adulterers and spreaders of pestilence? And a woman of such lineage, such wealth, and such chaste manners—why did you attempt to disgrace her as if she were like a woman from the stage, or as if you took her from the enemy as a slave? You will, therefore, receive a punishment worthy of your brazen act: as an evil man you will die an evil death."

After the eparch had so angrily threatened Eugenia, she 48 turned her face to the ground so that for the time being her father might not recognize a face so familiar, and said, "My God not only forbids the deeds of which at present you accuse me, but also ordains actions much loftier than these. As for me, He willed that I live in perpetual virginity and arranged for me to dwell with these male ascetics; He has thus preserved me inviolate even in this case, as is clear to Him and shortly will be to you as well. You threaten me with torment and death, not realizing that you are threatening me (as the saying goes) with a fear that causes no fear. For I would feel shame if I sought to defend myself because I dreaded those punishments and not because I dread that

τῶν Χριστιανῶν ὑμῖν εἰς διαβολὴν κεῖσθαι καὶ μυκτηρίζε-
σθαι. Πλὴν ἀλλ᾽ ἐχρῆν ὑμᾶς μὴ οὕτως εὐκόλους ὑπέχειν
τοῖς κατηγόροις τὰς ἀκοάς, μηδ᾽ ἐκ πρώτης ἑτοίμως καταγινώσκειν, ἀλλά, τὸ πρῶτον ἀμφοῖν διακούσαντας, εἶτα
καὶ τὴν ψῆφον ἐκφέρειν. Κἂν μὲν ἐγὼ τοιαῦτα δράσασα
φανερὰ γένωμαι, δικαίαν ὑπόσχω τὴν τιμωρίαν. Εἰ δὲ
ψεῦδος ταῦτα καὶ συκοφαντία σαφής, μίαν ἀντὶ πάντων
αἰτῶ χάριν, τὸ μηδὲν τὴν γυναῖκα ταύτην ὑποστῆναι δεινόν, μηδ᾽ εἰ πολλῷ τούτων χείρω διεξήει περὶ ἡμῶν· οὕτω
γὰρ ὅ τε ἡμέτερος κελεύει νόμος, καὶ ἡμεῖς πειθόμεθα μηδέποτε κακοῖς τὰ κακά, ἀλλὰ τοὐναντίον μᾶλλον τοῖς ἀγαθοῖς ἀμείβεσθαι. Τοῦτο γοῦν μοι καὶ μόνον πιστούσθω δι᾽
ὅρκου, καὶ οὔ τινων δεησόμεθα λόγων οὐδ᾽ ἀντιθέσεων,
ἀλλ᾽ αὐτὸ δὴ δείξει τὸ πρᾶγμα σαφῶς, καὶ οἱ σοὶ ῥᾷστα
δικάσουσιν ὀφθαλμοί."

49   Οὕτως εἰποῦσα, πρὸς τὴν Μελανθίαν ἰδιαζόντως (ἔτυχε
γὰρ ἐκεῖ καὶ αὐτὴ παροῦσα), "Εἰ καὶ πάντας," ἔφη, "λαθεῖν
δυνατόν, ἀλλὰ τό γε σὸν συνειδὸς πάντως οὐ λήσῃ. Μὴ
τοίνυν καὶ σεαυτὴν ἀγνοεῖν δόξῃς, καὶ ὀφθαλμῶν θείων
ὀλιγωρήσῃς, οἳ πάντα τε ὁρῶσι καὶ συκοφαντίαν ἐνδίκως
κολάζουσιν." Ἐπεὶ δὲ οὐδὲν ἧττον ἐκείνη Μελανθία ἦν,
οὐδ᾽ ὑφίει τῆς ἀναιδείας, εὐθὺς ἐκέλευε παραστῆναι τὴν
θεράπαιναν, ἣν ἡ Μελανθία μάρτυρα ἔφη γενέσθαι τῆς
βίας. Ἐκέλευε δὲ καλεῖσθαι οὐχ ὡς τἀληθῆ μαρτυρήσου-
σαν (πῶς γὰρ ἂν ἡ δούλη πρὸς τὴν δέσποιναν ἀντετίθει;),
ἀλλ᾽ ὥστε τὸ ψεῦδος ἐκ πολλοῦ διελεγχθῆναι τοῦ περιόντος, καὶ Μελανθίαν ὀφθῆναι οὐχ ὅπως μόνην, ἀλλὰ καὶ
μεθ᾽ ἑτέρων ἑλομένην συκοφαντεῖν.

the Christian faith might seem fair game for your slander and mockery. Indeed, you should have neither given credence to my accusers so easily nor passed sentence so readily and precipitously; you ought instead to have first listened to both sides and then made a decision. If it should become apparent that I did such things, I should be rightfully punished. But if these accusations should prove to be false and an obvious slander, I ask one favor above all: that nothing terrible befall this woman, not even if she should expound about us accusations much worse than these; for this is the command of our law, and we are persuaded that we should not repay evil with evil under any circumstance, but rather with good. Let this favor alone be vouchsafed to me by oath and we will not need any speeches or counterarguments; the deed itself will reveal the truth openly, and your eyes will judge most easily."

After she had spoken thus, she directly addressed Melan- 49 thia (who also happened to be present), "Although you may be able to hide from everyone, you will never hide totally from your own conscience. Do not pretend that you are ignorant of your own self, and do not belittle the eyes of God that see everything and justly punish calumny." But since Melanthia did not stop being Melanthia even in the least, nor did she abate from her shamelessness, Eugenia at once summoned the maidservant whom Melanthia said was a witness of the violation. Eugenia commanded her to be summoned not because she thought that she would tell the truth (for how could a slave contradict her mistress?), but so that the lie might be entirely exposed and that it might become evident that Melanthia chose to make her false accusation not alone but with the help of others.

50 Παραστᾶσα οὖν ἡ θεράπαινα, καὶ τῇ δεσποίνῃ χαρίζε-
σθαι βουλομένη, ψεῦδος τῷ ψεύδει συνείρειν οὐκ ἀμαθῶς
εἶχε, "Κἀμέ," λέγουσα, "ὁ μιαρὸς οὑτοσὶ πολλάκις ἐπείρα.
Εἶθ᾽ ἡ συνήθης ἀκολασία καὶ αὐτῇ ἐπιμανῆναι παρέπεισε
τῇ δεσποίνῃ, ᾗ, μὴ βουλομένῃ, βίαν ἐπῆγεν, ἕως ἡ μὲν ὡς
εἶχεν ἀνέκραγεν, ἐγὼ δέ, ἐπιστᾶσα καὶ ἄλλας μετακαλεσα-
μένη τῶν ὁμοδούλων, μόλις αὐτὸν τοῦ αἰσχροῦ ἐπέσχομεν
ἐγχειρήματος· αἳ καὶ βουλομένων ὑμῶν εἰ μετακληθεῖεν,
εἴσεσθε ὅπως τοῖς ἐμοῖς ἔσονται συνᾴδουσαι λόγοις."

51 Τότε ὁ μὲν ἔπαρχος, πικρότατα διαταραχθείς, ὕβρεσιν
ἔβαλλε τὴν Εὐγενίαν· καὶ δῆλος ἦν καὶ ἐπὶ τὰς βασάνους
ἤδη ὁρμήσων, ὡς οὐδενὸς ἔτι λειπομένου πρὸς ἔλεγχον.
Ἡ δὲ (ἀλλὰ προσεκτέον· ἡδεῖα γὰρ πρὸς ἀκοὴν ἡ διήγη-
σις), "Καιρός," εἰποῦσα, "παρρησιάσασθαι τὴν ἀλήθειαν,
ἵνα μὴ τὸ ψεῦδος αὐτῆς ἐπὶ πλέον κατακαυχήσηται, καὶ
εὐδιάβλητα Ἕλλησι τὰ Χριστιανῶν ᾖ," τί ποιεῖ; Ἀναγκά-
ζεται διὰ τὴν πολλὴν τῆς κατηγόρου ἀναίδειαν καὶ πέρα
τι τοῦ σεμνοῦ ποιῆσαι· καί, λαβοῦσα, διαρρήγνυσιν ἄνωθεν τὸν χιτῶνα· καί, μέρη τινὰ τοῦ ἱεροῦ τῷ ὄντι γυμνώ-
σασα σώματος, ἐδείκνυ πᾶσιν, ὅτι καὶ φύσει αὕτη καὶ ἀληθείᾳ γυνή. Λέγει τε πρὸς τὸν ἔπαρχον· "Κύριέ μου, σὺ μὲν
ἐμὸς κατὰ σάρκα πατήρ, ὁ Φίλιππος· Κλαυδία δέ μοι μή-
τηρ· καὶ ἀδελφοὶ οὗτοι, οἵ γε καὶ συγκαθέζονταί σοι, Ἀβίτας καὶ Σέργιος· ἐγὼ δὲ σὴ θυγάτηρ Εὐγενία, ἥτις, κόσμον εὐκόλως ἀποδυσαμένη πάντα καὶ τὰ ἐν κόσμῳ, μόνον
ἀντὶ πάντων ἐνεδυσάμην Χριστόν. Ἰδοὺ καὶ οὓς εὐνούχους

The maidservant came forward and not unskillfully wove   50
lie after lie, wishing to please her mistress: "This depraved
man," she said, "many times assaulted me as well. Then his
habitual lasciviousness convinced him to impose his mad
lust even on my mistress herself, forcing himself on her
against her will, until she cried out as loud as she could and I
came to her help, and with my fellow slave women, whom I
had called to my aid, we were barely able to restrain him
from his shameless attack; and if you want to summon them,
you will see how they will concur with my statement."

At that point, the eparch, bitterly disturbed, began to re-   51
proach Eugenia with insults; and it was clear that he was also
ready to subject her straightaway to torture, thinking that
there was nothing left to investigate. Eugenia (listen carefully! For this part of the story is a joy to hear!) first said,
however, "It is time to speak the truth boldly, so that her lies
may no longer exult over the truth and so that the Christian
faith may not be misrepresented by the Greeks." Then what
does she do? She was forced by the great shamelessness of
her accuser to do something beyond the bounds of modesty;
grabbing her tunic she ripped it apart from top to bottom;
and, exposing certain parts of her truly holy body, she
showed everyone that both by nature and in truth she was a
woman. And to the eparch she said: "You, my lord, are my
father according to the flesh, Philip; Claudia is my mother;
and these are my brothers who are sitting with you, Abitas
and Sergios; and I am your daughter Eugenia, who has readily stripped herself of all her worldly adornments and everything in the world, and donned Christ alone in place of them
all. And behold, these eunuchs that you see are Protas and

ὁρᾷς, Πρωτᾶς ἐστι καὶ Ὑάκινθος, οἱ καὶ παιδείας μοι καὶ βίου τοῦ κατὰ Χριστὸν κοινωνήσαντες."

52   Οὕτω πέρας ἐτίθει τοῖς λόγοις. Καὶ ὁ πατήρ, ὡς δὲ καὶ οἱ ἀδελφοί, τοῦτο μὲν ἀφ' ὧν διεξήει, τοῦτο δὲ καὶ μᾶλλον ἀπὸ τῶν ἐν τῇ ὄψει παρασήμων φωράσαντες τὴν ἀλήθειαν (ἀνέγνωσαν γάρ, ἐπιβαλόντες περιεργότερον τῷ προσώπῳ τὰς ὄψεις, ταύτην ἐκείνην εἶναι τὴν Εὐγενίαν), τὴν μὲν καρδίαν ἡδονῆς ἀρρήτου, τῶν ἐξ ἡδονῆς δὲ δακρύων πληροῦνται τοὺς ὀφθαλμούς. Ἔπειτα ἐπὶ τὴν ἀρχοντικὴν αὐτὴν καθέδραν ἀναβιβάσαντες, μονονουχὶ καὶ τὰς ψυχὰς ἐπ' αὐτῇ ἐξεκένουν. Καὶ τῷ φίλτρῳ ταύτην διεμερίζοντο, ἐντεῦθεν ὁ πατήρ, ἐκεῖθεν οἱ ἀδελφοί, ἀλλαχόθεν ἡ μήτηρ (παρῆν γὰρ καὶ αὕτη μαθοῦσα)· καὶ πρὸς ἀλλήλους τοῦτο μὲν περιπλοκαῖς, τοῦτο δὲ καὶ φιλοστόργοις ἡμιλλῶντο προσρήσεσι. Τίνα μὲν οὐ περιβάλλοντες μέλη; Τί δὲ μὴ πάσχοντες ἢ μὴ δρῶντες ἐξ ἀπορρήτου περιχαρείας; Ἢ τί τῶν διαγγελλόντων ἡδονὴν ψυχῆς διὰ τὸ πλῆθος ποιεῖν εὐλαβούμενοι;—τὸ γὰρ σεμνὸν τῆς ἀρχῆς καὶ τὴν ὅλην ἐκ περιφανείας κομψότητα ἡ φύσις παρευδοκίμει καὶ φανερῶς ἤλεγχεν. Ἔκραζον οὖν, οἷον ἐνθουσιῶντες, "Ἡ θυγάτηρ αὕτη"· "ἡ ἀδελφή"· "ἡ τῶν ὀφθαλμῶν ἡδονή"· "τὸ τῆς τύχης ἀγαλλίαμα"· "ἣν ἀνάρπαστον γενέσθαι ὑπὸ θεῶν νενομίκαμεν"· "ἣν ἡμεῖς οὐχ ὁρῶντες, οὐδὲ ὁρᾷν ὅλως φῶς ἠνειχόμεθα."

53   Ταῦτα καὶ ὁ δῆμος ἀκούοντες δηλαδὴ καὶ ὁρῶντες, "Εἷς Θεὸς ἀληθής, ὁ Χριστός," ἐβόων. Ὅσοι δὲ τῶν σπουδαιοτέρων Χριστιανῶν περιμένοντες ἦσαν, ὥστε μετὰ τὸν θάνατον τῶν μαρτύρων ἀνελέσθαι τὰ σώματα καὶ ταφῆς

Hyacinth, who have shared in both my education and my life in Christ."

Thus she put an end to her words. And her father, as well 52 as her brothers, discovered the truth, partly from what she said and, even more so, from the distinguishing features of her appearance (for gazing more carefully at her face, they recognized that she was indeed their Eugenia); their hearts were filled with unspeakable delight, while tears of delight filled their eyes. Then they sat her on the ruler's very chair and all but emptied their souls onto her. With intense affection, they were vying for a share of her, her father on this side, her brothers on the other side, her mother on yet another side (for she too had come, after hearing the news); and they contended with each other with their embraces and affectionate endearments. What parts of her body did they not embrace? What did they not feel or do in their unspeakable joy? Or what expression of their souls' gladness did they not show in spite of the crowd? For nature surpassed and clearly proved superior to the solemnity of office and every elegance that derives from social prestige. They cried out as though they were possessed, "This is my daughter"; "this is our sister"; "the delight of our eyes"; "the joy of good fortune"; "the one whom we believed was snatched up by the gods"; "the one whom, as we were unable to see, we could not bear to even see light at all."

When the people heard these things and, of course, 53 saw them, they shouted, "The true God is one, Christ." And those more zealous Christians who had been waiting to collect the martyrs' bodies after their deaths and give them

ἀξιῶσαι τῆς προσηκούσης, οὗτοι δέ, πυθόμενοι τὴν οὕτως
ἀθρόαν τοῦ ἐπάρχου δήπου καὶ τοῦ δήμου μεταβολήν,
εἰσπηδῶσι μετὰ τῶν ὄχλων, "Τίς μέγας ὡς ὁ Θεὸς ἡμῶν,"
γεγωνοτέρᾳ τῇ φωνῇ βοῶντες, "ὁ ἀνακαλύπτων βαθέα καὶ
ἀπόκρυφα, καὶ τῇ αὐτῶν πανουργίᾳ τοὺς σοφοὺς δρασσό-
μενος;" Ὁ μέντοι πατὴρ καὶ ἄκουσαν Εὐγενίαν διαχρύσῳ
περιβαλὼν στολῇ (ἠβούλετο γὰρ κοινωνοὺς πάντας τῆς
εὐφροσύνης λαβεῖν), ἐφ᾽ ὑψηλοῦ τε ἀνεβίβασε θρόνου· καὶ
ὀφθῆναι πᾶσι πεποίηκε.

54   Ἐν ᾧ δὲ ταῦτα ἐπράττετο, καὶ αὐτὸς ὁ ἐν οὐρανῷ Θεός,
ἢ μᾶλλον (τὸ τοῦ θείου Ἰὼβ φάναι) ὁ *ἐν οὐρανοῖς* Εὐγενίας
μάρτυς, ὁ ἐν ὑψίστοις συνίστωρ αὐτῆς, πῦρ αἰφνίδιον οὐρανόθεν ἀφείς, τὸν Μελανθίας οἶκον εἰς ἅπαν ἀνάλωσε· ἐκείνην γὰρ τῷ αἰωνίῳ μᾶλλον ἐταμιεύσατο. Καὶ τὸ γεγονὸς
τοῦτο ἐπιστρέψαι πολλοὺς πρὸς τὴν ἀλήθειαν παρεσκεύασεν.

55   Αὐτίκα γοῦν τοῖς Χριστιανοῖς ἤγετο ἑορτὴ κοινή· καὶ ἡ
μακρὰ κατήφεια μετεβάλλετο, τοῦ μὲν ἐπάρχου μετὰ τῆς
θυγατρὸς ἅμα καὶ τὴν εὐσέβειαν εὑρηκότος, Χριστῷ τε
προσελθόντος καὶ τῷ ἁγίῳ σημειωθέντος βαπτίσματι,
Χριστιανοῖς δὲ τῶν ἱερῶν εὐθὺς ἐκκλησιῶν ἀναδοθεισῶν,
καὶ ὧν εἶχον πρὸ τοῦ τιμῶν τε καὶ προνομίων. Οὐ μόνον
δὲ τοιούτων ἐτύγχανον, ἀλλὰ καὶ ἀδεῶς αὐτοῖς ἐφεῖτο τὰς
πόλεις οἰκεῖν. Φίλιππος γὰρ τοῦτο αὐτοῖς περιεποιήσατο,
τοῖς κρατοῦσιν ἀνενεγκών, Σευήρῳ τε καὶ Πίῳ τῷ Ἀντω-
νίνῳ, ἀλυσιτελὲς εἶναι τῇ Ῥωμαίων ἀρχῇ Χριστιανοὺς ἀπ-
ελαύνεσθαι, ἅτε δὴ μὴ ἐν ὀλίγοις χρησίμους τῷ κοινῷ γι-
νομένους. Καὶ συνιόντων, ἦν ὁρᾶν αὖθις τὴν Ἀλεξανδρέων

a fitting burial, these people, hearing about this sudden change in the attitude of the eparch and of the crowd, sallied forth among the masses, shouting with loud voices: "*Who is great as our God, who discovers deep things* and secrets, and catches the clever in their evildoing?" As for the father, he dressed Eugenia, against her will, in a golden robe (for he wanted all to take part in the jubilation) and set her up on a high throne; he made it so that all could see her.

Meanwhile, God himself in heaven, or rather (to use the 54 words of divine Job), Eugenia's *witness in heaven,* her *advocate on high,* suddenly cast fire down from heaven and consumed Melanthia's house completely; as for her, He saved her rather for the eternal fire. This event caused the conversion of many people to the truth.

Immediately thereafter, all Christians celebrated a feast 55 together; their long grief was transformed to its opposite; the eparch found both true faith and his daughter, drew near to Christ, and was sealed with holy baptism; the Christians immediately regained their sacred churches as well as their former honors and privileges. Not only did they receive such benefits, but in addition they were permitted to live without fear in the cities. Philip secured this right for them by appealing to emperors Severus and Antoninus Pius that the persecution of Christians was unprofitable for the Roman rule, especially since Christians were useful for the state in many respects. When Christians started

ὥσπερ ἐκ δευτέρου πάλιν οἰκιζομένην. Ἐν ὁμοίαις δὲ ταῖς ἀνέσεσι καὶ ταῖς εὐθηνίαις, καὶ αἱ κατ' Αἴγυπτον πόλεις ἦσαν. Καὶ πάλιν τὰ Χριστιανῶν ἤνθει, διέλαμπέ τε καὶ ὑπερήρετο.

56 Ἀλλ' ἐπειδή, καλῶς οὕτω τῆς ἀρετῆς ἐχούσης, τὴν κακίαν ἔμπαλιν συνέβαινεν ὑπορρεῖν, πλήττεσθαί τε τὸν αὐτῆς αἴτιον ἰσχυρῶς, οὐδὲ τανῦν φέρει ὁ τοῖς καλοῖς ἀντικείμενος. Ἀλλὰ τῶν Ἀλεξανδρέων τινὰς ὑπελθών, οἳ πλούτῳ μὲν καὶ περιφανείᾳ περιττῶς εἶχον, ὑπὸ δὲ τῆς περὶ τὰ εἴδωλα μανίας κραταιῶς εἴχοντο, πείθει τὰ βασίλειά τε καταλαβεῖν, καί, τοῖς κρατοῦσι προσελθόντας, τὸν μὲν πρὸ τοῦ χρόνον εἰπεῖν ἅπαντα καλῶς τε τῇ ἀρχῇ τὸν Φίλιππον ἐπιτρέψαι, καὶ εὐσεβέστατα διατεθῆναι τὰ περὶ τοὺς θεούς· "Νυνὶ δέ," φησί, "δέκατον ἔτος, οὐκ οἶδ' ὅ τι παθών, ἑαυτόν τε καὶ πᾶσαν ἡμῶν τὴν πόλιν ἀνατρέψαι διενοήσατο, τὴν τῶν μεγίστων θεῶν τιμὴν εἰς ἑνὸς ἀνθρώπου λατρείαν μεταγαγών, ὃν ἐν Παλαιστίνῃ πρὸς Ἰουδαίων ἀνεσκολοπίσθαι λέγουσι. Ταύτῃ τοι καὶ ἔλυσε μὲν ἔθη πάτρια· ἐτίμησε δὲ νόμους καινούς· προετίμησε δὲ τοὺς ἀσεβεῖς ἡμῶν· καί, συνελόντας εἰπεῖν, οὐδὲν τῶν εἰς ἀνατροπὴν ὅλως ἡμῶν τε καὶ θεῶν ἀπολέλοιπε."

57 Ταῦτα οἱ βασιλεῖς διακούσαντες, ἐπιστέλλουσι τοιάδε Φιλίππῳ· "Ὁ μὲν πρὸ ἡμῶν θειότατος Αὔγουστος θεραπευτὴν ὄντα σε τῶν θεῶν εἰδώς, καὶ περὶ τὰς τούτων τιμὰς σπουδαῖον, μεγίστην σοι καὶ αὐτὸς παρέσχετο τὴν ἀρχήν, καί, ὥσπερ βασιλέα μᾶλλον ἢ ἔπαρχον, πάσης ἄρχοντα τῆς Αἰγύπτου κεχειροτόνηκε· καὶ μηδέποτέ σε, μέχρι καὶ διατελεῖς ζῶν, τῆς ἀρχῆς ταύτης ἀποχειροτονηθῆναι

234

assembling, it looked as if Alexandria was founded a second time. Other cities too in Egypt enjoyed the same license and prosperity. Christianity blossomed again, shone forth, and was raised high.

As virtue thrived in this way and wickedness began to slip 56 away once again, with its instigator dealt a forceful blow, this adversary of all good could bear none of what was now happening. Rather, stealthily worming his way into some citizens of Alexandria, who possessed abundant wealth and prestige, but were also firmly possessed by the folly of idolatry, he persuaded them to go to the imperial palace and appear before the emperors in order to say that, until recently, Philip had always distinguished himself in employing authority well and dispensed the matters of the gods most piously. "Yet now," he said, "in his tenth year—who knows what happened to him—Philip decided to ruin himself and our whole city by transferring the veneration of the greatest gods to the worship of a single man, who, they say, was crucified by the Jews in Palestine. With this worship he dissolved the customs of our fathers; he honored newfangled laws; he preferred those impious people to us; and, to put it briefly, he took every step to overthrow us and our gods completely."

When the emperors heard these words, they sent the fol- 57 lowing letter to Philip: "Our predecessor, the most divine Augustus, knew you to be a servant of the gods, and zealous for their honors. He in turn invested you with a very important position and appointed you to rule over all of Egypt, more like an emperor than an eparch; he also ordered that, as long as you live, under no circumstances should you be

διεκελεύσατο, ἀλλὰ συνδιαμετρηθῆναι τῷ βίῳ καὶ τὴν ἀρχήν. Ἡμεῖς δέ σοι καὶ ταύτας διασεσώκαμεν, καὶ ἑτέρας οὐκ ὀλίγας τῶν τιμῶν προστεθείκαμεν. Ἀλλὰ ταῦτα, μέχρις οὗ καὶ αὐτὸς φίλος τοῖς θεοῖς ἐτύγχανες ὤν. Ἐπεὶ δὲ νῦν διατεθρύλληται περὶ σοῦ, τά τε πρὸς θεοὺς μεταβαλεῖν σε, καὶ τὰ πρὸς ἡμᾶς οὐκ εὐνοϊκῶς ἔχειν, προστάττομεν ἤ, ἐχόμενόν σε τῶν προτέρων, ἔχεσθαι καὶ τῆς τιμῆς, ἤ, ἀποστέρξαντα τὸ περὶ τοὺς θεοὺς σέβας, παυθῆναι καὶ τῆς ἀρχῆς, οὐ μὴν δὲ ἀλλ᾽ ἀφαίρεσιν ὑποστῆναι καὶ τῆς οὐσίας."

58 Ταῦτα δεξάμενον καὶ ἀναγνόντα τὸν Φίλιππον, νόσον ὑποκριθῆναι, ἕως διαπωλήσαντα τὴν οὐσίαν διχῇ διελεῖν· καὶ τὰ μὲν ἐκκλησίαις, τὰ δὲ πτωχοῖς διανείμασθαι, τοῖς ἀνὰ πᾶσαν τὴν Ἀλεξάνδρειάν τε καὶ αὐτὴν Αἴγυπτον περιοῦσιν. Ἦν δὲ οὐ περὶ τὸ λέγειν μόνον ὁ Φίλιππος ἐνεργὸς τὴν γλῶτταν, ὡς πολλοὺς τῶν Ἑλλήνων πειθοῖ ταύτης μεταμαθεῖν τὴν εὐσέβειαν, ἀλλὰ καὶ τὸν βίον θεοφιλέστατος καὶ φιλοσοφώτατος, ὥστε πᾶσαν τὴν Ἀλεξανδρέων κοινῇ ψήφῳ πρὸς τὴν ἐπισκοπὴν αὐτὸν μετακαλεῖσθαι. Ὅτι δὲ καὶ περὶ τὴν πίστιν ἦν θερμότατός τε καὶ στεγανώτατος, ἡ δήλωσις ἐκ τοῦ τέλους· τελευτᾷ γὰρ τὸν βίον μαρτυρίου στεφάνῳ κοσμήσας τὴν κεφαλήν.

59 Πέμπεται γοῦν διάδοχος αὐτῷ τῆς ἀρχῆς Τερέντιος. Ὃς ἅμα τε τῇ Ἀλεξανδρέων ἐπέβη, καὶ πάντα κάλων ἐκίνει, Φιλίππῳ τὴν ἀναίρεσιν σκαιωρούμενος. Ἐπεὶ δὲ μὴ ἠδύνατο φανερῶς αὐτὸν ἀνελεῖν (πολὺ γὰρ ἦν τὸ περὶ Φίλιππον τῆς πόλεως φίλτρον), λάθρα κακουργεῖ τὴν μιαιφονίαν· καί τισι τῶν προσποιήτων Χριστιανῶν τὰ τοῦ

divested of this power, but that you should rule for your entire lifetime. And we both retained these privileges for you and granted you not a small number of other new honors. Yet this was the case only so long as you yourself also happened to be a friend to the gods. Since now, however, it is rumored that you have changed your attitude toward the gods, and are also not inclined favorably toward us, we command that either you maintain your previous ways and thus also keep your honors, or, if you reject reverence to the gods, you should also be deprived of your power and, moreover, be indeed subjected to the confiscation of your property as well."

Having received and read the letter, Philip feigned illness 58 until he sold his property, dividing it in two; one part he gave to the churches, the other he distributed among the poor who lived throughout Alexandria and also Egypt. Not only was Philip's tongue capable of effective speaking, so that many among the heathens converted to the true piety, but he also conducted his life in the manner most pleasing to God and most philosophical, so that the entire city of Alexandria by a solid vote summoned him to become its bishop. And that he was most fervent and most steadfast in his faith is clear from his death, for he ended his life by adorning his head with the crown of martyrdom.

And so Terentios was sent as a successor for Philip's of- 59 fice. As soon as he disembarked at Alexandria, he let out the rope of every sail in contriving Philip's murder. Since, however, he could not kill him openly (the city's love for Philip was strong), he worked the evil deed of assassination in secret; he entrusted the enactment of the deed to the hands

δράματος ἐγχειρίσας, ἐπὶ τὸν φόνον παρώρμησε—τῶν βασιλέων αὐτῷ τοῦτο μᾶλλον ἐπιτρεψάντων. Οἳ καὶ κρύφα
πρὸς Φίλιππον εἰσελθόντες, εὐχῇ καὶ δεήσει τῇ πρὸς Θεὸν
προσκείμενον ἀναιροῦσι.

60   Φοβηθεὶς δὲ Τερέντιος μὴ καὶ ὁ δῆμος τὸ πραχθὲν μι-
σήσας κατ᾽ αὐτοῦ κινηθῇ (καὶ μάλιστα φίλτρῳ τοιούτῳ
πρὸς Φίλιππον ἡρμοσμένος), συλληφθῆναι τοὺς ἀποκτεί-
ναντας αὐτὸν καὶ φρουρᾷ δοθῆναι προστάττει, ἐπιπλάστῳ
πράγματι συγκρύψαι τἀληθὲς μηχανώμενος, ὑπόνοιάν τε
διασπείρων, ὡς μὴ κατὰ γνώμην αὐτῷ προβῆναι τὸν φόνον. Ἔπειτα μικροῦ παρελθόντος χρόνου, τῶν βασιλέων
δῆθεν οὕτω κρινάντων, ἀνίησιν αὐτοὺς τῶν δεσμῶν. Οὕτω
Φίλιππος ἐτελεύτα, ἡμέρας τρεῖς μετὰ τὴν πληγὴν ἐπιζή-
σας. Τυγχάνει δὲ ταφῆς εἴσω τῆς πόλεως ἐγγύς που τοῦ
καλουμένου Ἰσείου, ὅπου αὐτὸς περιὼν ἔτι οἶκον ἱερὸν
ᾠκοδόμησεν.

61   Εὐγενία δὲ μετὰ τὸν ἀναγνωρισμόν, συνάμα καὶ ἄλλαις
παρθένοις, ἁγνείας τε καὶ τοῦ κατὰ Χριστὸν εἴχετο βίου.
Ἡ δέ γε μακαρία Κλαυδία—ἣν Φιλίππου μὲν γαμετήν,
Εὐγενίας δὲ μητέρα ὁ λόγος φθάσας ἐδήλωσεν—καὶ ἕτερον οἶκον εἰς ξένων ὑποδοχὴν τῷ ὑπὸ τοῦ ἀνδρὸς ἤδη
γενομένῳ προσῳκοδόμησε, πλῆθος ἐν αὐτῷ χρημάτων
ἀφιερώσασα, εἰς χορηγίαν τῶν προσηκόντων τοῖς ἐπιξε-
νουμένοις ἐπιτηδείων.

62   Ἀλλὰ ταῦτα μὲν οὕτω· καὶ τοιαύτην Εὐγενία τὸ μέχρι
τοῦδε τὴν περὶ τὸν βίον ἔσχεν οἰκονομίαν. Βούλεται δὲ ὁ
λόγος καὶ λαμπρότερον αὐτῆς ἐπιδεῖξαι τὸ τέλος, ἅτε καὶ
μαρτυρικῷ στεφάνῳ δεδοξασμένον. Χρόνῳ γὰρ ὕστερον

of certain sham Christians, inciting them to the killing—it was, rather, the emperors who allowed him to do it. These men stole into Philip's room and killed him while he was offering prayer and supplication to God.

As Terentios feared that the citizens would recoil at his 60 deed and therefore revolt against him (especially because they had such a love for Philip), he ordered that the killers be arrested and put in jail; thus he contrived to plaster over the true deed with a sham, spreading the insinuation that the murder happened against his will. Not long after he released them from their bonds, supposedly because the emperors decreed it. This is how Philip died, living on for three more days after the attack. He was buried within the city near the so-called Isium, where he himself had built a church, while he was still alive.

After her identity was revealed, Eugenia, along with other 61 virgins continued to adhere to chastity and the life according to Christ. Meanwhile, the blessed Claudia—who was mentioned earlier as Philip's wife, and as Eugenia's mother—had a house constructed in addition to the one her husband had built, for the purpose of providing hospitality to foreigners; to this she consecrated abundant resources, to provide what was necessary for the immediate needs of the guests.

Well, this is how all this transpired; and, up to this point, 62 such was the divine arrangement of Eugenia's life. But this account wishes to also portray her even more brilliant end, given that it was glorified with the crown of martyrdom. At

μετὰ τελευτὴν Φιλίππου, ἡ σύνευνος Κλαυδία τοὺς παῖδας παραλαβοῦσα—Ἀβίταν φημὶ καὶ Σέργιον, πρὸς δὲ καὶ τὴν Εὐγενίαν—εἰς τὴν μεγάλην ἐπάνεισι Ῥώμην. Καὶ ἡ πατρὶς αὐτὴν εὐμενῶς δέχεται· καὶ ἡ τῶν Ῥωμαίων βουλὴ πρὸς ἀρχὰς ἐπισήμους τοὺς παῖδας χειροτονεῖ, Ἀβίταν μὲν τῆς Καρθαγένης ἀνθύπατον, τῆς Ἀφρικῆς δὲ τὸν Σέργιον οὐ-ϊκάριον. Εὐγενίᾳ δὲ ἦρκει τοῦτο μόνον ἀξίωμα τῶν πάν-των μεῖζον, ἡ ἀρετή, καὶ τὸ ὑπὸ Θεῷ ζῆν, καὶ ἄλλας τῶν τῆς βουλῆς θυγατέρων μεθ᾽ ἑαυτῆς ἔχειν, τοῦ ἴσου ζήλου καὶ σκοποῦ μεταποιουμένας. Ἐν αἷς καὶ μία τις ἦν πολλῷ τῶν λοιπῶν διενεγκοῦσα, ἡ θαυμαστὴ τῷ ὄντι Βασίλλα, ἐκ βασιλικοῦ τοῦ γένους καταγομένη· ἥτις καὶ παραπλη-σίως Εὐγενίᾳ διέλαμψεν, ὡς αὐτίκα ῥηθήσεται.

63   Αὕτη γὰρ Χριστόν τε καὶ τὰ τοῦ Χριστοῦ θαύματα παραλαβοῦσα δι᾽ ἀκοῆς, οὐ μὴν ἀλλὰ καὶ περὶ Εὐγενίας ἀκούσασα, τοῦ παντὸς μὲν ἠξίου τὸ παρὰ ταύτην φοιτῆσαι καὶ τῶν θείων λόγων αὐτῆς μετασχεῖν. Τούτου δὲ εἰργο-μένη, διά τε τὸν μνηστῆρα (Πομπηΐῳ γὰρ ἐμνηστεύετο), διά τε τὸν διωγμόν (ἤδη γὰρ Χριστιανοῖς μέγας ἀνήπτετο), ἄνδρα τινὰ πιστὸν πορθμέα τῶν λόγων εὑρίσκει, καί, δι᾽ αὐτοῦ πέμπουσα, οὐκ ἀνίει πολλὰ δεομένη τῆς Εὐγενίας, γράμμασιν αὐτῇ πάντα τὰ περὶ τῆς θείας πίστεως γνώριμα θέσθαι.

64   Ἡ δὲ καλῶς εἰδυῖα, ὅσον τὸ ἐξαλλάττον ἐστὶ γραφῆς καὶ φωνῆς, καὶ ὅτι οὐχ᾽ ὁμοίως ἄν τις πείσειεν ἢ διδάξει ἐπιστέλλων, ἢ περὶ τηλικούτων διαλεγόμενος, ἐπεὶ καὶ πολὺ τὸ μέσον ἐμψύχων λόγων καὶ ἀψύχου καὶ νεκρᾶς εἰσ-ηγήσεως, βουλὴν βουλεύεται συνετὴν ὁμοῦ καὶ νεανικήν.

some point after Philip's death, his wife Claudia took her children—Abitas, I mean, and Sergios, and Eugenia as well —and returned to the great city of Rome. The fatherland received her favorably; and the Roman senate appointed her young sons to illustrious magistracies: Abitas became proconsul of Carthage; Sergios became vicar of Africa. But for Eugenia this single distinction, the worthiest of all, sufficed, namely virtue, and a life subject to God, and to have with her other daughters of senators, converted in equal zeal to her purpose. Among these there was also one who was particularly outstanding compared to the rest: the truly marvelous Basilla, descended from the royal family; this woman also shone forth similarly to Eugenia, as will be explained forthwith.

Having learned through hearsay about Christ and Christ's 63 miracles, and then hearing also about Eugenia, Basilla sought above all to become her disciple and partake of her divine teachings. Prevented, however, from this, both because of her fiancé (for she was betrothed to Pompey), and because of the persecution (which had already been kindled with great intensity against the Christians), she found a trustworthy man to act as a purveyor of messages, and through him did not cease to send request upon request, entreating Eugenia to make everything about the divine faith known to her in letters.

But Eugenia knew well how great the difference is be- 64 tween writing and speech, and that one would not be as persuasive or could not teach such elevated topics as well in letters as in a colloquy, and that there is a significant disparity between animated speech and inanimate, dead instruction; she thus devised a clever and, simultaneously, daring

Πείσασα γὰρ τοὺς περὶ Πρωτᾶν καὶ Ὑάκινθον σχῆμα δου-
λικὸν ὑποδῦναι, δῶρον αὐτοὺς τῇ Βασίλλᾳ ἐκπέμπει,
πάντα γενέσθαι ἀντ᾽ ἐπιστολῆς αὐτῇ σπεύδουσα, μᾶλλον
δὲ αὐτοὺς ἐκείνους ἐπιστολὴν ἔμψυχον. Τούτους οὖν καὶ
λίαν ἀσμένως ἡ Βασίλλα ἐκδεξαμένη, οἷά τινας ἀποστό-
λους προσεκύνει Χριστοῦ. Μαθὼν δὲ τὰ κατ᾽ αὐτὴν καὶ
Κορνήλιος, ὁ μέγας ἐν ἐπισκόποις ἀστήρ, ὑπὸ νύκτα διὰ
τὸν διωγμὸν ἀφίκετο παρ᾽ αὐτήν, καὶ τοῦ θείου ταύτην
ἀξιοῖ βαπτίσματος.

65   Οὕτω μὲν οὖν Βασίλλα καὶ Εὐγενία δεσμῷ τινι ἀρρήτῳ
τῇ διὰ Χριστὸν συνδεθεῖσαι φιλίᾳ, ζεῦγος ἡρμόσθησαν τῷ
Θεῷ, αὐταῖς ψυχαῖς ἀλλήλων ἠρτημέναι καὶ νοερῶς συγ-
γινόμεναι, οὐ μὴν ἀλλὰ πολλὰς καὶ ἄλλας εἰς τὸν αὐτὸν
ζυγὸν ἐφελκόμεναι. Ὢ πόσας μὲν τῶν παρθένων ἐκεῖναι,
πόσας δὲ τῶν χηρῶν ἡ σεμνὴ Κλαυδία, πόσους δὲ τῶν
ἀνδρῶν Πρωτᾶς καὶ Ὑάκινθος τῷ κοινῷ Δεσπότῃ προσήγαγον!

66   Πλὴν ἀλλ᾽ οὕτω μέχρι πολλοῦ τῆς Χριστιανῶν ὑπεραυ-
ξομένης πίστεως, ὁ τοῦ Πονηροῦ φθόνος ἐπὶ μεῖζον κατὰ
τῶν εὐσεβῶν ἤρετο· Οὐαλεριανοῦ γὰρ καὶ Γαλλίου τὴν
Ῥωμαίων ἀρχὴν διεπόντων, αὐτὸς τοὺς πολλοὺς ὑπιὼν
Ῥωμαίων, πονηρὰ σπέρματα ταῖς αὐτῶν ἐνέβαλε διανοί-
αις. Καὶ στάσις ἀνήπτετο κατὰ Χριστιανῶν χαλεπή· καὶ ἡ
τῆς στάσεως ὕλη Κορνήλιος δήπου καὶ οἱ περὶ αὐτὸν
ἦσαν, ὅτι "πάσῃ χειρὶ καὶ γνώμῃ τὰ Χριστιανῶν πλατύνειν
προῃρημένοι, οὐ μόνον Ῥώμην αὐτὴν μικροῦ πᾶσαν, ἀλλὰ
καὶ τὰς κύκλῳ πόλεις τε καὶ χώρας τῆς τῶν θεῶν λατρείας
ἀπέστησαν, καὶ τὸν ὀνομαζόμενον παρ᾽ αὐτοῖς Χριστὸν

scheme. She persuaded Protas and Hyacinth to dress as slaves and sent them to Basilla as a gift, eager that they take the place of a letter for her, or rather, that they themselves become a living letter. Basilla received them with exceeding gladness and revered them as if they were Christ's apostles. When Cornelius too, that great star among bishops, learned of her actions, he came to her residence at night (due to the persecution) and deemed her worthy of divine baptism.

Thus Basilla and Eugenia were joined by the ineffable 65 bond of friendship for Christ, a pair yoked in God, with their entire souls dependent on each other, uniting with one another in spirit, as well as drawing many other women beneath the same yoke. How many virgins did those two, how many widows did the revered Claudia, how many men did Protas and Hyacinth lead to the Master of all!

But as the faith of the Christians expanded greatly and 66 widely, the envy of the Evil One against the pious increased even more; when Valerian and Gallius held power in Rome, he stealthily wormed his way into many of the Romans and sowed seeds of evil in their minds. A terrible animosity was kindled against Christians. Its fuel was Cornelius and his colleagues, because, they said, "having chosen to spread Christianity with all their might and mind, they drew not only most of Rome away from the veneration of the gods, but also the cities and the countryside around Rome, and they are endorsing the one they call Christ as their common

κοινὸν Δεσπότην καὶ Θεὸν ἐπιγράφονται." Παραχρῆμα
τοίνυν βασιλικὸν ἐξεφωνεῖτο θέσπισμα, καὶ διὰ πάσης τῆς
Ῥωμαίων ἐφοίτα πανταχοῦ, πάντας τοὺς τῶν Χριστιανῶν
ἐκκρίτους τε καὶ τοῦ δόγματος εἰσηγητὰς συλλαμβανομέ-
νους θανάτῳ δίδοσθαι. Ἀνῃροῦντο γοῦν ἄλλοι μὲν ἄλλη,
Κορνήλιος δὲ διελάνθανε, μάλιστα μὲν τῷ καὶ τῇ συγ-
κλήτῳ διὰ τιμῆς ἄγεσθαι, καὶ παρὰ τῶν ἐν αὐτῇ πρώτων
ὥσπερ ὑπό τινων προβόλων περιφρουρεῖσθαι, ἤδη δὲ καὶ
τῷ τηρεῖν αὐτὸς ἑαυτὸν ἐπὶ πολλῶν σωτηρίᾳ.

67   Συνεκρότουν δὲ ἀλλήλας πρὸς τὸν ἀγῶνα Βασίλλα καὶ
Εὐγενία· αἵ, μὴ φέρουσαι τὴν ἀπὸ τοῦ τόπου διάστασιν,
ἐπεὶ κατὰ ψυχὴν ἀλλήλαις ἥνωντο, καὶ τῷ τόπῳ συνάπτον-
ται, καὶ λόγων κοινωνοῦσιν ἀλλήλαις. Ἡ μὲν οὖν Εὐγενία
πρὸς τὴν Βασίλλαν ἄλλα τε πολλὰ τοῦ προκειμένου χάριν
ἀγῶνος διέξεισι καὶ ὡς ἐπιδήλως αὐτῇ ὁ Κύριος τὰ περὶ
αὐτῆς ἐκκαλύψειεν, ὅτι τὸν τοῦ μαρτυρίου δρόμον ὅσον
οὔπω δραμεῖται, καὶ στέφανον ἐν τῷ τέλει γενομένη λήψε-
ται. Ὁμοίως δὲ καὶ Βασίλλα τοῖς ἴσοις αὐτὴν ἠμείβετο, ὅτι
καὶ αὐτῇ τὰ περὶ Εὐγενίας ἐγνώρισεν ὁ Χριστός, καὶ ὅπως
διπλῷ μέλλει στεφάνῳ τὴν κεφαλὴν κοσμηθήσεσθαι, ἑνὶ
μὲν τῷ ὑπὲρ τῶν κατὰ τὴν Ἀλεξάνδρειαν καὶ τὴν ἄλλην
Αἴγυπτον κινδύνων καὶ πόνων, ἑτέρῳ δὲ τῷ ὑπὲρ τοῦ μαρτυρίου καὶ τῆς δι᾽ ἐκεῖνον σφαγῆς.

68   Ταῦτα ἀλλήλαις τε συνθέμεναι καὶ ἀλλήλων ὑπερευξά-
μεναι, ἀλλὰ καὶ τῶν περὶ τὴν Εὐγενίαν παρθένων τὰς
ψυχὰς ἀρρενώσασαι, καὶ θανάτου διὰ Χριστὸν ἀμελεῖν
πείσασαι, διΐστανται τό γε νῦν ἔχον σωματικῶς, ἑτέρα

Master and God." Immediately, an imperial edict was promulgated and proclaimed through the entire Roman empire that all the leaders of the Christians and those who preach that faith should be arrested and executed. Many people in many different places were thus killed, but Cornelius remained safe, surely because he was held in honor by the senate and was protected by the senatorial leadership as though by bodyguards, but also because he preserved himself for the sake of the salvation of many.

Basilla and Eugenia strengthened each other's resolve for 67 the contest; unable to bear their physical separation since they were really one in spirit, they joined together in one place and conversed with each other. Eugenia said many things to Basilla concerning the struggle ahead and also how the Lord had clearly revealed Basilla's fate to her: that she would soon run the course of martyrdom and would receive a crown at the end. Basilla answered her in the same way, saying that to her as well had Christ made known Eugenia's fate: that her head would be adorned with a double crown, one for the dangers and toil in Alexandria and the rest of Egypt, and the other for her martyrdom and death for His sake.

After making these pledges to each other and praying 68 for one another, and also after they urged the souls of the virgins who were with Eugenia toward manly courage, convincing them to disregard death for the sake of Christ, they separated for now physically, each letting many tears flow

πόθῳ τῆς ἑτέρας πυκνὰ τῶν ὀφθαλμῶν ἀφιεῖσα δάκρυα, ὥσπερ οὐκ ἀνεχομένων αὐταῖς τῶν ὄψεων τῆς ἀλλήλων ἀποστῆναι θέας.

69   Ἐπεὶ δὲ ἔδει καὶ πέρας ἕξειν τὰ ὑπὸ τοῦ Κυρίου περὶ αὐτῶν προηγορευμένα, τῆς μὲν Βασίλλης κατεῖπε πρὸς τὸν Πομπήϊον μία τις τῶν ἐφεπομένων αὐτῇ παιδισκῶν, ὡς εἰ μὴ σπουδῇ πάσῃ καὶ βασιλείῳ χειρὶ τὴν μνηστευθεῖσαν αὐτῷ Βασίλλαν, ὡραίαν ἤδη γάμου γεγενημένην, πρὸς τὸν οἶκον ἀγάγηται, οὐκέτι τὸ μετὰ ταῦτα γυναῖκα τὴν εἰρημένην ἕξει. "Χριστιανήν τε γὰρ ἴσθι," φησί, "τοῖς τῆς Εὐγενίας γεγενῆσθαι λόγοις, καὶ οὐ γάμῳ μόνον, ἀλλὰ καὶ κόσμῳ παντὶ ἀποτάττεσθαι· ταῦτά τοι καὶ τὸν πάτρωνα ταύτης Ἕλενον πρὸς τοὺς γάμους μέλλειν, κἀκεῖνον Χριστιανὸν ὄντα, καὶ τοῦ ὁμοίου σκοποῦ γινόμενον· οὐ μὴν ἀλλὰ καὶ οὕς," φησιν, "εὐνούχους ἡ Εὐγενία ὡς δούλους αὐτῇ πέπομφεν· οὗτοι δὴ καὶ πάντων μάλιστα τῆς μαγικῆς ἔχονται τέχνης, καὶ οὕτω ταύτην κατεγοήτευσαν, ὥστε νῦν δεσπότας αὐτοὺς ἔχειν ὁμολογεῖν καὶ ὡς ἀθανάτους θεοὺς σέβεσθαι."

70   Οὕτω τῆς πονηρᾶς δούλης Πομπηΐῳ προσαγγειλάσης, ἄντικρύς τε τῷ Διαβόλῳ τὴν γλῶσσαν ἐγχειρισάσης, καὶ τοιαῦτα κατὰ τῶν Χριστιανῶν φθεγξαμένης, ἀνήφθη σφόδρα τὸν θυμὸν ὁ Πομπήϊος καὶ κατὰ τοῦ Ἑλένου βαρὺ πνέων ἐχώρει. Καὶ πρῶτα μὲν ἐπιδεῖξαι αὐτῷ τὴν κόρην ἀνάγκην ἐπῆγεν, εἶτα καὶ τοὺς γάμους τελέσαι, "εἴ γε μὴ καὶ αὐτός," φησίν, "ἐχθρὸς εἶναι τῶν αὐτοκρατόρων φανερῶς βούλοιτο."

71   Ταῦτα τοῦ Πομπηΐου λέγοντος, οὐκ ἔλαθε μὲν τὸν

from her eyes out of longing for the other, as though their eyes could not bear to leave the sight of each other's faces.

Then, since it was necessary that what the Lord had pre- 69 scribed for them would come to pass, one of the female slaves in Basilla's retinue informed Pompey that if he did not, in all haste and by the king's hand, marry Basilla, who had been betrothed to him and was now ripe for marriage, he would no longer be able to have the aforementioned as his wife. "Know that she has become," she said, "a Christian because of the words of Eugenia, and that she is renouncing not only marriage but also the whole world; Helenos, her guardian, who is also a Christian, is going to delay the wedding, sharing the same goal; in agreement," she said, "are also those eunuchs whom Eugenia sent to Basilla as servants; they practice the art of sorcery more than anyone else and they have bewitched her so that she now contends that they are her masters and she worships them like immortal gods."

When the wicked slave woman had spoken thus to Pom- 70 pey, openly giving her tongue over to the Devil, and uttering such things against Christians, Pompey was wildly incensed with anger, and breathing heavily against Helenos went to him. He demanded that Helenos should first show him the girl, and then conduct the wedding ceremony, "if indeed he too," Pompey said, "does not wish to openly become an enemy of the emperors."

As Pompey said these words, Helenos realized the source 71

Ἔλενον ὅθεν ἡ προδοσία· ἐλευθέραν δὲ ὅμως καὶ δικαίαν τὴν ἀπόκρισιν ἐποιήσατο, "Ἐγώ," λέγων, "τῆς κόρης ἐπιτροπεύειν λαχών, μέχρι μὲν ἦν ἐν παισίν, ὑπ' ἐμοί τε τρεφομένην εἶχον, καὶ θελήματι τῷ ἐμῷ ζῶσαν. Ἐπεὶ δὲ ἡλικίας ἐπέβη, καὶ χρόνον ἤδη τὸν ἔννομον ἀπειλήφει, οὐκέτι θελήματι αὕτη τῷ ἐμῷ ἕψεται· ἀλλὰ γνώμῃ τῇ ἰδίᾳ στοιχοῦσα, ὅπως ἂν καὶ βούλοιτο δράσει."

72   Ταύτην ἐπεὶ Πομπήϊος ἐδέξατο τὴν ἀπόκρισιν, πρὸς τὴν τῆς Βασίλλης οἰκίαν παραχρῆμα ἐχώρει· καί, κόψας τὴν θύραν, τῷ θυρωρῷ ἐκέλευε προσαγγέλλειν. Ἡ δὲ ἠρέμα διὰ τοῦ παιδὸς αὐτὸν ἀπωθεῖτο, μηδὲν ἔτι κοινὸν εἶναι λέγουσα Βασίλλη καὶ Πομπηΐῳ, ἀλλὰ μὴν οὐδὲ αὐτὴν ὅλως τὴν ἄφιξιν αὐτῷ ἔχειν ἀμέμπτως. "Πῶς γὰρ ὅς γε γυναικὶ παρθένῳ ἐπῆλθε, καὶ ἰδιάζουσαν ὁμιλίαν ἐπιζητεῖ, ἥτις μικροῦ πάντων ὀφθαλμοῖς ἀρρένων ἐστὶν ἄψαυστος;"

73   Ἐκμαίνεται τοῖς ῥήμασιν ὁ Πομπήϊος· καὶ πρῶτα μὲν εἰς τὴν βουλὴν παρελθών, ἐδεῖτο ταύτης. Ἔπειτα καὶ τούτους παραλαβών, τῶν ποδῶν τοῦ κρατοῦντος οὐκ ἄδακρυς ἥπτετο· καὶ ὥς τι κοινὸν ἀτύχημα τὸ ἴδιον ὠλοφύρετο, "Ὑπὲρ ὑμῶν," λέγων, "αὐτῶν, ὦ θειότατοι Αὔγουστοι, ὑπὲρ ὑμῶν αὐτῶν διανάστητε καὶ τῶν ὑμετέρων θεῶν· καὶ ὃν ἐξ Αἰγύπτου νῦν Εὐγενία ἐπεισήγαγε νέον θεόν, τῆς ὑμετέρας πόλεως ἀπελάσατε. Πολλὰ μὲν γὰρ καὶ ἄλλα τοῖς πράγμασι λυμαίνονται Χριστιανοί, καταγελῶντες βασιλέων, καταφρονοῦντες νόμων, τοὺς εὐμενεῖς καὶ σωτῆρας θεοὺς ὡς μάταιά τινα χειροποίητα διαπτύοντες. Νυνὶ δὲ καὶ τοῦτο αὐτοῖς ἐπινενόηται τὸ ἀσέβημα καὶ τοὺς τοῦ

of the treachery; nevertheless, he made a response that was both liberal and just, saying: "Assigned to be the girl's guardian, I both raised her myself and she lived in accordance with my will, for as long as she was a child. But since she came of age and reached the number of years prescribed by law, she will no longer follow my will; rather, she will do as she might wish in accordance with her own will."

When Pompey received this answer, he immediately set out for Basilla's house; after knocking on the door, he ordered the doorkeeper to announce his arrival. Yet Basilla gently sent him away with the servant as her go-between, saying that Basilla and Pompey no longer had anything in common, and that even his coming there was not entirely without fault. "For how could he approach an unmarried woman and seek a private audience with her, a woman who is almost untouched by the eyes of all men?" 72

At these words Pompey became furious; proceeding first to the senate house, he entreated the senators. Then, taking them along with him, he tearfully clasped the emperor's feet and bewailed his personal misfortune as though it were one shared by all. "On your own behalf," he said, "O most divine Augusti, on your own behalf rise up, and on behalf of your gods; and drive away from your city the new god whom Eugenia has now imported from Egypt. For the Christians commit many different outrages, mocking the emperors, disregarding the laws, spitting upon the kindly and salvific gods as though they are useless works of artifice. But now they have thought up this new irreverence: they dissolve 73

γάμου διαλύουσι νόμους, καὶ τὰς συζυγίας ἀπαγορεύουσι·
τὰς γὰρ νυμφευθείσας ἢ καὶ νυμφευθῆναι μελλούσας τῶν
ἀνδρῶν διασπῶσι· μᾶλλον δὲ τούτους μὲν ἐκείνων ἀποστε-
ροῦσιν, ἑαυτοῖς δὲ περιποιοῦσι καὶ ἀσέμνως φθείρουσι.
Τί οὖν ἔτι, τί λοιπὸν γένοιτο, καὶ ποῖ τις τράποιτο, εἰ γάμος
ἐστὶ μηδαμοῦ; Τὸν μὲν γὰρ παρὰ νόμον οἱ νόμοι, τὸν δὲ
κατὰ νόμον Χριστιανοὶ κεκωλύκασιν, ἀλάστορές τινες, ὡς
ἔοικεν, ἐπελθόντες καινοὶ καὶ τὴν τῶν ἀνθρώπων ἀναι-
ροῦντες γένεσιν. Οὗ δὴ προβάντος, ἔρημος ἔσται πάντως
ἀνθρώπων ἡ γῆ. Πῶς δὲ τοῦ λοιποῦ καὶ τὸ στρατιωτικὸν
ὑμῖν ἕξει; Καὶ πῶς οὐκ οἰχήσεται; Τίνων μὲν βασιλεῖς
ἄρξουσιν; Ὑπὸ τίνων δὲ πολεμίων κρατήσουσι; Πῶς δὲ
πολιτεία ὅλως καὶ ἀνθρώπων συστήσεται βίος;"

74   Οὕτω τοῦ Πομπηΐου μεθ᾽ ὅσης ἀγορεύσαντος τῆς περι-
παθείας, συνεφθέγγετο ἅμα καὶ ἡ βουλή, ὥστε, συναλγή-
σαντα τὸν κρατοῦντα, ὀξεῖαν ἐπενεγκεῖν τὴν ἀπόφασιν·
Βασίλλαν, ἢ τῷ ἑαυτῆς μνηστῆρι γάμου συναφθῆναι
νόμῳ, ἢ τῇ διὰ ξίφους ὑποβληθῆναι σφαγῇ. Ἐπεὶ δὲ καὶ
περὶ Εὐγενίας ἠκηκόει, καὶ περὶ αὐτῆς εὐθὺς ἀποφαίνεται·
ἢ πεισθεῖσαν θῦσαι, ἢ βασάνοις παραδοθεῖσαν βιαίως ἀπο-
θανεῖν, κοινῇ δὲ καὶ πάντας τιμωρεῖσθαι τοὺς ἄλλους, οὐ
Χριστιανοὺς μόνον, ἀλλὰ καὶ τοὺς ὅσοι Χριστιανοὺς ὑπο-
δέχονταί τε καὶ ἀφανεῖς εἶναι παρασκευάζουσι.

75   Ταύτης ὡς ἤκουσε Βασίλλα τῆς ἀποφάσεως, ἡ βασιλὶς
ὄντως ἐκείνη καὶ γλῶτταν καὶ τὴν ψυχήν, ὀξυτέραν καὶ
αὐτὴ τὴν φωνὴν ἤπερ ἐκεῖνος εὐθὺς ἀπεφήνατο. Εἶχε δὲ
οὕτως· "Τῷ Βασιλεῖ τῶν βασιλευόντων καὶ Δημιουργῷ

the laws of marriage and they forbid matrimony; for they wrench away from men those women who have been engaged or are going to be engaged to them; or, rather, they deprive those men of them, preserving the women for themselves and corrupting them in a debauched way. What else, what is left for one to do, and where might one turn, if mating is nowhere to be found? Union outside the law is prohibited by the laws, and legal marriage is prohibited by the Christians, those new and encroaching evil spirits, as it seems, that are destroying the human race. If this were to continue, the earth will be completely empty of people. How will your army survive then? How will it not disappear? Whom will emperors rule? And with what leaders will they defeat their enemies? How will the empire and the entire human society be sustained?"

Pompey spoke with such passion, and had the immediate 74 support of the senate, that the emperor, sharing in their agitation, made a swift decision: Basilla would either be joined to her suitor by the law of marriage, or she would be subjected to death by the sword. Since he had also heard about Eugenia, he instantly pronounced a verdict for her as well: either she would be convinced to sacrifice to the gods, or she would be subjected to torture and die a violent death, and all others were to be punished in the same way, not only Christians, but also all those who received Christians and enabled them to hide.

When Basilla, that truly royal woman in both speech and 75 soul, heard this proclamation, she responded, she too in a voice sharper than that of the emperor. She spoke as follows: "As I am betrothed to the King of kings and Creator, I

νυμφευθεῖσα, φθαρτοῦ ἀνδρὸς κοινωνίαν ἥκιστα παραδέ-
χομαι, εἰ καὶ τῷ κάτω βασιλεῖ τοῦτο δοκεῖ· φοβερὸν γὰρ
τῷ ὄντι φοβερὸν τὸ ἐμπεσεῖν εἰς χεῖρας ἀληθινοῦ Βασιλέως
καὶ ζῶντος Θεοῦ." Ἅμα δὲ τῷ "Θεοῦ" προῆκε τῆς γλώττης,
καὶ τοῦ σώματος εὐθὺς ἡ κεφαλὴ ἀπετέμνετο.

76   Ἀλλὰ τοῦτο μὲν ἔσχεν ἡ Βασίλλα τὸ τέλος. Συλλαμβά-
νονται δὲ καὶ Πρωτᾶς καὶ Ὑάκινθος· καὶ πρὸς τὸν ναὸν
τοῦ Διὸς ἀπάγονται, θύειν ἐκείνῳ τῷ βδελύγματι βιαζόμε-
νοι. Στάντες οὖν ἐπ᾽ ὄψει τοῦ δοκοῦντος θεοῦ, κατηύ-
ξαντο· καί, παραχρῆμα, πρὸ τῶν ποδῶν αὐτῶν καταπίπτει
τὸ εἴδωλον· καὶ λεπτύνεται παραδόξως· καὶ εἰς κόνιν καὶ
χοῦν διαλύεται.

77   Ἐπεὶ δὲ τοῦτο Νικήτιος ὁ ἔπαρχος ἔγνω, καὶ αὐτῶν
ἐκτμηθῆναι προστάττει τὰς κεφαλάς, Εὐγενίαν δὲ παραστῆναι κατὰ τὸ βασιλικὸν προστάγμα. Ἐπεὶ δὲ παρέστη,
"Πόθεν," φησὶν ὁ ἔπαρχος, "οὕτω τὴν μαγικὴν τέχνην εἰς
ἄκρον ἐξεπονήθητε, ὥστε καὶ αὐτῶν δύνασθαι κατάρχειν
τῶν μεγίστων θεῶν;" Τοῦτο λέγων, ἐλάνθανε τοῖς περὶ
Πρωτᾶν καὶ Ὑάκινθον περιφανὲς πλέκων ἐγκώμιον, ὅτι
προσευχῇ μόνῃ τὸν παρ᾽ αὐτοῖς μέγιστον τῶν θεῶν εἰς
χοῦν κατέρραξαν, καὶ κόνιν παραχρῆμα λεπτὴν ἔδειξαν.

78   Ἀμέλει καὶ ἡ θεόπνευστος Εὐγενία μετὰ πολλῆς ἀπ-
ήντηκε τῆς συνέσεως, "Τοῦτο μέν," εἰποῦσα, "πανάληθες
εἴρηταί σοι, ὦ ἔπαρχε, τὸ ἡμᾶς ῥᾳδίως κατάρχειν τῶν ὑμετέρων θεῶν. Ἐκεῖνο δέ σοι καὶ παντελῶς ἄτοπον καὶ εὐ-
έλεγκτον, τὸ μαγικῇ ταῦτα ἐπιγράφειν τέχνῃ, ἀλλὰ μὴ
θείᾳ τινὶ καὶ ἀμάχῳ δυνάμει τοῦ παρ᾽ ἡμῖν ὄντως μόνου
Θεοῦ. Εἰ γὰρ μάγοι μέν, ὡς ὑμεῖς φατέ, ἀκαθάρτους δή

can scarcely accept union with a mortal man, even if this seems right to the king on earth. For, indeed, it is a fearful thing, *a fearful thing to fall into the hands of* the true King and *living God.*" As soon as her tongue uttered the word "God," her head was severed from her body.

And so Basilla met this end. Protas and Hyacinth were 76 also arrested; they were taken to the temple of Zeus, where they were forced to sacrifice to that abomination. As they stood facing that supposed god, they prayed; and, immediately, the idol fell at their feet; *it* miraculously *began to diminish in size* and dissolved into dirt and *dust.*

When the eparch Niketios learned of this, he commanded 77 that their heads too be cut off, and that Eugenia appear in accordance with the emperor's decree. When she appeared, the eparch said: "Where have you learned the art of sorcery to such perfection as to be able to command even the greatest gods themselves?" In saying this, he was unaware that he was weaving glowing praise for Protas and Hyacinth, that by prayer alone they had shattered into *dust* the most powerful of their gods and in no time rendered him *fine* dirt.

At any rate, Eugenia too, inspired by God, answered him 78 with great prudence. "You have spoken the absolute truth in this respect, O eparch," she said, "namely that we can easily command your gods. But it is entirely absurd and can be easily refuted that you ascribe this to sorcery and not to some divine and invincible power of our God who is truly the only one. For if sorcerers, as you say, summon impure

τινας καὶ ἐνύλους ἐπικαλοῦνται δαίμονας, οὗτοι δὲ τῶν παρ᾽ ὑμῖν ἐπικρατοῦσι θεῶν, μᾶλλον δὲ τοῦ πρώτου τῶν οὐρανίων, οὐκέτ᾽ ἂν φθάνοιτε πάντα πάλιν στρέφοντες καὶ τὰ ἄνω κάτω ποιοῦντες, τοῖς μὲν μείζοσι θεοῖς τὴν κάτω μοῖραν ἀποκληροῦντες, καὶ οὐδὲ θεοὺς ἀλλὰ δούλους αὐτοὺς ποιοῦντες, καὶ δούλους δαιμόνων, τοὺς δαίμονας δὲ θεοὺς καὶ πρώτους θεῶν. Ὃ δὴ καὶ καθ᾽ ἕτερον ἀληθεύει τρόπον· τούτους γὰρ ὑμεῖς ὡς ἀληθεῖς θεοὺς προστησάμενοι, καὶ ἀγαθοὺς εἶναι νομίζοντες, διαπορεῖτε, τί δή ποτε τῶν πονηρῶν ἡττῶνται δαιμόνων, οὐκ εἰδότες ὅτι αὐτοὶ μὲν ἀληθῶς οἱ κακοποιοί τε καὶ πονηροὶ δαίμονες, εἷς δὲ ἐπὶ πᾶσι Θεός, οὗ καὶ ὄνομα μόνον οὗτοι μὴ φέροντες, ὡς κηρός, ᾗ φησιν ὁ θεῖος Δαυίδ, *ἀπὸ προσώπου πυρὸς τήκονταί τε καὶ ἀπολλύονται*."

79   Ταῦτα ἀκούων Νικήτιος, ἐξίστατο μὲν αὐτὴν τῆς μεγαλονοίας, ὅλος δὲ τῆς τῶν εἰδώλων μανίας γινόμενος, καὶ οὐδὲν ἕτερον ἢ τὸ ἐκείνοις ἀρέσκειν διασκοπῶν, εἰς τὸν ναὸν αὐτὴν τῆς Ἀρτέμιδος ἀπαχθῆναι κελεύει, ἐφέπεσθαι δὲ καὶ τὸν σπεκουλάτωρα, τὸ ξίφος αὐτῇ ἐπισείοντα, καὶ τοῦτο μὲν παραινοῦντα, τοῦτο δὲ καὶ διαπειλούμενον, ὅτι, μὴ θύουσαν, τὸ ἐν χειρὶ μετελεύσεται, δεικνύντα τὸ ξίφος. Ἡ δέ, ἐπειδὴ ἧκεν εἰς τὸν ναόν, στᾶσα κατὰ πρόσωπον τοῦ ἀγάλματος ἐν σχήματι προσευχῆς, τῆς τῶν εἰδώλων κατηύχετο ἀπωλείας, "Ὁ Θεός," λέγουσα, "ὁ αἰώνιος, ὁ τῷ σῷ μὲ βουλήματι ἀξιώσας καὶ φῦναι, καὶ τραφῆναι, καὶ παρθένον ἄχρι καὶ νῦν διατηρηθῆναι, νύμφην τε τοῦ μονογενοῦς σου δειχθῆναι Υἱοῦ, καὶ συμπαρεῖναί μοι τὸ πανάγιον Πνεῦμα, καὶ ἐν ἐμοὶ βασιλεῦσαι παρασκευάσας,

and material demons, and these overpower your gods, especially the first among your heavenly ones, you had better hurry and change all order and turn everything upside down, since you are granting to the greatest gods the humble lot, rendering them no longer gods but slaves, and slaves of demons, and making the demons gods and, moreover, the first among gods. This is proven true also in another way: by positing them as true gods and assuming them to be good, you wonder why they are defeated by evil demons; you ignore the fact that these in truth are the maleficent and evil demons, and that there is one God who is above all things, whose name they cannot even bear to hear but, rather *as wax,* as the divine David says, *before the fire they melt and perish.*"

When he heard these words, Niketios was stunned by the greatness of her mind, but, being completely overcome by the madness of idolatry, and thinking of nothing else besides pleasing them, he ordered that she be taken to the temple of Artemis, and that the executioner should follow, brandishing his sword at her, half warning and half threatening that, if she did not offer sacrifice, she would die by what he was holding in his hand—showing his sword. But when Eugenia arrived at the temple, standing face to face with the statue in a posture of prayer, she prayed for the destruction of the idols. "O God," she said, "the eternal one, who, by Your will, deemed me worthy to be born, and raised, and preserved me a virgin to the present day, and made me a bride of Your only begotten Son, You who have arranged for the all-holy Spirit to be present inside me, and to govern me, be with me

αὐτὸς πάρεσό μοι καὶ νῦν ἐν τῇ ὑπὲρ σοῦ ταύτῃ ὁμολογίᾳ, παράδοξα ἐκτελῶν, ὅπως οἱ μὲν σεβόμενοί σε δοξασθῶσιν, αἰσχυνθῶσιν δὲ πάντες οἱ τῷ ἀλάλῳ τούτῳ καὶ κωφῷ βδελύγματι προσκυνοῦντες, καὶ τοῖς γλυπτοῖς αὐτῶν ἐγκαυχώμενοι."

80   Ταῦτα προσευχομένης, κινεῖ μὲν ὁ Θεὸς τὴν γῆν ἰσχυρῶς· καταστρέφεται δὲ ὁ ναός· συντρίβεται δὲ τὸ εἴδωλον· τὰ λοιπὰ δὲ ὁμοῦ συνταράσσονται. Ἐξίστανται οἱ ὁρῶντες· φθάνει καὶ τοὺς πόρρω τὸ θαῦμα· καὶ ἄλλος ἄλλοθεν συρρυέντες, ὅσοις μὲν νοῦς ὑγιῶς ἔχων καὶ φρένες ἦσαν, διὰ θαύματος τὸ γεγονὸς ἐποιοῦντο, καὶ θείας ἔργον ἡγοῦντο δυνάμεως, ὅσοι δὲ μετὰ τοῦ δόξης ὑγιοῦς ἐστερῆσθαι καὶ τοῦ φρονεῖν ἀπελείποντο, οὗτοι, πολλαῖς ὕβρεσι τὴν Εὐγενίαν βάλλοντες, ἔτι καὶ μάγον ἐκάλουν. Ἀκούει ταῦτα καὶ βασιλεύς· καὶ τιμωρὸς οἷα γενέσθαι τῶν αὐτοῦ θεῶν ἐπειγόμενος, λίθον μὲν βαρύτατον κελεύει τοῦ τραχήλου ταύτης ἐξαρτηθῆναι, ῥιφῆναι δὲ αὐτὴν κατὰ ποταμοῦ τοῦ Τιβέριδος.

81   Ἀλλ᾽ οὕτω μὲν οἱ *συλλαμβάνοντες πόνον καὶ τίκτοντες ἀνομίαν·* ἄπρακτον δὲ αὐτῶν ποιεῖν τὸ ἐπίταγμα τῷ Θεῷ μέλλον ἦν. Ὅθεν ὁ μὲν λίθος τοῦ τραχήλου αὐτῆς ἀπελύετο, αὐτὴ δὲ οἷα Πέτρος ὁ μέγας ἀπταίστως τοῖς ποταμίοις ἐβάδιζε νάμασιν. Εἶτα κρείττω φανεῖσαν τοῦ ὕδατος, πυρὶ κολάζειν αὐτὴν διεσκέψαντο· καὶ κάμινος ὑπεδέχετο τὴν μεγάλην. Ἀλλ᾽ ὁ φρουρῶν αὐτὴν Κύριος καὶ τανῦν ἐνταῦθα παρῆν· καὶ τὸ πῦρ, οἷα τὴν φύσιν ἀποβαλόν, εὐθὺς διηλέγχετο· καὶ τὸ σῶμα ταύτης ἀπαθὲς διεσώζετο.

82   Τί τὸ μετὰ ταῦτα; Σκότει κολάζεται βαθυτάτῳ, πρὸς τῷ

now in this confession of my faith in You, and perform miracles so that those who worship You may be glorified, and all those who bow down to this mute and deaf abomination and exult in their sculptures may be humiliated."

As she made this prayer, God shook the earth mightily; 80
the temple was destroyed; the idol was shattered; everything else was thrown into confusion. The onlookers were amazed; word of the miracle even reached people far away; they gathered from different places, and those with healthy mind and wits considered the event to be a miracle and the work of God's power, while those who were deprived of a healthy mind and were unable to think straight cast many insults at Eugenia and continued to call her a sorceress. The emperor heard these things as well; and as though rushing to be the avenger of his gods, commanded that an extremely heavy stone be hung from her neck and that she be thrown into the river Tiber.

These were the plans of those who *conceive mischief* and 81
bring forth lawlessness; yet God made sure that it would be impossible for them to carry out the order: the stone slipped from her neck and she, like the great Peter, walked surefootedly through the currents of the river. Since she proved to be stronger than water, they then decided to punish her with fire; and a furnace received the great Eugenia. But the Lord, her protector, was with her now as well; and the fire was immediately proven ineffective, as though discarding its nature; and her body remained unscathed.

What happened next? She was punished with the deepest 82

σκότει δὲ καὶ λιμῷ· καὶ οἰκία ταύτην ἐσχάτως ἐλάμβανεν ἀφεγγής, μηδὲ τροφῆς ὅλως κοινωνοῦσαν. Ἠγνόουν δὲ πάντως μετ᾽ αὐτῆς εἶναι τὸν τοῦ φωτὸς Κύριον, ὑφ᾽ οὗ καὶ πρώϊμον αὐτῇ, κατὰ τὸν προφήτην, ἐρράγη τὸ φῶς· καὶ φωτὶ θεϊκῷ ἅπας ὁ οἶκος περιελάμπετο. Οὐ φῶς δὲ μόνον ἐδίδοτο, ἀλλὰ καὶ θεία τις ἄνωθεν ἐχορηγεῖτο τροφή, ἄρτος ἑκάστης ἡμέρας παραδόξως ἑτοιμαζόμενος, λευκότερος μὲν χιόνος, τὴν ἡδονὴν δὲ θεσπέσιος. Τὸ δὲ μεῖζον· αὐτὸς ἐκεῖνος ἐφίσταται ὁ Σωτήρ, "Ἐγώ εἰμι," λέγων, "Εὐγενία, ὃς καὶ σταυρὸν διὰ σὲ καὶ θάνατον ἠνεσχόμην· δι᾽ ὃν καὶ σὺ ταῦτα προείλου παθεῖν. Τοιγαροῦν καὶ μεγίστῃ σε δόξῃ περιβαλῶ· καὶ πολλῶν ἐμπλήσω χαρίτων. Ἔστω δέ σοι καὶ τοῦτο τῆς περὶ σὲ τιμῆς σύμβολον· αὕτη γὰρ ἡ ἡμέρα πρὸς τὴν ἄνω σε παραπέμπει ζωήν, ἥτις κἀμὲ εἶδε τοῖς κάτω ἐπιδημήσαντα."

83   Οὕτως εἰπών, ὁ μὲν ἀπ᾽ αὐτῆς ἀπέστη. Οὐ μακρὰν δὲ καὶ τῶν λαληθέντων ἀπήντα τὸ πέρας· στέλλεται γάρ τις τῶν ἀσεβῶν, τὸ τῶν μοναχῶν ἐκεῖνος σχῆμα ὑποκρινόμενος, ὅς, εἴσω γενόμενος τοῦ δεσμωτηρίου, κατ᾽ αὐτὴν ἄρα τὴν ἡμέραν τελειοῖ τὴν μάρτυρα τῇ διὰ ξίφους σφαγῇ, καθ᾽ ἣν καὶ ἡ τῶν Γενεθλίων τοῦ Σωτῆρος ἡμῶν ἤγετο ἑορτή. Τελέσαντες οὖν ὅσα θέμις ἦν ἐπὶ θυγατρὶ τοιαύτῃ καὶ ἀδελφῇ, ἥ τε μήτηρ, φημί, καὶ οἱ ἀδελφοί, τὸ ἱερὸν αὐτῆς λείψανον ἐν τόπῳ μὲν κατατίθενται οὐ μακρὰν ἀπέχοντι Ῥώμης, "ἡ Ῥωμαία" δὲ "ὁδὸς" ἐπικαλουμένῳ.

84   Οὕτω μὲν Εὐγενία ἐβίω, σεμνῶς· οὕτω δὲ ἀπεβίω καθὰ καὶ κέκλητο, εὐγενῶς· ὥστε μηδ᾽ ἕτερον μᾶλλον ἔχειν ἡμᾶς θαυμάζειν, τὴν ἐν Χριστῷ ζωήν, ἢ τὸν ὑπὲρ Χριστοῦ

darkness and, in addition to darkness, with starvation; a building without light was the last to receive her, where also she was denied any food. They did not know at all, however, that with her was the Lord of light from whom *the light,* according to the prophet, *broke forth* for her *as the morning;* and the whole building was illumined by divine light. And not only was light given but also some divine nourishment was supplied from above, bread which was miraculously prepared every day, whiter than snow, and with taste that was divine. And this was greater still: the Savior himself appeared to her, saying, "It is I, O Eugenia, who endured both the cross and death for you; I, because of whom you too have chosen to suffer. Therefore I will clothe you also in the greatest glory; and I will fill you with many gifts. Let this too be a symbol of your honor; the day that will convey you to the heavenly life will be that very day which also saw me come dwell on earth."

After speaking thus, He left her. And it was not long be- 83 fore His words came to pass: an impious man, disguised in a monk's habit, was sent, came inside the jail, and killed the martyr with a blow of the sword on the very same day that the feast of the Birth of our Savior was being celebrated. Having carried out all rites as were proper for such a daughter and sister, her mother, I say, and her brothers buried her holy remains in a place that was not far from Rome and which was called "the Roman Way."

This is how Eugenia lived, honorably; and this is how she 84 departed from life, nobly, just as her name indicated. The result is that we cannot choose at what to marvel more: her life in Christ or her death for Christ. Indeed, not long

θάνατον. Ὅθεν καὶ ὅσης αὕτη τῆς δόξης ὑπὲρ ἀμφοτέρων
ἠξίωται, δῆλον οὐ μετὰ πολὺ γέγονε.

85 Δισσοῖς γὰρ τοῖς πάθεσι μεριζομένης αὐτῇ τῆς μητρός,
καὶ τῷ μὲν διὰ Χριστὸν τυθῆναι χαιρούσης, ἀλγούσης δὲ
τῷ θυγατρὸς διαζυγῆναι τοιαύτης, καὶ τὸν χωρισμὸν ἥκιστα πράως ὑπομενούσης, ὄναρ ἡ μάρτυς αὐτῇ ἐφίσταται,
οὕτω μὲν ἐστολισμένη λαμπρῶς, ὡς μηδὲ προσβάλλειν
αὐτῇ τὸν ὀφθαλμὸν ἱκανῶς ἔχειν, τοιαύταις δὲ παρθένοις
προπεμπομένη φαιδραῖς, ὡς μηδεμίαν αὐτῇ τῶν βασιλί-
δων παραβεβλῆσθαι δύνασθαι.

86 Οὕτω τοιγαροῦν ἐπιστᾶσα, ἐῴκει τῇ μητρὶ λέγειν, "Ἵνα
τί, ὦ μῆτερ, οὕτω σοι τὸ δεινοπαθεῖν, πολλοῖς ὑπὲρ ἡμῶν
τοῖς δάκρυσι τηκομένη; Οὐ θρήνων, ἀλλ᾽ εὐφροσύνης
ἄξια τὰ ἡμέτερα· ἴσθι γὰρ ὡς ἐγώ τε καὶ ὁ πατὴρ Φίλιππος
ἐν ἀρρήτῳ τινὶ τῶν μαρτύρων εὐφροσύνῃ ζῶμεν, συν-
όντες Χριστῷ καὶ συμβασιλεύοντες. Ὃς καὶ σὲ οὐ πολλαῖς
ὕστερον ἡμέραις εἰς τὴν ζωὴν ταύτην μετακαλέσει. Τοῖς
δὲ ἐμοῖς ἀδελφοῖς, φυλάξαι τὴν ἐν Χριστῷ σφραγῖδα βε-
βαίαν, καὶ ἀδελφοὺς ἐμοὶ γενέσθαι καὶ τὰς ψυχάς, συνεχῶς
παραίνει, ἵν᾽ οὕτω γένος ὅλον καλὸν δῶρον τῷ Δεσπότῃ
προσενεχθῶμεν."

87 Ταῦτα παρὰ τῆς Εὐγενίας ἡ μήτηρ ἤκουσεν· ἐλέγετο δὲ
καὶ ἀγγέλων ἐπιστασίαν ὁρᾶν, ὧν τὸ σχῆμα χαρᾶς τε ἦν
ὁμοῦ καὶ αἰδοῦς σύμβολον, ὥσπερ ἐνδεικνυμένων αὐτῶν,
ὅτι καὶ τιμῆς ἄξιοι ἐκεῖνοι, ἀλλὰ καὶ ἀλήκτου χαρᾶς κοι-
νωνοί. Ἧς γένοιτο καὶ ἡμᾶς πάντας ἀξιωθῆναι, χάριτι καὶ
φιλανθρωπίᾳ τοῦ Κυρίου ἡμῶν Ἰησοῦ Χριστοῦ, ᾧ πρέπει
πᾶσα δόξα, τιμὴ καὶ κράτος, νῦν καὶ ἀεί, καὶ εἰς τοὺς
αἰῶνας τῶν αἰώνων. Ἀμήν.

afterward, it became clear of what great glory she was deemed worthy on both accounts.

For her mother was torn by two emotions: she rejoiced 85 that her daughter had been sacrificed for Christ, but was pained to be separated from such a daughter, and bore the separation most ill; the martyr thus came to her in a dream, so brightly clad that her mother could not even lay her eyes on her, and also escorted by such brilliant virgins that not even any of the empresses could be compared to her.

Appearing to her mother in this way, she seemed to say to 86 her, "Why, O mother, do you suffer so grievously over me, melting away with so many tears? My situation is not worthy of lamentations, but rather of joy; you should know that I as well as my father Philip are living in that inexpressible joy of martyrs, together with Christ and sharing in His royal state. And, in a few days, He will summon you too up to this life. As for my brothers, continually exhort them to maintain firmly their seal in Christ and to become my brothers also in their souls, so that our entire family might thus be offered as a good gift to our Master."

These were the words that the mother heard from Euge- 87 nia; and it is said that angels also appeared before her eyes in a posture that symbolized both joy and reverence, as if to show that those martyrs were worthy of honor and also shared in unending joy. May it be possible for all of us to partake in this joy by the grace and love of our Lord Jesus Christ, to whom all glory, honor, and dominion is due, now and forever, and unto the ages of ages. Amen.

Abbreviations

BHG = François Halkin, *Bibliotheca hagiographica Graeca,* 3rd ed. (Brussels, 1957); see also François Halkin, *Novum auctarium bibliothecae hagiographicae Graecae* (Brussels, 1984)

Blampignon = Aemilius Blampignon, ed., *De sancto Cypriano et de primaeva Carthaginensi ecclesia* (Paris, 1862), 172–203

CPG = Ernst L. von Leutsch and Friedrich G. Schneidewin, eds., *Corpus Paroemiographorum Graecorum,* 2 vols. (Göttingen, 1839–1851); repr., 3 vols. (Hildesheim, 1958–1961)

Ehrhard, *Überlieferung* I, II, III = Albert Ehrhard, *Überlieferung und Bestand der hagiographischen und homiletischen Literatur der griechischen Kirche,* 3 vols. (Leipzig, 1937–1939)

Euthymios, *Barlaam and Ioasaph* = *Die Schriften des Johannes von Damaskos,* vol. VI/2, *Historia animae utilis de Barlaam et Ioasaph (spuria). Text und Zehn Appendices,* ed. Robert Volk (Berlin, 2006)

Flusin-Paramelle = Bernard Flusin and Joseph Paramelle, eds., "La Vie métaphrastique de Pélagie: *BHG* 1479," in *Pélagie la pénitente: métamorphoses d'une légende,* ed. Pierre Petitmengin, vol. 2, *La survie dans les littératures européennes,* 28–40 (Paris, 1984)

Gebhardt-Dobschütz = Oscar von Gebhardt and Ernst von Dobschütz, eds., *Die Akten der edessenischen Bekenner Gurjas, Samonas, und Abibos* (Leipzig, 1911), 149–99

Gregory of Nazianzos, *Or.* 4 = *Grégoire de Nazianze: Discours 4–5 contre Julien. Introduction, texte critique, traduction et notes,* ed. and trans. Jean Bernardi (Paris, 1983)

Gregory of Nazianzos, *Or.* 7 = *Grégoire de Nazianze: Discours 6–12. Introduction, texte critique, traduction et notes,* ed. and trans. Marie-Ange Calvet-Sebasti (Paris, 1995)

Gregory of Nazianzos, *Or.* 24 and 25 = *Grégoire de Nazianze: Discours 24–26. Introduction, texte critique, traduction et notes, avec la collaboration de Guy Lafontaine,* ed. and trans. Justin Mossay (Paris, 1981)

Gregory of Nazianzos, *Or.* 40 = *Grégoire de Nazianze: Discours 38–41. Introduction, texte critique et notes,* ed. Claudio Moreschini, trans. Paul Gallay (Paris, 1990)

Gregory of Nazianzos, *Or.* 43 = *Grégoire de Nazianze: Discours 42–43. Introduction, texte critique, traduction et notes,* ed. and trans. Jean Bernardi (Paris, 1992)

Halkin, *Catalogue* = François Halkin, *Catalogue des manuscrits hagiographiques de la Bibliothèque nationale d'Athènes* (Brussels, 1983)

Heliodoros, *Ethiopian Tale* = *Héliodore. Les Ethiopiques (Théagène et Chariclée),* ed. and trans. Robert M. Rattenbury, Thomas W. Lumb and Jean Maillon (Paris, 1960)

Høgel, *Metaphrastes* = Christian Høgel, *Symeon Metaphrastes: Rewriting and Canonization* (Copenhagen, 2002)

Omont, *Catalogus* = Henri Omont, *Catalogus codicum hagiographicorum graecorum Bibliothecae nationalis parisiensis* (Brussels, 1896)

PG = Jacques-Paul Migne, ed., *Patrologiae cursus completus, series Graeca,* 161 vols. (Paris, 1857–1866)

PmbZ = Ralph-Johannes Lilie et al., *Prosopographie der mittelbyzantinischen Zeit,* 2 Abt., 8 vols. (Berlin, 1998–2013)

Suda = Ada Adler, ed., *Suidae lexicon,* 5 vols. (Leipzig, 1928–1938)

SynaxCP = Hippolyte Delehaye, ed., *Synaxarium ecclesiae Constantinopolitanae: Propylaeum ad Acta sanctorum Novembris* (Brussels, 1902)

Tsames = Demetrios G. Tsames, ed., *Τὸ μαρτυρολόγιο τοῦ Σινᾶ* (Thessalonike, 2003), 312–31

Note on the Text

Unfortunately, no Metaphrastic text exists in a modern critical edition, in the full sense of the term—namely, an edition that takes into consideration the entire manuscript tradition, a formidable task. Three of the texts included in this volume *(Pelagia; Galaktion and Episteme; Euphemia)* have been edited critically before, but in an eclectic fashion: their editors took into consideration only a limited number of manuscripts in order to present a reliable text. I have used, but also improved, these editions and also followed their example in editing all six texts anew by collating only a representative number of eleventh-century Metaphrastic manuscripts as well as by examining some manuscripts of the late Byzantine and post-Byzantine periods. The manuscripts and modern editions used to prepare each text are listed below.

As became evident during the collation process, by the end of this first hundred years of their history, the Metaphrastic texts became remarkably stable, without much variation from manuscript to manuscript. This stability legitimizes the choice to print here a version of Metaphrastes as it exists in the majority of the collated eleventh-century manuscripts, and not to attempt either to reconstruct the "original" version or to present the full history of the text.

The later Byzantine manuscripts (and then the nineteenth-century editions) introduced almost exclusively mistakes into the text; these were the result of mishearings (upon dictation), misreadings (upon copying), omission, or careless editing. None of these later mistakes as well as the (relatively few) mistakes of the eleventh-century manuscripts are recorded here; they have been corrected silently instead.

The stability of the manuscript tradition also legitimizes the choice to record in the frugal Notes to the Text only those few variations that seem to reflect, to the extent that this can be surmised, either: (1) conscious rewriting, on a minor scale (variation, expansion, or reduction), by eleventh-century scribes after the text had become fixed (for instance, manuscript *G* for the month of October); or (2) an alternative version of the text (for instance, manuscripts *O* and *Υ* for the month of December). It remains unclear whether this alternative version goes back to the time of the composition, when different scribes were involved in the production of the Metaphrastic corpus (Flusin-Paramelle 22–23), or predates (or perhaps is) a second "edition" likely created during the early eleventh century (Høgel, *Metaphrastes* 130–34), or reflects the somewhat "fluid" state of the text in the early stages of its transmission, previously unobserved by the students of Metaphrastes but confirmed by my collation. The existence of this last variety is confirmed by the earliest dated manuscript that preserves Metaphrastes's *Barbara:* Koutloumousiou gr. 25, written in October 1011 by Theophanes of the Athonite monastery of Iveron. Though apparently based on the early Metaphrastic version(s), Koutloumousiou gr. 25 presents such remarkable variation in its wording that I have decided not to take it

into consideration for the present edition. Such and further similar issues can be fully resolved only when the immense number of Metaphrastic manuscripts have been studied closely anew and, then, the future editor evaluates all the available evidence. Still, the Greek text printed here corresponds closely to the form that it had acquired for a majority of its Byzantine readers.

Some technical matters: Biblical citations refer to the Brenton edition of the Septuagint and the Farstad edition of the New Testament. When Metaphrastes quotes from the Bible, the Greek text and translation are both italicized, and the biblical reference is indicated in a note to the translation. Often he has slightly modified the quotation, by changing the form of a noun or verb in order to put it in the mouth of a new speaker. In these cases, I have indicated that the quotation has been modified slightly by the addition of "see" in front of the biblical reference (for example, "see Psalms 7:15"), though the reader will have to compare the biblical passage with Metaphrastes to see the change he has made.

My basic principles of punctuation of the text are the following:

1. Virtually every punctuation mark in the manuscripts has an equivalent mark in the edition, with a few exceptions: (a) those cases where in the manuscripts punctuation separates the verb either from its subject or from its direct object; (b) a few instances where a punctuation mark would not only seem superfluous but also cause confusion (for instance, in certain paratactic structures); (c) cases where I have

added a punctuation mark, absent from the manuscripts, again to facilitate comprehension.

2. The most common punctuation mark of the manuscripts, namely the so-called middle dot, has been interpreted variously (as comma, semicolon, full stop, or, in a few instances, question mark) on a case-by-case basis, since the medieval middle dot does not correspond exactly to any single modern punctuation mark.

Manuscripts Consulted

I note paleographical information only when relevant to the pages used for this present edition:

A   Lesbos, Leimonos Monastery 13a, 11th century (second half?) (folios 5r–6v added by a later hand [14th century?]); folios 5v–21r *(Kyprianos and Ioustina);* 48v–53r *(Pelagia)*

B   Lesbos, Leimonos Monastery 56, 11th century (second half); folios 6r–23r *(Kyprianos and Ioustina);* 61r–67v *(Pelagia)*

C   Lesbos, Leimonos Monastery 19, 11th century (second half); folios 5v–15v *(Kyprianos and Ioustina);* 36v–40v *(Pelagia;* text partly mutilated)

D   Lesbos, Leimonos Monastery 48, several hands; folios 44r–50r *(Galaktion and Episteme;* [early?] 11th century); 149v–53v *(Euphemia;* mid-15th century)

E   Paris, Bibliothèque nationale de France, gr. 1494, 11th/
       12th centuries (scribe from southern Italy or Epirus?);
       folios 3r–4v (*Kyprianos and Ioustina;* a fragment); 22v–
       26v *(Pelagia)*

F   Paris, Bibliothèque nationale de France, gr. 1495, 11th
       century (second half; from Bithynia); folios 4r–18v
       (Kyprianos and Ioustina); 49v–55r *(Pelagia)*

G   Athens, National Library of Greece, gr. 2099, 11th cen-
       tury (last quarter; scribe: *Le copiste du Métaphraste*); fo-
       lios 3r–14r *(Kyprianos and Ioustina);* 36v–40r *(Pelagia)*

H   Paris, Bibliothèque nationale de France, gr. 1020,
       (mid-?)11th century; folios 87r–95v *(Galaktion and Epi-
       steme);* 290r–300v *(Euphemia)*

I   Paris, Bibliothèque nationale de France, gr. 1522, 11th
       century (first half?); folios 83r–94r *(Galaktion and Epi-
       steme);* 347v–56v *(Euphemia;* end missing)

J   London, British Library, Add MS 36636, 11th century
       (first half?); folios 34v–42r *(Galaktion and Episteme)*

K   Athens, National Library of Greece, gr. 1054, 11th cen-
       tury (second half; scribe: Euthymios in the team of the
       Copiste); folios 65r–73r *(Galaktion and Episteme);* 256v–
       64v *(Euphemia;* end missing)

L   Florence, Biblioteca Medicea Laurenziana, Plut. gr.
       11.10, 11th century; folios 2r–11v *(Barbara)*

M   Paris, Bibliothèque nationale de France, gr. 1501, 11th century (first half?); folios 1r–5v (*Barbara;* beginning missing)

N   Paris, Bibliothèque nationale de France, gr. 1461, 11th century; folios 1r–8r (*Barbara*)

O   Paris, Bibliothèque nationale de France, gr. 1466, (early?) 11th century; folios 40r–48v (*Barbara*); 211r–37v (*Eugenia;* folios 234r–37v are written by a different, later hand)

P   Paris, Bibliothèque nationale de France, supp. gr. 563, 11th century (first half?); folios 229r–44r (*Eugenia*)

Q   Paris, Bibliothèque nationale de France, Coislin 148, 11th century (first half?); folios 176v–200v (*Eugenia*)

R   Paris, Bibliothèque nationale de France, gr. 1496, 11th century (first half?); folios 1r–7v (*Barbara;* folios 1r–2v were added by a later 14th-century hand); 319r–40r (*Eugenia*)

S   Paris, Bibliothèque nationale de France, gr. 1535, 11th century (first half?); folios 97r–118r (*Eugenia*)

T   Paris, Bibliothèque nationale de France, gr. 921, 11th century (first half?); folios 44v–59v (*Eugenia*)

U   London, British Library, Add MS 22733, 11th century (second half); folios 146v–72v (*Eugenia*)

V^2 Vatican, Biblioteca Apostolica Vaticana, gr. 1995, 11th century (second half); folios 1v–13v (*Kyprianos and Ioustina);* 47v–55r (*Pelagia*)

V^3 Vatican, Biblioteca Apostolica Vaticana, gr. 2037, 11th century (second half); folios 74v–85r (*Galaktion and Episteme*); 299v–309v (*Euphemia*)

V^5 Vatican, Biblioteca Apostolica Vaticana, gr. 2038, 11th century (second half); folios 1r–3v (*Barbara;* beginning missing)

V^6 Vatican, Biblioteca Apostolica Vaticana, gr. 2040, 11th century (second half); folios 142v–74v (*Eugenia*)

X Athens, National Library of Greece, gr. 2809, 11th century (second half?); folios 98r–109v (*Galaktion and Episteme*)

Υ Athens, National Library of Greece, gr. 2106, 11th century (second half?); folios 1r–6v (*Barbara;* beginning missing); 302r–23v (*Eugenia*)

For further information on the copyists of manuscripts G and K, see Irmgard Hutter, "*Le Copiste du Métaphraste.* On a Center for Manuscript Production in Eleventh Century Constantinople," in *I manoscritti greci tra riflessione e dibattito*, ed. G. Prato (Florence, 2000), 535–86.

FURTHER MANUSCRIPTS CONSULTED

While preparing the critical edition, I also collated the following later manuscripts. Since they provide only inferior readings (omissions, misspellings, rearrangement of phrases, and the like), their variants are not recorded in the notes, nor are they furnished with an abbreviation sign, but are listed here in order to offer the reader a full picture of the evidence that was utilized:

NOTE ON THE TEXT

Athens, National Library of Greece, gr. 987, 16th century, folios 3r–10v *(Barbara)*

Florence, Biblioteca Medicea Laurenziana, Plut. gr. 11.1, year 1327, folios 65r–73r *(Galaktion and Episteme)*

Florence, Biblioteca Medicea Laurenziana, Plut. gr. 11.11, 16th century, folios 1r–6r *(Barbara)*

Lesbos, Leimonos Monastery 15, late 15th century, folios 78r–87v *(Galaktion and Episteme);* 287v–98v *(Euphemia)*

Lesbos, Leimonos Monastery 16, 15th century, folios 5v–28v *(Kyprianos and Ioustina);* 78v–87r *(Pelagia)*

EDITIONS OF TEXTS IN THIS VOLUME

The six texts in this volume were edited anew based on previous editions, whose full references can be found in the bibliography, and a new collation of relevant manuscripts. The editions and manuscripts consulted for each are as follows:

Kyprianos and Ioustina: This edition is based on a collation of the manuscripts *A, B, C, E, F, G,* and *V²*. I have also consulted the edition of Blampignon.

Pelagia: The text is based on the edition of Flusin-Paramelle, which has been tested against five early witnesses not utilized by Flusin-Paramelle: *A, B, C, G,* and *V²*. I have followed the punctuation and paragraphing of the manuscripts and recorded some significant later variations (especially in *G*), but the interested reader should consult the critical apparatus of Flusin-Paramelle for a fuller image of what the editors

have identified as a second "version" of the text, as mentioned above.

Galaktion and Episteme: This edition is based on the edition of Tsames, which has been improved (also in terms of punctuation and paragraphing) by collating the manuscripts *D, H, I, J, K, V³,* and *X.*

Euphemia: The text reproduces the edition of Gebhardt-Dobschütz, whose punctuation and paragraphing have been improved by collating the manuscripts *D, H, I, K,* and *V³.*

Barbara: This edition is based on a collation of the manuscripts *L, M, N, O, R, V⁵,* and *Υ.* I have also consulted the edition in the PG.

Eugenia: This edition is based on a collation of the manuscripts *O, P, Q, R, S, T, U, V⁶,* and *Υ.* I have also consulted the edition in the PG.

Notes to the Text

Title   Βίος καὶ μαρτύριον τοῦ ἐν ἁγίοις ἱερομάρτυρος Κυπριανοῦ καὶ
τῆς ἁγίας Ἰουστίνας G

1   περιχαρῶς: *omitted* G
ἐκθρέψαντας: θρέψαντας G

2   ἀκολουθοῦσα: ἐπακολουθοῦσα G
ἀσθένειαν καταγινώσκειν ἤρξατο: ἤρξατο καταγινώσκειν
ἀσθένειαν G

4   ὀφθῆναι: ἐλθεῖν G

5   τεχνιτῶν: τεχνητοῖς G
θιασώτας: στρατιώτας G

6   πατήρ: πατήρ σου G
πορεύεσθαι τὸ λοιπόν: λοιπὸν πορεύεσθαι G

7   ὑπεσήμαινεν: ὑπεσήμανεν G
ὁ πατὴρ αὐτῷ: αὐτῷ ὁ πατήρ G

8   οὐκέτι διαμφιβάλλων: διαμφιβάλλων οὐκέτι G
φρουρίῳ τούτους περιτειχίζει: τούτους περιτειχίζει φρουρίῳ G

9   Πάντως δὲ οὐκ ἦν: οὐκ ἦν δὲ πάντως G

10   ἔλαχεν: ἔτυχεν C
ἐδόκει: *omitted* F G
ἄξια F Blampignon: ἀνάξια *all other manuscripts*

11   ἀπατηλοῖς: *omitted* G

12   πάσης: ἁπάσης G

13   θανάτου βαρύτερον: βαρύτερον τοῦ θανάτου G
ἀπεδύετο: ἀποδύεται G

16   ὁρμήν: *omitted* G

σοι ταῦτα: ταῦτα σοι G
17   ἔβλεπε: ἔβλεψε F G Blampignon
πάντων: ἀπάντων G
18   ὅλας πόλεις: πόλεις ὅλας G
20   τὴν ἧτταν ὁμολογῆσαι: ὁμολογῆσαι τὴν ἧτταν G
21   ἐκεῖνο καταγνωσθέν: ἐκείνου καταγνωσθέντος F
22   ὠδίνω … πόθον: καὶ αὐτὴ πόθον ὠδίνω σοι G
παρὰ σοῦ: omitted G
24   μεγάλα: μεγάλαυχα C
τῆς τοιᾶσδε: τῆς τοιαύτης B
25   δαίμων: τῶν δαιμόνων ἄρχων G
26   Φέρειν: χαίρειν E F
οὖν εἰπὼν: οὖν ταῦτα εἰπὼν C; οὖν ταύτας εἰπὼν G
καταλαμβάνει τὴν ἐκκλησίαν: omitted A
28   εἰσήνεγκε: ἤνεγκε G
ὑπολειφθῆναι: ἀπολειφθῆναι G
29   Τοσούτῳ τε: τοσοῦτον δὲ G
προσφέρειν: προφέρειν F Blampignon
31   ἐντός: ἑστῶτας ἐντός G
32   βάλλειν … φιλονεικεῖς: τῆς ἐκκλησίας φιλονεικεῖς βάλλειν G
33   τὸ πρᾶγμα θεῖον ἀκριβῶς: θεῖον ἀκριβῶς τὸ πρᾶγμα G
34   καλῶς: καλὸς G
37   προσκαίρου καὶ: omitted G
38   χρώμενος … γοητείᾳ: καὶ ἀφύκτῳ τῇ γοητείᾳ χρώμενος G
40   τε καὶ ἀνεθάρρυνεν: omitted G
41   ἀπηξίου, τὴν σύζυγον: ἀπηξίου τὸν σύζυγον G
ταύτην ἀκλινῶς ἔχουσαν: ταύτης ἀκλινῶς ἐχούσης C
ἀντιπράττουσαν: ἀντιπραττούσης C
42   πάντα πράττειν τῷ δοκεῖ: τῷ δοκεῖν πάντα πράττειν G
43   Διὰ ταῦτα … ἐπάλαιον: omitted G
παρ’ αὐτῇ εἶναι: εἶναι παρ’ αὐτῇ G
44   δαιμονίῳ: δαιμόνων G Blampignon
46   δυνάμενος σώζειν: σώζειν δυνάμενος G
47   ὡς αὐτὴν: ὡς αὐτὴν μὲν G
53   εὐθὺς: εὐθέως G
54   ἔλεγε, "σφόδρα: σφόδρα ἔλεγε G

55 συμβουλὴν: βουλὴν G
    ἐνέλιπες: ἔλιπες G
56 πολλῆς . . . ἀπολαύοντας: ἀπολαύοντας τοὺς ὑπὸ τὴν σὴν
    ἐξουσίαν G
57 τῆς αὐτῶν ἀνοχῆς: τῆς αὐτῆς ἀνοχῆς G
    πολλούς τε: καὶ πολλούς G
58 ἡττᾶτο: ἡττᾶται G
    ἐπαινοῦντας: συναινοῦντας G
61 ἀτίμῳ θανάτῳ: θανάτῳ ἀτίμῳ G
62 παρά τινων ἀποκλαπῆναι ταῦτα: ἀποκλαπῆναι ταῦτα παρά
    τινων G
    ἐπὶ τὴν Ῥώμην: ἐν Ῥώμῃ G

Pelagia

Title Βίος καὶ πολιτεία τῆς ὁσίας μητρὸς ἡμῶν Πελαγίας τῆς πρώην
       πόρνης ἐν Ἀντιοχείᾳ G; Βίος καὶ πολιτεία καὶ ἀγῶνες τῆς
       ὁσίας μητρὸς ἡμῶν Πελαγίας V^2
1   ὅσῳπερ: ὅσῳ περὶ A B
       φύσιν φιλοτιμήσαιτο: φιλοτιμήσαιτο φύσιν G
       ἦν: ἢ F G
2   παραβλάπτεσθαι: πρότερον παραβλάπτεσθαι V^2
       πλῆθος ἀκολούθων: ἀκολούθων πλῆθος πολύ G
       ὑπαγομένη: ἐπαγομένη G
3   οὗτος ἦν: ἦν οὗτος A B C and several witnesses in the critical appa-
       ratus of Flusin-Paramelle
       ἱεροῦ: ἱεροῦ καὶ θείου G
4   ἰδόντες χορός: χορὸς θεασάμενοι G
5   μηδὲ γηράσκουσα: μὴ φθειρομένη μηδὲ γηράσκουσα V^2
6   προεδείκνυ: παρεδείκνυ G
7   ἤδη δὲ ταύτης: ταύτης δὲ ἤδη G
       οἷος omitted Flusin-Paramelle
8   ἱερὸς ἀνὴρ: ἱερεὺς G
       ἐπὶ τὸν ναὸν: πρὸς τὸν ναὸν G
       τὴν δὲ Καινὴν . . . Εὐαγγέλιον: τὴν καινὴν δὲ λαβὼν διαθήκην,
       τὸ θεῖον φημὶ Εὐαγγέλιον G

9   ἡ ψυχή: τῇ ψυχῇ συμφέρει, τίς δὲ ἔστιν αὕτη G

10   χρῆται πρὸς σωτηρίαν: πρὸς σωτηρίαν χρῆται G

    τοῦ ἱεροῦ τῷ Νόννῳ: τῷ Νόννῳ τοῦ ἱεροῦ G

    ἀπαγγέλλειν: ἐπαγγέλλειν A B C

11   τὸ προσταχθὲν: πρὸς τὸ προσταχθὲν V²

    του τῶν: που τῶν G

    βλέπειν στέγει: στέγει βλέπειν G

    τοιούτου: τοιοῦτος V²

14   ἔλεγεν: *omitted* V²

    καὶ ἀναγεννήσῃς: *omitted* V²

17   μετασχηματισθεὶς: καὶ μετασχηματισθεὶς G

    διετείνετο τὰ μέγιστα παρ' αὐτοῦ: τὰ μέγιστα παρ' αὐτοῦ
     διετείνετο G

18   πάλιν δὲ βάλλεται τῷ σταυρῷ: *omitted* A

    εὐθὺς: *omitted* V²

    τοῦ δυσμενοῦς: δηλαδὴ τοῦ ἀντικειμένου G

20   ἐμφώτειον: ἐμφώτιον Flusin-Paramelle

    τρύχινόν: τρίχινόν Flusin-Paramelle

    ἐπείγεται: ἠπείγετο G

25   πλεῖον ἀπενεγκαμένη: ἀπενεγκαμένην πλεῖον B

27   θαρρείτω: καὶ θαρρείτω G

GALAKTION AND EPISTEME

Title   καὶ ἐνδόξων: *omitted* K; ἐνδόξων τοῦ Χριστοῦ H J

10   σέβας μεταβληθήσεται: μεταβληθήσεται σέβας V³

16   πάλιν πρὸς ταῦτα τοῦ θαυμασίου: μᾶλλον πρὸς ταῦτα πλέον
    τὸν ἄνδρα ὑπαλείψαντός τε ὁμοῦ καὶ X

    τοῦ θαυμασίου: τοῦ θείου καὶ θαυμαστοῦ V³

19   ἐπράττετο: εἰσεπράττετο V³

22   ἀχώριστον: *omitted* K V³

23   διαστῆναι: διαναστῆναι Tsames

28   φυσικῶς: καὶ φυσικῶς H I K V³

31   ἐγγίζουσα: ἐγγίσασα J

36   ἀπαυθαδίζεσθαι: ἀπαυθαδιάζεσθαι X Tsames

37   διαμένειν: μένειν K V³

41   τιμὴ πᾶσα: τιμὴ καὶ προσκύνησις K V³

EUPHEMIA

Title   *omitted* K; τὸ περὶ τὴν κόρην θαῦμα τῶν ἁγίων I; ἄθλησις τοῦ
ἁγίου μάρτυρος Ἀβίβου *sic* H; Θαῦμα τῶν ἁγίων ὁμολογητῶν
Γουρία, Σαμωνᾶ καὶ Ἀβίβου *Gebhardt-Dobschütz*

BARBARA

Title   Ἄθλησις τῆς ἁγίας καὶ καλλινίκου μάρτυρος τοῦ Χριστοῦ
Βαρβάρας: Μαρτύριον τῆς ἁγίας καὶ ἐνδόξου τοῦ Χριστοῦ
μάρτυρος Βαρβάρας R; Μαρτύριον τῆς ἁγίας καὶ ἐνδόξου
μεγαλομάρτυρος τοῦ Χριστοῦ Βαρβάρας O; Ἄθλησις τῆς
ἁγίας ἐνδόξου καὶ καλλινίκου μεγαλομάρτυρος τοῦ Χριστοῦ
Βαρβάρας N PG
4   μελετώμενον: μελετώμενος N PG
5   διώσατο: ἀπώσατο N PG
      προσαγάγῃς: παραγάγῃς O
6   αὐθέκαστον: ἀκάθεκτον O
7   Ἐμβραδύνοντος: ἐμβραδύναντος L M V⁵
8   "τὰς τρεῖς," ἔφη: *omitted* O
13   ἀπῄει: ἐπῄει O Υ
22   ἐδηλοῦτο: παρεδηλοῦτο L R V⁵
24   ξυστῆρσι: ὄνυξι V⁵
25   Δέσποτα: *omitted* L
27   δούλην: φίλην L
      ἐκάλει: ἐπεκάλει L
33   οὐρανόθεν παραδόξως: παραδόξως οὐρανόθεν L
      ἐνωτισθεῖσα: ἀκροασαμένη V⁵
      ἀναφανεῖσα: ἀναφυεῖσα L

EUGENIA

Title   Μαρτύριον τῆς ἁγίας μάρτυρος Εὐγενίας O Υ PG; Βίος καὶ
πολιτεία καὶ ἄθλησις τῆς ἁγίας ὁσιομάρτυρος τοῦ Χριστοῦ
Εὐγενίας V⁶
1   Ἀβίτας: Ἄβιτος O
2   Ἀλεξάνδρου πόλιν: Ἀλεξάνδρειαν T

τὴν μεγάλην: *omitted* Q U

3 ἐλευθερίως: ἐλευθερίοις O

7 ἐστι Θεὸς: θεός ἐστιν T P G

11 Δεσπότην καὶ Πατέρα: καὶ πατέρα U; δεσπότην καὶ σωτῆρα Υ

12 ἀποκείρατε τῆς ἐμῆς: τῆς ἐμῆς ἀποκείρατε P

13 προαγαγεῖν: προσαγαγεῖν O

15 ψάλλουσιν αὐτὴν: ψάλλουσιν αὐτίκα ἑαυτὴν O Υ

     αὐτὸς διετέλει: διετέλει O

16 ἐκεῖθι: ἐκεῖσε O; ἐκεῖθεν T

     μάτην αὐτῷ: μάτην ἑαυτῷ O Υ

18 πρὸς τοὺς λόγους: καὶ πρὸς τοὺς λόγους O

     ἀναφθῆναι: ἀφεθῆναι O

19 καὶ ἡ φλὸξ . . . συνείχετο: *omitted* U

     τοῦτο καθ᾽ ἑαυτόν: καθ᾽ ἑαυτόν O Υ

21 ἐξεπλήττετο . . . ἐδέετο: *omitted* Q

22 καὶ τοῦτο νομίζεσθαι: *omitted* U

     καὶ ἴσα Θεῷ νομίζεσθαι: *omitted* U

24 παραστῆναι: παραστῆσαι O

25 νικῴης: νικοίης O Υ

     γυναικείαν σοι: γυναικείαν σου O Υ

30 προπορευομένοις: πορευομένοις O Υ

     ἐπεὶ καὶ τὸ ζῷον: ἐπεὶ οὖν καὶ τὸ ζῷον O Υ

31 προσέδραμον: συνέδραμον O Υ

33 Ὡς δὲ οὐκ ἦν: Ὡς δὲ οὐ O

     ἀνηρπάσαντο: ἀνήρπασαν O Υ

     Ἀβίτας: Ἄβιτος O Υ

     τοῖς λεγομένοις: τοῖς εἰρημένοις U

34 ἦν οὖν ἡ: καὶ ἦν οὖν O Υ

36 ἐπιτρέψασα: *corrected from* ἐπιτρέψαντας O P Q S V⁶ Υ; ἐπι-
     τρέψαντος R T

38 οἶκτος οὖν . . . Εὐγενίαν: *omitted* U

     καθαρᾶς: καθαρῶς P Q R S T U

44 ἔρως: ὑβρισθεὶς ἔρως O Υ

45 πρῶτον: πρῶτα O Υ

46 γυναῖκα οὕτω τε: γυναῖκα τὲ οὕτω O

47 ἡτοιμάζοντο θῆρες: *omitted* O Υ V⁶

48 μόνον: μόνα O Υ

49   οὐδὲν ἧττον: οὐδὲν ἥττων *P R S T U V*[6]
   τοῦ περιόντος . . . ὀφθῆναι: *omitted* ℚ
50   ὁμοδούλων: δούλων *O Υ*
51   ὁρμήσων: χωρεῖν *T*
   Ἀβίτας: Ἄβιτος *O Υ*
53   κοινωνοὺς πάντας: πάντας κοινωνοὺς *O Υ*
55   ἡ μακρὰ: *omitted T*
56   ἐπιπρέψαι: ἐπιτρέψαι ℚ *Υ V*[6]. Ἐπιπρέψαι *is a rare infinitive that*
   appears also in the letters of Symeon Magistros Logothetes (perhaps
   identical with Metaphrastes); see, for instance, Letter 86.2.
57   τῶν θεῶν εἰδώς: εἰδὼς τῶν θεῶν *T*
58   τὸν Φίλιππον . . . ἕως διαπωλήσαντα: *omitted* ℚ
59   διάδοχος αὐτῷ: αὐτῷ διάδοχος *O*
60   ταφῆς: ταφεὶς *O Υ*
62   ὁ λόγος: ὁ χρόνος *O*
   Ἀβίταν: Ἄβιτόν *O Υ*
   Ἀβίταν: Ἄβιτον *O Υ*
   ὑπὸ Θεῷ: ὑπὲρ Θεοῦ *O*; ὑπὸ Θεοῦ *Υ*
63   πάντα τὰ: πάντα *O* ℚ *Υ*; τὰ *V*[6]
64   τηλικούτων: τούτων *O Υ*
   ἐκδεξαμένη: δεξαμένη *O T PG*
67   τῷ ὑπὲρ τῶν: τῶν ὑπὲρ τὴν *O Υ*; τῷ ὑπὲρ *V*[6]
70   γλῶσσαν: γλῶτταν *O*
71   Ἐγώ: ἀλλ᾽ ἐγώ *R*
   δράσει: διάγει *T*
73   τούτους: ταύτας *V*[6]
81   πόνον καὶ τίκτοντες: *omitted* ℚ
82   ἐσχάτως: *omitted O T*
   παραδόξως: *omitted O*
   λέγων: *omitted* ℚ
84   μεριζομένης αὐτῇ: μεριζομένης *O U*
   ἐστολισμένη λαμπρῶς: λαμπρῶς ἐστολισμένη *T*
86   ᾧ πρέπει . . . κράτος: ᾧ πρέπει δόξα, τιμὴ καὶ κράτος *Υ*; ᾧ πρέπει
   πᾶσα δόξα κράτος τιμή *U*; ᾧ πρέπει πᾶσα δόξα, τιμὴ καὶ
   προσκύνησις *S U* PG; ᾧ πρέπει πᾶσα δόξα, τιμὴ καὶ
   προσκύνησις, ἅμα τῷ Πατρὶ σὺν τῷ Ἁγίῳ Πνεύματι *O*

Notes to the Translation

KYPRIANOS AND IOUSTINA

Title   *BHG* 456; feast day: October 2. The story is set in Antioch on
the Orontes (near the modern city of Antakya, Turkey) during the reign of Decius (249–251), while the martyrdom takes
place in Nikomedia (modern İzmit, Turkey), during the time of
a ruler called Claudius (see note to chap. 41 below); in other
versions, the story is set in Pisidian Antioch (northeast of Yal-
vaç, Turkey), during the reign of Diocletian (r. 284–305). The
text confounds tales about the martyrdom in 258 of the Latin
Church father Cyprian, bishop of Carthage, with a legendary
"magician" from Antioch and his romance with (and subsequent conversion to Christianity because of) a virgin, a story
with a long tradition in European literatures, echoed in the
German legend of Faust. See further Hippolyte Delehaye,
"Cyprien d'Antioche et Cyprien de Carthage," *Analecta Bollandiana* 39 (1921): 314–32.

Leaving aside hymns and poems and an abundant tradition
in Latin, Syriac, Arabic, Ethiopic, Coptic, and Slavonic, the hagiographical dossier in Greek is very rich: see *BHG* 452–61f,
which includes a *Confession* by Kyprianos, an encomium (*Or.* 24)
by Gregory of Nazianzos (329/30–ca. 390), and a poem by the
empress Athenais-Eudokia (ca. 400–ca. 460). Metaphrastes
reworks, expands, and combines two earlier texts: the *Acts*
(*BHG* 452–52c), in chapters 1 to 34, and the *Passion* (*BHG* 454–
55p), in chapters 35 to 62.

1   *that people became Christians:* In fact, it was not Luke who said this, but Paul, in Acts 11:26.

       some thirtyfold, some hundred, some sixty: See Matthew 13:8, 23; Mark 4:8, 20.

3   *within her hearing:* This scene of Ioustina listening ("through a window," in the earlier versions) to the good news of the Gospel is highly reminiscent of the initiation of Saint Thekla into Christianity.

4   *Iousta:* Before becoming a deaconess (see chap. 34 below), Ioustina's name was Iousta.

       on the tablets of her heart: See 2 Corinthians 3:3.

5   *A short time had passed:* A variation on a common formula in Metaphrastic narrative, possibly originating in Gregory of Nazianzos (*Or.* 4.31 and 25.8).

       the precious pearl: An allusion to Matthew 13:45.

7   *Fighting with sleep:* Ὑπνομαχῶν, a learned word used by Aristophanes, Xenophon, and Synesios of Kyrene and anthologized in Byzantine lexica.

       "Come to me": Matthew 11:28.

8   *blessed with the same office:* A reference to Aidesios's becoming a priest.

       he praised Christ in the assembly of the elders: See Psalms 106(107):32.

9   *The virgin showed no ignoble emotion:* Holy women who overcome their feminine emotional frailty are common in Metaphrastes; see, for instance, *Passion of Saint Euphemia* 10; *Life of Saint Xenophon and His Children Ioannes and Arkadios* 16 (PG 114:1029C–D); *Passion of Saint Iouliane* 6 (PG 114:1444A); *Passion of Saint Sophia and Her Daughters Pistis, Elpis, and Agape* 9 (PG 115:505C); and also chapter 47 below—all passages with similar wording.

10   *There was a certain lawyer:* The Greek word *(scholastikos)* could also mean simply someone educated ("schooled") or, even, a learned simpleton, such as the butt of most of the jokes included in the late antique collection of anecdotes titled *The Laughter-Lover (Philogelos)* that was read in Byzantium.

       perhaps due to his beauty: "Aglaïdas" literally means "beautiful,

splendid." A similar explanation about the name of the female saint Aglaïs is provided in Metaphrastes's *Passion of Saint Boniphatios* 2 (PG 155:241B).

11   *since unrequited desire is heavier and more violent:* In manuscript V^2, this phrase is marked as a γνώ(μη) ("maxim"; notably, Blampignon prints mistakenly τιτρωσκόμενος γνώμη). For a similar maxim, see *Eugenia* 44 as well as Metaphrastes's *Passion of Saint Iouliane* 6 (PG 114:1444A).

   moved every stone, as the proverb says: CPG 1:146, 1:293, and 2:201.

12   *that most chaste and most courageous man:* See Genesis 39, for the story of Joseph who staunchly resisted the repeated aggressive attempts of Potiphar's wife to seduce him. In Byzantium, this was a paradigmatic story of male steadfastness against female aggression; Symeon Metaphrastes himself, for instance, included a relevant passage from Basil of Caesarea in his anthology of passages from Basil (PG 32:1348A–B) on a section on "Temperance and Insolence." Perhaps expectedly, next to this sentence, in the margin, *C* marks "ση(μείωσαι)" ("note").

   sign of the cross before her like a weapon: a favorite image in Metaphrastes; see also chapter 53 below as well as the *Passion of Saint Euphemia* 6 and 7.

   the one who was stealthily attempting to wage war: Namely, the Devil.

15   *when Decius held the imperial reins:* Decius (201–251) ruled from 249 to 251. Many Christian martyrs were thought to have died during his persecutions.

   His occupation . . . sharpness of mind: There is an obvious effort here to soften the negative image of Kyprianos as a magician; compare, for example, the entirely negative figure of the Persian magician and teacher in Metaphrastes's *Passion of Saint Anastasios the Persian* 1; see also the depiction of Zareas in *Eugenia* below (chaps. 16–20).

16   *It is to this man that Aglaïdas came:* In the earliest version of our story, as evident in Gregory of Nazianzos (*Or.* 24.9), it is Kyprianos himself, and not Aglaïdas, who falls in love with Ioustina.

he looked into his books . . . then summoned one of the evil spirits: This phrase, and many others, was borrowed from Metaphrastes and employed verbatim in Euthymios, *Barlaam and Ioasaph* 30.39–40.

of the evil spirits . . . such wicked plans: Employed verbatim in Euthymios, *Barlaam and Ioasaph* 29.20–22.

18 *If everything . . . useless:* Employed verbatim in Euthymios, *Barlaam and Ioasaph* 29.99–100.

19 *kidneys:* The seat of the desirous part of the soul, according to Byzantine thought.

"I remembered Your name in the night, O Lord": Psalms 118(119):55.

"and felt delight": Psalms 76(77):3.

"They have prepared a trap for my steps and have overwhelmed my soul": See Psalms 56(57):6.

"While they troubled me, I wore sackcloth and humbled my soul with fasting and my prayer shall return into my lap": Psalms 34(35):13.

"In this, I knew that You wanted me: since my enemy will not rejoice on my behalf": Psalms 40(41):12.

"May their sword enter into their own hearts, and may their bows be crushed": See Psalms 36(37):15.

20 *The demon returned to Kyprianos, but was ashamed to confess his defeat:* Similar phrasing employed in Euthymios, *Barlaam and Ioasaph* 31.4.

and although he was fond of lying: Employed verbatim in Euthymios, *Barlaam and Ioasaph* 31.5.

22 *What happened next?:* A common Metaphrastic formula; see, for instance, *Passion of Saint Anthimos, bishop of Nikomedia* 10 (PG 115:181B); also *Pelagia* 7 below.

in the guise of a woman: Next to this passage, manuscript *C* marks "ση(μείωσαι) γ′ (= τρίτος) πειρασμός" ("note, this is the third temptation").

24 *bearing on his face clear signs of his defeat:* Employed verbatim in Euthymios, *Barlaam and Ioasaph* 31.5–6.

25 *Then, the demon . . . been completed:* Employed with some variation in Euthymios, *Barlaam and Ioasaph* 31.8–13.

26 *immediately turned against his books . . . for demonic delight and devo-*

tion: Employed with some variation in Euthymios, *Barlaam and Ioasaph* 32.142–44.

Anthimos: Otherwise unattested.

among the flock of Christ's sheep: Here manuscript *C* notes "Ἀρχὴ τῆς σ(ωτη)ρίας τοῦ Κυπριανοῦ" ("The beginning of Kyprianos's salvation").

28   *Immediately, great remorse . . . until very recently:* Employed with some variation in Euthymios, *Barlaam and Ioasaph* 32.98–102.

29   *He poured the dust of shame on his head:* A common expression of grief and lament used in Heliodoros, *Ethiopian Tale* 1.13 and 4.19, but also by Basil of Caesarea, in a passage that was included in Metaphrastes's anthology of passages from Basil (PG 32:1233C), in a section on "Repentance." Chapter 29 in its entirety appears with some variation in Euthymios, *Barlaam and Ioasaph* 35.47–53.

he experienced the good conversion: See Gregory of Nazianzos, *Or.* 40.40; see also Psalms 76(77):11. Metaphrastes employs the same phrase also elsewhere; see, for instance, *Passion of Saint Boniphatios* 13 (PG 155:257A–B).

now that he had experienced . . . to virtue: Here (fol. 13v), at more or less the middle of *Kyprianos and Ioustina,* manuscript *B* marks "κάθ(ισμα)" ("seating"), perhaps suggesting that a break in the reading aloud of the text must be made.

30   *Kyprianos came to the church:* The Greek term used here for church is *kyriakon,* literally, "place of the Lord."

31   *"Christ redeemed us from the curse of the Law, having become a curse for us":* Galatians 3:13.

"You saw, O Lord, do not pass by in silence! O Lord, do not stay far from me": Psalms 34(35):22.

"Behold, he will understand, my beloved son whom I have chosen": See Isaiah 52:13; Matthew 12:18.

32   *As it was the time that the catechumens were asked to step outside the church:* A practice in Byzantine liturgy that had gone out of fashion at the time of Metaphrastes.

You have not yet become perfect: That is, Kyprianos had not yet been baptized.

33   *a man most skilled in saving a soul . . . with the holy baptism:* Employed with some variation in Euthymios, *Barlaam and Ioasaph* 32.148–52.

on the thirtieth, he included him among the deacons: An unusually rapid promotion.

34   *not simply a promotion, but a motivation toward progress in virtue:* See Gregory of Nazianzos, *Or.* 24.18.

By following the narrow and rough path . . . : An allusion to Matthew 7:13–14; Luke 13:24.

36   *ruler of the Romans at that time:* See chapter 15 above.

37   *Neither enfeebled by promises of riches nor persuaded by threats of abuse:* A topos in hagiographical discourse; see, for example, Georgios Pisides, *Life, Conduct, and Passion of Saint Anastasios of Persia* 32, in Flusin, *Saint Anastase le Perse.*

38   *Eutolmios:* Unattested elsewhere. A *komes* was among the highest ranking officers in the empire, but the title "komes of the East" did not appear before the fourth century CE; the anachronism exists in the original *Passion* and is reproduced by Metaphrastes.

40   *Solemn stature:* A common locution in Metaphrastes; see, for example, *Passion of Saint Euphemia* 6.

41   *from Claudius's clan:* It is not clear if this is supposed to be the emperor Claudius (r. 41–54 CE), or some other third-century Roman emperor (see Gregory of Nazianzos, *Or.* 24 and 25, 20), namely, the "ruler/Caesar" (a quasi-historical personality?) mentioned in chapter 56. The same(?) name is then again mentioned in a positive light and associated with Matrona Rufina in chapter 62.

42   *like a mouse attacking a lion or a beetle challenging an eagle to fight:* See the titles of two Aesopian fables in *Corpus fabularum Aesopicarum*, vol. 1, fasc. 1, *Fabulae Aesopicae soluta oratione conscriptae*, ed. August Hausrath (Leipzig, 1959), nos. 155 and 3: *The Mouse and the Lion* and *The Eagle and the Beetle.*

46   *like a man pulled by his nose:* A proverbial expression; see *CPG* 2:670.

I sought, and I found; I knocked, and the door was opened for me: An allusion to Matthew 7:7; Luke 11:9.

the light of knowledge: An allusion to Hosea 10:12.

47   *hanged and flayed:* A common type of torture in martyrdom tales; see Metaphrastes's *Passion of Saint Mamas* 17.

nothing ignoble nor what one would expect of her female and weak gender: See chapter 9 above.

49   *"If indeed you think . . . for which I am the cause":* Next to these sentences, manuscript *C* notes "ὅρα εἰρωνείαν" ("note the irony").

monastery of Terentine: An otherwise unattested monastery.

51   *For this reason, though you have eyes . . . you will not comprehend:* An allusion to Matthew 13:13; Mark 4:12; Luke 8:10.

52   *he began to embolden her with words:* That the male martyr offers words of encouragement to his female and, as convention would demand, somewhat weaker companion is a commonplace; see, for instance, Metaphrastes, *Passion of Saints Eulampios and Eulampia* 9 (PG 115:1064A–B); also, below in *Galaktion and Episteme,* chapter 32.

53   *As if with a weapon:* See the note on chapter 12 above.

55   *those two righteous ones:* An allusion to Matthew 27:19.

56   *this was Claudius:* See the relevant note on chapter 41 above.

57   *I did not seem to be dealing with a man, but rather with a statue:* See a similar thought in Metaphrastes, *Passion of Saint Anastasios the Persian* 24.

59   *the river Gallos:* A river in Bithynia.

62   *belonging to the proud lineage of Claudius:* See the relevant note on chapter 41 above.

PELAGIA

Title   *BHG* 1479; feast day: October 8. Antioch and Jerusalem provide the setting for the story, which includes no internal temporal specifications but is set in a fifth-century Syro-Palestinian context. A popular account, with wide diffusion in the late antique and medieval periods, the story of Pelagia seems to have appeared first in Greek; for the various versions in Greek, Latin, Syriac, Arabic, Armenian, Georgian, Slavonic, and then various European vernaculars, see Pierre Petitmengin, ed., *Pélagie la pénitente: métamorphoses d'une légende,* 2 vols. (Paris, 1981–1984).

Metaphrastes reworks the pre-Metaphrastic version γ (*BHG* 1478; Petitmengin, *Pélagie la pénitente,* 1:94–130), by reducing its size, decreasing the emphasis on the bishop Nonnos, and also removing the first-person perspective of the original text, which is narrated by Iakobos (see chap. 21 below). For a French translation of the Metaphrastic version, see Flusin-Paramelle, 2:29–41.

1   *a comparable vice:* A reference to the original sin for which Eve was regarded as primarily responsible in Christian thought.

Pelagia whom the sea of God's love made known to us: As is usual in the Metaphrastic corpus, a pun is occasioned by the characters' names; here there is wordplay between the name "Pelagia" and the "sea" *(pelagos)* of God's love.

2   *city was that of Antiochos:* That is, Antioch.

harlots: For the usage of the Greek word μαινάς (maenad) to denote a prostitute, see Metaphrastes's *Life of Saint Daniel the Stylite* 23.

3   *one's will alone is sufficient for one to become good:* A patristic commonplace, especially in the popular writings of John Chrysostom; see, for example, *Homilies on the Statues* 8.3 (PG 49:101.9–10), or *Homilies on Paul's Letter to the Hebrews* 16.3 (PG 63:127.21–22).

the incumbent to the priestly throne in Antioch: That is, the patriarch. The corresponding Greek phrase, τοῦ ἐν . . . τὸν ἱερατικὸν διέποντος θρόνον, is among those learned expressions (a genitive absolute here) favored in the Metaphrastic corpus. The text from this line of chapter 3 through the first sentence of chapter 6 was reproduced in the *Evergetinos,* a monastic anthology created by Paul, the abbot of the monastery of Evergetis in Constantinople (1048/49–1054); see Flusin-Paramelle, 18–19; the passages are cited as an example of how "spiritual men redirect even worldly and wicked matters into good thoughts."

Nonnos, a man admirable in all respects and angelic in his ways: It is unclear whether this Nonnos of the pre-Metaphrastic and Metaphrastic texts on Pelagia should be related to a Nonnos, "bishop of Edessa," mentioned as participant in the *Acts* of

PELAGIA

the Council of Chalcedon in 451, ed. Eduard Schwartz, *Acta conciliorum oecumenicorum,* vol. 2.1.1–2.1.3 (Berlin, 1933–1935). Metaphrastes omits the additional information, present in his model (version γ), that Nonnos had previously excelled as a monk in the cenobitic monastery of Tabenna (in Upper Egypt, founded by Saint Pachomios, ca. 292–348). The *SynaxCP* cites a "holy father Nonnos who catechized saint Pelagia" (November 9, col. 205).

Ioulianos the martyr: An important saint (and church) in Antioch.

5   *bitter pleasure:* A commonplace in patristic and, then, middle Byzantine rhetoric; for an example close in time to Metaphrastes, see *The Homilies of the Emperor Leo VI,* ed. Theodora Antonopoulou (Leiden, 1997), 30.37–38.

6   *These were his words:* Metaphrastes has omitted a long section (γ 11–13) that includes a prayer by Nonnos.

       they: That is, he and his fellow Christian hierarchs.

       until the priest invited the catechumens to leave: Namely, that moment in the middle of the divine liturgy, after the Gospel has been read and those not yet baptized are asked to leave the church.

7   *And then, what happened?:* See note above on *Kyprianos and Ioustina,* chapter 22.

8   *The holy man:* This is simply Iakobos, the narrator, in version γ.

11   *'I did not come to call the righteous, but sinners to repentance':* Matthew 9:13; Mark 2:17; Luke 5:32.

       that He dined with publicans . . . the Seraphim do not dare even to look: Commonplaces in Byzantine patristic writing with biblical referents.

12   *like the Gospel's harlot:* An allusion to Luke 7:36–50.

       beautiful, proclaiming . . . the good tidings of peace: See Romans 10:15.

       baptism of tears: An expression that was picked up (likely from Metaphrastes) in twelfth-century Byzantine novels; see, for example, *Theodori Prodromi De Rhodanthes et Dosiclis amoribus libri IX,* ed. Miroslav Marcovich (Stuttgart, 1992), 9.275.

13   *their sorrow was mixed with astonishment and pleasure:* The mixture of emotions is typical of Metaphrastes's novelistic approach.

14   *"a pure bride to the pure bridegroom, presenting me to Christ":* The

spiritual union with Christ (especially for female saints) is a
common theme in Metaphrastes and hagiographical literature
in general; for an early example, see *Life of Saint Synkletike* 49–
50, 70–73 (Labrini G. Abelarga, ed., *Ο βίος της Αγίας
Συγκλητικής: Εισαγωγή – Κριτικό κείμενο – Σχόλια.* [Thessalo-
nike, 2002]).

15   *Pearly:* In Greek, *margarito,* namely, "made of pearls."

16   *and she partook of the undefiled and bloodless sacrifice:* That is, she
received Holy Communion.

17   *the Evil One usually becomes more ruthless when he is defeated:* In the
margin of manuscript *C,* this phrase is marked as a "γνώ(μη)"
("maxim"); the description that follows is also noted with the
following remark: "look at the deceptive scheme of the Devil,
the hater of goodness."

18   *her godmother—her name was Romana:* As her godmother, Romana presented Pelagia at baptism, sponsoring, as it were, her
conversion. In the pre-Metaphrastic versions she is a deaconess.

20   *baptismal garment:* The phrase originates in Gregory of Nazianzos, *Or.* 40.25.

21   *Iakobos:* This man, a deacon, is the main narrator of the story in
the pre-Metaphrastic versions.

23   *his pilgrimage there:* According to the pre-Metaphrastic versions
his main goal was to visit the church of the Holy Sepulcher, a
building that dated to the reign of Constantine I (r. 306–337).
her eyes had become hollow: A sign of illness or deficient nutrition,
according to ancient and medieval medical treatises.

25   *Not long after:* For this common Metaphrastic formula, see the
note above to *Kyprianos and Ioustina,* chapter 5.
Nikopolis: Another name for the city of Emmaus in Palestine.

Galaktion and Episteme

Title   *BHG* 666; feast day: November 5. The story is set in Emesa
(modern Homs, Syria) at an undetermined pre-Byzantine date.
Metaphrastes reworks a late antique *Passion* narrated by a certain Eutolmios (*BHG* 665; Tsames 228–47; see also Anne P. Al-

wis, *Celibate Marriages in Late Antique and Byzantine Hagiography: The Lives of Saints Julian and Basilissa, Andronikos and Athanasia, and Galaktion and Episteme* [London, 2011], chap. 5 and also pp. 279–308, where an English translation and extensive annotation can be found). Apart from turning Eutolmios's first-person narrative into a third-person account, Metaphrastes has also removed most of the direct discourse (dialogical exchanges, etc.) that prevailed in the pre-Metaphrastic version. To the rather small hagiographical dossier of the story (which does not seem to have circulated outside the Greek world), we should add an unedited hymn (a *kanon*) by Joseph the Hymnographer (d. 866?); see Eutychios Tomadakes, Ἰωσὴφ ὁ ὑμνογράφος· Βίος καὶ ἔργον (Athens, 1971), 123, item 81. For a modern Greek translation of the Metaphrastic version of this *Passion*, see Tsames 313–31.

1   *Kleitophon . . . Leukippe:* The couple's names (and perhaps also their extraordinary qualities) are borrowed directly from the fictional world of the Greek novel; Kleitophon and Leukippe are none other than the protagonists in Achilleus Tatios's *Leucippe and Clitophon,* dated to the second century CE. Metaphrastes makes this borrowing even clearer, since in the pre-Metaphrastic version the name of the female protagonist appears (either mistakenly or intentionally) as Gleukippe. For a similar case of Christianization of a novel's protagonist, see Tomas Hägg and Bo Utas, *The Virgin and Her Lover: Fragments of an Ancient Greek Novel and a Persian Epic Poem* (Leiden, 2003), 65–75 (on the *Martyrdom* of Saint Parthenope).

she was subjected to many insults by her husband: The pre-Metaphrastic text dwells much more on this marital abuse. See also Metaphrastes's *Life of Saint Daniel the Stylite* 2 for a similar case of the mother of a future saint suffering from infertility and the consequent reproach.

2   *Sekoundos:* Otherwise unattested.

7   *raise up children even from stones:* Matthew 3:9.

you will benefit . . . as their heritage: See Gregory of Nazianzos, *Or.* 7.4 (on the mother of Gregory and Kaisarios).

8   *her earlier defilements:* Perhaps an allusion to Leukippe's love af-

fair (however chaste) with Kleitophon, as described in Achilleus Tatios's homonymous novel.

13   *O sweetest husband:* For this form of address by a wife to her husband, which exists also in the pre-Metaphrastic version (chap. 5), see Metaphrastes's *Life of Saint Stephen the Younger* 87; see also Elizabeth Jeffreys, ed. and trans., *Digenis Akritis: The Grottaferrata and Escorial Versions* (Cambridge, 1998), 2.120 (Grottaferrata Digenis).

15   *to walk honestly in day:* See Romans 13:13.

17   *Galaktion:* The name means, literally, "milky," thus "white" or "pure."

       his wisdom surpassed his age: The emphasis on Galaktion's secular learning is noticeable, though in the pre-Metaphrastic version it is even more detailed and elaborate, listing grammar, "the art of Homer" (that is, poetry), rhetoric, philosophy, and astronomy.

18   *Episteme:* The name means "Science" or "Knowledge."

20   *grace of a liberal sort:* Perhaps a phrase from Plutarch, in whose texts *"eleutherios charis"* is common. See *Themistocles* 2.2; *Agis and Cleomenes* 32.1; *How to Tell a Flatterer from a Friend* 64B.

24   *Eutolmios, the most well-disposed among all their servants:* This is the (first-person) narrator of the story in the pre-Metaphrastic version (chap. 6) and most likely a fictional character.

       mountain which is called Pouplion: This mountain is nowhere else attested, though a mountain called Episteme near Sinai is mentioned from the eighteenth-century onward; see the discussion in Alwis, *Celibate Marriages*, 302–3.

26   *the man holding imperial authority:* According to the *SynaxCP* (November 5, col. 193), this ruler was Diocletian (r. 284–305); according to other versions, this was Decius (r. 249–251).

27   *stung by these words as if by a gadfly:* A proverb repeated, in its Metaphrastic form, verbatim in Konstantinos Manasses, *Hodoiporikon* 1.68 (Konstantin Horna, "Das Hodoiporikon des Konstantin Manasses," *Byzantinische Zeitschrift* 13 [1904]: 327) and alluded to in Denis Sullivan, ed. and trans., *The Life of Saint Nikon* (Brookline, Mass., 1987), 3.24–25.

28   *steward of the monastery:* According to the pre-Metaphrastic ver-

sion (chap. 11), this was the abbot of the monastery where Galaktion resided.

29   *Only two monks:* It is unclear who this other monk was (Eutolmios perhaps?). The pre-Metaphrastic version (chap. 12) tells us that Galaktion was the only one who stayed.

30   *deaconess:* The leader of Episteme's convent in the pre-Metaphrastic version.

31   *what she wanted:* In the pre-Metaphrastic version (chap. 12), the deaconess wants Episteme to model herself on Saint Thekla.

32   *his exhortations toward piety:* For a similar encouragement from the male to the female companion in martyrdom, see above, *Kyprianos and Ioustina,* chapter 52.

33   *The interrogator:* His name was Oursos (that is, "Bear") according to the pre-Metaphrastic version (chap. 13).

    sullen and morose: See Heliodoros, *Ethiopian Tale* 3.18.2, 4.14.1. The interrogator alludes to his monastic and ascetic appearance.

34   *flogged with rawhide whips:* Literally, "whips made of an ox tendon," a common implement of torture in martyrdom tales.

35   *young limbs:* "Beautiful limbs" in the pre-Metaphrastic version (chap. 13).

39   *false gods:* A common expression in Metaphrastes; see the *Passion of Saint Euphemia* 1.

EUPHEMIA

Title   *BHG* 738, a reworking of a pre-Metaphrastic story (*BHG* 739–39k), which itself originated most likely in a (fifth-century?) Syriac legend; for this legend, see Francis Crawford Burkitt, *Euphemia and the Goth with the Acts of Martyrdom of the Confessors of Edessa* (Oxford, 1913). Though the earlier versions were sometimes transmitted independently, Metaphrastes's *Miracle* was usually attached as an appendix to his martyrdom account of the three Syrian "martyrs and confessors" of Edessa (Urfa, in modern Turkey), celebrated jointly on November 15: Saints Gourias and Samonas, who had died during the reign of Diocletian (r. 284–305), and Abibos, who was martyred under Li-

cinius (r. 308–324) and was buried together with the other two (*BHG* 736–37, pp. 102–47). For the cult of the three saints, the story that follows, its wide circulation (within as well as outside the Byzantine tradition), and the way Metaphrastes reworks the original text, see Messis and Papaioannou, "Histoires 'gothiques' à Byzance."

1   *the saints:* Namely, Gourias and Samonas.

From that point on . . . grant pardon to the Christians: This entire sentence paraphrases Arethas, *Encomium of the Saint Confessors Gourias, Samonas, and Abibos* (= *Or.* 6), in *Arethae archiepiscopi Caesariensis Scripta minora,* ed. Leendert G. Westerink (Leipzig, 1968), 62.17–20. Constantine I (272–337) was emperor from 306 to 337 and sole emperor from 324 after defeating and executing Licinius, his coemperor since 313.

2   *Long after the death of the martyrs . . . plundered its hinterland:* The vague reference to "Long after the death of the martyrs" replaces the very precise date of the "707th year according to <the calendar based on> Alexander the king of the Macedonians" (= 396 CE), provided in the pre-Metaphrastic as well as the Syriac versions. By contrast, Metaphrastes's usage of a classicizing ethnonym—"Ephthalite Huns" as opposed to simply the "Huns" in the pre-Metaphrastic and Syriac versions— is part of his attempt to highlight his learning as well as historicize his narrative according to contemporary tenth-century historiographical references to the Ephthalite Huns (also known as White Huns, a confederation of nomadic peoples from Central Asia), in the *Excerpta* of Constantine VII Porphyrogennetos; for these references, see Messis and Papaioannou, "Histoires 'gothiques' à Byzance," 38–39. Metaphrastes's phrase "the Ephthalite Huns, . . . neighbors of the Persians" (Οὖννοι Ἐφθαλῖται, Περσῶν ὅμοροι) is repeated almost verbatim in Michael Attaleiates, *The History,* ed. and trans. Anthony Kaldellis and Dimitris Krallis, Dumbarton Oaks Medieval Library 16 (Cambridge, Mass., 2012), chapter 8.1, but Attaleiates uses the alternative name "Nephthalite."

the emperors of the Romans: A vague reference, absent from the earlier versions of the story.

the image of our Lord Jesus Christ was sent to Abgar first in Edessa: Metaphrastes refers to the most important Edessene relic, the famous Holy Mandylion, a towel that, according to several Byzantine legends, preserved the authentic likeness of Christ, an image authorized by Christ himself. The relic had been recently brought to Constantinople (in 944 CE), and its triumphant arrival was henceforth celebrated every year on August 16, commemorated by a text attributed to Constantine VII Porphyrogennetos and included in the Metaphrastic menologion (PG 113:423–53; *BHG* 794–95); that text mentions the "words of Christ," who in a letter to King Abgar prophesied Edessa's eternal protection from the barbarians (PG 113:429C). Notably, Constantine VII Porphyrogennetos was also responsible for the translation of the head of Saint Abibos from Edessa to Constantinople.

3   *the Romans sent reinforcements to the Edessenes:* Unlike the pre-Metaphrastic version, according to which Edessa is explicitly within Byzantine territory, Metaphrastes seems to suggest that Edessa is an autonomous city.

of barbarian manners: The "barbarism" of the Goth is highlighted by Metaphrastes; see further the similar comments in Metaphrastes's *Passion of Saint Niketas the Goth* (PG 115:705A; *BHG* 1340).

happened to be among them: Goths were commonly employed as mercenary soldiers in the Roman army in this period.

newly-sprouted scion: For this expression, see Gregory of Nyssa, *Funeral Oration in Honor of the Empress Flacilla,* ed. Andreas Spira, in *Gregorii Nysseni opera,* vol. 9.1, ed. Günther Heil et al. (Leiden, 1967), 481.11; also Michael Choniates, *Epistulae,* ed. Foteini Kolovou (Berlin, 2001), *Ep.* 100.30, likely inspired by Metaphrastes's usage of the phrase. See also Eustathios of Thessalonike, *Commentarii ad Homeri Iliadem,* ed. Marchinus van der Valk, vol. 3, *Praefationem et commentarios ad libros K–II complectens* (Leiden, 1987), 191.17.

fair countenance and extraordinary beauty: For the same expression, see the tenth-century *Chronicle* of Symeon Logothetes (most likely identical to Metaphrastes), *Symeonis Magistri et Logothetae Chronicon,* ed. Stephan Wahlgren (Berlin, 2006), 13.20–21. Metaphrastes's phrase is also repeated verbatim in a late eleventh-century (?) defense of the cult of saints written by Ioannes the Deacon and Maistor (line 213), a text that includes a brief summary of our story along with high praise for Metaphrastes (lines 202–18); see Jean Gouillard, "Léthargie des âmes et culte des saints: un plaidoyer inédit de Jean Diacre et Maistôr," *Travaux et Mémoires* 8 (1981): 173–79.

9   *the confessors:* That is, Saints Gourias, Samonas, and Abibos.

12 In the twelfth century, this entire episode (chs. 12–17) inspired one of the rhetorical exercises of Nikephoros Basilakes, which imagines the words of Euphemia after her deception by the Goth; see *The Rhetorical Exercises of Nikephoros Basilakes: Progymnasmata from Twelfth-Century Byzantium,* ed. and trans. Jeffrey Beneker and Craig A. Gibson, Dumbarton Oaks Medieval Library 43 (Cambridge, Mass., 2016), Ethopoeia 27.

    This part of the story (chaps. 12–19) may be compared to the ancient Greek story of Cassandra, Agamemnon's ill-fated captive.

13 *abominable head:* A learned expression; see *Suda,* μ 1025.

14 *gave out a loud and deep moan:* A topos of intense emotional expression in Metaphrastic texts (see, for example, *Passion of Saint Anastasia* 16 [PG 116:588B]; *Life of Saint Xenophon and His Children Ioannes and Arkadios* 6 [PG 114:1020B]; *Eugenia* 9, below), possibly borrowed from Heliodoros's *Ethiopian Tale,* 1.10.3, 2.14.5, 7.9.3, 10.7.4. The topos later became popular, likely also via Metaphrastes, in post-Metaphrastic Byzantine high-style rhetoric.

18 *those who had suffered on behalf of Christ:* That is, the three Edessene martyrs.

19 *"for erotic desire strikes up friendship, it does not create separation":* This phrase is marked as a "γνώ(μη)" ("maxim") in manuscripts *H* and *V³*.

20   *She conceived mischief because of this and gave birth to iniquity:* See
         Psalms 7:14.

23   *her mischief returned upon her own head; and her violent dealing came
         down upon her own pate:* See Psalms 7:16.

         she fell into the ditch she made: See Psalms 7:15.

         she was justly captured in the net in which she hid: See Psalms 9:15.

27   *like another prophet Habakkuk:* According to a story in the Apoc-
         rypha (*Bel and the Dragon* 34–36), the prophet Habakkuk was
         transported miraculously by an angel from Judea to Babylon in
         order to provide food in the lion's den for Daniel, a noble Jew-
         ish youth who had been taken captive by Nebuchadnezzar.

         like Philip the disciple: An allusion to Acts 8:39–40.

         the church of the confessors and martyrs: Such a church is attested in
         Edessa already around the year 350.

29   *"Our God in heaven and upon earth has done whatsoever He has
         pleased":* Psalms 113(115):3.

         "He sent from heaven and saved me": Psalms 56(57):3.

         "who saves those who put their hopes in You": See Psalms 16(17):7.

         *"My weeping may have endured for a night, but joy came in the morn-
         ing":* See Psalms 29(30):5.

32   *they tried to calm each other down:* For a similar scene of reunion,
         see *Eugenia,* chapter 52 below.

35   *Lord God . . . rendered a reward to the proud:* See Psalms 93(94):1–2.

40   *Without even addressing a word to him:* Mirroring perhaps the at-
         titude of the Goth's wife; see above, chapter 18: "the worst evil
         was that she would not even deign to speak to her."

         Eulogios: Mentioned already in the Syriac version, this Eulogios
         may refer to a known Eulogios, bishop of Edessa from 379 to
         387, thus somewhat earlier than the supposed dates of our
         story.

43   *He rendered retribution to the arrogant ones:* Psalms 93(94):2.

         Amen: In two of the manuscripts that transmit the pre-
         Metaphrastic version, the story ends with Euphemia becom-
         ing a saint herself by leading a "solitary life" of "fasting and
         prayers" in the church of the Edessene martyrs; see Gebhardt-
         Dobschütz, 199.

BARBARA

Title   *BHG* 216; "passion" translates here the Greek term *athlesis,* which is an alternative title for the genre of *martyrion* and literally means "struggle." The story of Saint Barbara (feast day: December 4) is set in Helioupolis, an important Roman city in Syria (modern Baalbek, Lebanon) at the time of the emperor Maximian (on whom see the following note). The diffusion of the story of Barbara and, accordingly, her cult is impressive— both within the Greek-speaking world and in, for example, Latin, Syriac, and beyond; for the most important Greek texts in her hagiographic dossier, see *BHG* 213–18q. Metaphrastes reworks an anonymous late antique *Passion* (close to *BHG* 213– 14); he also makes much use of a still unedited *metaphrasis* (the earliest of its kind) of her martyrdom tale by the bishop Ioannes of Sardeis (ca. 815)—an edition of this text with a discussion of Barbara's dossier is being prepared by Daria Resh. Metaphrastes capitalizes on Ioannes's text and heightens its rhetorical style. For a Modern Greek translation of Metaphrastes's text, see Georgios D. Papademetropoulos, Συμεών του Μεταφραστού, Η άθληση και το μαρτύριο των αγίων Αγάθης – Βαρβάρας – Ευφημίας – Θέκλας – Ιουλιανής – Σοφίας και των θυγατέρων της (Athens, 2002), 53–73.

1   *Maximian, the impious emperor:* The name could refer to several emperors: emperor Maximianus (r. 286–305 as Augustus, or senior emperor, in the West and Constantine I's stepgrandfather); Maximinus Daia (r. 305–308 as Caesar, or junior emperor, in the East under Galerius; r. 310–312 as Augustus in the East), known for continuing Diocletian's persecutions of the Christians; or the earlier emperor Maximinus Thrax (r. 235–238). The most likely contender, however, is another persecutor of the Christians, Galerius (ca. 260–311), whose full list of names included Maximianus; between 293 and 305 Galerius served as Caesar under Diocletian in the East, and then became Augustus from 305 to 311. Along with Diocletian, some-

times jointly with him, and conflated perhaps with the above
emperor Maximianus, Galerius is referenced usually as simply
Μαξιμιανός in a great number of Greek martyrdom accounts,
set in the eastern parts of the Roman empire (as is Metaphrastes's *Barbara*). In the context of martyrology, that is, "Maximian" is almost a symbolic name for Galerius, who was the second, after Diocletian, major pre-Constantinian persecutor of
Christians.

2   *Helioupolis:* Roman city in Syria (modern Baalbek, Lebanon).
Different versions of the story mention other places, such as
Nikomedia or a village called Gelasion or Gelassos, near Euchaita (in the "land" or "island" [!] of Helioupolis). Gelassos is
mentioned in our story as the burial place of Barbara (chap. 35
below).

3   *he built a high tower, fashioned chambers inside, and placed Barbara to
live there:* This episode has parallels in other stories. It echoes
the myth of Danaë, a virgin daughter imprisoned by her father
and yet visited and seduced by a divine force, namely Zeus,
while there; for Byzantine references, see Georgios Kedrenos,
Compendium Historiarum, ed. Immanuel Bekker, vol. 1 (Bonn,
1838), 1:39.15–21; and *The Rhetorical Exercises of Nikephoros Basilakes* (DOML 43), Fable 5 and Ethopoeia 17. It is also echoed in
the story of Saint Christina, who was similarly imprisoned by
her father: see *SynaxCP* (May 24); *BHG* 301y–2b. Euthymios
the Iberian uses relevant phrases in his late tenth-century
Greek version of *Barlaam and Ioasaph* (3.17–21). The rather classical name of Barbara's father, Dioskoros, perhaps further ac-
centuates the classical antecedents.

untouched by the eyes of all men: see Gregory of Nazianzos, *Or.* 4.87.
the grace of the Paraclete . . . made the true God known to her: Employed almost verbatim in Euthymios, *Barlaam and Ioasaph*
5.38–40.

4   *shared with her . . . his plans about it:* Employed almost verbatim in
Euthymios, *Barlaam and Ioasaph* 16.109–10.

5   *She, however, did not even wish to hear:* μηδὲ ἄκροις ὡσί (literally,

"not even upon the tips of her ears"), a phrase which seems to become proverbial after Metaphrastes, as many later references attest.

rejected it as something discordant and absurd: Repeated in Euthymios, *Barlaam and Ioasaph* 16.111.

"you will not be called 'father' any more": Echoed in Euthymios, *Barlaam and Ioasaph* 24.168–69.

9   *until this very day the sign of the cross, engraved by her finger, can be seen etched in the marble:* A pseudo-historical detail, present also in the earlier versions of the story; Metaphrastes's "until this very day" does not necessarily indicate his own present.

the streams of the Jordan, or the spring of Shiloh, or even with the pool of Bethesda: Legendary biblical sites of healing; see, for instance, Matthew 3:13 on the Jordan; Joshua 18 for the spring of Shiloh; and John 5:1–5 for the pool of Bethesda.

10   *"Let them become like you":* See Psalms 113(115):8, 134(135):18.

11   *Not much time had passed:* For this common Metaphrastic formula, see the note above to *Kyprianos and Ioustina,* chapter 5.

12   *"illuminate every man coming into this world":* See John 1:9.

the Holy Trinity: Here, manuscript N adds a small circle with a pointed ray looking upward and to the right, namely, the marginal sign called "σημεῖον ἡλιακόν" ("sign of the sun"). This sign was borrowed from earlier astronomical treatises and was used in Byzantine manuscripts, especially those with the homilies of Gregory of Nazianzos, to highlight references to the Trinity.

13   *"Look, this is the Father, the Son, and the Holy Spirit":* In the margin of manuscript N, the "sign of the sun" is again inserted.

tyrant and murderer: Reproduced verbatim in Euthymios, *Barlaam and Ioasaph* 24.172.

14   *just as He had saved Thekla . . . by ordering the rocks in her way to split open and envelop her:* A reference to one of the most famous Christian female saints in late antiquity, often alluded to as a model in stories of virgin martyrs. According to her vita (which existed in various versions), Thekla was saved miraculously from her persecutors when God opened a fissure in the rocks

of a cave and then closed it immediately; see *Miracles of Saint Thekla,* in *Miracle Tales from Byzantium,* trans. Alice-Mary Talbot and Scott F. Johnson, Dumbarton Oaks Medieval Library 12 (Cambridge, Mass., 2012), 199.

15   *original murderer of humankind:* See John 8:44.

used his keeping of that oath as vindication for evil pleasure: Metaphrastes refers to Herod who gave an open "oath" to a daughter of Herodias and then, in keeping it, had John the Baptist beheaded at her request; see Matthew 14:1–12; Mark 6:14–29. The thought that a smaller sin would be better than a graver crime and the allusion to Herod are possibly borrowed here from patristic writing: see, for example, *Saint Basil, Letters 186– 248,* ed. and trans. Roy J. Deferrari (Cambridge, Mass., 1930), *Ep.* 199.29 (p. 120).

turned into scarab beetles, they are a perpetual reminder of the crime: Another pseudo-historical detail that appears with some variation in the earlier versions.

16   *Markianos:* Otherwise unattested.

18   *"my sacrifice of thanksgiving":* See Psalms 115(116):17.

"heaven and earth, and all that is therein": See Psalms 145(146):6.

"the idols of the heathen are silver and gold, the work of men's hands": Psalms 113(115):4, 134(135):15.

"all the gods of the nations are demons": Psalms 95(96):5.

20   *"For I am with you":* See Isaiah 41:10; Acts 18:10.

"the shade of my wings": See Psalms 56(57):2.

His healings sprang forth speedily: See Isaiah 58:8.

her wounds . . . there before: A very similar complete miraculous restoration of health after the initial set of tortures appears in Metaphrastes's *Passion of Saint Euphemia* 6; there too the miracle does not change the torturer's attitude. See also Metaphrastes's *Passion of Saint Charitine* 3 (PG 115:1000B).

Joy and exultation: Luke 1:14.

everlasting gladness was upon her head: Isaiah 35:10.

23   *"Christ, Son of the living God":* See Matthew 16:16.

25   *knower of hearts:* See Acts 1:24; a common form of address to God, especially in the prayers of saints and martyrs.

"*Do not forsake us*": See Psalms 26(27):9, 37(38):21.

26   *the spirit is willing, but the flesh is weak:* Matthew 26:41.

      the breasts of both women be cut off: The mutilation of breasts occurs very frequently in martyrdom accounts of female saints. See, for instance, Metaphrastes's *Passion of Saint Sophia and Her Daughters Pistis, Elpis, and Agape* 7 (PG 115:505A).

27   "*Hide not Your face from us*": See Psalms 26(27):9, 68(69):17, 101(102):2, 142(143):7.

      "*and take not Your all-holy spirit from us. Restore unto us, Lord, the joy of Your salvation; and uphold us with Your directing spirit*": See Psalms 50(51):11–12.

29   "*who cover the heaven in clouds*": See Psalms 146(147):8.

      "*swathe the earth in mist*": See Job 38:9.

      heard out of His holy temple: Psalms 17(18):6.

32   *she said:* The following is marked as "εὐχ(ή)" ("prayer") on the margin of *N* and *R*.

      the heavens as a curtain: See Isaiah 40:22.

      the earth above the waters: See Psalms 135(136):6.

33   *a good fruit that miraculously appeared from a wicked tree:* An allusion to Matthew 7:17, 19; Luke 3:9.

35   *a village called Gelassos, which lies twelve miles from Euchaita:* See note to chapter 2 above.

EUGENIA

Title   This text (*BHG* 608) was translated by Stratis Papaioannou together with Stevie Hull, Daria Resh, and Zachary Rothstein-Dowden.

      Metaphrastes first describes Eugenia's and, eventually, her family's complete transformation into models of Christian life and then narrates the events that led to her martyrdom on Christmas day of an unspecified year (her feast day is December 24). The first part, chapters 1 to 61, is set in Alexandria during the reigns of Commodus (180–192) and Severus (193–211) and, probably, Caracalla (198–217); the second part, chapters 62 to 87, supposedly takes place in Rome under the rule of Vale-

rian and Gallienus (253–260). This chronological discrepancy is, as was the case with *Kyprianos and Ioustina,* the result of conflation of two different stories that occurred already in the original Latin version of Eugenia's legend and was repeated, without comment, in the late antique translations of the story into Greek; for the Greek dossier, see *BHG* 607w–8e with Hippolyte Delehaye, *Étude sur le légendier romain: les saints de novembre et de décembre* (Brussels, 1936), 171–86. Since none of these early Greek versions has been edited, it is difficult to say with certainty what was the exact model for Metaphrastes's inspired reworking. It seems, however, that he has combined and thoroughly updated in his novelistic style two separate texts: Saint Eugenia's *Acts* (*BHG* 607x = Metaphrastes, chaps. 1–65, including the "return to Rome") and her *Passion* (*BHG* 607z = Metaphrastes, chaps. 66–87), which are transmitted together and in sequence in the manuscripts (Paris, Bibliothèque nationale de France, gr. 1491, early 10th century, fols. 169v–82r and 182r–86r; Vatican, Biblioteca Apostolica Vaticana, gr. 1608, early 11th century, fols. 51v–61r and 61r–64v). That Metaphrastes does not fix the chronological discrepancy is thus not the result of "sinking into the swamp of vulgar epic martyrdom," as Alexander Kazhdan suggested in his close and otherwise insightful reading of *Eugenia* (*A History of Byzantine Literature,* 2:242–44), but of understandable respect for a well-established storyline.

Like most of the stories in this volume, *Eugenia* had a long and complex tradition in multiple languages in the Middle Ages, including an Old English version, contemporary to Metaphrastes, written by Ælfric of Eynsham around 996/97 and included in his *Lives of the Saints.* Metaphrastes's version has been translated twice into a modern language: Russian, Sophia V. Poliakova, *Vizantiĭskie legendy* (Leningrad, 1972), 225–43; modern Greek, Georgios D. Papademetropoulos, Συμεών του Μεταφραστού, Ο βίος και το μαρτύριον των Αγίων Αικατερίνης και Ευγενίας μετά των ασματικών ακολουθιών των Αγίων (Athens, 1997), 82–127.

1   *Commodus:* Lucius Aurelius Commodus (r. 161–192; sole emperor
        180–192), son of Marcus Aurelius (121–180; r. 161–180).

        Philip—one of the eminent men: Philip is cited as a historical figure
        and identified with a homonymous eparch under the emperors
        Pupienus Maximus and Balbinus (April 22–July 29, 238) in the
        chronicles of Georgios the Monk and Symeon Logothetes,
        respectively: for Georgios, see PG 110:545.11–15; for Symeon
        Logothetes, most likely identical to Metaphrastes, see *Symeo-
        nis Magistri et Logothetae Chronicon,* 75. The twelfth-century
        historian Ioannes Zonaras rightly criticizes the chroniclers'
        view: *Ioannis Zonarae Epitome historiarum,* ed. Ludovic Dindorf
        (Leipzig, 1870), 3:131.

        Abitas: This version of the name has been retained, since it is
        transmitted by the majority of the manuscripts; "Abitos," pre-
        served in *O,* is, however, the most common form of this name
        and is also the form transmitted by the pre-Metaphrastic ver-
        sions.

        noble: In Greek, *eugenes,* a wordplay on Eugenia's name.

2   *the great city of Alexander:* That is, Alexandria in Egypt.

3   *he also raised his daughter Eugenia in liberal learning:* For another
        example of a father educating his children in the best possible
        secular learning, see Metaphrastes's *Life of Saint Xenophon and
        His Children Ioannes and Arkadios* 3 (PG 114:1016B), and *Galak-
        tion and Episteme* (above, chap. 17 and note).

        it seemed to have been engraved on her heart as if on bronze tablets:
        Nikephoros Kallistos Xanthopoulos, who is generally indebted
        to Metaphrastes's *Menologion,* cites this phrase verbatim in the
        Encomium of Andronikos II Palaiologos, which prefaces his *Ec-
        clesiastical History* (PG 145:569C). See also 2 Corinthians 3:3,
        where the image of "tablets of the heart" is found.

4   *propriety of character:* See a similar notion in Metaphrastes's *Pas-
        sion of Saint Euphemia* 6.

6   *prominent in lineage:* a phrase and concept dear to Metaphrastes;
        see, for instance, his *Passion of Saint Sebastianos* 2.

7   *only in her soul:* That is, before being baptized.

8   *"All the gods of the nations are demons; but the Lord made the heavens"*: Psalms 95(96):5.

9   *an intense and deep moan from her heart:* A topos of intense emotional expression in Metaphrastic texts; see, for instance, *Passion of Saint Anastasia* 16 (PG 116:588B); *Life of Saint Xenophon and His Children Ioannes and Arkadios* 6 (PG 114:1020B); and *Euphemia* (above, chap. 14 and note).

    Proteas: In all its later appearances in Metaphrastes's text, this name appears as "Protas," which seems to be consistently also the form in the pre-Metaphrastic Greek versions. Protas and Hyacinth (along with their mistress Basilla, who appears later in our story; chap. 62) are mentioned already in fourth-century martyrologies and appear to have had a developed cult early on. It is also worth noting that Theophylaktos Hephaistos, bishop of Ochrid (ca. 1050–after 1126) lists "Hyacinth and Proteas" among the exemplary eunuch saints; see his *Discourse on Castration,* in *Theophylacte d'Achrida. Discours, traités, poésies,* ed. Paul Gautier, vol. 1, *Opera* (Thessalonike, 1980), 327.9–10.

    knowledge of being: An echo of one of the Byzantine definitions of philosophy; see, for example, John of Damascus, *Philosophical Chapters,* in *Die Schriften des Johannes von Damaskos,* vol. 1, ed. Bonifatius Kotter (Berlin, 1969), 8.2–3 (p. 160): "Philosophy is the knowledge of beings *qua* beings."

10   *"there are many gods, superior and inferior":* A Christian argument against pagan philosophers put forward, for example, by Eusebios; see *Eusebius Werke,* vol. 8.1, *Die Praeparatio Evangelica,* ed. Karl Mras (Berlin, 1954), 7.11.13.

    "All the gods of the nations . . . The Lord made the heavens": Psalms 95(96):5.

11   *"I will no longer behave toward you as a mistress . . . since we will have God as our common Master and Father":* A similar idea and wording in Metaphrastes's *Life of Saint Eusebia, Renamed Xene* 3 (PG 116:984C).

12   *dress me in man's garb:* For a similar assumption of the male monastic habit by a woman, see, for example, Metaphrastes's *Life*

    of Saint Theodora of Alexandria 4 (PG 115:669B). See also above, *Pelagia* 23.

13   *Helioupolis:* One of the most ancient Egyptian cities, located beneath the northern part of modern Cairo.

    "The path of the righteous has been made straight": Reminiscent of Isaiah 26:7; no manuscript identifies this as a biblical quotation, as the Greek text translates the Latin original of the *Life of Eugenia.* The passage from the Septuagint differs slightly.

14   *as well as those of David:* See above, chapter 8.

15   *worth both telling and remembering:* The same expression is also found in Metaphrastes's *Passion of Saint Sebastianos* 13.

16   *Zareas:* This image of Zareas may be compared with the depiction of Simon, the most famous and, at that, stereotypical presentation of a magician as an evil character in Metaphrastes; see *Acts of Peter and Paul* (BHG 1493).

18   *the agreed-upon day:* The Greek word *(kyria)* could also mean "Sunday."

20   *putting on the helmet of Hades:* A proverb; see *Suda,* α 675; *CPG* 2:4, 649, for those who attempt to conceal themselves by various devices.

23   *bound together:* An echo of Matthew 8:10.

24   *the first one is called Protas:* a pun in Greek between "first" *(protos)* and Protas.

26   *the second Adam:* That is, Christ; a common theme in patristic exegesis, Byzantine homiletics, and hymnography.

27   *you slaves no more, but friends:* See John 15:15.

29   *would in no way deserve to be passed over:* A common Byzantine narrative formula, used also elsewhere by Metaphrastes; see *Life of Saint Stephen the Younger,* line 2761.

30   *In the dead of night:* In chapters 30 to 33, Metaphrastes backtracks in his narrative in order to follow the events in Alexandria after Eugenia's departure (chap. 8) and her decision to join Theodoros's monastery (chap. 11 onward).

31   *with what great . . . joy:* a phrase used elsewhere by Metaphrastes; *Life of St. Sampson* 8 (PG 115:288A).

inebriated by grief: An expression from patristic rhetoric; see, for
example, Basil of Seleucia, *Discourse on Joseph* (PG 85:113.34–35).

32 *poured dust on their heads:* See the note to *Kyprianos and Ioustina,*
chapter 29.

33 The scenario in this chapter has no exact equivalent in Greek
mythology, with the exception of Ganymede, who was ab-
ducted by Zeus and brought to Mount Olympos.

34 *rejoiced with those faring well:* See Romans 12:15.

35 *her unfeigned love for everyone:* Love *(agape)* is, in fact, a rare virtue
in the Metaphrastic corpus, where endurance seems to prevail.

After not much time had passed: For this common Metaphrastic
formula, see the note above to *Kyprianos and Ioustina,* chapter 5.

36 *she concealed:* "She" could possibly be translated as "it," that is,
her virtue.

When the book was opened at random: Seemingly randomly chosen
biblical passages that prefigure or prompt specific action are
frequent in Byzantine literature; see Stratis Papaioannou, "Re-
marks on Michael Attaleiates' *History*," in *Pour l'amour de Byzance: hommage à Paolo Odorico,* ed. Christian Gastgeber (Frank-
furt, 2013), 157–60.

*"If anyone among you wants to be first, let him be last of all, and the
servant of all":* Mark 9:35.

37 *"reaching forth," as divine Paul says, "unto those things which lie
ahead":* See Philippians 3:13.

38 *Melanthia:* This stock character of the temptress echoes, as
will become clear below, the behavior of Potiphar's wife, who
falsely accused Joseph (see Genesis 39, and note to *Kyprianos
and Ioustina,* chap. 12 above). The name Melanthia itself, which
literally means "dark flower" and is the word for black cumin,
echoes the Homeric male name Melanthios (see, for example,
Odyssey 17.247) and reappears in the female form (as in Eugenia's story) in Byzantine vernacular novels: see, for instance,
Jeffreys, *Digenis Akritis,* 5.68 (p. 138); Panagiotis Agapitos,
ed., Ἀφήγησις Λιβίστρου καὶ Ροδάμνης. Κριτικὴ ἔκδοση τῆς
διασκευῆς a (Athens, 2006), 4545.

38   *long-lasting and grievous disease . . . shivering on every fourth day:* This seems to have been a quartan fever caused by a mild form of malaria.

40   *the old saying is true that nothing is as close to another as virtue is to evil:* These sentences are marked as "γνώ(μη)" ("maxim") in *S* and *U;* for the reference, see Gregory of Nazianzos, *Or.* 43.64.

43   *she plugged her ears with wax:* A common ancient and Byzantine proverb; see *CPG* 2:478.

      the very venom of the ancient serpent: A reference to the story about the Devil as serpent in Genesis 3.

44   *for desire is hard to bear:* Marked as "γνώ(μη)" ("maxim") in manuscript *V⁶*. A similar maxim is found in *Kyprianos and Ioustina,* chapter 11 above, as well as in Metaphrastes's *Passion of Saint Iouliane* 6 (PG 114:1444A).

45   *Thus shameless Melanthia dared:* A common ploy of spurned lovers in the ancient novel; see, for instance, the false accusations that Demaenate constructs against Knemon, notably (like Melanthia) using a female slave to accomplish her target, in Heliodoros, *Ethiopian Tale* 1.10–12.

48   *with a fear that causes no fear:* A proverb; see *Suda,* α 434.

      we should not repay evil with evil under any circumstance: See Romans 12:21; 1 Thessalonians 5:15; Matthew 5:38–42.

49   *But since Melanthia did not stop being Melanthia even in the least:* See note to chapter 38 above.

52   *With intense affection, they were vying for a share of her:* For scenes of family reunion, presented in comparable effusive rhetorical emotionality and similar wording, see Metaphrastes's *Life of Saint Xenophon and His Children Ioannes and Arkadios,* chapters 25 and 28 (PG 114:1037B and 1042A); see also *Euphemia,* chapter 32 above.

53   *"Who is great as our God, who discovers deep things":* Psalms 76(77):13.

      "who discovers deep things": See Job 12:22.

54   *witness in heaven, her advocate on high:* See Job 16:20.

55   *Severus and Antoninus Pius:* Septimius Severus (145–211; r. 193–211) and, probably, Caracalla (188–217; r. 198–217), who bore also the

name of Antoninus Pius, rather than the earlier emperor Antoninus Pius (86–161; r. 138–161).

56   *the matters of the gods:* In the context of the high Roman empire, civic officials (along with emperors and priests) were responsible for matters pertaining to civic cults and religion.

he said: That is, the Devil through his envoys.

57   *"Our predecessor, the most divine Augustus":* Commodus (161–192; r. 180–192), mentioned at the beginning of the text.

58   *most philosophical:* That is, ascetic.

59   *Terentios:* An otherwise unattested eparch of Alexandria.

he let out the rope of every sail: A very common expression, meaning "to use every effort." See *Suda*, κ 259, ν 602, and π 222; see also *CPG* 1:145, 372, and 2:86, 104, 145, 177, 287, and 600.

60   *the so-called Isium:* A temple apparently dedicated to the Egyptian goddess Isis; for the city of Isium, see *Stephan von Byzanz. Ethnika,* ed. August Meineke (Graz, 1958), 338.3–8.

62   *vicar:* A "deputy of a praetorian prefect, vicar of an imperial diocese," according to Lampe; the title is mentioned, for example, in the letters of Basil the Great and Gregory of Nazianzos.

descended from the royal family: A pun (Βασίλλα, ἐκ βασιλικοῦ γένους), repeated also later. On Basilla see note to chapter 9 above.

64   *that they themselves become a living letter:* See 2 Corinthians 3:2. The image is absent from the pre-Metaphrastic version.

Cornelius too, that great star among bishops: Cornelius, pope of Rome (251–253), a well-known figure among Byzantine historiographers and chroniclers, especially for his fight against the Novatianist heresy; see *Suda,* ν 50.

65   *the Master of all:* Here is where Metaphrastes's likely model, Eugenia's *Acts* (*BHG* 607x), ends; chapter 66 begins Metaphrastes's reworking of Eugenia's *Passion* (*BHG* 607z).

66   *when Valerian and Gallius held power in Rome:* Valerian (193/95/200–260/64; r. 253–260) and Gallienus (218–268; r. 253–268).

68   *After making these pledges to each other:* Metaphrastes here greatly condenses a long and moving speech by Eugenia that is present

in the pre-Metaphrastic *Passion* (see Paris, Bibliothèque nationale de France, gr. 1491, fols. 182v–83r; *BHG* 607z).

to leave the sight of one another's faces: A similar image is found in
Achilleus Tatios, *Leucippe and Clitophon* 1.4.

74   *death by the sword:* For a similar case of a betrothed virgin who
spurned her fiancé for the sake of Christ and was then led to
martyrdom because of him, see Metaphrastes's *Passion of Saint
Iouliane* (PG 114:1437–52).

75   *"a fearful thing to fall into the hands of the true King and living God":*
See Hebrews 10:31.

76   *the temple of Zeus:* Perhaps the famous temple of Jupiter Capitoli-
nus.

*it miraculously began to diminish in size and dissolved into dirt and
dust:* See Psalms 17(18):43.

77   *they had shattered into dust . . . rendered him fine dirt:* This image,
present also at the end of the previous paragraph, alludes to a
Psalmic verse (Psalms 17(18):43) and is used in a similar fashion
also in Metaphrastes's *Passion of Saint Sebastianos* 12, and *Passion
of Saints Eulampios and Eulampia* 6 (PG 115:1060C).

78   *"as wax, as the divine David says, before the fire they melt and perish":*
See Psalms 67(68):2.

79   *the temple of Artemis:* Perhaps the temple of Diana upon the
Aventine Hill.

mute and deaf: A common notion in Metaphrastes; see *Passion of
Saint Euphemia* 3.

81   *conceive mischief and bring forth lawlessness:* See Psalms 7:14.

walked sure-footedly through the currents of the river: See Matthew
14:29.

82   *the light, according to the prophet, broke forth for her as the morning:*
See Isaiah 58:8.

83   *"the Roman Way":* Any attempt to locate such a shrine has proved
futile.

Bibliography

EARLIER EDITIONS AND TRANSLATIONS

Kyprianos and Ioustina

Blampignon, Aemilius, ed. *De sancto Cypriano et de primaeva Carthaginensi ecclesia.* Pages 172–203. Paris, 1862.

Pelagia

Flusin, Bernard, and Joseph Paramelle, eds. "La Vie métaphrastique de Pélagie: *BHG* 1479." In *Pélagie la pénitente: métamorphoses d'une légende.* Vol. 2, *La survie dans les littératures européennes,* edited by Pierre Petitmengin, 28–40. Paris, 1984.

Galaktion and Episteme

Tsames, Demetrios G., ed. *Τὸ μαρτυρολόγιο τοῦ Σινᾶ.* Pages 312–31. Thessalonike, 2003.

Euphemia

von Gebhardt, Oscar, and Ernst von Dobschütz, eds. *Die Akten der edessenischen Bekenner Gurjas, Samonas, und Abibos.* Pages 149–99. Leipzig, 1911.

Barbara, Eugenia, and Pelagia

Migne, Jacques-Paul, ed. Patrologia Graeca. Vol. 116. Pages 301–16, 609–52, 907–20. Translated into Latin by Gentien Hervet. Paris, 1891.

Additional Metaphrastic Editions

Life of Saint Daniel the Stylite. Delehaye, Hippolyte. "Vita S. Danielis Stylitae." *Analecta Bollandiana* 32 (1913): 121–214.

Life of Saint Stephen the Younger. Iadevaia, Francesca, ed. and trans. *Vita di San Stefano Minore.* Messina, 1984.

Passion of Saint Mamas. Berger, Albrecht. "Die alten Viten des Heiligen Mamas von Kaisareia. Mit einer Edition der Vita BHG 1019." *Analecta Bollandiana* 120 (2002): 280–308.

Passion of Saint Anastasios the Persian. Flusin, Bernard, ed. and trans. *Saint Anastase le Perse: et l'histoire de la Palestine au début du VIIe siècle.* Vol. 1, *Textes.* Pages 305–59. Paris, 1992.

Passion of Saint Euphemia. Halkin, François. *Euphémie de Chalcédoine: légendes byzantines.* Pages 141–62. Brussels, 1965.

Passion of Saint Sebastianos. Lequeux, Xavier. "La Passion métaphrastique inédite de S. Sébastien, martyr à Rome (BHG 1619z) et son abrégé (BHG 1620). Présentation et édition des textes." *Analecta Bollandiana* 123 (2005): 241–88.

Secondary Sources

Beck, Hans-Georg. *Kirche und theologische Literatur im byzantinischen Reich.* Munich, 1959.

Efthymiadis, Stephanos, ed. *The Ashgate Research Companion to Byzantine Hagiography.* 2 vols. Farnham, UK, 2011–2014.

Høgel, Christian. "Hagiography under the Macedonians." In *Byzantium in the Year 1000,* edited by Paul Magdalino, 217–32. Leiden, 2003.

———. "Symeon Metaphrastes and the Metaphrastic Movement." In Efthymiadis, *Ashgate Research Companion,* 2:181–96.

Kazhdan, Alexander. *A History of Byzantine Literature (850–1000).* 2 vols. Edited by Christina Angelidi. Athens, 1999–2006.

Messis, Charis. "Fiction and/or Novelization in Byzantine Hagiography." In Efthymiadis, *Ashgate Research Companion,* 2:315–44.

Messis, Charis, and Stratis Papaioannou. "Histoires 'gothiques' à Byzance: le saint, le soldat et le Miracle de l'Euphémie et du Goth (BHG 739)." *Dumbarton Oaks Papers* 67 (2013): 15–47.

Patterson Ševčenko, Nancy. *Illustrated Manuscripts of the Metaphrastian Menologion.* Chicago, 1990.

Index